psychology

of personality

SIX MODERN APPROACHES

Edited by J. L. McCary, Ph.D., University of Houston

GROVE PRESS INC.   NEW YORK
JOHN CALDER LTD.   LONDON

COPYRIGHT© 1956 BY LOGOS PRESS, INC.

All Rights Reserved

This edition is published by arrangement with

Logos Press

Grove Press Books and Evergreen Books

are published by Barney Rosset at Grove Press Inc.

795 Broadway   New York 3, N. Y.

Distributors in Great Britain:

John Calder Ltd., 17 Sackville St., London, W.1

MANUFACTURED IN THE UNITED STATES OF AMERICA

contents

contributors

Leopold Bellak, M.D.
Clinical Assistant Professor of Psychiatry, New York Medical College; Lecturer in Psychology, New York School for Social Research

Raymond B. Cattell, Ph.D., D.Sc.
Research Professor in Psychology and Director, Laboratory of Personality Assessment and Group Behavior, University of Illinois

George S. Klein, Ph.D.
Associate Professor of Psychology and Director, Clinical Laboratory of the Research Center for Mental Health, New York University

David C. McClelland, Ph.D.
Professor of Psychology, Harvard University

Margaret Mead, Ph.D., D.Sc.
Associate Curator of Ethnology, American Museum of Natural History

Nevitt Sanford, Ph.D.
Professor of Psychology, University of California, Berkeley; Coordinator, Mary Conover Mellon Fund for the Advancement of Education, Vassar College

PREFACE

Widely varied approaches to the problem of understanding personality have bombarded the literature during the past decade. Although few have withstood careful scrutiny and investigation, several have weathered criticism better than most. Of these, six approaches have been selected for presentation here.

This book is an outgrowth of the Annual Lecture Series in Psychology held at the University of Houston. In 1954 the series included a symposium in personality by six leaders in the field: Leopold Bellak, Raymond B. Cattell, George S. Klein, David C. McClelland, Margaret Mead, and Nevitt Sanford.

For this volume, each was asked to present his position in the terminology and organization best suited to his own theoretical approach, since marked differences in orientation prevent uniformity. Such presentation should give the reader a better view and understanding of each method, and lessen the likelihood of confusing one with another.

Each contribution is presented as an integrated and detailed system by itself. The authors are presented alphabetically, except for McClelland. His chapter is placed last because it undertakes some measure of integration by indicating similarities among the various methods before presenting his own viewpoint for understanding personality.

Many persons, a number of whom are not mentioned here, have contributed time, effort, and funds to the lecture series and to the presentation of this book. The suggestions and efforts of L. T. Callicutt, R. I. Evans, Charles Moore, Lois Rommel, Grace Ware, Kenneth Ware, Alvin Weinstein, and Elizabeth Weinstein have been especially helpful.

J. L. McCARY
University of Houston

INTRODUCTION

Emphasis on the relationship between theory and research has been rapidly increasing throughout the entire field of psychology in recent years. More especially has this emphasis been found in the specific area of personality, where a bumper crop of theories and subsystems have been produced—although separating wheat from chaff is still somewhat difficult.

During the earlier days of development in the field of personality study—undoubtedly as a result of the tendency to view each system as being complete within itself, much like a closed system of philosophy—new theories sprang up in numbers directly proportional to the number of psychologists interested in experimentation. More recent work in personality has evinced a trend towards consolidation of subtheories and integration of the broader systems. With time, theorists have become aware of similarities among the various systems and have recognized each other's contributions. In order to evolve a more complete and satisfactory over-all theory, some have broken through the seemingly impervious boundaries between systems by incorporating data, concepts, and viewpoints from approaches previously ignored.

This tendency toward organization of personality data has been rewarding, and in a practical way. Personality theory, as it exists today, is composed of a body of general, abstract principles which taining to the behavior of the individual. This body of theories has resulted from attempts to systematize and unify concepts per- facilitates the organization and representation of current knowl- edge of existing facts in abstract terms, and also serves as a ref- erence point for efforts to advance toward a better understanding of behavior. Yet none of the present single theories of personality seems entirely adequate, even though current attempts to con- struct a science of personality suggest that, by a process of suc- cessive approximations, together with an integration of these ap- proximations, a useful theory is gradually being developed.

Assessing contemporary progress and delimiting its problems becomes easier if one examines the historical background and the sequence of events which antedate personality theory formula- tions. Moreover, a viewing of personality theory in perspective and within a broader context should also be of value in giving direction to the present integrative trends.

The history of scientific thought in general has meaning for the study of the individual. Before scientific objectivity became a goal, man's perceptions were governed by animism and super- sitition and, later, by religion and mysticism. These forces in- fluenced the direction and degree of progress in every field. Only recently have we recognized that scientists like others are affected by limitations and distortions in perception and thinking which are functions of their own personalities and cultures. Ideas about the physical world were the first to change as a result of the scientific method of critical observation. The next advance came in chemistry, then in biology. The emancipation of objective science from older religious and ethical considerations has been gradual, however, and only recently has modern biology freed itself from religion. In conjunction with this trend, it might be postulated that man has become progressively freer in his study of himself. Having first gained some knowledge of his environment, he began to examine an area in which ego involvement was greater: his relation to this environment. Finally, with the de- velopment of psychology, and with personality theory, man has dared to investigate scientifically an area which has for centuries withstood his best efforts: himself.

Since the science of personality investigation is the most recent, earlier concepts still hamper objectivity in it to some extent. For example, the field of biology has for some time exerted a disproportionate influence upon many theories of personality. Having been developed from this science, the new discipline neither denies nor abandons the biological aspects of the organism, but, rather, emphasizes that the investigator must also take into account psychological aspects of the individual. The development of the nervous system, acquisition of behavior, and adaptation of behavior to environment all show the principle of the expansion of a primarily integrated total pattern, and of the individuation of partial patterns within it. It has been postulated that endogenous stimulation in a nervous field, such as that found in the brain, has implications for the motivation of behavior. This hypothesis has been carried even further in the suggestion that the antagonistic processes of integration and individuation may be the organic basis of psychic conflict. In keeping with this hypothesis, the concept that the time of physical injury influences the result of the injury has been applied to explain psychological as well as physiological effects. Thus, the psychological concomitants of brain injury illustrate the holistic principle. For example, the brain-injured patient's need to have his life well ordered is viewed as not only a manifestation of the physical insult, but a psychological defense mechanism as well. On the other hand, certain descriptions of behavior organization stress the importance of the biological aspects of the organism in the development of behavior, although the psychological and sociological factors are also acknowledged.

Further emphasizing the biological thesis is the concept that need, stress, and frustration are dependent on homeostasis. This concept is used to explain the individual's behavior in biopsychological terms. This orientation has also been used to describe the characteristics of learning. On the other hand, other investigators have emphasized the psychological and sociological determinants of behavior, but within a biological frame of reference.

The preceding statements reflect a difficulty which has been central in psychology: man, while a biological organism, is not merely that, but something more.

Some investigators have endeavored to resolve this problem of man's nature, seemingly a dualistic problem, by means of statements demonstrating the basic integrity of man's biological nature and his reason. These statements have been, to a great extent, concerned with isomorphism. For each object perceived, there is a corresponding neural mechanism; and, corresponding to this mechanism, there is an idea.

To describe the total adjustment of the organism, there is no need for a dichotomy of *biological* and *psychological*. While much effort is expended to bridge this dichotomy, the mode of thinking persists. On the lower-order level, the organism receives the impact of stimuli from its surroundings to which it may respond immediately, as long as there are commissural fibers to join the two functions. Thus, even the neonate is able to make a simple adjustment to his environment. Where the impinging stimuli are more pronounced and sustained, a higher level, the autonomic, may function as an energizer, causing an emergency force to go into operation and produce or facilitate sustained, pronounced responses which may serve to correct the disturbance. At a still higher level, the central, both peripheral and autonomic functions may be governed. Meanings may be attributed to perceptions. Autonomic functions may be set in motion before mechanical contact has been made with impending stimuli. It is even possible, through central functions, to obliterate the stimuli and to inhibit potential responses to them. Moreover, the central level may function so as to avoid, through prediction, the need to adjust to the full impact of noxious stimuli. In short, then, there is little distinction, as current theory sees the problem, to be made between body and mind. All areas of the organism function together, some controlling others, so that the functions of one facilitate and overlap the functions of others. From the standpoint of theory, this stratification of systems reflects the unity of the organism. It also provides a new orientation in concepts relating to all functions of the organism, for example, the concept of disease. This suggests that any illness is an illness of the whole person, an idea which, of course, has strong implications for the development of personality theory.

Another important development is that personality theory now takes greater cognizance of the interaction of the organism and its environment in all stages of development. This interaction has implications for the order of the libido stages as posited by Freud. The communication between the organism and the environment has even broader connotations, in that psychological interaction, and especially incorporation, can be viewed as analogous to biological incorporation and exchange. This position gives insight into such aspects of personality theory as oral incorporation and identification, and the introjection of the parents in a psychological sense to form the superego as defined in psychoanalytic theory.

Thus strong integrative trends are developing in contemporary personality theory, as exemplified by a breakdown in the separation between the biological and the psychological aspects of the organism, and between the organism and its environment. Still other dichotomies are becoming obsolete, at least in theory, such as that which viewed the individual and his society as isolated entities, and that which drew sharp distinctions between personality and culture. Current thinking asserts that knowledge of a society rests upon knowledge of the individuals who are its members and who share its culture. Some approaches even maintain that individuals can be defined only as they may be seen against the social and cultural background of which they are a part: the individual and his society, now thought of as constituting a single field, can be dealt with separately only in abstraction. By the same token, personality and culture are seen as part of the same process of interaction.

Today, then, to a much greater extent than at any previous time, attempts to understand man—to understand his personality —are drawing together. Still, widespread differences in viewpoint prevent the synthesis of a single approach to understanding personality which will be even halfheartedly accepted by a majority of the theorists in the field. The process of integrating and combining theories of personality to even the present inadequate point has taken much thought, experimentation, research, work, and patience. But even at best, the science—if it be that—of personality is in its earliest infancy. To contribute further to the understanding and betterment of mankind, psychologists must apply infinitely more thought, experimentation, research, work, and patience.

The personality branch of the psychology tree is large and complex. The job of pruning and grafting this mass of personality theories to isolate six of the most representative and most generally accepted approaches required the omission of some significant theories from this book. While the six approaches differ, the gaps among them have been narrowed considerably. The summary chapter of McClelland is a step toward an even greater integration, and has, in a sense, indicated the direction of a greater understanding of personality structure.

McClelland has shown how seemingly divergent personality theories when analyzed can be incorporated into larger, more inclusive theories in such a way that none loses its value. The process of integration which McClelland has used is not intended to produce an overall theory of personality which will be happily accepted by all, but rather to contribute toward such a theory of personality.

Each of the six authors contributed significantly to the foundation or development of the approach he presents. None believes his approach is the only answer to the problem of personality; each believes that his contribution offers a significant part of the sought-for, but elusive, total understanding.

J. L. McC.

psychoanalytic theory
of personality

notes toward a systematic textbook of

psychoanalysis

LEOPOLD BELLAK, M.D.

LEOPOLD BELLAK, M. D.

Dr. Bellak is clinical assistant professor of psychiatry at New York Medical College, lecturer in psychology at the New School for Social Research, past president of the New York Society for Projective Techniques, and private practitioner in psychoanalysis and psychiatry. He studied medicine and psychoanalysis in Vienna and New York, and psychiatry at St. Elizabeths Hospital, Washington, D. C., and graduated from the New York Psychoanalytic Institute. He has also done graduate work in psychology at Harvard. His publications include a number of scientific articles and books, among which are his *Dementia Praecox* and *The TAT and CAT in Clinical Use*.

Dr. Bellak states that, at best, one can learn psychoanalysis only through tracing the development of its concepts historically. With this view in mind, he utilizes a historical approach in his "Psychoanalytic Theory of Personality," thus giving the reader an understanding of some of the basic principles of psychoanalysis.

Believing that the purpose of an attempt to restate psychoanalytic concepts in an orderly fashion is (as is the function of every hypothesis) to facilitate the understanding, prediction, and control of events, Dr. Bellak perceives his task as one of reviewing and clarifying systematically psychoanalytic concepts, in the hope that such an approach will lead not only to more orderly and accurate generalizations, but also to new ideas which will permit better understanding and prediction of human behavior, and, ultimately, better control through therapeutic intervention.

Dr. Bellak does not accept the premise of those analysts who state that psychoanalytic theories, concepts, and processes cannot lend themselves to ordinary scientific methodology. To the contrary, he emphasizes the importance of research with psychoanalytic concepts and processes and gives some of his thoughts concerning systematic investigation and research in this field.

INTRODUCTION

A quantitative measure of the genius of a man might well be derived from the length of time it takes for the rest of the world to replace or modify his creations with significantly better ones. By this measure Sigmund Freud has gone well beyond the half-century mark already, and is likely to go much longer.

Freud was a clinician who elaborated a general theory of personality; eighteen volumes of his own work and countless others derived from them attest to his tremendous creativity. Few people have read his books carefully enough. Only those who have sincerely attempted to understand him, and particularly those who have tried to go beyond, know the tremendous depth and *Prägnanz* of each of his statements. Having once spent two years of experiments and cogitation trying to restate Freud's concept of projection, because it seemed too limited, I found finally that he had already conceived of it in as broad a way as possible and tucked his insight away in what amounts to little more than a footnote [15].

I am indebted to Drs. R. Holt, A. Reich, and H. Schlossman for having critically read this manuscript and made many helpful suggestions. Of course, the responsibility for all material is the author's.

Nevertheless, Freud and his one life had to have some limitations; as with Moses, it is hard to forgive such a great man even one shortcoming. Like a good scientist, Freud created working hypotheses which he then tried out with what he learned from his patients on the couch. He reshaped his model when it did not fit perfectly and recorded his observations late into the night. Sometimes he did recall his earlier formulations and bring the new insight and the new formulation into tune with the entire rest of his system (as in the case of the successive theories of anxiety), but very frequently he did not integrate one concept with another and all of them with each other. Nor did he find it possible to define his concepts operationally or to work out textbook definitions.[1]

The result is that at best one can learn psychoanalysis only if one traces the development of its concepts historically, and only he who knows all of it knows anything about it at all, because concepts are defined—insofar as this has been done—differently in different papers, or even inconsistently within one publication. In a recent experiment [7] some colleagues and I have tried to judge and conceptualize recorded psychoanalytic sessions, only to find that even though we were all properly trained psychoanalysts, graduates of the same psychoanalytic institute, we had the greatest difficulty in arriving at agreements on the precise meaning of some basic events and the terms to describe them, such as "identification," "transference," "acting out," etc.

To be sure, we had no doubt about what was going on in the patient, what needed to be done, and even what to expect in his development. And, to be sure, the patient progressed satisfactorily. But from the standpoint of scientific conceptualization the conclusion to be drawn was clear: psychoanalytic concepts need definition, need systematic restatement in scientific language which will permit one to verify what is useful and what is not, and to progress toward further valuable formulations.

A most impressive fact is that every good analyst works con-

---

[1] In the opening paragraphs of "Instincts and Their Vicissitudes" Freud discusses the formulation of progressive models of thought as lucidly as it is discussed anywhere: "It is only after more searching investigation of the field in question that we are able to formulate with increased clarity the scientific concepts underlying it and progressively so modify these concepts that they become widely applicable and at the same time consistent logically. Then indeed, it may be time to immure them in definition."

tinuously with covert concepts, sound enough, but never spelled out, and therefore hardly teachable. In attempts at experimentation, the writer has dictated after each analytic hour the propositions upon which were predicated his statements or his silences. It was amazing to find how complex were the reasons for even a brief remark, which may have been made quite correctly, but still intuitively.

The purpose of an attempt to restate psychoanalytic concepts in orderly fashion must be clear: it is the function of every hypothesis to help understand, predict and control events. It would be sterile labor indeed to restate concepts merely for the purpose of enabling them to be experimentally verified. Albeit this is a criterion to be met, equally significant is the fact that clarification of concepts may lead to more orderly generalizations with exclusion of the erroneous and discoveries of new vistas. Psychoanalytic hypotheses permit understanding of human behavior, prediction (implicit in the treatment situation, as we shall have occasion to discuss later), and control in the sense of therapeutic interventions by means of carefully formulated interpretations.

The present attempt, confined to one chapter, must be seen only as a very limited, very preliminary venture into the task. This paper is indeed fragmentary and uneven, in that at times it will be necessary to deal naïvely with elementary problems and at other times refer to complex inferences which can hardly be understood without the experience of psychoanalytic practice. A more integrated approach would have to be the work of a lifetime and should preferably be the task of a special research team on definition and methodology of the American Psychoanalytic Association. Such a team, aided by the few psychoanalysts who are acquainted with scientific methodology and the few psychologists and methodologists who are acquainted with psychoanalysis, could serve an immeasurably useful purpose.

SOME BASIC PRINCIPLES OF PSYCHOANALYSIS

Every scientific concept is embedded in a larger frame of philosophical assumptions, as a general rule implicitly rather than explicitly, and is not unrelated to the cultural milieu. This also holds true for psychoanalysis.

Determinism

Freud was probably the first to use the principle of causality in a truly thoroughgoing way in the psychology of personality in the form of psychic determinism: the axiom that each behavioral act is determined by a specific cause or causes (and is itself a cause again to other effects). His theory and practice of free association is based on the assumption of causal connections via unconscious motivations. Freud's genetic viewpoint is a function of the consistent application of the law of causality to the shaping of the personality. As Kaufman [30] suggests, it may be better to speak not of a law of causality since "the principle of causality is 'no law at all' but rather a declaration of the resolution not to renounce the search for causes in any instance and of the belief that this search will not be in vain." The laws of classical physics, including the statements about causality, still hold for macroscopic events, while quantum physics is said to need some special treatment. Einstein still held, though, that "God would not have played dice with the world"; classical principles are still useful for the new science of psychology.

The entire theory and practice of psychoanalysis is in fact predicated upon determinism;* in turn this is related to a number of allied propositions. Logically, the next step is a concern with the *nature* of determining factors. They may be divided into two principal classes: socio-psychological-environmental determinants, genetic-constitutional-prenatal-somatic-maturational ones, and countless complex interactions between these factors.

Determinism is a necessary assumption for therapy, predicated on the proposition that the contemporary "neurotic personality" is a result of early events and can be restructured.

Overdeterminism

Overdeterminism is but a special case of determinism: that a given event, for example, a dream or a spoken sentence, is the final common path of many genetically and contemporaneously derived

* This does not necessarily mean rigid one-to-one relationships; restatement in terms of probability theory is possible.

forces. Strange as this concept may sound at first, it is of course also necessary for the physical world: the course of an object through space is determined by its weight, its size, space, air currents, the impetus given, gravity, etc., and the history of whether it was magnetized or exposed to a radioactive field: in a sense of course all forces are contemporary ones, in psychology as well as in physics, but as a convenience of description and for the best understanding of the interrelation of forces, a historical viewpoint can be adopted. Obviously, the entire concept of "working through" is particularly predicated upon the principle of overdeterminism.

Metapsychological Principles

The metapsychological principles themselves are predicated upon the principle of determinism. Each psychological event, in order to be understood, must be examined from the dynamic, structural and economic point of view. Of all these dimensions, we will concern ourselves here only with the economic one.

The *economic* assumptions are part of the libido theory. Libido itself is the form of energy of the system, and its cathexis (investment, charge) in various libidinal aims and the countercathexis (in the defensive system) are a fundamental part of psychoanalytic theory and practice. Implicitly, each person seems to be considered a closed energy system by Freud, to which the law of conservation of energy seems to apply: that is, if libido is withdrawn from one area, the psychoanalyst asks himself to where it becomes diverted or in what reinvested. This is fundamental to the theoretical understanding of narcissism and object-cathexis, and of symptom formation.

A very mechanistic application of the economic viewpoint can be found in Freud's [18] theories concerning wit, humor, and the comic, which may be stated briefly as follows: A certain saving of expenditure of energy, which was previously used for repression, becomes available by the use of the trigger mechanisms of wit, and the amount of energy thus available is "laughed off" and expended in somatic activity of the diaphragm and the facial muscles. Similarly he conceives of humor as due to a saving of expenditure of energy for affective tone and thinks of the pleasure of the comic as the saving of expenditure of energy incidental to the fact that the spectator feels that he could perform the "comic" task with much less exertion than the comic manages to.

It has been impossible so far to measure quantities of cathectic energy in any direct way but I do not believe that this affects the heuristic importance of the concept. The most notable attempt along the lines of libidometry has been made by Bernfeld and Feitelberg [9]. The problem of measurement may be simpler than it seems. When we speak of measurement generally, we have in mind reference to a metric scale. We know, however, that there are other types of scales, of which the simplest is the nominal scale, where we do not deal with more than the identity of the sign ascribed to an object; in other words, where we deal only with naming things. The next type of scale is the one we feel is useful and meaningful for libidinal energies, namely, the ordinal scale. In such a scale the statement made concerns the identity and the position in the scale of the datum dealt with. All one can say is something is greater or lesser than something else. This type of scale has been useful in various forms of sensory psychology and in the psychology of hedonic tone, and it could be used in experiments on libidinal cathexis, e.g., in ranking the liking of different people at different times [6].

A possible way of actually submitting the libido theory to quantitative measurement is discussed later (see Research on Libido Theory). From the evidence of Ernest Jones's biography [29] there can be little doubt that Freud practically grew up with the formulation of the thermodynamic laws. In fact, he relates the controversial theory of the death instinct to the concept of entropy (the second thermodynamic law).

The Reality Principle—Pleasure Principle

The term "pleasure principle" is probably a particularly unfortunate one from the standpoint of the academician, but peculiarly enough, Freud from the very earliest days of 1892 [26] had about as broad and academically acceptable a concept of this principle as one could imagine. Freud had then already spoken of "constancy" and the tendency towards constancy of organismic and psychic phenomena, anticipating broadly the later physiological concept of homeostasis advanced by Cannon and present-day applications of the concept of homeostasis to psychological phenomena.

In essence, the pleasure principle implies that the organism has a tendency toward drive gratification, or even broader, toward a state of equilibrium, perceptually, physiologically, and otherwise.

The reality principle, so dramatically opposed to the pleasure principle in Freud's system of polarities, is nothing but the fact that the learning of detour behavior of the ego inhibits the immediate and direct gratification of drives. As has been pointed out by Freud [16] and Hartmann *et al.* [26], instincts lead to gratification and survival in animals while in men the ego needs to mediate between drives and reality to achieve this aim. Freud's contention in *Civilization and Its Discontents* could briefly be summarized here as saying that increasing civilization implies increasing interaction between individuals and thus increasing regulation of individual behavior and thus increasing conflict in turn which requires more frequent and more complex detours for unpunished drive gratification.

Symptom formation, in this sense, may be seen as unstable compromise efforts at drive gratification on the one hand and inhibition of the drive by learned (ego and superego) behavioral patterns on the other.

Unconsciousness and Continuity of Personality

Unconsciousness is but a necessary construction, subsidiary to another basic principle practically never discussed; namely, the continuity of the personality. The interpretation (of the unconscious content) of a dream in essence means the ordering into a continuum of the dream thoughts and concerns with the thought processes of the preceding day (the day residue) and the subsequent day (e.g., that the patient got up tense and with a headache, etc.), aside from relating the other aspects of the dream to genetic and dynamic material. In other words, unconsciousness was necessary to bridge the discontinuity of manifest behavior, one of the most startling tasks psychoanalysis performs successfully every day. Additional hypotheses are concerned with the nature and reasons of unconscious material and its fate. Parapraxes (misnaming, misspelling, etc.) belong to the simplest examples of continuity-discontinuity.

The concept of continuity of personality has not been stated explicitly by Freud. Implicitly, he has stated it in his contention that all the essentials of the personality are established by the fifth year. Manifest differences of behavior in later life are presumably to be explained by shifts in the intrapsychic system, a quasi-closed system in that the person is in constant interaction with the environment. It is better to say, then, that the theory of continuity of personality of psychoanalysis implies that, after age five, responses to the environment take place only over a certain range or in a finite number of variations predicated upon established intrasystemic variables.

These assumptions become most conspicuous clinically in the concept of the *repetition compulsion*, the *return of the repressed*. It is met most frequently clinically in the problem of marriage, where repeated choice of mates is likely to be made along the same personality patterns (with some dynamic variations—e.g., a masochistic choice instead of a sadistic choice, but definitely a sado-masochistic relationship each time).

Theories of testing, e.g., with the Rorschach and the TAT, are founded upon such a concept of the continuity of personality. Testing is an experimental sampling of behavior based on the assumption that the personality is continuous and that the sample obtained will be representative. If one permits the dangerous practice of analogy, and should choose for this instance to compare psychological testing with public health assays of the waters of a stream (by taking a pailful of water at regular intervals for analysis), one can easily see why tests sometimes fail: if one test samples the surface water (paper and pencil tests) and another the ground current, they are likely to come up with different content. Similarly, if a pailful is taken very near to the entrance of even a small tributary (such as a disturbing recent event, including a not properly structured testing situation), one is likely to be woefully wrong.

SOME BASIC CONCEPTS

The Libido Theory

The pre-Freudian meaning of libido in medical science referred to a person's sexual interests, in the sense that a patient suffering from some endocrine disorder associated with gross pathological effects on his sexual life was and is referred to as suffering from increased or deficient libido. It is probably from this usage that Freud took one of the two major aspects of the psychoanalytic meaning of libido, namely the concept of libido as drive energy.

The second major aspect of the libido theory was (aside from Freud) shaped by Abraham. A well-trained embryologist before he became a psychiatrist and psychoanalyst, Abraham applied some concepts of segmental development to his new field and conceived of an orderly sequence of stages of libidinal development, from the oral zone (active and passive) to the anal zone (retentive and aggressive-ejective) to the genital. To a certain extent, thus, the libido theory is concerned with maturational processes. To this is added the effect of upbringing and relative emphasis or frustration of the various zones and aims, the timing of the stimulation (earlier or later in life), the subsequent effects upon the personality in terms of fixation, regression, symptom formation and object relationships, and the reversibility of any adverse effects.

The libido theory could then be described as a series of interlocking propositions:

1. Propositions concerning the sequence of maturation of bodily zones with a positive hedonic tone (erotogenic zones) and specific aims of gratification (libidinal aims).
2. Propositions concerning the perception of oral, anal, and genital stimuli and the reaction of significant figures to such stimulation (early anal training, masturbation, and prohibition).
3. Propositions concerning specific effects of the maturational and learned aspects on later development (object relations, character formation).
4. Propositions concerning the timing of maturation and learning (the same maternal act at different times in the child's life will have different effects); in recent discussions by Anna Freud and others

at the Arden House Conference, 1954, these propositions were discussed under the term of "phase specificity" of child-mother interactions.

5. Propositions concerning the interaction of events learned at different times (the relationship of trauma sustained in infancy to trauma sustained in latency to trauma sustained in puberty).

All the above propositions are conceived in quantitative terms; that is, a conception of constitutional variation of the strength of drives, variations in the strength of stimulation or lack of stimulation, and quantitative differences in the nature of learning.

Psychoanalytic therapy is predicated upon propositions concerning the reversibility of the perceptual learning and its effects on behavior.

Let us now examine the propositions about libidinal zones, aims, and objects more closely and attempt to restate them further.

The Libidinal Zones

The earliest stage of libidinal investment is very appropriately conceived of as a diffuse cathexis of the whole body, both splanchnic and in the skin surface [35]. This is increasingly focused (in a way that has not yet been specified) into a greater specific hedonic tone of the oral zone, to be followed and overlapped by the anal area. This is followed and superimposed at the end of infancy by the phallic stage as the early aspect of focusing on the genital zone, to be interrupted by the latency period and to be matured into the genital zone proper as the preferred zone of pleasure-seeking with the end of puberty. (For a more detailed discussion of the concepts involved, see "Libidinal Aims." To be sure, the sequence does not imply that the earlier zones be entirely abandoned.)

These propositions can be stated as *an orderly maturational sequence of preferred loci of stimulation*. As such, the proposition still needs clear-cut observational verification and more specific statement; e.g., if oral, anal, and genital preferences were to be drawn as curves, how would the relationship of each curve to the other have to be drawn, if time were the abscissa and "libidinal units" the ordinate?

The early oral (passive) phase is presumably present at birth. Suckling movements of a nonnutritive nature have been observed soon after birth. The active oral (aggressive, incorporating) phase is probably associated with the eruption of the teeth. Inasmuch as the eruption of the first lower incisors is usually put at six months, plus or minus two months, it was arbitrarily entered at that point. Similarly, the retentive phase of the anal period was entered later, roughly related to the time of voluntary control of the anal sphincter.

Figure 1

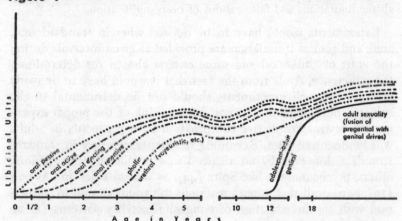

The phallic phase is generally conceived as developing fully somewhere between the third and fourth year, possibly closer to the end of the third. The urethral phase is not separately represented here, nor are other partial drives.

Greenacre has recently suggested that it is useful to conceive of the various phases of the partial drives as being more or less accentuated at certain times rather than their being absent and suddenly emerging or re-emerging; therefore, the drives are presented as starting parallel to the baseline.

The latency period, usually considered lasting from five to ten is subdivided again by Bornstein into a period from five, to eight and one-half, to ten. In the first part the superego is considered by her to be still extremely severe and to hinder the ego and those sublimations which are associated with latency: only between eight and one-half and ten can the ego really function freely.

The area of pre-puberty is drawn as it is in the figure, since as Anna

Freud stated, no qualitative changes happen, only quantitative ones: there is a reinforcement of the pregenital drives (children becoming dirty, unruly, etc.) after the lull of latency.

From the period of adolescent-adult-genitality on not only the truly genital impulses and cathexes of the genital area should be considered, but also the admixture of the pregenital drives. In accordance with psychoanalytic theory, the adult sexual drive includes the partial or pregenital components, and for this reason the lines converge in our figure. (Only when the pregenital drives become primary and supersede the genital one as goal, do we speak of a sexual disturbance.)

It must be remembered that this graph is nothing but an attempt at a schematic approximation of psychoanalytic theory and as such has all the limitations and falsifications of oversimplification.

Experiments would have to be devised wherein standard oral, anal, and genital stimulation are provided at given intervals during the years of childhood and some criteria chosen for determining the preference. Aside from the fact that it would have to be made certain that such experiments should not be detrimental to the subject's development, it is not easy to think of the proper experimental design. Postdictive confirmation by experiments in adults will be discussed later. Recording of infants' reaction to standard stimuli is, however, by no means a new or difficult idea. Among others, psychoanalysts like Spitz [44], as well as Fries and Woolf [19], have studied children's reactions to various stimuli in connection with the investigation of congenital activity patterns (in response to a loud noise, etc.).

Libidinal Aims or Modes of Pleasure Finding

Aside from defining the somatic areas which are preferred as foci of gratification, the libido theory includes statements concerning the *nature of the operations involved in gratification* of libidinal aims at various stages of development. These are also spoken of as partial or component sexual aims, since they may be part or components of later adult genital activity. Thus the theory of libidinal aims is a set of propositions concerned with the sequence, interaction and fate of preferences for gratifying operations throughout life. These operations may be in part a function of maturational processes of the endocrine-nervous system and in part related to learned stimulus-response patterns. With Lashley [32] one might think of these aims as perceptual choices *in response to deficit states.* "Perceptual choices" and "stimulus response" should not be understood in primitive conditioned reflex terms but rather in form of complex interactions of configurations (Gestalten), as will be discussed further below.

1. Corresponding to the earliest *undifferentiated* zone (which for classification purposes is included in the oral phase, since the relationship between feeding and skin sensation at the mother's breast has been shown) are undifferentiated aims of skin stimulation, rhythmic muscular activity, and of splanchnic gratification, already related to the oral phase's aim of sucking.
2. More specifically, the *oral* aims are subdivided into the passive (sucking) subphase and the active oral (incorporating, biting) subphase.
3. The *anal* phase is subdivided into the aim to retain and the aim to expel (aggressively). Sadistic-masochistic aims are considered characterologic derivatives of this phase.
4. The *early genital* or *phallic* phase, including urethral phase, was added by Freud to his pregenital and genital conceptions [16] with these words: "I later (1925) altered this in that I interpolated a third phase into the development of the child after the two pregenital organizations, one which indeed deserves the name of a genital, one which reveals a sexual object and a measure of convergence of the sexual strivings upon this object, but which differs in one essential point from the definitive organization of sexual maturity. That is, it knows only one sort of genital, the male. I have therefore called it the *phallic* stage of organization." [2] Its biological prototype according to Abraham is the homogeneous genital *Anlage* of the embryo undifferentiated for either sex.

It is of interest to note again the reference to Abraham's suggestion of the biological equivalent, to which one might add the cultural correlate of phallic worship in many religions as the symbol of productive activity.

The basic assumption of the phallic phase of libidinal development is that the aim and modes of gratification are now focused on the penis and its biological equivalent, the clitoris. (Clinically there are many forms of an illusory phallus, e.g., fecal; and adult female patients often seem to conceive of the cervix as an indwelling phallus). The implication for object relations is that in contrast to the autoerotic pregenital phase, phallic gratification is

[2] The clitoris may play the role of the phallic organ for the girl.

desired from an external object, from one specific object originally.

From the standpoint of learning, the phallic phase may be of
particular importance for the development of a girl. If the little
girl has a brother who is greatly favored, she may feel that it would
be better to be a boy and she may become "fixated" at the
phallic level. Not only is she a tomboy as a child, but she stays
identified with masculine activities, viewpoints, and aims into
adulthood. She may possibly be overassertive denying the lack of
a phallus, she may be particularly aggressive toward males whom
she envies the phallus and wants to "castrate," or she may make
male object-choices (of boy friends, husbands) who have a large
feminine component. Other learning experiences may also fixate[3] a
girl at the phallic phase of gratification. If the role of the mother
is a particularly suffering one, e.g., at the hands of a sadistic husband; or if the child is particularly exposed to parental intercourse
(primal scene) or has particularly realistic reasons for a sadistic
conception of things done to the mother; if the situation is so
structured that the child becomes particularly aware of menstrual
bleeding and connects this with ideas of genital traumatization of
the female. All these learning experiences may tend to arrest her
at the level of attempts to maintain that she is a boy rather than
a girl. This may culminate clinically in extreme cases in her becoming one of those Lesbians who wear or use rubber phalli.

The *urethral* phase is sometimes treated as an independent intermediary stage between the pregenital and the phallic and sometimes as part of the phallic. The latter designation seems to us
more appropriate clinically and logically and is therefore discussed
at this point.

The urethral phase is usually conceived of as twofold: the active
form, accompanied by fantasies of penetration and exhibitionism,
and the more passive form of "letting flow." The latter is clinically
often seen related to the oral phase, e.g., in cases of premature
ejaculation in which the patient reports a pleasant feeling of the
penis being enveloped by the vaginal walls "like a body being
embraced" and associations further relating to being fed and
loved by the mother. Ejaculation in such cases frequently takes

[3] The term "condition" or "fixate by conditioning" could be substituted for
this usage of "fixate."

place from an unerect penis and without a feeling of climax, the patient reporting that "it really was more like urinating."

In more detail, the aims of the urethral phase of gratification are not only that of urinating, but often urinating competitively (seeing who can aim higher), and wanting to be admired for one's prowess. To be sure, the intermediary position of the phallic phase is also borne out by the fact that some of the urinary pleasures may be more of an autoerotic nature, while others are definitely object-related. On the other hand the more definitely phallic connotations appear in the fact that little girls at this time often want to "urinate like boys" standing up and by this activity stake their claims to phalli.

Learning propositions enter in, for instance, where the child is early submitted to severe urinary training, or where there is general overemphasis on urinary functions. Again, frequent occasions for comparison with an older male, or reasons for excessive masculine identification in a female child (e.g., in a strong homosexual relation to a sister) may reinforce urethral aims to a point where they predominate in character formation or in the creation of neurotic syndromes.

Characterologically, the psychoanalytic proposition is that urethral aims will later manifest themselves in the wish to be looked at (exhibitionism) and to look (voyeurism, e.g., for comparison of genitals). If such aims are sublimated, acting on the stage, or looking, as a microbiologist, may be a resultant. More diffusely, a urethral character would be one who is very ambitious, competitive, show-offish.

The degree to which this aim is expressed in behavior depends alike on how early the urethral aim was strengthened by mother's conditioning and other environmental circumstances. That is, if the urethral aim is excessive, it is considered apt to produce pathological manifestations (from perversions to premature ejaculation, to character disorders, to sublimated character traits). However, as an example holding true for other statements concerning libidinal propositions, we should state here that these propositions are made appropriately much more complex by other propositions: the isolated event of increased urethral aims must be seen in the total pattern of the personality. Similarly other statements concerning libido theory have to be qualified. For instance, even if a mother should particularly stress urethral performance but should otherwise afford the child a "healthy" psychological climate, the urethral problem might appear only in a sublimated or at least nondisturbing pathological form (e.g., a [voyeuristic] hobby such as collecting opera glasses in an otherwise well-functioning person), while the same maternal behavior in an otherwise pathogenic environment might lead to a specific urethrogenic psychopathology, while again in a third environment of extreme pathogenicity a schizophrenic picture might be produced in which the urethral pathology belongs to the least of the patient's troubles.

ς. *The latency period* belongs to the more embattled of the psychoanalytic concepts. This is mostly so because Freud originally ascribed it to phylogenetic influence. Nearly all psychoanalysts have given up this speculation and hold that ontogenetic propositions adequately explain its existence. Another point of contention has concerned its lawful appearance: there are those who maintain it reflects ontogenetic maturational processes, and those who maintain that the latency period is strictly the result of (cultural) learning.

In short, the proposition concerning aims of gratification in the latency period (roughly from the fifth to the tenth year) means that there is an inhibition of direct pregenital or phallic aims; i.e., these aims are not observed or are observed less than before and after this period. Instead, what is observed and is presumed to be causally related to the erstwhile manifest phallic aims (now inhibited by the superego) are sublimations of this aim, manifesting themselves in intellectual curiosity. The infantile aims are also sublimated in part, and in part reaction formations take place. The ego is strengthened, possibly by a maturational ebbing of active striving and resultant better control, in part by the emergence of the superego (out of the resolution of the oedipus complex).

Thus, a concept of the "latency period" involves at least the following:

a. The assumption, or postulating, or demonstrating of a biological, endocrine, maturational process characterized by a decrease in a sexual drive (in all its psychoanalytic submeanings).

b. A strengthening of the ego, partly secondary to the weakening of the id drives and partly due to the perceptual, motor, and intellectual growth of the ego (a strengthening of the "autonomous functions" as Hartmann calls them). The secondary strengthening of the ego is itself predicated upon a set of propositions: namely, that it is part of the ego's functions to mediate between drive demand and reality, and to exercise control generally, and that such control is "easier" when the drive demand is decreased. The further proposition involved is that if the ego can "spare some energy" from controlling the id, it can use this energy for other tasks, e.g., of sublimating the drive.

c. It involves the concept of sublimation: drives may change their mode of gratification, their aim from direct gratification to some detour behavior which is more consistent with the entire set of cultural demands and maturational change. For example, the wish to look at someone's genitals may be generalized into curiosity concerning the nature of the universe and learning generally, toward mastery of the environment.

6. *Adolescent-Adult genitality.*[4]   The aim of this phase is the one ordinarily associated with sexuality, namely, that there eventually be a union of the genitals in copulation. It is important for the concept of adult genital aims that psychoanalysis recognizes all preceding pregenital and early genital aims as appropriate components of the genital aim *per se*, provided the components play a secondary role and terminate in the genital union. Perversion, psychoanalytically, exists where any component pregenital aim supersedes the genital aim.

It should be pointed out that the mere fact of copulation with apparently good function and orgasm in either sex is not *ipso facto* evidence of genital sexuality. Psychoanalysts frequently find that such manifest genitality is accompanied by conscious, preconscious, or unconscious fantasies of a homosexual or anal nature, and that these factors contribute exclusively or primarily the aim and pleasure and that therefore the manifest genital activity does not represent genital activity, dynamically speaking. If frequency and even intensity of genital activity and orgasm were the criterion of psychodynamic maturity, manics would doubtlessly win the medal. However, such a criterion would be the result of fallacious reasoning which could only be compared to the proposition that if being married is a criterion of maturity, then being married five times means being five times as mature.

It is part of the concept of sexual aims that there may not only

[4] Preadolescence, roughly ages 10–12, shows an increase again of pregenital drives and interests, sloppiness and general unruliness.

be *progression* as described up to now, but also regression. Under
adverse circumstances *regression* to any earlier level may take place.
Clinically, it is of the utmost importance diagnostically and prog-
nostically for a psychonanalyst to know whether a patient ever
reached the genital level and, having reached it, regressed again, or
never reached it. The prognosis in the latter case is generally much
worse.

Libidinal Object-Choices and Their Cathexis

The third major proposition of the libido theory is concerned with
the nature of the object that is chosen in aiming for gratification
at various stages of maturation. Implicit in this proposition are the
quantitative economic formulations concerning libido as energy.
The proposition concerning object-choices states that the first object is the infant's own body (as yet undifferentiated from the
rest of the world) and designates this first state as *narcissistic*. The
second type of object-choice is described as an anaclitic object-
choice (anaclitic meaning "leaning against"): the child relates first
to that figure which supplies him with gratification of its needs,
and only the final achievement of cathexis of a person outside the
family is considered true *object-cathexis.*[5]

The economic implications are involved in the idea that the
"amount of libido" which was originally invested in the self is
decreased by the amount invested, say, in the mother figure. To
speak facetiously, if baby John started out with a total narcissistic
libido of 100,000 Freudian units, he may be investing 20,000
units in the mother. Thereupon baby John would be left only
with 80,000 Freudian units with which to keep house. John may
be expected to invest some of this in his father, his siblings, his
teachers, etc., but incidentally can never go completely bankrupt
according to another proposition never quite explicitly stated. In
the first place, some units always stay invested in his body and in
the various libidinal zones. (This, incidentally, could all be very
well stated in terms of Kurt Lewin's topological concepts, vectors,
etc.) Also, some units are intricately bound up in his defenses

[5] Probably the most significant advances in psychoanalysis in recent years have
to do with the increasingly detailed study of the development of early object
relations, and the related development of the ego. Cf. M. Mahler's work on
symbiotic psychoses, Spitz's research on anaclitic depressions and the work of
Kris, Katherine Wolf, and others.

and counter-cathexes and his entire intrapsychic system (ego, superego).

However, John's progress in libidinal object-choices could very well be traced quantitatively. For instance, with the final adolescent resolution of the oedipus constellation, John is expected to withdraw a considerable, not specified, number of units—say 15,000 of the 20,000 originally invested in the mother, and some 5,000 of those invested in sister, and an equal amount from those invested in brother and father, and now briefly but richly endow a series of objects (girl friends), and finally settle 30,000 Freudian units on his wife, at least during the active courtship, further increased by a withdrawal of 10,000 units from his own narcissistic reserves. Upon the birth of his first child, some further reinvestment from the family, from his own narcissistic pool, and possibly some withdrawal from the original heated investment in his wife may be expected to be placed upon the account of the baby. As he lives on he can be expected to decrease his narcissistic supply to the safe minimum necessary for intact operation, self-protection, and self-esteem, as much as any good business venture may be expected not to deplete its reserves below a safe minimum. At the same time, for maximal health, all expendable units should be freely circulating, expended on his own family, friends, the community, and his work.

The above roughly and very schematically constitutes the quantitative picture of the propositions concerned with choices and investments of objects of libidinal aims. It is an inherent part of psychoanalysis that health exists only under such circumstances. Again, the concept of progression or regression is paralleled by a concept of lack of progression. There are a great number of propositions concerned with the lack of progress from the narcissistic stage, which, if complete, will result in the narcissistic neurosis (*i.e.*, psychosis); or if less marked, and possibly in the presence of greater ego strength and other variables, may result in a narcissistic character disorder; or if even less, in a neurosis of the familiar field and garden variety.

Again, progression to true object-cathexis may be achieved and regression may take place due to disappointment or other adverse effects, for example, enforced separation in illness, war, jail, etc. Thereupon, reinvestment of the individual's own person and earlier aims and zones may take place.

Of crucial importance again will be the propositions concerning severity of interference with the progression of object-cathexes or their forced regression. Aside from constitutional defects, as recently posited most clearly by Mahler and Elkisch [35], who state that the mother-child relationship may in part be determined by characteristics of the newborn, and in part by the type of object the mother is (frustrating, punishing, giving, sadistic, affectionate), these will determine the early object relationship, and according to further propositions, all later ones. Spitz has spelled out most succinctly the devastating effects of early disturbance of object relationships in nearly quantitative terms [43, 44].

So far we have hardly touched upon the crucial processes involved in the shifts of object-cathexis during the oedipus complex and its resolution. In our schematic presentation, it will have to suffice to point out the quantitative assumptions involved. In terms of our hypothetical example the propositions concerning the oedipus complex can be illustrated by the following: John has invested 20,000 units in his mother as the object of his aim for genital (and other) gratification. He also has a considerable investment in his father (the nature of which we will not stop to specify here) and also in his own penis as the vehicle of his aim. Let us assume that the penis is invested with 30,000 units, and John feels he is in danger of losing it, plus the investment in his father if he does not forego—or rather withdraw—most of his investment in his mother. This obviously would be very bad business. He thereupon resolves the dilemma by withdrawing 15,000 from his mother, and changing the nature of his financial ambitions from one of primary control over the mother to one of sympathetic participation in a small way; he reinvests some of the units in the superego (those internal police forces which should protect him from getting so much out on a limb again), some in his father (sort of making friends with an enemy found valiant who becomes at the same time admired); he keeps the bulk of libido as ready working capital for a series of transactions of object-cathexis. This finally may alight more permanently in the wife, etc., as stated before.

The transactions are more complex in the case of the girl, but in our schematic discussion this need not concern us.

Again, a great number of further propositions are related to those of the oedipus complex. Learning experiences, such as over-seductive behavior on the part of the mother, may so increase the investment in her as to make withdrawal and reinvestment impossible without endangering the whole economic structure. A very frightening father may so discourage investment in the mother and, by the same token, in the penis as vehicle of the aim, that either this stage of the transactions is never reached, or if reached, there is regression to earlier investments of autoerotic aims and objects (zones).

To these propositions concerning the oedipus complex are tied even further propositions concerning the future pathology resultant from a great number of constellations of variables as briefly indicated above, pathology ranging from an inability to marry or to stay married to a general avoidance of competitive striving. If all attainment of success, for instance, is identified with possession of the mother, as it frequently is, any number of other clinical syndromes may result, such as a "success neurosis."

The Conception of Learning Implicit in the Libido Theory

Having briefly discussed some of the basic propositions of the libido theory, it behooves us now to examine more closely the nature of the learning processes interacting with the processes of maturation concerned with the changing of preferred choices of zones, aims, and objects of aims. It is our basic bias that such learning proceeds in a way consistent with a combination of some of the propositions advanced by the Gestalt school of psychology and some of the principles of conditioning.

In the theory of projection Freud [15] has really formulated a perceptual theory of learning:

But projection is not specially created for the purpose of defense, it also comes into being where there are no conflicts. The projection of inner perceptions to the outside is a primitive mechanism which, for instance, also influences our sense-perceptions, so that it normally has the greatest share in shaping our outer world. Under conditions that have not yet been sufficiently determined even inner perceptions of ideational and emotional processes are projected outwardly, like sense perceptions, and are used to shape the outer world, whereas they ought to remain in the inner world . . .

The thing which we, just like primitive man, project in outer reality, can hardly be anything else but the recognition of a state in which a given thing is present to the senses and to consciousness, next to which another state exists in which the thing is *latent*, but can reappear, that is to say, the co-existence of perception and memory, or, to generalize it, the existence of unconscious psychic processes next to conscious ones.

Freud says in essence, then, that percept memories influence the perception of contemporary stimuli and not only for the narrowly defined purposes of defense, as stated in the original definition of projection. We are compelled to assume that *all* present perception is influenced by past perception, and that indeed the nature of the perceptions and their interaction with each other constitutes a large part of the field of the psychology of the personality.

Apperception was defined by Herbart [27] as follows: "The process by which new experience is assimilated to and transformed by the residuum of past experience of any individual to form a new whole. The residuum of past experience is called apperceptive mass."

This, however, would necessitate two theories: one to explain the first perception; and another one, the one of apperceptive distortion, to explain all the rest of the perceptions. Luckily, no such monstrosity is necessary. It is generally agreeable to psychoanalysts (who arrive there via reconstructions from psychotics' experiences), to academic psychologists (from the nature of assumptions concerning *Gestalten*), and to neurologists (from their knowledge of the organic substratum) that the original perception of infants is likely to be poorly defined (poor figure and ground definition) with many sensory data overlapping. By the time an infant is able to have accurate perceptions, they are already apperceptions, i.e., structured by the vague perceptual precursors.

Schematically speaking then again, within the frame of the libido theory, an infant being suckled would have a diffuse apperception of the mother suckling him: tensely or relaxed, loving or impatient, frustrating or satisfying or overindulging. Again, he would have images of mother cleaning him or training for cleanliness, and later mother talking, mother in relation to the other siblings, to father, etc. It is part of the implicit learning theory of the libido theory to say that, all other things being equal, the *law of primacy* will determine the dominance of an image; that is, the earlier an apperception, the more controlling an effect it will have on later apperception. The *law of frequency* is also generally implied: all other things being equal, the more frequent maternal behavior will have a more marked organizing effect on later apperceptions.

In fact, nearly all the tenets of conditioning theory are really implicit in the covert assumptions concerning learning in the libido theory; namely, that the degree of reinforcement (e.g., a mother severely punishing uncontrolled defecation, or aggressively insisting on enemas) will determine the degree of influence of one series of apperceptions on other apperceptions.

Within the genetic framework of the libido theory is the covert assumption that every contemporary apperception is determined by all previous apperceptions. To be more specific, in the contemporary apperception of a woman, for example, the wife will be determined by all the previous apperceptions of mother, sister, and other significant figures. Techniques like the TAT are specifically predicated upon such assumptions.

Free association could be described as a systematic way of recapturing the genetic structuration of contemporary apperception. The contemporary images are best seen like a composite photograph of, say, the average American if 160 million profiles had been superimposed on each other. If one should want to ascertain the origin of one particular feature, one would have to examine each of the profiles that may have contributed to the final picture. For this process, the laws of Gestalt formation hold true; e.g., the final resultant picture is not a mere sum total but a new configuration where quantitative factors have produced qualitative changes (after Hegel's concept of Transformation of Quantity into Quality).

Psychoanalytic propositions concern the lawful relationship of certain contemporary manifest features of behavior to the acquisitions of apperceptions—e.g., of premature ejaculation to urethral experiences or apperceptions of castration threats or both in rela-. tion to each other, or agoraphobia to apperceptions of ambivalence on the part of the mother (and ambivalence in the child). (See discussion of reaction formation under "The Defenses.")

The Ego

The novelty in psychoanalysis was originally its introduction of the unconscious in the sense of the unconsciousness of feelings, the unawareness of previously experienced events, the covert nature of motivations, and the hidden meaning of dreams and symptoms. Slowly attention focused on the forces responsible for this unconsciousness, notably repression. Particularly with Anna Freud's book, *The Ego and the Mechanisms of Defense,* a new era started in psychoanalysis, dedicated to the analysis not only of the unconscious but of the ego and its defenses. The pendulum has swung nearly full cycle, in that there is so much talk about ego psychology today that the forces of the unconscious are possibly already somewhat in disregard. Many a psychologist who would not want to be found dead close to a volume of Freud will quite happily write about the study of the ego—as if the latter alone could at all be sensibly studied without the entire dynamic psychoanalytic context. It seems that ego psychology is the part of psychoanalysis most easily found socially acceptable.

Theoretical assumptions concerning the ego are twofold, being in part based upon constitutional, genetic, maturational processes, and in part upon principles of learning. Even though Freud stated quite clearly that there is no reason why there should not be primary, congenital ego variations, it is only now that these two basic assumptions are being made somewhat overt, e.g., in Hartmann's paper [23] and Anna Freud's discussion of it [14].

Enlightened behavioral science has a certain reluctance to consider the significance of genetic and congenital factors; this is in part a reaction to earlier overemphasis on genetics and in part an aspect of our cultural era. Birth and heredity were so all-determining in past centuries that the Declaration of Independence found it necessary to proclaim that "all men are created equal." Much of the sentiment in American psychology against the genetic orientation of psychoanalysis, its determinism and biological orientation, is influenced by these cultural trends.

The ego can be described by its history, by its functions, and possibly best by the extent to which it fulfills its functions in a quantitative way (see section on investigation of the ego, this chapter). Spitz probably has put historical events most clearly. There is observational evidence, and it seems likely on neurological and general development grounds (Melanie Klein notwithstanding) that there is little differentiation of psychic function in the infant prior to the sixth month [43, 44]. The infant at first probably has only poorly defined sensory impressions, without a differentiation of its own body from the rest of the world or differentiation of its proprioceptive and other subjective perceptions from reality *per se*. There is in fact observational and experimental evidence that body and mind are one in the sense that perceptual stimulation seems necessary for somatic development: Spitz speaks of the "somatopsyche" up to the sixth month *[43, 44]*, and has shown hospitalism and anaclitic depressions as clinical syndromes related to this construction.

Only when the perceptions become well enough differentiated into figure and ground so that the child can differentiate the surface of its own body from the rest of the world, can the child be expected to tell the difference between subjective and objective phenomena. It is then presumably that one may speak of an ego. Freud *[17]* in 1923 in his book *The Ego and the Id* said: "The ego is first and foremost a body ego; it is not merely a surface entity but it is itself the projection of a surface."

Thus, starting with the perception of the body as figure and the rest of the world as ground, psychoanalysis refers to the ego as that aspect of mental functioning concerned with the ordering of reality into figure and ground and the awareness of this and other intricate relationships between apperceptions and their memory. In the most severe disturbances of the mental functioning, the psychoses, this differentiation of body and the rest of the world in parts breaks down again. As Federn *[11]* has pointed out, the ego boundaries are disturbed in psychosis and thus cosmic delusions and hallucinations of any kind are possible.

This function of the organism has recently been interestingly related to the brain. Linn *[34]* has studied perceptual functions in the brain-injured and observed defenses as Freud described them. Subscribing to the concept of "scanning" of Pitts and McCulloch *[38]*, Linn believes that the ego tests apperceptions (in a scanning operation) as long as it is intact but that the efficiency of that scanning may be interfered with by brain defects. He does not say so, but one might surmise that this takes place in accordance with Lashley's concept of mass action and equipotentiality of the brain. Linn leaves the relationship to "functional" ego defect open, though this seems unnecessary. The scanning function of the ego can easily be understood as interfered with if circumstances so strongly revive past apperceptions as to distort each contemporary apperception to a point where it may not be perceived clearly as figure and ground any more. The phenomenon of *déjà vu* in normals (at times of anxiety in a new environment) or in certain schizophrenics, who feel with every person they meet that they have seen him before or that he looks like somebody seen before, most clearly illustrates this function.[6]

Thus the *reality-testing function* can be seen as a structural capacity of the ego; namely, its ability to keep the effect of all but a few selected pertinent past apperceptions upon the contemporary apperception to a minimum (selective inattention); that is, to apply those apperceptions which have been learned as useful in dealing with a reality situation only. If inappropriate apperceptions gain access to the conscious perceptual and motor apparatus, feelings and behavior inappropriate to reality may result.

We speak of this reality-testing function as associated with a structural aspect of the ego for this reason: if the personal history is of such a nature that apperceptions were clearly articulated (good configurations), and if the child developed good object relations, was exposed to consistent handling and not persistently disturbed by libidinal and aggressive stimuli, then the *structural* organization of the apperceptions is a firm one and not easily disrupted by disturbing contemporary apperceptions or drives. The healthy ego, because of the "good" organization of the memory traces and past apperceptions, keeps a firm grip on reality even in adversity or under monotonous circumstances. (Related to the reality-testing function is the ego's function as a barrier against excessive external and internal stimuli.)

As already indicated in the discussion of the learning of stimuli as postulated in the libido theory, it is consistent with the psychoanalytic theory that all structured mentation starts with perception. The ego comprises those apperceptions which are conscious or can easily become conscious* and which are continuously part of the contemporary apperceptions in a way which permits one to differentiate (by experience) various figure and ground judgments, e.g., external versus internal, and permits one altogether to exercise "good judgment" founded upon past experience (memory traces

---

[6] Wilder Penfield's reported eliciting of discrete memories, inclusive of affect, upon electrical focal stimulation of the brain, also supports the entire psychoanalytic theory of memory.

* Some aspects of ego functioning are unconscious, however.

of past apperceptions) as to what is safe and what not, what is probable and what not. In this context there can be no doubt that intelligence may enter in as the ability to form new "wholes" out of old "parts" and to find solutions to new problems never before met as such. In that sense intelligence truly becomes an organizing function.

It is part of the assumptions made about the ego that certain maturational factors are involved, correlated to the maturation of the motor and neurological apparatus. That the ego is correlated to the brain was always implied without too much overt statement. Freud did think of it as primarily akin to the cortex. Recent psychoanalytic work in connection with lobotomies, as well as the previously quoted observations of Linn, suggest to us the quantitative relations to mass action of the brain previously mentioned.

Only lately have constitutional differences between egos been clearly stated by Hartmann *[21]*, though Freud made reference to them. Hartmann speaks in this context of "autonomous functions of the ego," a concept including intelligence and in essence providing a conceptual roof for the assumption that some inherent organismic qualities of nonspecified, though possibly genetically transmittable, factors may also influence the tendency toward "good" organization of apperceptions (and thus in our terms, a strong ego). The study of epileptics with their ego disturbances (of perception, of the muscular apparatus, of impulse control, and obsessive defenses against the impulses and hypothesized synaptic disturbances) might be the best link to be studied between the neurological and the psychological level.

The ego is also said to have *executive functions* concerning the motor system. Presumably they are related to the early apperception of kinesthetic stimuli and their differentiation from external and other stimuli and the reactivation of kinesthetic memory images in the process of bodily manipulation.

Thinking, considered by Freud a form of trial action, can at least in part be conceptualized as the recall of past apperceptions —visual, auditory, etc. Problem solving presumably occurs by closure concerning past apperceptions and the contemporary apperceptions of the "problem." Intuition, so long a matter of speculation, probably simply refers to the fact that a new configuration may occur on the one hand as more than just the sum of the parts that went into it; and on the other hand, without conscious awareness of the process of restructuration or even conscious awareness of the parts that went into it; just as any visual stimulus may be apperceived as a whole without conscious awareness of the parts that make up the total picture.

Into the ego's development go many learning experiences, inasmuch as the reality that is tested differs greatly in different cultures. In fact, even the degree of differentiation of contemporary apperception from past apperception and of that of subjective and objective differs in different cultures. Probably people without psychosis could have hallucinations in other cultures, since what may be socially acceptable behavior in one culture has to be rejected by the ego as unacceptable by another culture.

Ego Strength

The concept of ego strength is discussed in more detail in the section on Research. Briefly it can be defined as being measured (on an ordinal scale) by the degree to which the ego manages to perform its many functions of reality testing, stress tolerance, motor functions, etc.

Many, if not all, phenomena of ego weakness can be shown to be primarily characterized by perceptual disturbance, specifically a disturbance of the differentiation of past apperceptions from contemporary ones. For instance, in the normal weakening of ego strength associated with falling asleep we speak of hypnagogic phenomena, following Varendonck [45] and Silberer [42]. There the apperception of reality is distorted by the memory traces of past apperceptions. Dreams themselves may be so understood, particularly if we consider the case where an external stimulus, e.g., pressure on the body, becomes apperceptively distorted by past apperceptions into some nightmarish imagery.

The clinical diagnosis of conditions characterized by extreme ego disturbance—that is, ego weakness—is primarily done by phenomenological characteristics, whether clinical or by tests. Clinically, phenomena of unreality, and evidence of the primary process in apperception, are evidence of structural weakness—i.e., lack of clear definition of the apperceptions disturbed by the past. The Rorschach diagnosis is of course predicated precisely on the apperceptive disturbance of the contemporary images of the blots by past apperceptions. If images are seen poorly, i.e., where the response is obviously more determined by memory traces than by what consensus agrees to be "reality," the diagnosis of ego weakness has to be made.

The concept of strength or weakness of the ego, in terms of its apperceptive clarity, can be further likened to physical structures. As much as stability of apperception constitutes ego strength (a matter unwittingly demonstrated by experiments of optical ambiguity by Eysenck *et al.*), so much does rigidity constitute an aspect of weakness, and flexibility an aspect of strength. The simile that comes to mind is the architecture of bridges, or even of steel and concrete skyscrapers, which are built to allow a certain flexibility and thus fare much better than structures built as rigidly as possible. The rigid apperceptive construction of the obsessive-compulsive sacrifices adaptability for the sake of some stability. The firmness of organization of images may be overdone, particularly in the obsessive. The ego of the hysteric with its fluctuating ego boundaries in conversions and hypochondriasis stands on the other side of the center. Alcohol and other anesthetics in their effect on brain function may loosen the arrangement—"weaken the ego."

For a number of normal functions a measure of flexibility of apperception is necessary. Creativity, artistic or scientific, can come about only if figure and ground relationships may change freely. This is most easily observable, of course, in the painter and photographer, but holds true even for functions such as telling stories in the TAT, or being able to free-associate *[4]*. Kris *[31]* has spoken of regression in the service of the ego, which is closely related to Hartmann's *[22]* concept of self-exclusion. In both cases a measure of control is relinquished. This is a measure of strength.

For free-associating, it is necessary that one permit a poor definition of the contemporary apperception, precisely in order that past images may emerge. In what the writer has previously called the "oscillating function" of the ego, it is at the same time necessary that one be able to compare the past apperception with the contemporary apperception (in reality testing in analysis) and observe the differences. Similarly, as Hartmann and Kris have pointed out, the ability of the ego to exclude itself and regression in the service of the ego, respectively, is necessary for falling asleep, intercourse, and creativity: permitting a "soft focusing" of the ego, as it were.

The Defenses

The defenses were originally entirely anthropomorphized concepts, particularly the concept of the "censor" responsible for repression in dreams, etc. Defenses can probably be entirely conceptualized, however, in terms of apperception. *Repression*, as the main and oldest form of defense, is truly inherent in the entire concept of unconsciousness. We have already stated that unconsciousness, in the meaning of unawareness of parts that go to make up the new configuration, is a basic proposition of Gestalt formation. Thus, the fact that some characteristics of mother or some memories of her behavior are "repressed" is part of the construction of the composite photograph.

The idea of "defense" has a perfectly good correlate in the "buffer systems" of the bodily organism, viz., the alkali reserve. Cannon's concept of homeostasis had its early forerunner in Freud's thinking [26, 29] and is now freely used by psychoanalysts [36]. It is probably consistent with the perceptual principles of the tendency toward the "good Gestalt" (*Prägnanz*) which on the other hand finds its equivalent in the formation of crystals and the formation of globules in fluid in such a way that the most stable form is the one where all forces are "equalized." The psychoanalytic concepts of defense can probably be understood as a tendency to achieve the most stable system, or to permit minimum disturbance of an established system of forces in an apperception. The latter embodies in essence the concept of the ego as a barrier to excessive external or internal stimulation.

One may also state it this way: defense mechanisms may be restated as the selective and structuring effect of certain image properties upon the effect of past apperceptions on present apperceptions. Each separate defense mechanism formulated by psychoanalysis constitutes a hypothesis concerning some lawfulness of interaction of images under certain circumstances.

The mechanism of *denial*, for example, can probably most easily be understood as the apperception of a contemporary situation in a way least likely to upset a (precarious) apperceptive balance. For some of the other defenses, psychoanalysis has actually covertly laid down principles of Gestalt formation which are probably experimentally verifiable, as for instance, in the concept of reaction formation. When a mother has aggressive feelings for her child along with affectionate feelings at the same time, one of the possible results of this conflict of sentiments is described by psychoanalysis as *reaction* formation: the aggressive feelings are repressed and become unconscious and only excessive affection is manifest. It is possible to restate this analytic concept in Gestalt language: when a "good" image and a "bad" image are simultaneously apperceived, the resultant will be a reinforced "good" image modified by some aspects of the "bad" image. But mother love as the result of the reactive formation has the destructive features of overprotectiveness; i.e., some of the originally coexistive aggression manifests itself in the new guise. This was experimentally investigated upon the writer's suggestion by Finn *[12]. Projec tion* also can be by far best understood as a phenomenon of apperceptive distortion of contemporary images by past apperceptions *[4]*.

The Id

The id was Freud's term, borrowed from Groddeck, which originally stood for all that was felt as ego alien—"it makes me feel like crying." Freud himself *[17]* has suggested that the term may originally go back to Nietzsche. Conceptually speaking, the id became the hypothetical locus and mainspring of the drives and, covertly, the psychoanalytic concept of the id is part of the psychoanalytic theory of *motivation*. It is not, however, the entire theory of motivation, as some would mistakenly have it, since psychoanalysis deals very complexly with a motivational system that takes into account not only the complex assumptions concerning drives (as already discussed in part as the libido theory) but also their genetic and dynamic and economic interaction with each other, with the superego, the ego, and the environment.

The concept of the id primarily implies the assumption of primary organismic drives. Psychoanalysis then formulates specific hypotheses concerning maturational changes of these drives, and the impact of environmental learning upon them and interaction with them. As far as the primary drives are concerned we can safely expect biologists, experimental psychologists and neurologists to advance the soundest hypotheses, which then should lend themselves to the additional specific hypothesis which psychoanalysts know about best.

However reluctant psychologists may have been to acknowledge any strictly biological nature of drives, it is impossible to form a sound theory of personality without it. Perhaps most helpful will be the formulation of inherent *Anlagen* to react to deficit with a certain neural pattern, as Lashley *[32]* demonstrated experimentally.

Again, psychoanalysis has made a few formal statements of a principle often implied, namely that there are probably congenital id variations, primarily in the strength of the drives.[7] Thus, one person's ego may be predestined for a more difficult time simply because this particular person starts out life with a more vigorous id than the next person's. The excellent observations of Fries and Woolf on congenital activity patterns come closest to this formulation *[19]*. They justly suggest that this activity pattern might be one of the early determinants of ego activity, in particular helping to determine the choice of symptoms, defenses and character structure.

Beyond the most basic conception of the nature and functioning of drives and aside from the theory of aggression, the psychoanalytic theory of libido and its vicissitudes, which has already been discussed, constitutes the conception of the id.

The Superego

The superego is the structural concept of psychoanalysis concerned with "moral" behavior, insofar as this moral behavior is based upon unconscious, early learned behavioral patterns. Alexander's suggestion to speak of conscience in distinction to superego when we speak of conscious, ego-syntonic precepts of social behavior is probably a widely accepted one.

There are analysts who maintain that the superego also has genetic, constitutional aspects aside from what we could readily identify as learned components. This seems difficult to accept—un-

[7] Greenacre has discussed this topic in a paper on "Some Factors Producing Different Types of Genital and Pregenital Organization," in Greenacre, P., *Trauma, Growth and Personality*.

less it be made part of a broader concept; namely, that some organisms seem to have less drive demand than others and that this is not primarily a function of lack of drive but of excess of control (if this can be at all differentiated). The difficulty lies in the assumption that "moral control" would be constituted separately from those control factors usually identified with the ego.

From a learning standpoint the superego is the totality of a great number of complexly learned inhibitions of drive aims. Psychoanalysis posits, for instance, that the earliest and most severe learned inhibitive behavior (often appearing self-punitive) stems from the anal phase, related to excessive cleanliness training. That is, a child severely trained to be clean, may be excessively afraid of any "dirtiness" including verbal abuse, may grow up into an adult always feeling "dirty" (guilty), and may in essence suffer from an "inner voice of conscience" which is the persistent unconscious apperception of the nagging and reprimanding voice or look of the mother. In this sense "moral masochism" may be understood as a continuous effect of apperception of such an "anal-sadistic" mother upon one's apperception of one's contemporary feeling, thinking, and behavior.

One should hurry to emphasize that of course psychoanalytic hypotheses are by no means so naïve or oversimplified as to assume that cleanliness training is in a one-to-one relationship to the formation of the superego, or for that matter that it constitutes all of the causal factors. On the contrary, there are dozens of factors—e.g., the learning involved in the correct apperceptions of the dangers of the oedipus constellation and the related inhibition of aims directed toward mother as object become a powerful further contribution to the set of regulators.

The apperceptions pertaining to the superego appear in pure culture—in the hallucinations of a schizophrenic whose voices may accuse him, frequently in a clearly parental voice, of any number of infractions. Again, the self-accusations of the melancholic can be understood in linear continuity (instead of appearing senseless) if one interpolates the sets of hypotheses psychoanalysis has postulated for this syndrome, with particular reference to a distortion of the patient's contemporary feelings or behavior by past apperceptions associated with control and punishment for aggressive aims.

Aggression

Psychoanalysis is generally considered to advance a dual theory
of drives, sexual (generally equated with libidinal) and aggressive. This is primarily another instance of unnecessary semantic
confusion in that psychoanalysis indeed discusses very many partial drives, primarily as part of the libido theory; e.g., the drives
toward acquisition incorporated in the concept of the oral stage,
or all the other partial components such as the wish to see, to
exhibit, etc. Murray's [37] need system probably constitutes the
best elaboration of the covert diversity of drives subsumed under
psychoanalytic libido theory.

The theory of aggression was in an even less satisfactory state
than the libido theory. Freud came to be concerned with aggression only belatedly, and then first in terms of his concept of the
need for mastery as one aspect of sexual wishes; then later as
part of the concept of ego drives (which had to be abandoned
when the id was considered the locus of drives; what Freud considered ego drive of self-preservation is really the concept of the
ego as the testing aspect of mental functioning), and finally in
the concept of the death instinct, which is rejected by the majority of analysts.

The only major systematic paper on aggression in psychoanalysis is the paper by Hartmann *et al.* [26]. They interpret and
extend Freud's conception into a systematic statement in essence
paralleling the conceptualization of the libido. These authors,
with Freud, say that beginning in the undifferentiated phase of
infancy the self becomes differentiated from the "not self" by
virtue of the latter being identified with unpleasure and the self
with pleasure. By such means the "not self" becomes invested with
aggression and becomes the object of aggression. Hartmann *et
al.* say also that aggression may be described by stating impetus,
source, aim, and object, similar to libido theory.

By impetus is meant the amount of force, the quantity of
aggression. There seems to be some difficulty in identifying the
source of aggressive drive (in the libido theory drive is closely
linked with zone). Freud described the strong relationship between skeletal musculature and aggression, but Hartmann *et al.*
point out that the muscular system is as well related to libidinal
discharge. It would seem, as is pointed out in more detail below,

that we do not deal with a specific drive but instead with one aspect of an organismic reaction to environment (ordinarily subsumed under cathexis) which only later becomes more specific by maturation and learning, e.g., specifically aggressive. There is some support for this notion in the physiological fact that adrenalin release and the related biochemical changes (blood sugar, clotting time, etc.) are responses as much tied to aggression as to any simple work or any additional demand on the organism to respond to the environment.

This same basic tenet seems to hold for a discussion of the aim of aggression. As much as the source is nonspecifically organismic, so much is the aim originally a nonspecific relationship to the environment, only later modified into mastery, involving as much acquisition as rejection, removal or destruction. The object of aggression (Hartmann *et al.* quote from Freud, and one can only heartily agree) "is the most variable thing about a drive and is not originally connected with it but becomes attached to it only in consequence of being peculiarly fitted to provide satisfaction."

Hartmann *et al.* also provide a beautifully systematic discussion of four types of conflict through which the aims of aggression are modified: (1) "Instinctual conflict—aggression and libido may be involved in conflict when the cathexis of both drives is vested in the same object" (that is, when one object arouses both aggressive stimuli and libidinal ones, either by conditioning or by memory traces of past apperceptions and most likely indeed by a coexistence of both processes). (2) "Conflict with reality" (when there is a coexistence of an aggressive drive and learned inhibition related to self harm). (3) Structural conflict, involving the ego. "This danger (to the individual) may be anticipated by the ego, which is in part already identified with the object, and the ego might be opposed to the completion of aggressive acts" (when there is a coexistence of an aggressive drive and learned inhibition, the latter being predicated upon apperceptions of the self, superimposed on and integrated with apperceptions of the object). (4) Structural conflict involving the superego: "The conflict may involve moral values" (which means to me a coexistence of aggressive drive and learned apperceptions concerning culturally acceptable modes of behavior.)

These authors also speak of four types of processes which modify

the impact of aggression, which hardly need any redefinition:
(1) by displacement of aggression to other objects; (2) by
restriction of the aims of the aggressive impulses; (3) by sublimation of aggressive energy; and (4) by fusion of aggressive drives
with libidinal drives. The only point needing further elaboration is
the one dealing with sublimation of aggressive energy, for which incidentally the authors suggest the term "neutralization" (as equivalent to "sublimation" of libidinal energy). Either concept—involving the redirection of an aim to a socially acceptable object,
or the inhibition, restriction, or modification of the mode of
gratification—is difficult to redefine in terms of learning except in
terms of conditioning, which still is not quite satisfactory.

As stated they parallel the libido concept by insisting that a form
of sublimation must be posited for the aggressive drive, and
speak of it as "neutralization of aggression" and of neutralized
aggressive energy, paralleling the concept of sublimation and
sublimated energy of the libido theory. They believe that the ability
to neutralize aggressive energy is as much an aspect of ego strength
as the ability to sublimate, and as necessary for the creation and
maintenance of permanent object-relations.

Clinically, this above assumption makes excellent sense. One is
reminded of Schopenhauer's parable of the porcupines: Two porcupines beheld each other on a cold winter day and decided to
move close together to give each other warmth. Soon they found
that they stung each other with their quills and so moved apart,
only to find that they became cold again. Moving back and forth,
they finally found that optimum distance at which they could
give each other some warmth and yet find the sting of their
quills bearable. This may serve as an excellent parable on social
relations, involving both the libidinal needs (warmth) and the interfering aggressions (and fear of libidinal needs). Actually, it
seems that selection of mates may be as much influenced by the
amount of distance or tolerance of closeness that two people can
bear as by their libidinal needs. (Clinically, this is often primarily
a function of their narcissism.) At any rate, the disturbance in
social relations is frequently related to a lack of neutralization
of aggressive energy. The paranoid has to move on to frequently
changing positions because his tremendous hostility (aside from
arousal of homosexual wishes allied with it) drives him. In fact,
a recent research program in the work rehabilitation of post-

hospital psychotics seems to involve primarily a situation designed to increase the tolerance of ambivalence in these patients [8].

One can probably state the psychoanalytic theory of aggression fairly easily in academically acceptable terms. Aggression as described at first by psychoanalysis is one aspect of oral (aggressive, incorporative) behavior (later also anal). More generally, all movement is related to contact with and mastery of the environment, either in the form of acquiring or pushing away. Hoffer [28] has suggested that in a disturbance of ego development, the hand, instead of being an instrument (of aggressive mastery) in infants, may be an object of (oral) aggression, as in self-biting as he observed in a mentally deficient child of one year. Aggression can be conceptualized as being the direct outcome of motility,[8] moving to grasp by mouth or otherwise. The frustration-aggression hypothesis as a sole explanatory principle has already been roundly discredited. It again was an attempt to deny primary biological mechanisms for the sake of an all-inclusive learning theory. If aggression is originally identical with any outward-going movement—as appears in Mira's and other expressive techniques —it may again be related to the activity patterns of Fries and Woolf [19] and possibly even to the somatotypes of Sheldon et al. [41].

Psychoanalysis does state that in the beginning libidinal and aggressive behavior are inextricably fused [13]. This means that we are really introducing a conceptual artifact when we speak of aggressive aims and other aims (libidinal) of gratification toward an early object. Only as the child clearly perceives the outside world and learns frustration of a more specific and clearly perceived aim to incorporate, to reject, to be warmed, to be held, to be free of discomfort, does it differentiate specific movement in the service of producing the desired effect. In other words, in the theory of aggression too we must differentiate a basic motor and perceptual, organismic factor, and a series of later learned behavior.

The organismic perceptual factor is again a nearly protoplasmic one of reaction to stimuli. The human nervous system is so constructed that we can learn to react discriminatingly. Part of the acquired discrimination has to do with the differentiation of

[8] Anal expulsion might be seen as an extension of the body.

body from the outside world, and, as Hartmann *et al.* [26] suggest, the identification of the outside world as the source of nonpleasure. Further learned behavior, in the nature of both trial and error and better perception of figure and ground, then deals with differentiation of movements toward or away from these objects—acquisitive, rejecting, destructive. The psychoanalytic theory of aggression, we can then state again, is concerned with the maturational order of progression of differentiated response and with the formulation of specific learning of aggressive responses and their effect on adult personality. The primary existence of the reaction to stimuli obviates a simple frustration-aggression hypothesis. On the other hand, it seems to make unnecessary the postulation of a specific primary aggressive drive. As stated in the libido theory, we assume a reaction to stimuli which becomes modified by maturation *and* by learning into aggressive and other forms of behavior.

In that sense it may be easily acceptable that, after the oral aggressive phase, expulsion of the feces may acquire an aggressive meaning in the sense of rejecting by the ejection of material causing proprioceptive tension. Psychoanalysis states that if anal ejecting behavior is severely punished, an early learning of non-direction of aggression toward outside objects is established and redirection of aggression toward the child's own body (head-banging, etc.) is the first substitutive behavior. This is later modified into aggression against the ego (that is, an apperception of external, originally maternal, authority's disapproval—felt, thought, or expressed aggression). Thus, there is the psychoanalytic theory of the anal, obsessive-compulsive character trait with its inhibition of overt aggression and severely moral character. One hardly needs to caution again that this is a schematic representation and that psychoanalysis does not posit such a one-to-one relationship. This was isolated for the purpose of description, but is intricately bound up with hundreds of other apperceptions, each having a modifying character, as discussed in connection with other concepts.

The Theory of Dreams

The dream theory is indeed justly considered the cornerstone of Freud's theory. Significantly enough, none of the neo-Freudian schools has been able to alter substantially or to contribute to Freud's dream theory. None, in fact, could advance any cogent theory in terms of their supposed novel formulations.

Any dream theory has to explain in essence the nature of the manifest content, probably best by assuming a latent content. It has to explain the specific lawful relationship between the manifest and the latent, and the specificity of the occurrence of this particular dream in this person—i.e., order the dream behavior into a meaningful sequence within the continuity of a personality and that person's contemporary situation. To date, this has been accomplished only by Freud's theory which has also done much more than that.

Freud's formulation lends itself with particular ease to a restatement in terms of learned apperceptive distortion. Dreams consist primarily of pictures, sometimes of auditory, olfactory, or kinesthetic apperceptions; for purposes of simplicity we will speak of pictorial apperceptions only, though it will be readily apparent that any other dimensions could as readily be used as a model.

In this case, the dream pictures can best be understood as configurations structured by a series of learned earlier apperceptions and a contemporary apperception (the genetic aspects of dreams and the day residue). It is inherent in our previously stated concept that the dream will be overdetermined since a whole series of past apperceptions will structure the imagery. The primary process quality of the dream (its "nonsensicalness") is predicated upon decreased ego functioning (see discussion under "Ego Strength"), and thus the lessened tendency towards formation of "good Gestalten." The "secondary elaboration" is indeed precisely the structuring of the primary process by the waking ego into "good Gestalten." The wish-fulfilling element can simply be restated (see discussion of the pleasure principle, this chapter) as being the expression of drive aims in apperceptions consistent with the principle of achieving an equilibrium of forces.

The analyzing of the latent content into the manifest content, as referred to below, is the general problem of free association.

Free Association

"Free association" is probably rarely "free" or for that matter strictly "association" in the clinical situation. It is a complex and little-discussed phenomenon which we are considering in detail elsewhere [5].

Suffice it to say here that by means of association, the contemporary composite apperception of a male superior figure, for example, is shown to be the result of all previous apperceptions of male superior figures (father, older brothers, uncles, teachers, policemen, grandfather, phallic mother or aunts, etc.). In analyzing a patient's neurotic anxiety or aggressive behavior toward, say, his boss, we arrive by means of associations at the various genetic constituents of his contemporary Gestalt. Associations, as it were, lead to and constitute the component parts of our contemporary composite (see discussion of therapy and discussion of experimental investigation of psychoanalytic concepts, this chapter).

Psychoanalytic Theory Concerning Personality "Types" and "Traits"

Generally, the formulation of personality types and traits is one inconsistent with the dynamic approach to personality; however, within the dynamic framework of psychoanalysis there are actually a number of concepts which constitute "types" and "traits" as syndromes or clusters of variables associated in a way that assumes certain principles of psychodynamics. This fact actually permits infinitely richer understanding and predictions of many personality characteristics than for instance a factor analysis approach.

The main dynamic syndromes which one may lift out as constituting psychoanalytically formulated personality types are: the oral personality, the anal personality, the phallic and the urethral type. This classification is primarily founded upon the genetic dynamic propositions of the libido theory. However, predicated upon the outstanding pathological trait, personality types are often also referred to by analysts as the "phobic type," or the "obsessive-compulsive type" of personality, or the "voyeur," or the "exhibitionist." Similarly, "oral," "anal," "phallic," are used as adjectives to refer to personality traits; these, incidentally, need not imply a clinical disorder. These traits may be integrated aspects of the character structure which may lead neither to subjective discomfort nor to objective impairment, but simply constitute modes of operations which are discernible as having more of an organizing effect on an individual's behavior than other characteristics which he also possesses. Psychoanalysis has advanced the concept of "anal character," for example, to describe a personality in which anal traits are outstanding in a nonpathological way. Such character types are not always clearly differentiated, but should be, from "character disorder," in which the same traits exist to an extent where they cause difficulties to the environment—for example, to the patient's wife or husband or employer—and get the patient into difficulty with the environment without in themselves causing him subjective discomfort. The psychoneurosis (e.g., a compulsion neurosis), on the other hand, is characterized primarily by subjective difficulties. The word "primarily" has to be noted, in that clinically admixtures of character disorder and psychoneurosis are very frequent.

In essence, the concept of "oral personality," for example, permits one the following minimum of propositions (we are not differentiating further into active and passive oral):

1. *Behavioral propositions:* an excessive response to food (overeating, usually, with anorexia under specific circumstances); impulsivity; passive-dependent behavior with a great need for affection; low frustration tolerance; little patience; mood swings; flexibility, often including inventiveness, hand in hand with carelessness.
2. *Pathological propositions:* tendency toward depression; use of mechanism of denial and elation; obesity; frequently premature ejaculation in males; great sensitivity of feelings, easily hurt, etc.
3. *Genetic propositions (postdictions):* a childhood deprived of affection in any number of ways. This may be difficult to quantify except by rank-ordering a number of people. It should then be possible on the basis of such rank-ordering of deprivation (all other things being equal) to predict degree of oral characteristics, which could easily be experimentally investigated (frustration tolerance, etc.). The plain fact of the existence of the syndrome has been experimentally confirmed by Goldman [20]. (See section on experimental investigations, this chapter.)

Actually, the above is but a short schematic presentation; much more complex propositions can be derived simply from the diagnosis, "severe oral type." Lewin [33] has formulated the oral triad which has already been abundantly confirmed clinically: the wish to devour, the wish to be devoured, and the wish to sleep constitute a syndrome. Thus, oral people usually like to sleep, may in adversity take to sleeping long and frequently, and if depressed may wish to be dead. This last idea is almost always one of sleeping peacefully. Diagnostically, this can be of the greatest importance, since this type of suicidal idea in the absence of other characteristics is usually benign in distinction to others.

Similar to the oral type or trait, the other traits involve complex propositions, which interlock with other concepts concerning defenses, relations to objects, and every other variable of personality. Research establishing the clustering as postulated by psychoanalysis will not be enough. Prediction of complex experimental behavior should go further to verify and enlarge the usefulness of the concepts.

Psychoanalytic Treatment

Schematically speaking again, psychoanalytic treatment can be said to take place in a situation with a minimal apperceptive structure: the patient knows little about the psychoanalyst, the office may be nondescript, and the patient does not see the analyst sitting behind him. In this setting, in which the attempt is to treat the situation as a constant and the patient as the only variable,[9] again schematically speaking, one may differentiate these processes: communication, interpretation, insight and working through.

Communication from patient to analyst in classical psychoanalysis is primarily carried out by free association, but also by bodily expression and other behavioral variables. By such means the analyst becomes acquainted with the patient's history of apperceptions and his contemporary distortions.

For instance, if a patient in the first hour lies down on the couch with the feet dangling to the floor and head turned back as far as possible, the analyst may roughly infer that the patient apperceives the analytic situation as dangerous, is keeping a lookout on what possible attack to expect from his rear, has some passive anal wishes and fears, and is ready for flight. If the patient then associates and says that there is a funny smell in the room that reminds him of the time he had his tonsils out when he was five

[9] This is experimental support for the orthodox analytic insistence that the analyst remain nondescript—a bare projection screen, at least an ambiguous stimulus structured by the patient.

years old, the analyst further knows that this patient associated the situation with one in which one might be made unconscious and hurt. This patient will lead the analyst to postdictions and predictions totally different from those coming from the patient who lies down on the couch comfortably, states that the couch suits him well and that he feels like falling asleep and hopes that when he wakes up all his troubles will be over. In the second case we have a patient with a great deal of oral passivity who will expect the analyst to help him by magic, as he always wished that his mother (or father) would do things for him, etc.

It is the job of the analyst to wait until evidence accumulates for a particular pattern of behavior and then, following a set of complex rules, tell the patient about those aspects of his behavior which it seems best to point out at that moment. We call this latter step *interpretation*, the analyst pointing out to the patient a certain common denominator in the apperceptive distortions related to his behavior. Now to be sure, it would be just as inaccurate to say that interpretation is the only way in which the analyst communicates with the patient as to assume that free association is the only way the patient communicates with the analyst. Actually, silence or an impassively friendly tone or facial expression upon the patient's leaving may also be a means of communication. Also, the analyst makes many preparatory statements which serve as stimuli to which the patient reacts and only these secondary responses may lead to interpretation on the part of the analyst.

At any rate, the interpretations follow an intricate pattern. In essence, one starts with the minor apperceptive distortions relatively close to consciousness and the contemporary scene and slowly progresses, in many a back and forth movement, to the genetically earliest and the least conscious apperceptive distortions. The process of tracing the constituents of each apperception leads to a loosening of the figure-ground relationships in the patient. That is, he cannot any longer deal with contemporary situations using his stable apperceptive distortions as he had learned to deal with them, and this process leads to anxiety and attempts to use even earlier learned responses. This is the process classically called analysis of the defenses and regression in the analytic situation. The interpretations by the analyst may pertain to behavior and perceptive distortions in relation to the past, the present contemporary scene, and, in fact, specifically to the relationship to the analyst. In the process of analyzing apperceptive distortions into their constituents, the patient's attempts to deal with the environment in terms of earlier learned responses also involve the analyst. Analyzing the patient's distortion of the analyst by means of earlier genetic apperceptions is classically called the *analysis of the transference situation.*

Insight is the word we use when the patient is able to apperceive a new figure and ground relationship, specifically, if he is able to apperceive some form of contemporary behavior in relationship to earlier learned apperceptions. In this process he indeed learns, or in other words comes to restructure his apperceptions. It is almost as if an operation had repaired an ocular defect and the previously astigmatic patient were now able to see things in proper proportions. Making the unconscious conscious means to trace the figure constituents, make the patient aware of their contribution to the total (almost as in a Mueller-Lyer figure) and thus break up the particular destructive Gestalt formation. It is because of the long history of the adult patient that analysis takes so long: a long time is required to restructure such a multitude of images.

Insight again will have to take place with regard to contemporary, genetic, and transference distortions. It must be remembered that the affective tone of an apperception is part of its Gestalt, and that unless the appropriate emotion accompanies the analytic process, it will not lead to real restructuring in a stable new system.

Working through is the term connoting a repeated attempt on the part of the patient to try out his new optical correction in a variety of experiences. Just as a previously blind person or someone disturbed kinesthetically or in any other sense modality will try out his newly gained learning in a variety of situations, so the analytic patient will try to fit his new apperceptions on contemporary figures, e.g., his boss, his wife, etc. He will also try to apply the newly gained insight to his analyst and attempt to understand the apperceptions he had of his analyst in light of the new discovery. Similarly, an apperceptive distortion into which he has gained insight concerning, say, his relationship to his father, he may wish to extend to apperceptive distortions concerning his older brother, a high school teacher, a local policeman, etc. Again, the affective tone must be considered an integral part of the apperception and the corrective experience.

By such means, psychoanalytic treatment may be perceived schematically as a long process of studying apperceptive distortions in all their complexity, and attempts to change them by interpretation, insight, and working through. Thus, problems of technique could profitably be viewed in the light of facilitating or interfering with this aim. Technical considerations can be reduced to discussions of the best means to restructure apperceptive distortions most efficiently and most lastingly. Questions of diagnosis involve the nature and extent of apperceptive distortions (considered genetically, dynamically, and economically), and prognosis is concerned with estimating the likelihood and the extent of restructurating and the probable stability of such new Gestalten.

The Psychoanalytic Theory Applied to Related Fields

It may be expected that a useful theory of personality not only help one understand, predict and control all forms of individual behavior and its pathology, but also that it contribute significantly to the understanding of productions such as literature and other forms of art, that it be able to contribute to education and pedagogy. Above all, with the progress and integration of social science, a useful theory of personality must be able to help conceptualize the behavior of men in groups.

Group psychotherapy is in large part one of the outcomes of psychoanalysis. The study of prejudice and political opinion in psychoanalytic terms is best exemplified in the work of Adorno *et al.* [2]. Making explicit the concepts of psychoanalysis as to maturational assumptions and learning perceptions should facilitate greatly the orderly relationship of psychological science to other social sciences, such as anthropology and sociology. In essence it will help differentiate the effect of learning within each cultural subgroup as related to the underlying organic substratum.

Freud pioneered the application of psychoanalysis to all these fields. *Totem and Taboo, The Future of an Illusion, Civilization and Its Discontents, Group Psychology and the Analysis of the Ego* show his interest in anthropology and sociology. His study of Leonardo da Vinci, of Jensen's Gradiva and many other literary creations pioneered a rich field of psychoanalytic study of the arts. His entire work had a direct bearing on education and the upbringing of children.

RESEARCH

Research concerning psychoanalysis has been controversial and complex and difficult. Research by psychoanalysts themselves is primarily of a clinical, empirical, subjective nature. While extremely valuable in providing hypotheses, it cannot satisfy the tenets of ordinary scientific inquiry. Some analysts, in fact, have gone so far as to maintain that psychoanalytic theories, concepts, and processes cannot lend themselves to ordinary scientific methodology. Surely the untenability of this idea is steadily becoming more obvious; the concepts of the uniqueness of the unconscious were mostly at the basis of it, and now we may understand what seems to be the scientifically lawless nature of the unconscious well enough to see the lawfulness in it. Psychologists, on the other hand, erred by isolating psychoanalytic concepts inappropriately and in poorly understood ways in laboratory experiments which failed to bear out the contentions the psychologists misconceived as Freudian. The situation has vastly improved, and there seems little doubt that even the most complex psychoanalytic phenomena may be investigated experimentally without undue distortion.

Investigation of the Psychoanalytic Process

It has often been said that medicine took a turn toward the scientific only with the use of post-mortem examinations. Conversely, it has been stated that psychoanalysis (and psychiatry in general) suffers from the lack of such a model for learning. Though some have held that psychoses observed in *status nascendi* may somewhat fill this need, we can do better than that.

If an entire psychoanalysis is recorded from beginning to end, the available material can then be correlated to independently assembled information about the patient's history and a follow-up after the end of the analysis. That is, the treating analyst could make systematic predictions and postdictions* (concerning earlier events) which could be objectively assembled. Even simpler, since a psychoanalysis is a long drawn-out procedure, a record permits one to make predictions (and postdictions) concerning the interaction of the patient and the psychoanalyst in terms of specifically stated psychoanalytic hypotheses from one time in the

---

* A term borrowed from G. W. Allport.

analysis to another. Since it can be expected that some of these can be verified or disproven the next hour, the next week, the next month, or the next year, the study of the record may serve to validate and further explore the usefulness of the concepts for understanding, predictions, and (therapeutic) control. Since the record can be studied independently by any number of observers who may predict and judge, the condition of "public repeatability" of the psychoanalytic process is thereby fulfilled (which was long considered a serious stumbling block). True, the typewritten records will not give all the variables. But with additional comments on occurrences not recorded audibly, such a major percentage of all variables is included as to be considered sufficient. Of course, movies and social observation may supplement a voice recording, but it must be questioned if the trouble is worth the additional gain, and if it does not by chance introduce more artifacts than it compensates for.

Such a record could be studied from any number of viewpoints, quantitatively and qualitatively. Any fraction of the record might be used as a basis for prediction and postdiction—one session, one dream, the first interview, etc.

Both experiments have been anticipated by informal procedure. In a seminar under J. van Ophuijsen the present author was one of those who presented the history of a patient while the rest of the seminar predicted the current symptomatology. Again, in a seminar conducted by Bertram Lewin, one participant would present notes concerning a single patient-hour, without any factual references; the rest of the seminar would usually quite successfully predict large portions of history and symptomatology from these random associations not manifestly relating to either.

However, such gallant but not sufficiently cautious procedures will not do. These predictions and postdictions must be made under the most rigorously controlled circumstances. Then this method may actually be at least the equivalent of the post-mortems in somatic medicine and similarly benefit the development of personality theory, its verification, and the development of psychoanalytic and psychotherapeutic techniques.

Therefore, the following experiment was undertaken [7]: A patient's sessions were recorded and typed. Two psychoanalysts received the typed material for one week's recordings (five hours), and were asked to make a great number of judgments of qualita-

Figure 2

Psychoanalytic Research Questionnaire

Part I: Standard Predictions (Quantitative)

The patient's	PRESENT STATUS		NEXT HOUR		NEXT WEEK*		NEXT MONTH*		OTHER	
	Consc.	Uncon.	Consc.	Uncon.	Con.	Uncon.	Con.	Uncon.	Con.	Uncon.
Transference										
positive										
negative										
Acting out	xxxxx		xxxxx		xxxxx		xxxx		xxxxx	
Insight		xxxxxxxx		xxxxx		xxxx		xxxxxxx		xxxx
Working through										
Resistance										
Anxiety										
Aggression										
Extra-										
Intra-										
Passivity										
Guilt										
Depression										
Elation										
Oral strivings										
Anal strivings										
Phallic strivings										
Oedipal strivings										
Genital strivings										

Homosexuality										
Scoptophilia										
DEFENSES:										
Repression										
Projection										
Rationalization										
Isolation										
Denial										
Intellectualization										
Displacement										
Reaction Formation										
Regression										
Reversal										
Identification with aggressor										

* I refer to the hour after this week's material, week after this material, etc. Present status should be indicated by 0–10. Please mark intensity in appropriate columns by 0–10.

Date material rated:

Sessions rated:

Name of rater:

tive and quantitative nature concerning the variables listed in Figure 2. They were asked to judge both the first hour and the whole week as to conscious and unconscious factors apparent. At the same time they were asked on a second page to consider each variable which they judged as changed from the previous status, and to put down the observed clinical facts that they considered relevant to the change, and beneath it to state explicitly the rationale and hypothesis for the judgmental change. On a third page they were asked to describe any significant genetic data which they had found brought up by the patient and in each case to indicate the presumed psychological significance tied to these data. On a fourth page they were asked to write down in a thumbnail sketch, entirely freely, what they believed went on in the week's analysis, what would result from it, what the reasons were for it in terms of genetic and dynamic propositions. At the same time, two other analysts were using one week's material (the week previous to the one being evaluated by the judges) to make specific predictions following a similar scheme on the same variables; that is, they were asked to judge the present status of conscious and unconscious variables in a patient and were then asked to predict what they thought the status would be the next hour and the next week. In the case of both judges and predictors they were asked to make these qualitative interpretations on a scale from 0–10. On a second page the predictors were asked to record for each variable in which they predicted a change:

1. The observed clinical fact,
2. The hypothesis underlying that prediction, and
3. The prediction itself in detail.

On a third page they were asked to make specific postdictions; that is, they were asked:

1. to describe the observed clinical fact,
2. to state the hypothesis explicitly concerning which they were making assumptions about the patient's past experiences, and
3. to spell out specifically their postdiction; namely, what genetic events were responsible for the contemporary variables.

On the fourth page, again, they were asked to write a thumbnail sketch.

In his part of the experiment the treating analyst recorded not only the sessions, but also his own statements and interpretations. In addition he dictated comments afterward concerning such variables as might not have become apparent from the record; namely, changes in voice, facial expression, or motor behavior. He also recorded reasons for the main features of his own behavior, that is, why he said what he said or did not say anything. This was made available to the judges and predictors and was considered part and parcel of the psychoanalytic process going on between patient and analyst. The treating analyst also recorded immediately after each hour his own predictions for the succeeding hour but this was not made available to the judges or predictors. In another part of the experiment multiple-choice questionnaires were made up concerning the main theme of the entire week. The treating analyst stated the theme of the patient under consideration, together with what he considered the themes of four other patients of his. Each week four analysts were also asked to judge or predict which of five themes they considered to hold true at the time or to hold true for the future (in case of predictors) for the patient of the experiment.

Each four weeks, judges and predictors changed roles. Many other experimental precautions were taken which need not be mentioned here in detail. After each four-week interval some simple statistical data on judgments and predictions made were reported to the group and discrepancies discussed. By such means differences in conceptualization and definition were made apparent and many long-cherished notions and covert hypotheses stated explicitly for the first time. By this technique any single variable or syndrome, genetic or dynamic hypothesis, can be examined without interfering at all in the psychoanalytic process itself and without having to isolate variables in the artificial setting of a laboratory in a way which has so often proved to defeat the entire purpose. The recording itself did not cause any major problem and what minor problems it did cause at various points were appropriate material for analyzing; i.e., some exhibitionistic fantasies with which it provided the patient in regard to other people's sharing in his experiences.

Research Concerning the Libido Theory

Interestingly enough, attempts to investigate the libido concept belong to the earliest of any attempts to verify psychoanalytic concepts experimentally: Bernfeld and Feitelberg [9] attempted extensively to derive measurement of libido from the Weber-Fechner law and from thermodynamic processes. Unfortunately they failed.

Some recent useful experiments include the one by Sears [39, 40] investigating the existence of the syndrome stinginess-obstinacy-orderliness as posited by the analytic concept of the anal character. Sears found low correlations but all positive and in the expected directions. Similarly, Goldman [20] investigated the existence of the trait cluster associated with the concept of the oral character and in essence confirmed the theoretical expectations. The most ambitious experiment bearing upon the theory of libidinal stages was made by Blum [10] by means of his Blacky pictures. This provided a flexible scheme and permitted verification of several sets of psychoanalytic hypotheses.

An even more systematic way of investigating the libido theory might involve a combination of the Szondi and the Blacky test principles. One might construct a series of pictures: One picture would depict gratification of a partial drive; e.g., a person looking through a keyhole might be a representation of voyeurism, while a nude near a window might be a picture of exhibitionism, and a wolf devouring an animal a picture of oral incorporation, while a picture of a land of milk and honey might constitute a representation of oral passivity. Erector sets might be representations of phallic drives, and water cascades stand for urethral wishes. It would not be too difficult to represent the genital aims. Aside from the aim presentations, there should also be representatives of the defenses against each drive aim. For instance, a blindfolded person (defense against voyeurism), a meticulously clean, orderly room (defense against anal-erotic drive), a picture representing anesthesia (defense against sadism—while a picture of medieval torture might stand for expression of sadism), and a picture of a nun or a monk (might indicate defense against genital drives), etc.

Actually, the pictures would have to be chosen with great care; the rather haphazard suggestions above are merely meant to illustrate the idea. Also, each drive and the defense against it should be presented several times, say five times at least—ten times including drive aim and defenses against it. If there should be an agreement on the use of fifteen or twenty variables, the set would have to include 150–200 pictures. These should be presented in groups with the request that they be selected and rank-ordered for their aesthetic value or artistic merit.

The hypothesis is, of course, that each person would select those pictures representing his aims, or his defenses against them which would be most important in his personality. Since each variable is represented several times, it should be possible to study internal consistency—e.g., that a person picked out all (manifestly different) pictures relating to anal sadism in the set of 150 as the worst and those representing defense against anal sadism as the best. If each subject is asked to rank-order the whole set several times at some intervals, validity and over-all reliability could be established. One might think of this as a Szondi on a rational basis, viz., the libido theory. The crux is concerned with establishing a rank-order system of hedonic choices representative of the zones, aims, and objects of the libido theory.

External validation could proceed by first choosing subjects who have been studied psychoanalytically. The analysts would have to fill out a chart corresponding to the variables tested by the pictures and state which drives are most important, secondary, tertiary, etc. By this means their judgment—which is in effect a prediction of the subjects' performances—could be used as the validating factor. Again, in other cases, analysts acquainted only with a detailed history of the subjects should again be able to predict the pictorial choices, within the framework of the libido theory.

Research Concerning the Ego

The ego and its functions can also be experimentally investigated. If the ego is defined by its functions, one can investigate experimentally how well it performs the functions; that is, design tests for reality testing, frustration and anxiety tolerance, rigidity, motor functions, etc.

A. The ego as defined by its *functions:*
   1. The ego organizes and controls motility and perception.
   2. The ego serves as a protective barrier against excessive external

and internal stimuli. (Here we might also include a statement made by Hartmann [1938] that it is part of the function of the healthy ego to *exclude itself*. For instance, in order that we may be able to fall asleep, the ego must be able to relinquish most or all perception, including subjective awareness, motility control, etc., or else insomnia ensues. In this context E. Kris' concept of "regression in the service of the ego" in artistic creativity, etc., has found wide usefulness and acceptance.

3. The ego tests reality and engages in trial action (Freud's formulation of thinking), and sends out danger signals (anxiety).

4. The ego is responsible for detour behavior in gratification.

5. Under "organizing and self-regulating functions," we comprise character, defenses, and the integrating function of the ego.

6. Etc.

B. The ego can also be defined by its *development*. Its development is characterized by:

1. *Primary, genetic, congenital,* and/or *constitutional ego endowments*: Hartmann speaks of autonomous factors in ego development, apparently referring to motor, perceptual, intellectual, and maturational equipment. He quotes from Freud's "Analysis Terminable and Interminable": "We have no reason to dispute the existence and importance of primal, congenital ego-variations."

2. *Environmental forces*: the child learns the control of id drives at first possibly by conditioning and later by more complex processes of identification with parental figures. Inconsistent training or impossibility of identifying with parental figures for purposes of integration (either because of their absence or because of their own inconsistency or inadequacy) may make for a weak ego, a factor to be discussed more fully below. A seductive environment may so strengthen the id drives as to make control of them (by the ego) very difficult, thus indirectly influencing or weakening the ego development.

3. *Influence of the id drives*: there probably are hereditary, congenital, constitutional, physiologic, pathologic, and psychogenic variations of the nature and strength of id drives. A psychogenic influence (a seductive environment, for example) has already been mentioned. Pituitary or thyroid deficiency might be instances of pathologic influences; latency, adolescence, and involution are examples of physiologic influences which affect the ego.

C. The ego could be defined by the *quality of its function*, or possibly by the *quantitative aspects of its performance* (often spoken of as *ego strength*).

Ego strength can be principally defined by the effectiveness with which the ego discharges its functions, namely, of coping with the id, the superego, and reality, and of integrating (as described earlier), and by the energy remaining to permit self-exclusion of the ego for purposes of creativity and *ad hoc* needs. This latter, one might call flexibility (in distinction to rigidity of the personality when the ego is very capable of mediating between id, superego, and reality, but only at the cost of utter impoverishment of its resources).

Ego strength must be considered a resultant of the developmental factors mentioned above.

The ego will be strong:—

1. If its *congenital, genetic, and constitutional equipment is "good."* If there are any hereditary aspects to the presence or absence of mental disease then it would seem that ego strength or its lack is what is inherited rather than specific psychiatric disorders. If statistics have shown anything at all convincing, then it is a greater incidence of all kinds of psychiatric disorders than of particular ones in certain families. It would also seem that actual libidinal and generally psychopathologic constellations would be secondary to the primary inherited defect (of ego strength) in such instances.

2. *If the environmental circumstances are such as to permit consistent learning.*

3. *If the id drives are not overwhelming.*

4. A fourth factor affecting ego strength may be the so-called *secondary factors* of physiologic, pathologic, environmental nature. The most obvious effects on ego strength were, for example, discussed by Bychowski in a paper on the study of the brain-wounded, and can be observed as well in lobotomies. Physiologic, variations are encountered in sleep, dream, hypnagogic phenomena (Silberer's functional phenomena) and in exhaustion (Varendonck's preconscious fantasies).

Ego strength must be seen as something *global* in the way in which, for example, Wechsler conceives of intelligence. No single ego function can be appraised by itself without consideration of all the other functions at the same time. Any attempt to test ego strength would actually have to consist of many subtests such as in the Wechsler-Bellevue Intelligence Scale, each item being properly weighted to afford meaningful final data. Ego strength can then be measured by the effectiveness of the organism in various aspects of ego functioning, as revealed in the study of the integrative capacities under the impact of disorganizing events (Luria experiments, Tomkins, Haggard) and under the influences of frustration (Holt) [45].

Experimental procedures would have to involve the hypothesis of quantitative factors and would have to take the following directions:

A. An *appraisal of libidinal status* (object relations):
  1. A weighted scale of data consisting of a psychoanalytic appraisal of the history and symptomatology.
  2. A weighted scale derived from projective test data.
B. An *appraisal of ego strength.*
  1. A weighted scale of data concerning history and symptomatology with regard to ego strength (study of defenses, etc.). In such a scale different weighted scores would be given to the history of a psychotic mother or a psychotic aunt: having had a psychotic mother would be weighted in such a way as to decrease the total degree of ego strength more than the presence of a psychotic aunt not closely related to patient.
  2. A weighted scale concerning medical history and somatic aspects of ego functioning.
  3. Psychologic tests concerned with frustration tolerance and anxiety tolerance (Luria, Tomkins, Haggard, Holt, *et al.*) as well as integration and flexibility.
  4. Physiologic tests of ego strength, such as hyperglycemic index, adrenergic response (Hoagland) to stress, autonomic balance tests, a study of "mental set" under sodium amytal, the behavior in the Baranyi chair, etc.

All these test data will have to be weighted so as to allow summation and conversion into what one might call a Diagnostic and Prognostic Index.

In order to construct the aforementioned tests and scales, each subtest will have to be tested for its validity and its reliability; like items in an intelligence test, each part will have to be validated for its ability to differentiate crucially. For this purpose each item will have to be administered to normals, neurotics, manic depressives, patients with organic brain diseases, and schizophrenics. The ability of these items to differentiate between those more ill and less ill must be assured. For this purpose, exchange and substitution of items will frequently be necessary [3].

All measurements refer to an ordinal scale.

CONCLUSION

Psychoanalytic theory is probably the internally most consistent and at the same time most ambitiously all-encompassing view of personality formulated at any time. It attempts to make discontinuous events parts of an orderly sequence by establishing the relationship of such diverse phenomena as dreams, slips of the tongue, humor, neurotic behavior, psychotic manifestations, events of everyday life, and human interrelations, to the individual life history. It sees ontogenesis following specific lawful propositions of a maturational, dynamic, and structural-economic nature, predicated upon concepts of determinism, quantification, and some hypothesis of dynamic interaction between various constituents of the personality, such as the id, ego and superego.

Though already very useful by empirical evidence, in understanding, predicting and controlling (therapeutically and otherwise) human behavior, psychoanalytic theory needs checking of specific hypotheses, better integration of various concepts, and experimental verification. Such endeavors are very likely to increase the general lawfulness of psychoanalytic propositions, and in alternation with clinical data will fulfill the continuous need of any science for an increasingly better fit of the model with empirical data.

BIBLIOGRAPHY

1. ABT, L., & BELLAK, L. *Projective Psychology.* New York: Alfred A. Knopf, 1950.
2. ADORNO, T. W., FRENKEL-BRUNSWIK, E., LEVINSON, D. J., & SANFORD, R. N. *The Authoritarian Personality.* New York: Harper, 1950.
3. BELLAK, L. *Manic-Depressive Psychosis and Allied Conditions.* New York: Grune & Stratton, 1952.
4. ———. *The TAT and the CAT in Clinical Use.* New York: Grune & Stratton, 1954.
5. ———. *Free Association, Its Nature and Pathology.* (To be published.)
6. ———, & EKSTEIN, R. The Extension of Basic Scientific Laws

to Psychoanalysis and Psychology. *Psychoanal. Rev.*, 1946, 33, No. 3.

7. ————, WITH SMITH, B., & ALLEN, A., EPSTEIN, D., GOSLINER, B., KAIRYS, D., & ZECKEL, A.   An Attempt at Experimental Investigation of the Psychoanalytic Process. Psychoanat. Quart., 1956, 26, No. 3.

8. ————, *et al.*   Rehabilitation of Post-Hospitalized Psychiatric Patients at the Altro Workshop. *J. of Orthopsychiat.* 1956, 25, No. 2.

9. BERNFELD, S., & FEITELBERG, S.   Bericht über einige psychophysiologische Arbeiten. *Imago*, Leipzig, 1934, 20, 224-31.

10. BLUM, G. S.   A Study of the Psychoanalytic Theory of Psychosexual Development. *Genet. Psychol. Monogr.*, 1949, 39, 3-99.

11. FEDERN, P.   *Ego Psychology and the Psychoses.* New York: Basic Books, 1952.

12. FINN, M. H. P.   An Investigation of Apperceptive Distortion in the Obsessive-Compulsive Character Structure by Three Methods, Verbal, Graphic-Emotional and Graphic-Geometric, with Special Reference to a Defense Mechanism, Reaction Formation. (Doctoral Thesis, New York University Library, 1953.)

13. FREUD, A.   Aggression in Relation to Emotional Development: Normal and Pathological. (*The Psychoanalytic Study of the Child*, Vols. 3, 4.) New York: International Universities Press, 1949.

14. ————.   The Mutual Influences in the Development of Ego and Id: Introduction to Discussion. (*Ibid.*, Vol. 7.)

15. FREUD, S.   Totem and Taboo, in *Basic Writings of Sigmund Freud*, ed. A. A. Brill. New York: Modern Library, 1938.

16. ————.   Three Contributions to the Theory of Sex. *Ibid.*

17. ————.   *The Ego and the Id.* Translated by J. Riviere. London: Hogarth Press, 1947.

18. ————.   *Collected Papers.* London: Hogarth Press, 1950.

19. FRIES, M. E., & WOOLF, P.   Some Hypotheses on the Role of the Congenital Activity Type in Personality Development. (*The Psychoanalytic Study of the Child*, Vol. 8.) New York: International Universities Press, 1953.

20. GOLDMAN, F.   Breast-Feeding and Character-Formation. *J. Pers.*, 1948, 17, 83-103.

21. HARTMANN, H.   Comments on the Psychoanalytic Theory of the Ego. (*The Psychoanalytic Study of the Child*, Vol. 5.) New York: International Universities Press, 1950.

22. ————.   Ego Psychology and Problems of Adaptation, in *Organization and Pathology of Thought*, ed. D. Rapaport. New York: Columbia University Press, 1951.

23. ————. The Mutual Influences in the Development of the Ego and the Id. (*The Psychoanalytic Study of the Child*, Vol. 7.) New York: International Universities Press, 1952.

24. ————, & KRIS, E. The Genetic Approach in Psychoanalysis. (*Ibid.*, Vol. 1.) 1945.

25. ————, KRIS, E., & LOEWENSTEIN, R. M. Comments on the Formation of Psychic Structure. (*Ibid.*, Vol. 2.) 1946.

26. ————, KRIS, E., & LOEWENSTEIN, R. M. Notes on the Theory of Aggression. (*Ibid.*, Vols. 3,4.) 1949.

27. HERBART, C. P. *Psychologie als Wissenschaft*, Part III, Sect. 1, Ch. 5, p. 15, as quoted in *Dictionary of Philosophy*, ed. Dagobert D. Runes. New York: Philosophical Library, 1942.

28. HOFFER, W. Mouth, Hand, and Ego-Integration. (*The Psychoanalytic Study of the Child*, Vols. 3,4.) New York: International Universities Press, 1949.

29. JONES, E. *The Life and Work of Sigmund Freud*, Vol. 1. New York: Basic Books, 1953.

30. KAUFMAN, F. *Methodology of the Social Sciences*. Cambridge: Harvard University Press, 1943.

31. KRIS, E. *Psychoanalytic Explorations in Art*. New York: International Universities Press, 1952.

32. LASHLEY, K. S. Experimental Analysis of Instinctive Behavior. *Psychol. Rev.*, 1938, 45, 445-71.

33. LEWIN, B. *The Psychoanalysis of Elation*. New York: W. W. Norton, 1950.

34. LINN, L. The Discriminating Function of the Ego. *Psychoanal. Quart.*, 1954, 23, No. 1.

35. MAHLER, M., & ELKISCH, P. Some Observations on Disturbances of the Ego in a Case of Infantile Psychosis. (*The Psychoanalytic Study of the Child*, Vol. 8.) New York: International Universities Press, 1953.

36. MENNINGER, K. Psychological Aspects of the Organism. *J. Amer. Psychoanal. Assn.*, 1954, 2, Nos. 1,2.

37. MURRAY, H. A. *Explorations in Personality*. New York: Oxford University Press, 1938.

38. PITTS, W., & McCULLOCH, W. S. How We Know Universals: The Perception of Auditory and Visual Forms. *Bull. Mathematical Biophysics*, 1947, 9, 127.

39. SEARS, R. R. Experimental Studies of Projection: I. Attribution of Traits. *J. soc. Psychol.*, 1936, 7, 151-63.

40. ————. Survey of Objective Studies of Psychoanalytic Concepts. (A report prepared for the committee on social adjustment. Social Science Research Council, New York, *Bulletin*, 1943, 51.)

41. SHELDON, W. H., STEVENS, S. S., & TUCKER, W. B. *The Varieties of Human Physique*. New York: Harper, 1940.
42. SILBERER, H. Report on a Method of Eliciting and Observing Certain Symbolic Hallucination Phenomena, in *Organization and Pathology of Thought*, ed. D. Rapaport. New York: Columbia University Press, 1951.
43. SPITZ, R. Anaclitic Depression, an Inquiry into the Genesis of Psychiatric Conditions in Early Childhood. (*The Psychoanalytic Study of the Child*, Vol. 2.) New York: International Universities Press, 1946.
44. ———. Hospitalism, an Inquiry into the Genesis of Psychiatric Conditions in Early Childhood. (*Ibid.*, Vol. 1.) 1945.
45. VARENDONCK, J. The Psychology of Daydreams, in *Organization and Pathology of Thought*, ed. D. Rapaport. New York: Columbia University Press, 1951.

personality and motivation theory based on structural measurement

RAYMOND B. CATTELL, Ph.D., D.Sc.

RAYMOND B. CATTELL, PH.D., D.SC.

Dr. Cattell is research professor in psychology, and director of the Laboratory of Personality Assessment and Group Behavior at the University of Illinois. He received the Ph.D. degree with Spearman at the University of London in 1929, and the D.Sc. degree at the same school in 1939.

Dr. Cattell has produced many original tests for clinical, educational, and industrial practice, among which is the "Culture-free Intelligence Test." He is also the author of some 140 published research articles and 10 books, including *Personality: a Systematic, Theoretical and Factual Study; Factor Analysis;* and *The Description and Measurement of Personality.*

Although he personally recognizes "trait" as a valid and useful concept, Dr. Cattell is reluctant to use the term, itself, in his theory because of misinterpretations which others frequently make. Despite his use of other terms as substitutes, however, Dr. Cattell is considered one of the leaders in "Trait Psychology."

The concept of trait, a pattern of covarying behavior elements, is essential, Dr. Cattell believes, for explaining and understanding the unities observed in personality; but an understanding of traits, or any other concept of human behavior for that matter, cannot be derived, recognized, or utilized properly without the development of accurate methods of measurement. For him, then, the measurement of personality is the central need in psychological production at the present time.

In his chapter, Dr. Cattell presents a set of methods of measurement, concepts, and results which he believes can lead to possibilities of investigation which have not been feasible with previous, less exact concepts. When these methods and concepts are properly applied, studied and analyzed, then—and only then—will it be possible to develop a complete description and understanding of basic personality structures.

MEASUREMENT AS A MEANS AND AN END

It would be hard to find anything more important to the advance of psychology at the present moment than the development of a meaningful methodology for measurement. It has been repeatedly pointed out that the various sciences began to make their real progress when measurement and weighing became possible. At this point, the vague, philosophic and verbal punditry which previously dominated the sciences was compelled to give way to exact laws, and, with the development of exact laws, came the construction of a genuine and effective theory. Theory not based on a foundation of well-proven laws is often a merely pretentious and wanton attempt to attain the status of science before that status is justified, and the attainment of the condition for status, namely, exact laws, is very rare in the absence of measurement.

Measurement is required both by applied psychology and by basic research. In the former area, it is evident that much has been claimed about the effectiveness of vocational guidance or about psychotherapy which was quite unjustified and has often left the practicing psychologist in a false position. Thus, Thorndike found that vocational guidance based on a lot of meaningless measurement had a validity little better than chance, and Eysenck [16] has recently demonstrated that the recovery rate among neurotics is practically the same when they are left to their own devices as when they are treated by any of the standard psychiatric methods of the present schools. In pure science elaborate theories, such as Freud's psychoanalysis, or Lewin's "topology," have been put forward without any basis of measurement. The best that can be claimed for them—and it is a cynical best—is that they kept psychology in business during the years in which psychologists had no real stock in trade. But now that some really effective objective psychological methods, concepts, and therapeutic practices are being developed, one should beware of confusing the mere social prestige of these older theories with scientific prestige. Indeed, those who have worked for a more objective, scientific, experimental basis for clinical psychology may well feel a little embarrassed at the persistence of this social prestige, and feel that the sooner the false public façade is forgotten the better.

Though the measurement of personality and process is thus the central need in psychological production at the present time, it must be stressed that there is no point in pointless measurement. Measurement and quantification are only useful if they are concerned with definite personality structures and processes. This is what is meant by saying that the measurement must be meaningful. It is of little use to define some "scale" from a dictionary, and to set up a measuring device for that particular arbitrary concept, without regard to whether such dimension exists in natural personality structure. For example, "rigidity" can be defined in a variety of different ways—indeed, it *has* been defined in about fifty different ways—but it does not follow that measurements of most of these will correspond to any existing functional unity, and it would be better if one first found out what the varieties of rigidity are and then set out to measure them separately.

The advance of science is a co-operative effort in which each investigator tries to build upon the findings of his predecessors. If this building is to go upward and outward in an architectonic synthesis, then the personality functions and structures to which measurements apply must be the same for different researchers, just as, in building a skyscraper, the nuts and bolts of the iron skeleton must be of the same size and pitch if girders are to be firmly joined. Since a purely artificial standardization would not work, in the case of natural science, the essential point is that the measurements should apply to clearly discovered, unitary traits and well-established structures. Actually, psychology, and to a still more deplorable degree the various social sciences, have been conspicuous for a lack of architectonic growth. The notorious source of this defect is the inability to make meaningful measurement such that one investigator can build upon the findings of another investigator. Measurement studies in psychology have not been lacking during the past thirty years. Indeed, the journals are strewn with these one-story edifices of measurement on which no second person can ever build. If, therefore, a first axiom has been that science depends on measurement, a second must be that the only useful measurement is measurement of unitary traits, not measurements of farragoes of unknown and indefinable composition.

There is an interesting circular relationship between measurement and structure. While it is essential in practice to base measurement upon known structures (for example, to say that such and such an individual is two standard deviations above another in, say, a defined function of superego strength), measurement is required in the first place as a means of determining what is meant by a structure (e.g., in this case in delineating the superego structure). To determine what is meant by a superego structure, one must observe the changes in several forms of personal behavior under various tempting or difficult situations and under various consulting-room responses to therapy, and then, by integrating or correlating observations, arrive at the notion of a certain thing called a "superego" structure. This means that, before one reaches the phase wherein he measures the right things, he must spend some time measuring relatively meaningless things. If this seems now to contradict what has just been said about not measuring pointless things, let it be added that it is possible to measure meaningless things either in a pointless way or in a way that is likely to lead to their becoming meaningful. This may be a subtle point, but it is an important one. It justifies giving fully a half of the presentation here to the logic of those methodologies, principally factor analysis, whereby one can hope to develop, out of a mass of initially tentative measurements, some idea of the structure of personality, upon which further measurement can be much more meaningful, economical, and predictive. Thus, before any useful *applied* measurement can ever be gotten, one must do a considerable amount of *research* measurement in which he applies factor-analytic and other processes with the aim of disentangling the personality structure and thus arriving at the measurement of things which are functionally significant and practically important in motivation or personality prediction. The first purpose, therefore, must be the use of measurement to determine structure.

THE STATISTICAL PROOF OF FUNCTIONAL UNITY

In psychology, measurement is concerned with types or traits, on the one hand, or processes, on the other. Personality measurement concerns itself principally with the former, i.e. with comparatively permanent characteristics of the individual such as are manifested in trait and type descriptions. Type and trait approaches are not incompatible, but are, indeed, only different ways of intellectually analyzing the same data. They correspond to nouns and adjectives in language, or to species and attributes in the biological world. A glance at the history of psychology shows a tendency to oscillate between these two approaches, though the type description has in the main belonged to the more primitive phases. However, as just indicated, it is important to remember that the type is defined in terms of attributes and that, therefore, in saying that a person belongs to a certain type, one says at the same time that he has certain degrees of various traits.

It is best initially to start with a study of traits, because the statistical problems in *properly* dealing with types are more complex than those involved in dealing with traits. That is to say, it shall be assumed for the present that all humanity belongs to one class, and that there is essentially a normal distribution of most of the attributes being dealt with. The problem now is to define a unitary trait.

The earlier investigators of unitary traits, such as Hartshorne and May [3] were disappointed because all the manifestations of the traits which they supposed to exist did not correlate perfectly, and this shook their faith in the existence of the trait, e.g., of honesty. Had they looked around at that time, they would have found that there was already in existence a theory to explain this finding, and that indeed, Spearman, in developing his statistical theories regarding the nature of intelligence, was developing a method which had relevance to all trait analysis [7]. The fact is that the existence of a unitary trait does not require that all the parts of that hypothesized unity should correlate perfectly.

In nature, generally, when one is recognizing a unity, he is influenced primarily by the fact that the parts of this unity appear together and disappear together, grow together and decline together, and become affected as a whole when anything affects one part. If one seeks for a concept of unity in psychology, he will find that he is compelled to accept these same basic philosophical and logical conditions. Conceivably there may be other meanings assignable to a unity, but this is the only one which is operational, incontestable and widespread in its applications. This may be summarized by saying that a *unity exists in a set of manifestations or parts when they all suffer the same fate.* Parenthetically, it is necessary to distinguish between the existence of a unity and perception of a unity, the latter being liable to certain particular laws in which the Gestalt psychologists have interested themselves.

However, in order to take a broad philosophical approach, it must be recognized that the notion of parts of a whole and of subdivisions in an infinite regression brings in the idea of varying *degrees* of unity. For example, a library is a whole, but so also is a bookshelf, a book or a page. Again, classifications into unities may cut across one another, as when humanity is divided into social classes, to satisfy the Marxists, or into national and racial groups, if one be interested in divergent culture patterns and the growth of cultures. This fact of the relativity of unities is met best by the notion which has been called elsewhere "the efficacy" of a unity [7].

The psychologist's search for operational, objective means of determining trait unities has suffered from that otherwise desirable gift of the human mind which is called intuition. By virtue of being human beings, all are psychologists, and have immediate perception of traits and characteristics in the people around them. The very fact that individuals can do this with such facility and confidence has long stood in the way of advancing to something beyond the level of the unaided senses. To this day, any psychological demagogue of average persuasiveness can set up an artificial typology or trait nomenclature and get a following of people by the convincingness of his descriptions and interpretations. The verbal approach to recognizing traits is a dangerous will-o'-the-wisp among the quagmires of subjectivity.

The mathematical approach to defining unitary traits began, as indicated above, with Spearman's concern around the 1900's to settle the disputed question about the unitary nature of intelligence. Of course, one can trace the idea back further than this, in some of the work of Karl Pearson on the correlation coefficient, or even, in a logical, if not a mathematical sense, to the work of J. S. Mill, with his principle of concomitant variations. Essentially, it may be said here that, if things correlate positively and significantly together, they have some common feature behind them; whereas, if they do not correlate significantly, then they can be considered as not belonging to the same unity of personality structure.

The most natural way of testing whether there is a functional unity in psychological data is by using the correlation coefficient or one of its derivatives. Following this, a number of variables are taken to see whether all of them are positively intercorrelated. For example, if one suspects that ability to handle problems in two dimensions is the same thing as ability to handle problems in three dimensions, then he sets together, say, three tests of two-dimensional problems and, say, three tests of three-dimensional problems along with tests of many other things such as verbal ability. He tests a sufficient population of people on them and intercorrelates the scores on the variables. Then, if there really is a unitary ability to think spatially that covers both of these areas, the half-dozen variables concerned with the problems in spatial thinking will all form a single cluster standing out from the other correlations among variables.

It was Spearman who initiated, and Thurstone who carried into multiple factorial form [27], the idea of factor analysis, performed upon a matrix of correlations among variables. By this means, Spearman was able to show that one may consider a general factor of mental ability as a unitary tendency and that he can separate off such separate additional unities as a verbal-ability factor and a practical or spatial-ability factor. When Thurstone and his coworkers carried the analysis further, as is now well known, he finished up with some six to eight primary mental abilities, such as verbal ability, spatial ability, numerical ability, etc., which are functionally independent in the main, though somewhat correlated among one another in a positive way.

The process of correlating tests made upon a population of people, and the subsequent factorization of such a correlation matrix is called *R-technique* factor analysis. It operates upon individual differences among people, and it argues that, where one person possesses more of one thing, and also possesses more of another thing, then there is a likelihood that those two things will have a common trait underlying them. However, it is also possible to use correlation and factor-analytic methods to determine the unity of a *process* rather than of a structure or development. In this case, one takes a single individual and measures him on certain manifestations of behavior over a series of occasions in time, and correlates the various variables, i.e., tests the agreement of their plotted curves. This longitudinal factor analysis of the single case is called *P-technique,* and the factors which it demonstrates are independent tendencies or processes the parts of which wax and wane together in the same individual in response to external or internal stimulus conditions. *P-technique,* as shall be seen later, has been most useful in determining the structure of drives and acquired motivation patterns. The student should distinguish R- and *P-techniques,* on the one hand, which are concerned with determining structure within the individual, from *Q-technique* on the other, which is concerned with recognizing types, and which correlates people one with another. These three forms of factor analysis are systematically interrelated in ways which the student specializing in this area can find discussed elsewhere [7].

Although it is not necessary for the student of personality to know the details of the factor-analytic process, it is desirable that he should understand the logic of it, and, at any rate, be able to distinguish a factor from a cluster. On the other hand, the *research* student, hoping to investigate personality structure, certainly needs to know the finer points of the factor-analytic method, particularly as further progress is made in this area, so that the hypotheses at issue become more refined and delicate in their statistical checks. The brief account of factor analysis which follows will assume only an understanding of the *logic* of correlation and of factor analysis, and, as far as possible, it will proceed without any reference to the particular operations involved in the computations themselves.

THE ESSENTIAL LOGIC OF FACTOR ANALYSIS

Spatial Representation of a Correlation

The *algebraic* presentation of the idea of factor analysis is somewhat forbidding to students lacking college mathematics; but the equivalent *geometrical* picture can be grasped readily by anyone fit for so complex a study as psychology and has recently been developed in a small book by Thomson [25]. In the first place, it is necessary to get used to the convention of representing correlation coefficients as angles, as in Figure 1.

Figure 1

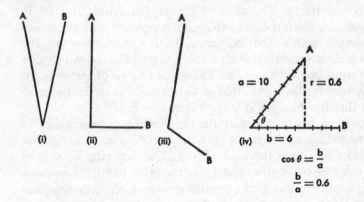

$$a = 10 \qquad r = 0.6$$
$$b = 6$$
$$\cos \theta = \frac{b}{a}$$
$$\frac{b}{a} = 0.6$$

(i)   (ii)   (iii)   (iv)

By this geometrical representation, if two trait variables A and B are highly correlated they will occur close together, as at (i) in the figure, separated by only a small angular distance. If they are quite uncorrelated they are set at right angles (ii) like the independent co-ordinates of a graph. If they are negatively correlated they are set at an obtuse angle, as at (iii). The convention is that the *cosine* of the angle is made exactly equal to the given correlation coefficient, as shown at (iv). This convention, faithfully followed through, continues to give results consonant with all that we know about the arithmetical behavior of correlation coefficients.

Factor as Co-ordinates

If now a group of trait elements have all possible correlations among them positive, as in the surface trait illustrated numerically in Figure 2, they will appear in the geometrical representation

Figure 2

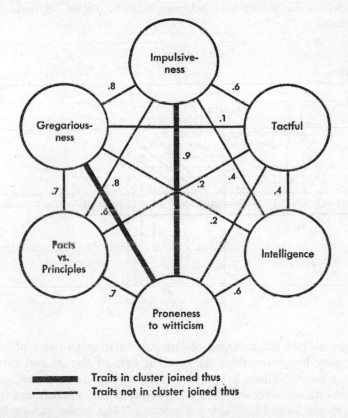

Traits in cluster joined thus
Traits not in cluster joined thus

as a bunched mass, like the ribs of a half-closed umbrella or a sheaf of arrows, as shown in Figure 3. Now if it should happen that this surface trait, like that in the example above, is the result of only *two* general factors, these factors can appear as the *co-ordinates* in Figure 3. To each of the trait elements—A, B, C, and D—there can now be given a *factor loading* representing the extent to which the given factor determines (for the average person) the extent of possession of that particular trait element. For example, the loadings of the four trait elements—A, B, C, and D —by Factor 1 are 0.80, 0.75, 0.60, and 0.56, as shown, while the loadings in Factor 2 correspond similarly to the projections shown on the second, horizontal co-ordinate. In short, the factors obtained by the complex processes of factor analysis are nothing more than the co-ordinates—the axes—in the space created by representing the correlations between tests as angles between "test vectors."

Figure 3

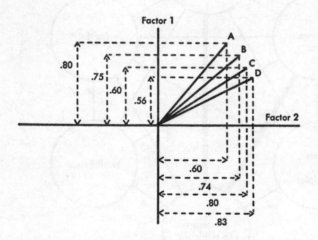

Some idea of the meaning of the particular magnitudes of loading may be gained from the familiar case of the general intelligence factor. There it is found that ability in mathematics is loaded about 0.8 or 0.9 with the general factor, whereas ability in drawing is loaded only about 0.3 or 0.4. (The reader can imagine that A and D are respectively problem arithmetic [mathematics] and drawing, in Figure 3, and that intelligence is Factor 1.) This means that a large part of the variability in mathematics is due to individual differences in the source trait "intelligence." Consequently, if a class of children were selected so that all had the same intelligence (mental age), the variability in mathematical performance would fall tremendously. On the other hand a group of people all of the same intelligence would still show almost as much variance in drawing ability as a group subtending the normal variability in intelligence.

The Meaning of Factor Loadings

From the facts behind Figure 3, it follows that the variability in any particular trait element can be broken down into variability in the two factors concerned, by an equation of the following form:

$$A = 0.8F_1 + 0.6F_2$$

and, as shall be seen later, this can be used for any particular person, i, to predict or estimate his possession of A from what is known about his personal endowment in the source traits F_1 and F_2, thus:

$$A_i = 0.8F_{1i} + 0.6F_{2i}$$

This means that, if his personal endowment in source trait F_1 namely, F_{1i}, is high, it will do more to help him in performance A than a high endowment in source trait F_2, for the loading of F_1 is greater in this situation, i.e., F_1 is more relevant to this particular performance.

Discovering the Number of Source Traits Involved

At this point the thoughtful student will ask, "But how did you know that there were just *two* source traits at work in the surface trait of Figure 3? And how do you find the *number* of factors at work in any given array of trait elements?" It should be clear that, in the first place, only the correlation coefficients are given that have been calculated among the various trait indicators (variables or subtests) measured in the experiment. These correlations, represented graphically, will arrange themselves in various experiments in different ways, giving some relatively isolated "test vectors" and also a number of clusters of vectors, called surface traits. The surface traits can be seen simply from inspection of the "rays" (vectors) drawn from the central origin. *But these same correlations (this same spatial "structure") will also tell how many factors are needed.*

Figure 4

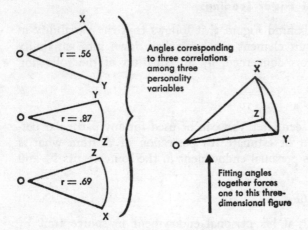

This fact can best be seen from an actual example. Consider the three correlations among trait elements X, Y, and Z as shown in Figure 4. The angles are already drawn in the proper convention such that their cosines are equal to the correlations found. Now if one were to cut out these angles with scissors, he would find that X, Y, and Z cannot be made to lie in a single plane, the plane of the diagram, as A, B, and C can in Figure 7. Instead, they force one to make a pyramid, so that the points X, Y, and Z can only be represented in three-dimensional space, as shown to the right of Figure 4. Three co-ordinate axes are now required, to fix the positions of X, Y, and Z. This means three factors. Consequently there will be three co-ordinate values for each point, i.e., there will be three factor loadings for each trait element and the *specification equation* for any one test performance, X, will be

$$X = aF_1 + bF_2 + cF_3.$$

Actually it is the rule rather than the exception for the correlations to force the model out into three-dimensional space or more (when there are many factors). If the student will experiment cutting out paper sectors to represent the correlations among any three or four variables known to him he may find some fitting in two dimensions, some fitting into three, but still others unrepresentable in three and requiring a model of four or more dimensions—a model in "hyperspace" which only a mathematician could conceive, for it cannot be visualized or constructed.

Since most models from personality and ability correlations would require more than two- or three-dimensional space, the discovery of the number of factors required and of the projections of the test points upon them is actually found from the correlations by algebraic methods. This process begins by finding the average correlation of each test with every other test, but its further steps need not be studied in this general text on personality and can be left for special technical reading.

The process of correlating trait elements and factorizing them may therefore be regarded as a search for the dimensions of personality, i.e., for the number of truly independent *directions* in which personality needs to be measured in order to describe it completely. Similarly there is a need, in describing any physical object, to know the number of dimensions involved, e.g., that a box requires numbers for each of three dimensions, but a lawn for only two. Incidentally, the student will find that the terms "factor," "vector" (but not "test vector"), "dimension," and "source trait" are used interchangeably by most writers, as they are here. Obviously the first great advantage of factor analysis is that it leads to a method whereby measurements on a few (about a dozen so far) factors are substituted for measurements on hundreds or even thousands of trait elements. The second advantage is that the source traits promise to be the real structural influences underlying personality, which must be dealt with in developmental problems, psychosomatics, and problems of dynamic integration.

The student will realize that what has been given here is only a skeleton outline of factor-analytic principles. If he is to proceed to research in personality measurement, he will need to know also how to extract factor loadings from the given correlations and how to find, by *algebraic*, analytical methods, the number of factors, i.e., the dimensions of space required. These facts can be found from the general textbooks on factor analysis in psychology now available [2, 7, 27]. However, it is sufficient for the essential understanding of personality measurement if the student knows that a factor is an independent direction of variation, discoverable from the examination of correlation coefficients. As such it *may* be considered an underlying *influence among* or *cause of* the observed correlations among trait elements. For, as research is now showing, these source traits correspond to real unitary influences—physiological, temperamental factors; degrees of dynamic integration; exposure to social institutions—about which much more can be found out once they are defined. Measuring behavior in factors is thus not only more economical and fundamental, but it also presents the first step in an analytic procedure aiming to discover the structure and function of personality.

THE VARIABLES AND POPULATION IN WHICH UNITARY TRAIT STRUCTURES ARE DISCOVERED

The terms "surface trait" and "source trait" have been applied respectively to correlation *clusters* and to *factors*. The correlation cluster is a relatively straggling thing which is difficult to delimit exactly. Moreover, it is possible that four or five clusters can be accounted for by only a pair of factors, or at any rate, by fewer factors than there are clusters. Thus the factor may be considered a more stable, underlying influence, *causing* certain clusters, and better corresponding to the psychological notion of functional unity. A cluster exists among achievements in a set of school subjects such as English, arithmetic, history, etc. It can be shown that this particular cluster is a composite one, as many clusters are, arising from the operation of two factors, and one could doubtless find other clusters arising from the operation of the same two factors. In this particular case, taken for example because it is psychologically easy to look into it, it is seen that people's scores will correlate highly in English, arithmetic and history for two distinct reasons: first, because those who are of higher intelligence will make more rapid progress in all three of these subjects, thus giving some degree of positive correlation among them; and, second, because anyone who has been longer at school and more interested in school work will also tend to achieve more, and this second cause will increase the correlation. Thus the correlations among them form a correlation *cluster*, which, however, must not be regarded as unitary, but as the result of *two* distinct factors. The computations of factor analysis would reveal that the observed surface correlation is actually due to the collaboration of two independent source traits.

It will be evident to the reader that a surface trait, in the realm of abnormal behavior, is typically referred to as *syndrome*. These syndromes were initially established without benefit of computation of correlations, but simply by the observations of keen-eyed clinicians that certain symptom manifestations tend to "go together." The present writer has shown elsewhere that there are about 25 to 30 abnormal syndromes recognized by psychiatrists, and the evidence now available shows that the correlations are on the whole rather low within these syndromes, and that the syndromes are somewhat difficult to separate. Such a measuring device as the MMPI is based on surface traits or syndromes, not upon factors or source traits, and it can readily be shown that the scales of the MMPI are not independent but correlate a great deal one with another. In addition to the 25 to 30 surface traits recognized in abnormal behavior, it can be shown that there are about 20 to 30 more that can be picked out in the *normal* ranges of behavior, and these include the well-known introversion-extroversion pattern as well as Sheldon's somatotypes, Jaensch's T- and B-types, James's Tender-vs.-Tough-minded, and so on.

Whether one deals with the surface structures found in clusters or the deeper functional unities demonstrated by factors, it is important to keep in mind the influence upon the pattern of the medium in which the original measures are made and the kind of population in which they are made. Observations may be made in just three media: behavior in real life, introspection, and behavioral reactions to actual test situations. The first is called *life record or behavior rating material*, because the correlations are carried out upon variables which represent measurements or rating of behavior as it occurs in *a natural life situation*. This is sometimes called *L-data* to indicate that it is life-embedded behavior, and is therefore frequently referred to as criterion data, though it may not deal with any criterion such as is commonly interesting to the industrial or educational psychologist.

The second type of data is questionnaire or *Q-data*, in which the person reports upon himself, as he sees himself, in a verbal questionnaire. This may also be called *mental interior* data, and it is typically upon this which clinical psychology has built, since it is the data of the consulting room. Thirdly is objective test data, usually called *T-data*. By an objective test is meant any sort of standard test situation in which the person's behavior is measured in such a way that two different observers can get the same score for him, and in which the subject is not asked to rate his own behavior. Objective tests thus include projective tests, miniature situation tests, stylistic tests, and a great variety for which there is yet no known name. The objective test data shares with *L-data* the quality of being true behavior rather than mere introspection as in the source of *Q-data*. However, it differs in essentials, which justify putting it in a second category. These essentials are that it is an artificial situation, transportable, perceived by the subject as something different from his natural real-life behavior, and therefore usually operates under relatively artificial motivation.

In the last ten years, personality measurement has made progress in discovering factors in all three of these media. One would expect that, if a source trait represents a real functional dimension of personality, it would show itself equally in all three realms of observation. This "indifference of the indicator" proves to be the case, up to a certain point. For example, one can recognize the cyclothyme-schizothyme dimension of personality, which has been of primary interest to psychologists since the days of Kraepelin and Bleuler, alike in behavior ratings, in questionnaire responses and in objective tests. However, as a methodological desirability, the factor analysis has typically been done separately in the three media. When the factors have been found, and checked in further researches within any one medium, it becomes timely to proceed further by measuring one population of persons in *all three media*, and to correlate the factors together, thus demonstrating the hypothesis that a certain factor found in behavior is the same as another factor found in mental interiors, or in objective tests. Thus, the psychologist's theory may eventually be sustained that a trio of factors in the three media is really the same behavior tendency manifesting itself in different circumstances of stimulus and response.

Before examining the actual factors found in these different media, the concept of the personality sphere must be dealt with. In all experimental work, including factor analysis, one can only get out relationships among variables that he has put in. But since factor analysis claims to be global, and wholistic, taking into account the total personality and accounting for more of the variance than is commonly done in experimental work, it is more important in factor analysis, when one is determining primary personality dimensions, to make some systematic attempt to sample all aspects of behavior. The personality sphere is an ideal concept of that multidimensional sphere the surface of which contains all the behavior manifestations of an individual. Ideally one should cut up the surface of this personality sphere into equal areas and take one variable from each area, thus being certain that the final factor analysis will yield primary dimensions for the total personality sphere.

Unfortunately, it is not so easy in practice as in theory to decide what is the principle by which the total area of human behavior may be included. The present writer has taken the view that language, which includes all the terms that people have developed over the centuries and millennia to describe the behavior of other human beings, must by now have symbols enough for all important aspects of human behavior. This being the case, the total set for statistical operations and experiment is derived by repeated condensations from the three thousand or more terms in the dictionary dealing with human behavior and personality attributes. Such a set of variables can be used in rating, but is not so readily applicable to questionnaire or objective tests; indeed, the variables in the latter cannot be set up to correspond in any dependable or precise sense to dictionary terms. Somewhat different principles must be sought in these areas. Meanwhile, since they lack this natural foundation in the symbolism of language, it was the design of the present writer to seek personality factors first in *behavior ratings*. Having so located the primary factors, the strategy called for setting up in questionnaire and objective test media the variables for factors which seem to correspond to those found in the behavior-rating field, but of course this can only be done approximately.

There are a number of difficulties in this last approach, notably the fact that behavior ratings are subject to a variety of distortions, and that they may distinguish behavior only to the extent of the powers of discrimination inherent in the raters. However, most of these difficulties can be overcome by special attention to procedures, as described elsewhere. Meanwhile, on such basis of behavior rating, there are now some eighteen factors found in the area of life record or criterion data, all of which have stood up in two or more factor analyses.

Since the critics of factor analysis have, in their last retreat, resorted to the criticism that there is disagreement among factor analysts about the nature of the factors found, it is desirable to dwell here on the methodology of factor recognition. When a psychologist says that a factor is invariant and confirmed, he may (and frequently *did* until recently) simply mean that he saw a factor in one study that seemed to him to have the same psychological nature as a factor found in an earlier study. This dependence upon mere human intuition, and "judgment of similarity," is not satisfactory in scientific work. Accordingly a number of indices have been developed, such as the pattern similarity coefficient *[4]* and the salient variable similarity coefficient *[12]*, which test the actual similarity of a pattern found in a study B to the pattern found in study A. With a given number of variables common to the two studies and a given similarity of loadings, it is possible to calculate the chance likelihood of having achieved the degree of similarity observed. The confidence limits achieved in recent work seem to indicate definitely that it is possible to reproduce the same personality factors in different studies, *providing they are on reasonably similar populations of human beings, and providing one uses in factor analysis such a principle as that of simple structure, which insures that the factors are psychologically meaningful rather than mere mathematical conveniences.*

THE TWELVE BEST-ESTABLISHED SOURCE TRAITS

The factors which have been confirmed in two or more research studies will be examined now. Each factor will be represented primarily by a letter index indicator, since the nature of the factor is not known well enough for one to depend on a verbal description or to settle on the final label for it. This practice merely follows the practice of the other sciences, such as physiology in its study of vitamins. First is located a certain pattern of behavior which one confirms while hanging on to the identity of the pattern by the symbol of a particular letter. The letter symbols were chosen in the first place to represent, by a later alphabetical *position*, a diminishing order of contribution of the factors to the total variance in personality, so that Factor A is far more important in accounting for individual differences than Factor Z would be.

However, most people prefer to have a title also, and so at present titles are also used, but mainly in a descriptive way, though in certain cases they are interpretive, as in the case of cyclothymia-schizothymia and superego strength. Naturally these interpretations await confirmation or rejection by further research, and the title would then need to be changed, though the letter could be preserved. Since starting off with the letter symbols, a need has arisen to use some universal index, which can be internationally recognized and which would greatly simplify discussion, and avoid confusion in research. (Different laboratories have sometimes used different letter symbols, and the alphabet is likely in the end to fall short of the number of factors established.) Accordingly, a universal index has been proposed in each of the three media [9], and each factor is therefore preceded by a sign, as for example *UI, Number X*, indicating its number in this universal index series. Committees will ultimately decide upon additions to these indices as new factors are discovered.

Both the source-trait title and the constituent trait elements below are always listed in *bipolar* fashion, corresponding to the plus and minus sign of the letter indicating the whole bipolar factor. This shows the character of the source trait at both of its poles, and reminds one that it is a "dimension" of personality. Unlike abilities, personality factors have appreciable negative loadings in many variables, i.e., there are many performances for which a particular personality source trait can be a disadvantage as well as an advantage. In these lists the negative variables have always been reversed, so that the pole listed in the left column is always positive with regard to the factor. The factors have almost identical patterns for men and women except for *C* and *E* which are different though recognizably the same. The trait variables have their ordinary dictionary meanings, though as supplied to the raters they were further defined by specific behavior, as indicated elsewhere [3].

Source Trait A: Cyclothymia vs. Schizothymia

The most highly loaded trait elements, in declining order are:

A+ POSITIVELY LOADED		A— NEGATIVELY LOADED
Easygoing	vs	Obstructive, cantankerous
Adaptable (in habits)	vs	Inflexible, "rigid"
Warmhearted	vs	Cool, indifferent
Frank, placid	vs	Closed-mouthed, secretive, anxious
Emotionally expressive	vs	Reserved
Trustful, credulous	vs	Suspicious, "canny"
Impulsively generous	vs	Close, cautious
Co-operative, self-effacing	vs	Hostile, egotistical
Subject to personal emotional appeals	vs	Impersonal
Humorous	vs	Dry, impassive

This trait is given more than a descriptive title because it is obviously related to the syndrome of "cycloid vs. schizophrenic" temperament which Kraepelin used in classifying mental disorder and to the cyclothyme-schizothyme temperament difference which Kretschmer *et al* described so skillfully on purely clinical observation [20]. It is probable that a certain liability to show prolonged ups and downs of mood, between elation and depression, also belongs on the left (positive) pole, and a "drive to work" on the right.

The student should bear in mind that the trait-element terms used are the extremes of a bipolar continuum, so that they sometimes seem to indicate abnormal behavior or to imply moral judgments, e.g., "obstructive" in the schizothyme pattern above. But in most of the schizothyme individuals one meets, short of a mental hospital, this trait element, for example, would probably be better verbally described only as "not very co-operative." Only the extreme, very seldom reached, pole is describable as actually "obstructive." In any case the psychologist should refrain from value judgments on temperament, for there are good, and, at any rate, likable aspects of both extremes, as well as special situations in which each is socially more valuable. It is possible, for example, that the above rather unpleasant picture of the schizothyme arises from the traits being rated on external behavior. Internally, as judged by the questionnaire pattern, the schizothyme "coldness" turns out to be partly shyness.

The above are the most highly loaded indicators, but almost *all* the trait elements in the personality sphere are affected to a lesser extent by this temperament trait. According to less exact, general observations, this source trait ramifies very widely indeed through personality and physiology. It is associated with differences in solidity of body build, the cyclothyme being more round-bodied and heavy-limbed, and there is now evidence of a high degree of inheritance [14]. In general, however, factors can just as readily be environmental mold patterns [3] produced by the culture pattern [23].

Cyclothymes, i.e., people with large *positive* endowment in this trait, according to Kretschmer [20], are more interested in people than in principles; make good organizers in business; as writers are humorous and realistic; as artists are more interested in color than form; are less able to abstract one thing alone from a percept; have a wider span of consciousness; are more disturbed, e.g., in reaction time, by irrelevant stimuli; and respond more vigorously to demands of the outside world. Schizothymes, on the other hand, are more interested in things than people; in abstract principles than particulars; seem to put more emphasis on moral principles than emotional appeals or temptations; do better in academic life than in business; as writers are idealistic; are sensitive lovers of nature; as artists are more interested in form than color and more frequently "classical" than "romantic"; are more tenacious ("one-track minds") in abstracting according to instructions from tachistoscopic exposures; have a faster, tenser personal tempo; have more rapid and extreme sympathetic nervous system reactions, e.g., flushing, stomach upsets from psychological causes; are less able to respond to sudden demands for speed of output; and are higher in verbal ability relative to general intelligence, especially relative to those aspects of intelligence entering into "adaptability to new situations."

Source Trait B: General Mental Capacity vs. Mental Defect

B+		B—
Intelligent	vs	Unintelligent
Thoughtful, cultured	vs	Unreflective, boorish
Persevering, conscientious	vs	Quitting, conscienceless
Smart, assertive	vs	Dull, submissive

It has been shown by tests that this is the factor of general intelligence (Spearman's "G" or Thurstone's "second-order factor") as it outcrops in the realm of personality. It is perhaps a little surprising that intelligence affects so much of the personality, including the character-like qualities of will and conscientiousness, as well as those of being merely well-informed and reflective (which one might expect).

Source Trait C: Ego Strength or Emotionally Stable Character vs. Neurotic General Emotionality

C+		C—
Emotionally stable	vs	Emotional, dissatisfied
Free of neurotic symptoms	vs	Showing a variety of neurotic symptoms
Not hypochondriacal	vs	Hypochondriacal, plaintive
Realistic about life	vs	Evasive, immature
Steadfast, self-controlled	vs	Changeable
Calm, patient	vs	Excitable, impatient
Persevering and thorough	vs	Quitting, careless
Loyal, dependable	vs	Undependable morally

This is one of the two most important source traits in determining character. Burt, describing its inverse as "General Emotionality," shows that it is one of the most diagnostic traits distinguishing delinquents and nondelinquents [1]. There is much scattered evidence that this is the trait which is conspicuously low both in delinquents and in neurotics. It is high in chosen leaders, in soldiers rated good combat buddies, and in more successful psychiatric technicians.

It may not be too speculative, even on the evidence yet available in the rating field, to interpret this factor as one of ego strength or well-integrated will power, as opposed to a poor dynamic organization of the ego. The individual at the lower pole experiences dissatisfaction and undischarged emotionality which he is unable to keep under control.

Factor D is omitted, as being insufficiently confirmed by independent researches.

Source Trait E: Dominance-Ascendance vs. Submissiveness

E+		E—
Self-assertive, confident	vs	Submissive, unsure
Boastful, conceited	vs	Modest, retiring
Aggressive, pugnacious	vs	Complaisant
Extrapunitive	vs	Impunitive, intropunitive
Vigorous, forceful	vs	Meek, quiet
Willful, egotistical	vs	Obedient
Rather solemn	vs	Lighthearted
Adventurous	vs	Timid, retiring
Insensitive to social disapproval, unconventional	vs	Tactful, conventional
Reserved	vs	Frank, expressive

This trait has been much investigated by those interested in leadership. Leadership is more complex than dominance, except among animals, but it seems true that highly dominant individuals like managing the affairs of others and are prone to organize and use people for superpersonal ends. The pattern seems to alter more than most with age. In children "disobedience" and "antisocial behavior" are more loaded, while in adults these take the forms of being unconventional and independent of group approval. Nature-nurture investigation gives a rather large role to early environment in determining this trait.

A similar pattern has been found in other mammals, notably chimpanzees and rats [21]. Here, as with humans, one finds both more sex expression and more curiosity or "enterprise" also associated with high dominance. However, at least in humans, there is no evidence that dominance is associated with intrinsically stronger sex urge, but only with more defiance of convention or religious authority.

Source Trait F: Surgency vs. Desurgency (or Anxious, Agitated Melancholy)

F+		F—
Cheerful, joyous	vs	Depressed, pessimistic
Sociable, responsive	vs	Seclusive, retiring
Energetic	vs	Subdued, languid
Humorous, witty	vs	Dull, phlegmatic
Talkative	vs	Taciturn, introspective
Placid	vs	Worrying, unable to relax
Resourceful, original	vs	Slow to accept the situation
Adaptable	vs	Bound by habit, rigid
Showing equanimity	vs	Unstable mood level
Trustful, sympathetic, open	vs	Suspicious, brooding, narrow

As the title indicates, the extreme low endowments in this source trait apparently correspond to the clinical syndrome of anxiety hysteria and, ultimately, agitated melancholia. The individual very low in F feels miserable for no reason, cannot be carefree, and becomes sensitively introspective. There is also evidence of correlation with compulsive anxiety, suspicion, anger, and disgust, with extreme correctness and conventionality of behavior, with increase of nervous habits and "general neuroticism." It is not certain, on the other hand, that extreme high F alone is mania—at least it may not be what Moore, Wittenborn and others have isolated as a "non-euphoric mania" factor [7, 28].

Probably people vary more from day to day in this trait than in any other; for it affects a group of trait elements probably identifiable with those affected by the mood changes which shall be called elation and depression. Nevertheless, it is certain that (a) interindividual differences are large compared with intraindividual differences, (b) that each individual tends to oscillate about a characteristic level, and (c) that certain physiological measures, notably alkalinity of saliva and low concentration of cholinesterase (a chemical affecting ease of nervous conduction), are correlated with surgency. Consequently, in spite of function fluctuation, the surgency-desurgency level has some tendency toward being a relatively constant individual temperament characteristic.

As the following section will show, surgency-desurgency is one of the most important and best-defined source traits in the realm of personality, whether measured in the medium of ratings or questionnaire responses, or objective tests. It is one of the three largest source traits in the surface trait of extraversion-introversion. Desurgency is positively correlated with age, at least over the late adolescent range.

Source Trait G: Superego Strength vs. Dependent, Noncompulsive Character

G+		G—
Persevering, determined	vs	Quitting, fickle
Responsible	vs	Frivolous, immature
Insistently ordered	vs	Relaxed, indolent
Attentive to people	vs	Neglectful of social chores
Emotionally stable	vs	Changeable

This factor has much resemblance to C on the one hand and K on the other, and it is sometimes difficult to separate it from either of them. However, it shows as an independent factorial dimension different from the mere emotional stability of C or the intellectual poise and integration of K, and is also distinguished from both by inner drive, high standards and good emotional integration of purposes. In some countries, notably Germany, and to some extent in American and the British Public Schools, it corresponds to the commonly understood meaning of "Character," and in psychoanalytic concepts to Superego Strength, though in normals it is noteworthy that "guilt" has small loadings.

Source Trait H: Immunity vs. Reactivity to Threat

H+		H—
Adventurous, likes meeting people	vs	Shy, timid, withdrawn
Shows strong interest in opposite sex	vs	Little interest in opposite sex
Gregarious, genial, responsive	vs	Aloof, cold, self-contained
Kindly, friendly	vs	Hard, hostile
Frank	vs	Secretive
Impulsive	vs	Inhibited, conscientious
Likes to "get into the swim"	vs	Recoils from life
Self-confident, debonair	vs	Lacking confidence
Carefree	vs	Careful, considerate

Just as there were three related factors—C, G, and K—in the realm of character so there seem to be three distinct influences—A, H, and L—in the cyclothyme-schizothyme region (or four, A, F, H, and L, in the surface trait of extroversion-introversion), but here the differences can be seen to have possible correspondence with existing clinical or other distinctions. For example, A–, H–, and L– have marked resemblance respectively to catatonic schizophrenia, simple or hebephrenic schizophrenia, and paranoid schizophrenia. They also have distinct questionnaire counterparts.

Descriptively the present factor, *H*, differs from A principally in carrying some adventurousness, seeking of the limelight, impulsiveness, frivolous, playful lack of conscientiousness, much positive interest in people, and strong sex interest, at the cyclothyme pole. At the same time the schizothyme pole loads *inflexibility* and hostility less, while withdrawing *timidity* and shyness more. Essentially there is here adventurous, carefree warmth opposed to an aloof, withdrawing, timid mistrustfulness.

Source Trait I: Mollity vs. Durity

I+		I–
Demanding, impatient	vs	Emotionally mature
Dependent, immature	vs	Independent-minded
Aesthetically fastidious	vs	Lacking artistic feeling
Introspective, imaginative	vs	Unaffected by "fancies"
Intuitive, sensitively imaginative	vs	Practical, logical
Gregarious, attention-seeking	vs	Self-sufficient
Frivolous	vs	Responsible

This source trait has not been foreshadowed by any type distinction in the history of psychology unless by some aspects of William James's *Tender vs. Tough-mindedness*. But it is well-confirmed by independent researches. It has distinct resemblance to what is commonly called the "artistic temperament" and also to femininity and perhaps to the clinical picture of hyperthyroidism.

There is, about the positive I-factor endowment, a suggestion of infantilism of sensitivity, and of that lability of mind which goes with far-ranging imagination. On the negative pole of this source trait we find maturity and responsibility but also a certain rigidity and smugness. The indications at present are that this is not a factor of goodness of dynamic integration or character soundness (like source traits C or G) but a factor of maturity and is very largely environmentally determined.

Source Trait J is as yet insufficiently confirmed for introductory study.

Source Trait K: Socialized, Cultured Mind vs. Boorishness

K+		K—
Intellectual interests, analytical	vs	Unreflective, narrow
Polished, poised, composed	vs	Awkward, socially clumsy
Independent-minded	vs	Going with the crowd
Conscientious, idealistic	vs	Lacking sense of any social duty
Aesthetic and musical tastes	vs	Lacking aesthetic interests
Introspective, sensitive	vs	Crude

Among the wider ramifications indicated are, on the left: greater resistance to suggestion, larger vocabulary (with less resort to slang clichés), inclination to study personalities, interest in current social problems, more interest in intellectual matters than in athletics (for their own sake), inclination to take the initiative and lead in group activities, and tendency to take an "advanced" rather than a conservative social viewpoint.

This source trait is shown by its correlations to be distinct from native intelligence (B factor) with which it might otherwise be confused. It is environmentally determined to a high degree and is probably the environmental-mold pattern arising from the influence of a more cultured home background and good education— though one must consider also a possible identification with the outward signs of strong superego development.

The remaining factors, of comparatively small variance, will be listed only briefly.

Source Trait L: Trustful Cyclothymia vs. Paranoia

L+		L—
Trustful	vs	Suspicious
Understanding	vs	Jealous
Composed	vs	Bashful

The independence of this factor, in relation to the other two schizothyme factors, raises the question of whether the abnormal extreme of this factor—presumably paranoia—should be recognized as a distinct disease entity from the schizophrenias.

Source Trait M: Ease vs. Concern

M+   M−

Unconventional, eccentric	vs	Conventional
Aesthetically fastidious	vs	Not so
Sensitively imaginative	vs	Lacking artistic feeling
Undependable	vs	Dependable
Undisturbed by practical considerations, unworried	vs	Responding to practical appeals, worried
Fitful hysterical upsets	vs	Unemotional

This is a somewhat subtle pattern, showing in M− apparent paradoxes such as social effrontery along with emotional dependence and exhibitionism. The term "bohemian" is carried temporarily as best indicating to most people the total pattern. Investigation of this pattern by factorizing new specially chosen variables is needed.

Source Trait N: Sophistication vs. Simplicity

N+   N−

Polished, socially skillful	vs	Clumsy, awkward
Exact mind	vs	Vague (sentimental) mind
Cool, aloof	vs	Attentive to people
Aesthetically fastidious	vs	Lacking definite artistic preferences

This, one of the more restricted factors, has shown itself most clearly in groups of women, but since it has questionnaire and objective-test associations among men too, it may be regarded as a general factor of some importance in personality. It appears to reflect some tendency to "hardheaded rationalism," independence of mind, and trained "efficient" thinking (but not love of culture or spiritual qualities).

RESEARCH ON THE INTERPRETATION OF FACTORS

A survey of the factors listed above will show that they seem realistic in that they agree with some of the principal functional unities observed clinically, e.g., ego strength, superego, dominance, schizothymia, while, at the same time, they also go beyond clinical knowledge in setting out additional dimensions. This is what one would expect, in that the method is far more sensitive and potent than the unaided memory of the clinician, just as in biology the microscope yields structures unknown to the unaided eye. Moreover, even in those unities which have been clinically observed, such as the cyclothyme-schizothyme dimension, the paranoid dimension, the ego-strength measure and the structure of the superego, the present method brings out the related manifestations with a reliability which is not possible by the clinical method alone. For example, when one looks at the patterns of variables which have been identified with the superego, he sees all the manifestations of conscientiousness, high moral standards, resistance to temptation, perseverance in face of difficulties, regard for other people, etc., but he does not see the associations of guilt and depression which the clinicians have frequently stated to be a function of the superego. This difference of viewpoint could be due to the clinician's lack of measurement, or to his being able to see relatively few cases in his lifetime (whereas the above analyses are now based in all on a thousand individuals), or to the bias generated by elaborate theories, or to the abnormal section of the population on which his conclusions are based.

The last explanation would be the most charitable one, and it is probably the most nearly correct. The clinicians see individuals who are in difficulties, specifically with conflicts between the id and the superego, and it is natural that a considerable amount of guilt would then be generated. The pattern of the superego as it appears here is, as it were, an average of the pattern of manifestations in all normal people, and, as such, it does not, of course, yield the picture of any specific individual's superego. The loadings indicate the extent to which this structure in the personality affects, for the average person, this and that kind of behavior. To be precise, the figures indicate the *fraction* of the variance, i.e., of the individual differences, in those modes of behavior which are accounted for by the strength of this functional unity. Thus, these studies reveal that the clinician has for a generation been foisting upon psychology a conception of the superego which is definitely distorted by the peculiar population with which he deals and which has consequently given false lead to conceptualization and experiment connected with the superego.

It may be asked by what process one interprets a particular factor or arrives at the conclusion, for example, that Factor G above corresponds to the superego. The answer is that he does so by the same methods as are used in any other attempt to relate observed behavior to a concept, except that he does so in quantitative fashion and with multiple checks. The nature of the superego, as a partly unconscious and irrational drive toward the requirements and moral standards of the culture, was originally inferred from various kinds of behavior which were observed to be simultaneously very strong in some clinical cases and very weak in others. The hypothesis which best meets this observation is the hypothesis of a unitary dynamic drive toward the moral standards implanted by the parents and society. Just so, there is here a definite pattern of behaviors which vary in strength together, in a way proving a common source, and with a content of moral and self-regarding standards. This hypothesis can be checked by reference to new variables, brought into further factor-analytic experiments, which confirm the general hypothesis that the pattern has to do with the positive things which society regards as desirable, with avoiding the things which society regards as undesirable, with being unselfish and attending to the needs of other people, with suppressing various kinds of behavior, etc.

In other cases the inference about the nature of the underlying tendency is not so clear, and further research is required with new variables to test a series of hypotheses. For example, the nature of one of the smaller factors above, such as M or N, remains rather obscure, because the loadings of the variables in that factor are still relatively low, and it may need many years of research, in cycles of hypothesizing, alternating with factorial experimentation, to find variables with such high loadings on the factor that its nature may be more exactly inferred. In addition, the nature of any factor can be tested by analysis-of-variance experiments, comparing dependent variables for individuals who are high in the factor and low in the factor, carried out without the complexity of factor-analytic design.

When the outline of the pattern, although confirmed, is faint and does not yield any highly loaded variables, it is important to preserve it in terms of the particular variables which mark it, and which are therefore called "marker variables," meanwhile keeping reference to the factor at a purely descriptive level. It will be seen that such postponement of interpretation is practiced in most of the titles above. They may, in consequence, be sometimes un-wieldy, but preserve the maximum amount of *description* in words. It would be premature, and would probably create more confusion than illumination, to take a title at the present moment as indicating a perfectly definite hypothesis, because further exper-iment might be biased by an interpretive title, and the many al-ternative possibilities might not then be investigated.

In research there are great opportunities today, for psychologists trained in the necessary factor-analytic techniques, to concentrate upon the interpretation of particular factors. It means trying new ratings, more subtle variables, and more accurately measured load-ings, in an attempt to get better practical measures of the factor. This is necessary for its experimental control and investigation, and also to make better inferences possible about the nature of the underlying influence concerned. However, even with the above brief background of factors observed in the life-record, time-sampling, behavior-rating variables, as observed *in situ*, it will be helpful for us now to turn to the factors found in questionnaires.

QUESTIONNAIRE MEASUREMENT SCALES AND THE CONCEPT OF VALIDITY

The conception of the personality sphere, as indicated, is not so easy to apply to the items of questionnaires, and indeed in the present writer's survey of factors indicated in questionnaires, in 1946, it was evident that questionnaires up to that point had dealt to an excessive degree with abnormal and clinical items. A fac-torization of items from all the existing questionnaires revealed, for example, no factor corresponding to intelligence or to dominance-submission, or to the above "I factor" of sensitivity. Accordingly, in the next studies carried out in the questionnaire field, immediately after the behavior-ratings factors had been isolated, an attempt was made to throw in items which would represent those of the behavior ratings which did not appear to be represented in existing questionnaires. The result was a scale for measuring sixteen personality factors, now known as the "16 Personality Factor Questionnaire," and which appears to measure the same twelve factors as were found in the first behavior-rating study, plus four factors which so far have been peculiar to questionnaire material. The task of factor-analyzing so many items is a very difficult one, as witnessed by the fact that there are still only two questionnaires in existence in which the items themselves have been factor-analyzed, and the progress in this area has only been possible by the help of the electronic computer and various advances in the techniques of factor analysis. However, the factors so found have been more "invariant," and more psychologically meaningful than those set up in terms of arbitrary scales. The actual sets of questions which form the pattern of particular factors will be set out below and can be compared for meaning with some of the rating factors set out above.

At this point one may conveniently compare the method of factor analysis with the methodologies of item analysis which had previously constituted the principal technique in questionnaire scale construction. The many methods of improving scale reliability and validity boil down essentially to two, namely the method of item analysis for consistency, and the Guttman method of the so-called "pure scale." The Thurstone method of attitude scaling should be related to these, but this must be left to the student [26]. So little information has yet accumulated regarding the practicability of the Guttman scaling outside attitude study that its role in personality is also best deferred. Suffice it to say that the evidence seems to show that what Guttman calls a "pure scale" may be quite impure, factor-analytically. Indeed, the basic weakness of this method is that it starts with the recipe, "Put together a pool of items of similar content." Except in the field of attitude study, or of specific achievement measures, such as those in scholastic work, this first recipe item is itself impossible. It is not known what the "content" of a personality dimension is. That is what must be found out first. Conceivably, therefore, this scaling method could be used to itemize material that has previously been factor-analyzed, but all this remains to be seen. Meanwhile, there is considerable experience—indeed some researchers think far too much of experience—in building scales by the classical "item analysis" techniques.

Typically each item is correlated in this classical item analysis with the pool of all the items or with some outside criterion. When the former is done, since no one knows what items should first go into the pool, the net effect of the item analysis is to concentrate the items about whatever center of gravity (in statistical technical terms, whatever "centroid") the pool of items initially put together happens to have. This may be concentrating a lucky shot, but is far more likely to be concentrating an error. It makes all the items internally more consistent but not more factorially unitary. In fact, a well item-analyzed scale is essentially the same as a correlation cluster or surface trait, discussed above. The chances are very great that any scale set up on subjective choice of variables will turn out to be factor-analytically composite, and indeed of quite high complexity. It would seem a much better principle of test construction first to factor-analyze, to obtain a unique simple structure position, and with such factorially defined factors set out to item-analyze within the items measuring a factor, thus obtaining still more concentrated measures of the factor.

The same is true of item analysis against an external criterion. In this case, of course, one is obtaining a set of questions which better predict the particular behavior of the criterion, with the population of that particular nature, that particular age, and under those particular conditions. Such prediction is quite uninformed and rigid, for one cannot relate it to general psychological principles as would be possible if one knew what factors were involved. For item analysis against a criterion still leaves the test itself factorially complex. Thus, one might obtain a set of items which would better predict scholastic performance than would an intelligence test, because they contain both measures of intelligence and also measures of various personality and interest factors which work together to produce scholastic achievement. However, this would be much less effective psychologically than having factorially pure measures of intelligence, together with factor measures of the personality factor of perseverance (or whatever it is that produces better achievement) and of the interest factors involved.

When measures of the psychologically meaningful, separate functional unities are possessed, it is possible to alter the weight of these different factors in the prediction according to the particular population variances and to one's psychological knowledge of which factors are likely to alter through the environment and which are likely to remain constant, and so on. Indeed, the prediction from a set of factors is a far more psychologically meaningful and technically satisfying procedure than the blind tagging of a particular test to a particular criterion, no matter how high the correlation between the two latter may be at the time of the first investigation (typically these correlations decline a lot with change of circumstance).

For a factor is not merely a measuring device; it is a statement about a functionally unitary, constitutionally or sociologically determined pattern within personality, about which the general progress of psychological research may be expected to yield a great deal of information. When the natural history of a factor is known, i.e., when one knows how far it is determined by heredity, what its curve of growth is through childhood or of decline in later life, how it is affected by various learning situations or by physiological changes, etc., the ability to understand and to predict is greatly increased. No arbitrary scale, however good, can ever be used with the insight and with the useful application of general psychological laws that is possible with a factor measurement.

With this completed excursion into concepts of scales and validation methods, which is required in any discussion of questionnaires, it is possible to return to personality factors and the theory of their interaction in the total personality. This excursion has shown that validity has two senses in any factor-analyzed questionnaire. In the first place, there is internal validity, the extent to which the particular set of questions measure the factor which they are intended to measure. Second, there is external or social validity, the degree to which the factor correlates with some of the standard criterion situations of life, e.g., progress in a school situation, prognosis in clinical neurotic issues, predictions regarding stability in marriage, etc. It is most desirable in discussions of validity that internal or essential validity should always be examined first and that no confusion should arise with external or social validity.

EXAMPLES OF FACTOR PATTERNS FOUND IN QUESTIONNAIRES

The factors found in questionnaire material need not necessarily be expected to correspond exactly to those found in behavior, but in the majority of cases they appear to do so. In the following three paragraphs are instanced three questionnaire factors, with the loadings found for items. These factors have been taken from the 16 Personality Factor Questionnaire, Form C [11], the standardization of which will show the percentile rank of any raw score obtained on these particular factors.

All questions have twice been factor-analyzed in two independently rotated factor analyses and have also been correlated, as factors, with the rating (criterion) factors.

Factor A

Cyclothymia

	LOADING*	ANSWER
1. In a factory would you rather be in charge of		
(a) mechanical matters?		
(b) talking to and hiring new people?	−.57	(b)
2. Would you rather be:		
(a) in a business office?		
(b) an architect, drawing plans of buildings?	.53	(a)
3. Could you stand living alone, far from anyone else, like a hermit?	−.48	No
4. Are you attentive in keeping appointments and keeping them on time?	.39	Yes
5. Are you slow in saying what you want to say, compared with other people?	−.37	No
6. Would you like a job where you listen all day to complaints from employees or customers?	.33	Yes

As would be expected from the rating, Factor A, with which this correlates, the essential feature is liking human contact (and, at this negative pole, a schizothyme withdrawal).

* The loadings are sometimes negative, because they are set out uniformly for the "yes" or "a" answer. Naturally they are positive loadings for the answers set out here.

Factor E

Dominance

		LOADING	ANSWER
1.	Would you feel embarrassed joining a nudist colony?	−.48	No
2.	Are you happy to be waited on by personal servants?	.46	Yes
3.	Can you deliberately lie to a friend and keep a straight face?	.46	Yes
4.	Are you annoyed by people who put on airs of superiority?	−.40	No
5.	Have people called you a proud, stuck-up, self-willed person?	.37	Yes
6.	Do you enjoy making life easy for waiters and waitresses?	−.34	No

Dominance should not be confused with such a mixture of factors as is involved in the arbitrary concept of the authoritarian personality, which is a surface trait varying a good deal from culture to culture and concept to concept. This dimension is largely concerned with independence of mind, unconventionality and disregard of group pressures, as shown also in the behavior-rating factors, e.g., in such work on men and animals as that of Maslow [21].

Factor F

Surgency vs. Desurgency

		LOADING	ANSWER
1.	Do you like large gatherings, as at parties or dances?	.50	Yes
2.	Do you feel awkward in company, so that you never seem to get on as well as you should?	−.47	No
3.	Have you ever been active in organizing a club, team or similar social group?	.43	Yes
4.	Do you crave travel?	.36	Yes
5.	Do you find it difficult to complain if your working conditions are poor?	.36	No
6.	At a party are you disinclined personally to start cracking jokes and telling stories?	.35	No

This is the well-known surgency pattern which, with cyclothymia, enters into the surface trait of extroversion-introversion. It has been found in several studies, including those of Guilford *[18]*.

Factor G

Superego Strength

		LOADING	ANSWER
1.	Do you think (a) some jobs don't need to be done as carefully as others? (b) any job should be done thoroughly if you do it at all?	.48	(b)
2.	Do you think people should observe moral laws more strictly?	.38	Yes
3.	Do you admire a clever but undependable man more than an average man with will power to resist temptations?	.36	No
4.	Have you ever come near fainting at a sudden pain or at the sight of blood?	.33	Yes
5.	If you find yourself with time between jobs, do you (a) fill it chatting with people or playing cards? (b) plan carefully to have some other work available at that time?	.33	(b)
6.	If you had more than enough income for your daily needs, do you think you should give most of the rest to your church or some other worthwhile cause?	.30	Yes

The identification of this factor with superego strength rests on the same basis as the clinical identification—the functional unity of a set of behaviors directed to ethical standards, to punishing the individual for sins of omission and commission, and particularly to regulating his social behavior. Furthermore this factor has been chosen to correlate with leadership and with various objective measures of dependability in social situations.

From these examples it will be seen that simple structure rotation yields psychologically meaningful "mental interiors," which can be aligned with the same dimensions as seen in behavior-rating factors.

THE THEORY OF TRAIT INTERACTIONS IN THE TOTAL PERSONALITY

As every graduate student with a statistical training knows, the factor analysis of variables leads to a specification equation, such as that already seen in its simplest form above (pages 68-71) which predicts the variance of any particular trait as follows:

$$R_{ji} = S_{j1}T_{1i} + S_{j2}T_{2i} + \ldots \ldots + S_{jn}T_{ni} + S_jT_{ji}$$

where R is the reaction in the stimulus situation j of the individual i. On the right of the equation the Ts correspond to the factors 1, 2, 3, by which the personality is measured, and the i indicates in each case that the amount of the factor is the standard score of the *individual* on that factor. The Ss are commonly known as loadings, in a statistical sense, but in the broader psychological interpretation are better called situational indices as the symbol S indicates. The situational index S_{j1} indicates the extent to which the personality factor trait 1 is involved in the reaction to the situation j.

It will be observed that here is essentially the formula proposed earlier *[3]* for personality, namely, R = F (OS), where O defines the properties of the organism and S the properties of the situation. But the S of the classical stimulus-response equation has become represented here by a whole series of Ss—S_{j1}, S_{j2}, etc.—and the O or organism has become represented by a pattern of dimensions, T_{1i}, T_{2i}, etc. It will be observed therefore that this is a way of representing both the environment and the individual as *patterns*. The pattern of the individual is a profile, presented by his standard scores on the primary personality factors. The pattern of the environment is a profile also, represented by the measures on the situational indices. Essentially, this statement is a measurement of the situation in terms of psychological significance, rather than in physical terms.

The beautiful universality of this formulation is that it permits throughout applied psychology a simple "two-file" system. With a file of profiles for situations, including the normal criterion situations of interest in clinical, educational and industrial psychology, and a file of personality profiles, the practitioner can perform any of the predictions which are commonly encountered in psychological work. One no longer needs to work with an enormous number of tests related to an enormous number of situations. Instead, there are a few tests, such as the 16 Personality Factor Questionnaire mentioned above, on which to measure the individuals on all important primary factors. Similarly, on the situational side, there is no need to examine thousands of correlations between criteria and specific composite tests; instead, there are the situational profiles for these standard factors (measurable by interchangeable test batteries) on all of the situations. It is required only that the pattern of measurements for the individual profile be inserted into the patterns of situational indices for the particular achievement in question in order that the best possible prediction can be made. An up-to-date, comprehensive survey of known factors has recently been made by French [17].

Although a fair number of personality factors are now measurable, so that batteries can be applied to give standard scores for any given individual, the examination of situations is still in its infancy. In the next twenty years one may expect a considerable increase in the cataloguing of situations according to their situational index profiles, and a whole set of useful generalizations about the meaning of stimulus situations can then be expected to arise.

It will be recognized that the Ss in the specification equation for a given criterion are a row out of the factor matrix, in which this and other criteria have been factorized along with the tests. There are quite a number of complications to the use of this equation which the statistically sophisticated student will want to take notice of. In the first place, most personality factors depart slightly from orthogonality, i.e., they are oblique, so that the weighting of tests in estimating a factor is not the same as the factor loadings, nor is the reference vector pattern the same as the factor structure [7]. But it is worth while losing some of the simplicity of orthogonal factors for the sake of the greater psychological universality of the factors used. Further, it will be noticed that use is made of a specific factor which, as Godfrey Thomson has pointed out, is essentially only a confession of ignorance. As time goes on the specific factors may be expected to break down into a number of new general factors.

The above specification equation applies as the means of estimating specific behavior from the total personality (T_1, T_2, etc.)

and from the total situation (S_1, S_2, etc.) alike for those Ts that are abilities and those which are temperamental or motivational traits, such as drives, or the self-sentiment, or complexes. However, there will be certain systematic differences in form. For example, it will be noticed also that, when temperament or motivational factors are dealt with, the situational indices may frequently be negative as well as positive, whereas in abilities it is usual for all loadings to be positive. It makes good psychological sense that a certain temperament trait may be an advantage in one situation and a disadvantage in another.

It is sometimes bemoaned that the factor analyst reduces the personality interactions to additive ones, whereas, in fact, they may be multiplicative or catalytic in some sense. It cannot be doubted that there are likely to be instances where one factor does not merely add itself to another, but greatly facilitates the second factor, as Saunders, for example, has brought out in his ruled surface regression [24]. Related to this is the general assumption of linearity, whereas again it is likely that in some cases the relation of the factor to the performance will be curvilinear. Properly regarded, these limitations are stimuli to fresh inquiry, but not criticisms of the factor-analytic method as such. One must walk before he can run. The fact is that the factor-analytic model in its present simple form certainly seems to give better predictions and greater constancy of analysis than any other design that has been tried. As it progresses, it will doubtless become modified to meet the special needs of the possibilities just indicated.

In sum, the psychologist, having taken the man to pieces, as it were, by factor analysis, puts him together again in the specification equation and obtains a wholistic picture of the response. It is true, as has been seen, that this oversimplifies in some respects, and, from the psychological point of view, the reader may object that so far the method has been exemplified with temperamental traits and abilities, but not with research on motivational traits which are an important part of the total picture. The omission of motivation does not arise from its being outside the model, but simply because the application of statistical structuring of personality to motivational data has been comparatively recent, and has been preserved for discussion in the special section we are now approaching.

Before the closing of this section, it should be noted that the profile of the individual upon his factors determines what in common speech is called the *quality* of his response to any particular situation. The same *quantitative* score on a given situational response may be achieved by a different combination of factors in different people, as has been illustrated at greater length elsewhere *[5]*. It is these difference combinations, or ways of achieving the same end result, which we typically refer to as a qualitative difference of act.

Yet another relationship that will eventually need to be taken into account in the factor-analytic representation is what Coombs has called *[15]* "lexicographic," but which we prefer to call "permissive," scaling, i.e., the fact that sometimes no action can take place whatever level has been reached on one factor unless a certain minimum level is reached on another factor. Such psychological situations actually exist, as Coombs's work shows, but it will take some time before this and related modifications can be accommodated by improved factor-analytic models.

OBJECTIVE PERSONALITY FACTOR TESTS: THE O-A BATTERIES

It has well been said that the objective testing of personality began methodologically at the wrong end. Typically, a variety of special tests and gadgets were invented, without any knowledge of personality structure in terms of such objective behavior measurements; and then personality structures or dimensions, e.g., the Rorschach categories, were further invented to fit the test, or, at best, a factor analysis of the test results was carried out to see what factors might reside in the test performances. The approach that has been advocated here by the present writer, as indicated above, is to obtain knowledge of personality by factoring behavior, then to invent tests, either questionnaire items or objective test devices, which may be expected to involve these general life dimensions of the personality.

The result of the mere test-centered approach has actually been a very disappointing one. The validities obtained from the tests have been poor and the areas of personality involved in a particular patent test have generally proved to be very limited. Yet, it is probably true to say, as of today, that for one clinical or industrial psychologist who knows about and is trained in the array of possible tests for measuring personality *factors* there are fifty who know the various gadgets and crystal balls used in clinical and industrial testing. It is this which accounts for the sad fact that, although good batteries are known for factor measurement at the research level, they have not yet been adapted to streamlined and standardized form for general use in applied psychology.

Factor measurement research, as carried out for example at the Laboratory of Personality Assessment at the University of Illinois, has now developed some three hundred or more tests for about twenty personality factors [10]. These have been externally as well as internally validated in certain cases. For example, in the work of Eysenck, in London [16], they have been validated against clinical criteria. In yet another direction of development one finds Thurstone using psychophysical experiment designs for factored personality tests. In the work of the present writer and his associates, the factors as found first in behavior ratings, i.e., in the general criteria of life, have been taken as the hypotheses for the design of new tests intended to cover the whole personality area. A recent survey [8] shows that some eighteen objective test factors have been found in various studies at least three times, though only about twelve of them can be considered confirmed at the level at which the questionnaire and behavior-rating factors are confirmed. The relation of these objective test factors to the factors in questionnaire and rating material, however, still awaits adequate research in order to clear up certain obscurities. The task in research is a formidable one, because it involves testing the same population (probably fewer than 300 would not be adequate) simultaneously upon a wide array of objective tests, upon the various questionnaire factors, and also upon rating factors in situations in which rating would be effective and reliable. This combination of circumstances is not easily achieved. Consequently, it has seemed best here, as in other media, to label the factors by universal index numbers [11], adopting this noncommittal symbolization instead of a descriptive label or letter which would tie them to the questionnaire and rating factors.

A sample of three objective test factors is given below:

Universal Index Factor No. 16

DESCRIPTIVELY LABELED: *Competent Assertiveness*

| | APPROXIMATE |
TITLE OF TEST	MEAN LOADING
Long exploratory distance in given time on maze	.40
Fast tempo of arm-shoulder swing	.40
Good "High Brow" taste in social and aesthetic environment	.35
Excessive use of circles on C.M.S. test	.28
Fast speed of letter comparison	.30
Many objects perceived in unstructured picture	.35
Little suggestibility to authority	.30

This factor is characterized by speed (which, of course, has nothing to do with intelligence since this is factored out), by independence of judgment, by assured good taste, and indeed by a general competence which resides in something distinct from ability. It may turn out to be some kind of energy or personality integration.

UI 17—Restraint-Timidity

Large mean P.G.R. deflection to all stimuli	.40
Absence of questionable reading preferences	.40
Slow speed of closure in Gestalt completion	.40
Tendency to perceive threatening objects	.40
Slowness to name object in dark adaptation	.30
High ratio of regularly to irregularly warned reaction time	.25

UI Factor 23: Neutral Reserves vs. Neuroticism

Low motor rigidity (classical perseveration or rigidity factor)	.40
Good two-hand co-ordination	.35
Low body sway suggestibility	.30
Slower decision on principles than particulars	.30
High dynamic momentum (cosatiation)	.30
Smaller P.G.R. response to mental than physical stimuli	.25
Little excess of aspiration over achievement	.25
Good immediate memory	.20

This factor has a consistent character of inhibition as shown for example in unwillingness to give judgment until certain, absence of questionable reading, and presence of anxiety, as shown in the larger P.G.R., the perception of threatening objects, etc.

These three factors are set out in terms of representative loadings just to illustrate the type of test given and the type of factor found. It is obvious that it is decidedly more difficult to infer the nature of the factor from the tests here than in the other two media. Knowledge that Factor 23 is essentially the inverse of neuroticism is due to Eysenck's criterion analysis of neurotic populations [16], where he has demonstrated that this particular factor is that which most highly distinguished neurotics from normals (the normal score high on the factor as it is set out above).

However, it is encouraging that the other factors which have been found also demonstrate at once a validity against outside criteria, i.e., they are not merely factors found among collections of artificial tests, at least not in most cases. Thus the competent-assertiveness factor has predictive value in relation to ability to stand the stresses of life as a pilot while factors A and G have been found important in clinical psychologists [19]. There are also indications that Factor 17 is associated with good scholastic performance for a given level of intelligence.

However, it is true that, in the main, the external validation of these factors must wait upon further research. Indeed, further research needs first to aim at raising the loadings of tests in the batteries by which it is proposed that the factors should be measured in the light of present knowledge. The "objective analytic" personality-factor batteries, recently published by the present writer [10], are indeed published primarily as research instruments, since it is clear that the factors are now being measured only with a validity of about .6 and .7. This perhaps is not surprising when one bears in mind that usually the factor is estimated only on between one and three dozen individual responses. In a questionnaire response, such as, "Are you reluctant to enter a meeting when everyone has sat down?" the responder is already averaging in this single item several incidents in his life. The objective test has the advantage of escaping the distortion of self-report, but it has the disadvantage that any part of it is in fact only a response measured on a single occasion, whereas the behavior rating or the questionnaire response is virtually an observation by time sampling over long periods.

However, it is the objective test medium that must be the ultimate goal of the psychologist. He cannot be content with ratings, which can be made with reliability in only about one setting in a hundred, nor can he continue to depend upon questionnaires indefinitely when, even with the use of supressor scales of various kinds a good deal of distortion still occurs. The ideal is to have batteries of objective, behavioral, personality tests, put together in various ways to measure specific factors. Fortunately, he is definitely at the beginning of the slopes that lead to this plateau of performance.

THE MEASUREMENT OF MOTIVATION AND MOTIVATION STRUCTURE

Although the clinician's inferences about dynamic connections are plainly based upon a nice, intuitive calculus of covariation, many years passed after the successful application of multivariate statistics to personality traits and ability traits before it was realized that the same tool would thus be expected effectively to analyze motivation structure. Possibly the reason for this delay was lack of insight into the observations and inferences by which a conceptualization of motivation is formed. Possibly, alternatively, the workers in the field of abilities were either not interested in motivation or feared that they would be dealing in interests and attitudes with something far more elusive, changeable, and hard to measure than had been dealt with successfully in the ability and achievement field. Be that as it may, the fact remains that it is only in the last five years that there has been seen the successful application of multivariate, factor-analytic methods toward unraveling those motivational connections which psychoanalysis and animal experimental psychology have handled either unreliably or crudely.

The first experiments on this approach to resolving dynamic structure were made between 1946 and 1950 by the present writer and his students, Heist, Unger, Maxwell, Stewart, Mccland, Light and others, who set out with 50 attitudes, the intensity of which was measured by new objective methods, shortly to be described, upon a population of 200 young men [5]. The attitude-interest variables were chosen deliberately to test certain hypotheses about drive structure. For example, the fear drive was represented by such attitudes as, "I want America to be protected against the terror of the atom bomb," and "I would like to see automobile driving made safer." Sex was represented by "I want to make love to a beautiful woman," and similarly with other interest statements. Each hypothesized drive was represented by a minimum of *two* attitude variables, as the technique of finding single factors in factor analysis requires. In addition, the study hypothesized the existence of various sentiments, toward the home, toward religion, toward one's country, toward one's profession, and so on.

The structure revealed by factor analysis of these variables was remarkably encouraging in one way and in another quite puzzling, because practically no trace of the sentiment structures could be found except that of the sentiment toward the self or the self concept. In regard to the drives, there was a beautifully clear confirmation of the ergic structures supposed by such writers as Mac-Dougall, Murray and Freud. Thus it was possible to distinguish the sex drive, the narcistic component of the sex drive, the fear or anxiety drive, and so on.

Before examining these drive patterns more closely, it is necessary to clarify further the technique described above as P-technique, or longitudinal factor analysis of the single individual. Two circumstances make the P-technique method peculiarly valuable to the study of motivation and to the clinician. First, motivational traits are especially liable to change from day to day under the influence of physiological conditions and the stimulus of outer circumstances, so that they establish their patterns by a more emphatic variance than is likely to be found with other kinds of traits. Thus that very "function fluctuation" which causes them to be unreliable in measurement of the ordinary kind is an advantage in the P-technique method of analysis. Secondly, the clinician is mostly interested in the *unique* pattern of the motivational traits within the individual, because his objective is to disentangle the unusual motivation pattern which has left a neurosis or some other personality abnormality. In regard to the first principle, it can be seen that, if the strength of the sex drive, or the level of anxiety, change from day to day with a hormone condition or with the external stimulus situation respectively, then one should expect that all the interest attitudes which subsidiate to these goals would change strength together with the strength of the basic need which they serve. The hypothesis, therefore, was that, if about fifty varied domestic, social, religious, recreational, professional and other interest attitudes were factor-analyzed, it would be found that the patterns within the individual also would correspond to the primary drives—or "ergs," in terms of this new operational basis.

Since the pioneer study first mentioned above was carried out, one further study using P-technique [13] and two further studies using R-technique have been carried out on adequate populations, and in fact the agreement of the P- and R-technique studies is extremely good, substantiating the patterns of:

Fear or Escape
Sex or Mating
Curiosity or Exploration
Appeal
Self-Assertion
Gregariousness
Narcistic Sex
Rest-Seeking
Construction
Protectiveness

The devices for objective measurement of drive have also independently been explored further by McClelland and Liberman [22]. Because of the danger of confusion of this purely operational concept of drive with various theoretical writings not founded on this same experimental basis, it was decided, as indicated above, to use the term "ergs" for the major motivational sources thus indicated. Presumably ergs will be found to be inherited patterns, but that has not yet been demonstrated, and additional research in psychological genetics is necessary to test this hypothesis further. An erg is meanwhile operationally defined as a covariation pattern found by simple structure, factor analysis in dynamic measures.

If one now examines the usual factor-analytic specification equation, but in terms of dynamic variables and factors, he sees that what is actually being done is the analysis of an interest or attitude into the ergs that achieve satisfaction through it. For example, the attitude, "I want to see a good movie or play every week," is found to be loaded principally in two ergic factors only. In fact, the specification equation says that the strength of interest in this course of action equals .54 times the strength of the sex drive plus .38 times the strength of self-assertion, while the coefficients for the remaining eight or nine drives or sentiments are practically zero. Presumably then, the more or less conscious Hollywood formula for fantasy satisfaction is predominantly one catering for identification by the onlooker in vicarious sexual and self-assertive expression. The formulation becomes as follows:

$$I_{ij} = S_{j1}E_{1i} + S_{j2}E_{2i} + \cdots \cdots$$

where I is the strength of interest (motivation) of the subject i in the course of action j, and E_1, E_2, etc. are the strengths of various ergic needs in the subject. The Ss, as usual, are loadings, or situational indices, in this case representing the extent to which the situation stimulates the ergs.

The rewards reaped from applying this method in an unusual way are indeed remarkable. In the first place there has been found in the specification equation the possibility of a real dynamic calculus, or quantitative psychoanalysis. The R-technique equation will state what interests go into a certain attitude in the case of the general population, but the P-technique analysis will give exactly that which the clinician is seeking in the clinical analysis of an individual, namely, the drive structure for the various satisfactions which the individual is capable of. Second, there is a means of assessing the strengths of drives in various individuals, by estimating their factor endowments, just as is done in the case of abilities, which similarly are factors. Third, there is a means of analyzing conflict, for it will be found that typically some of the factor loadings are positive and some are negative in any particular outlet, and the negative loadings mean that this factor is being suppressed or denied satisfaction in order to give satisfaction to the remaining drives. Fourth, there is a means of estimating the individual's degree of integration. If the loadings by P-technique analysis are compared from individual to individual, it will be found that some individuals have decidedly more negative loadings than others, though in every individual it is found that the positive loadings exceed the negative. This last means that the individual is succeeding in gaining a total satisfaction despite the various conflicts and suppressions which he has to carry. If the well-integrated individual be defined as one who succeeds in giving maximum harmonious expression to his drives, then an index of integration could be obtained by summing algebraically the loadings on a standard, comprehensive set of life situations.

In connection with this last index, and since there has been so much interest in recent years in the self concept and the role of the self, in personality psychology, it should be pointed out that here is a powerful instrument of investigation. A self-sentiment pattern emerges clearly in the studies so far carried out and it loads substantially such attitudes as "I want to be eminent in my profession," "I want never to do anything that would tarnish my reputation," "I want to avoid ever being a patient in a mental hospital," and "I want to feel that I can control my emotions and impulses adequately." This analysis, therefore, indicates more clearly than armchair psychology what attitudes and interests should be considered to be involved in the self concept, and it also provides the means of making comparison from person to person, or in the same person before and after therapy, in regard to the structure of the self concept and the functions which the self sentiment has.

Besides the theoretical developments just indicated, the new approach to dynamics involves a reformulation of attitude measurement in both a practical and a theoretical sense. First, in the above-mentioned researches all the attitude measurements were made by means of *objective* tests. Again, objective means tests in which the subject does not indicate the strength of this attitude by self-assessment, as in opinionnaire methods and most of those methods which have so far been subjected to our item-analysis developments. Instead, the attitudes are measured by employing various general psychological principles such as those in learning theory, retroactive inhibition, spontaneous attention, distortion of perception, distortion of belief, distortion of reasoning, increase of excitement level as measured by such devices as the psychogalvanic reflex, metabolic rate, etc. Altogether some fifty different principles and devices have been listed in reports on these researches. The misperception effects were discovered at about the same time in the Laboratory of Personality Assessment and Group Behavior by Heist, Stewart, Maxwell and others and at the same time by Bruner, Postman and others elsewhere; but in the present studies the more exacting test of significant correlation was applied rather than the mean-difference method as used by Bruner and Postman.

The second and theoretical change in attitude or interest measurement is one which shifts the measurement from a mere quantitative measurement along a pro-con continuum, to a true vector measurement. The independent ergic factors comprise a set of independent co-ordinates with respect to which an attitude can be considered to be oriented. Thus the attitude has both strength, which is represented by the length of the vector, and direction, which defines what kinds of drives enter into the attitude and indicates the "emotional direction," as it were, of the attitude. The pro-con continuum is an abstraction from the multidirectional emotional directionality, just as a black-and-white photograph is an abstraction from color.

Insofar as there is concern with practical problems of motivation, interest turns to the various objective devices mentioned above. In the research directed to improving these objective-motivation measures, the first step has been to measure a particular attitude with quite a variety of methods and to intercorrelate them to see which methods correlate most highly with the pool. This search for the demonstrable behavioral associates of strength of drive or interest has considerable importance for learning theory, in that at least half of the manifestations explored concern the effect of motivation on learning and forgetting.

But from the standpoint of personality theory, the conceptions which are likely to prove most valuable are those of vector measurement of attitudes and the representation of attitudes in the dynamic lattice [5].

More recent work has proved that with suitable objective test devices the sentiment patterns can also be brought out, as closely as those of ergs. Just as the factors corresponding to the ergs stand out most clearly when the measurements are measurements primarily of the id component in the motivation measures, so the sentiments stand out most clearly, as might be expected, when the objective test devices are those which are principally loaded in the ego motivation manifestation factor. Together with the self sentiment, which has previously been found, the list of demonstrated sentiments or metanergs now tolerably well demonstrated as common factors stands as follows [14a]:

The sentiment to religion.
The sentiment to career.
The sentiment to sports and games.

The sentiment of general mechanical interest.

The sentiment of patriotism.

The self sentiment.

There are also indications of an acquired structural pattern corresponding to the superego *[14a]*.

It has thus become possible to assign scores on the one hand to the strength of drives and on the other hand to the strength of sentiment structures. However, these are, essentially, two different kinds of measurement, the former expressed in terms of ergic need strength and the latter in terms of a social mold trait determined by frequency and degree of reinforcement and reward. With this it becomes evident that the direction of an attitude vector, in the spatial representation, includes not only its ergic quality, in terms of its direction in relation to the ergic co-ordinates, but also what might be called a sociological direction, in terms of its projections upon the standard common sentiment co-ordinates. If we represent in the specification the ergic need strengths by E, and the sentiment of metanerg factor measures by M, then the general equation for the strength of interest in the course of action defined by a given attitude is as follows:

$$I = s_{E1}.E_1 + s_{E2}.E_2 \ldots \mid s_{En}.E_n + s_{M1}.M_1 + s_{M2}.M_2 \ldots + S_{Mn}M_n.$$

It will be observed that the factor-analytic approach has independently led to a formulation which is strikingly parallel to that in learning theory. This formulation states that the strength of a habit, here expressed as the strength of an interest in a course of action, is a result of certain ergic need strengths multiplied by situational indices, plus a certain history of reward frequency or reinforcement, also multiplied by appropriate situational indices. The chief difference from the learning-theory formulation is that this *adds* the drive and reinforcement terms instead of multiplying them. Only time and more exact work can decide which is the better formulation.

If space permitted we could present arguments for stating that E, the ergic-need strength, is itself to be considered a composite. From a common sense point of view it will be realized at least that the covariation in the dynamic manifestations which produces a factor, when we are dealing with individual difference analysis or R-technique, could be produced by individual differences in constitutional strength of an erg, or by general situational differences in the degree to which an erg is stimulated, or by differences in the degree which a drive strength is discharged by satisfaction. And this can be formulated as follows:

$$E = S(K+C) - G.$$

where E is the erg-need strength, K is the constitutional strength of a drive, C is a physiological factor, partly determining the internal strength of the drive. And G is the normal amount of satisfaction being continuously obtained in a given situation defined by S. This S, incidentally, is the *total provocation of the drive in the life situation* and is not the same as the small s which enters into each specific, common, narrow situation when we are using the specification equation with the ergic strength derived from this equation. It will be seen that K + C corresponds to drive strength and, when multiplied by S, to tension level. This tension level, with the amount of satisfaction subtracted from it, gives the final ergic-need strength at a given time. It is this latter, which we measure at a given time by our objective tests of attitude-interest strength, and which consequently appears in the resultant factor.

Naturally, these developments are too recent to admit of confident assertion of their formulation, but the formulae are based on precise experimental measurements within at least three studies, and they certainly present symbolization in known operational terms which are therefore readily open to checking by further research.

SUMMARY OF FINDINGS AND CONCEPTS

The personality sphere, representing the total reactivity of the individual, can yield an explanation of these reactivities in terms of unitary source traits, by means of factor analysis. Applied to a population these factors define common traits; but on a single person, by P-technique, the structure is that of unique, individual trait patterns.

Statistical techniques now exist for checking the invariance and reproducibility of factors and it is now possible to measure over a dozen confirmed factors in ratings, questionnaires and objective tests. These have such meanings as ego strength, schizothyme tendency, dominance, neuroticism, superego strength and varieties of anxiety.

In addition to temperamental and integrative dimensions of the total personality factor, analysis has also isolated some nine drive patterns, or ergs, as well as the self sentiment, so that it is possible to predict a specific response in terms both of the temperamental (or ability) and the motivational states of the organism.

This last advance makes possible a quantitative psychoanalysis, in that (a) a given symptom or attitude can be resolved in its ergic quanta; (b) the strength of ergs or other discovered motivational structures can be plotted against stimulus conditions; (c) courses of action which engender maximum conflict can be recognized; and (d) an index of dynamic integration can be worked out for the individual in terms of a stratified sample of algebraic sums of specification equations.

In the above, certain approximations are made by the present mathematical model, such as the obtaining of the reaction strength by summation of drive strengths (as modified by situational indices). But, despite these, the factor-analytic calculation gives a wholistic treatment better corresponding with the results of experiment than does any other system.

The contribution here proposed is one of methods and concepts, using what little theory is dependable in psychology today. More ambitious attempts at universal theories in psychology at the present time seem to be undertaken largely because of a social need for psychology to have theories, rather than as a natural growth from findings. The striking historical fact about psychology is that it has far fewer dependable laws and concepts than any other true science. Until a sufficient number of regularities and laws have become established to make exact reasoning and inference possible, theories are worse than useless. Being insubstantial, they distract from the more modest objective of finding regularities in nature and fitting exact concepts to them. For example, learning theory has talked of drive in the abstract, but has demonstrated no way of recognizing and measuring particular drives (*a priori* definitions are not a suitable basis for measurement). It is conceivable that learning under the influence of some drives follows different laws from that of others. It is conceivable that objective measures of conflict as developed here will yield different and more interesting laws than those alleged to rest on rough clinical assessment.

What has been propounded here is essentially a set of measurement methods, concepts and results which can open up new possibilities of experiment and suggest exact ideas for testing in a way not possible with previous rougher concepts. For investigators having interest in genuine theory, these methods, and the laws to which they are capable of leading, will justify the patient statistical study necessary for their acquisition.

BIBLIOGRAPHY

1. BURT, C. L. *The Young Delinquent*. London: University of London Press, 1920.
2. ———. *Factors of the Mind*. London: University of London Press, 1940.
3. CATTELL, R. B. *The Description and Measurement of Personality*. New York: World Book Co., 1946.
4. ———. rp and Other Coefficients of Pattern Similarity. *Psychometrika*, 1949, 14, 279-98.
5. ———. *Personality: A Systematic Theoretical and Factual Study*. New York: McGraw-Hill, 1950.
6. ———. P-technique, A New Method for Analyzing the Structure of Personal Motivation. *Trans. N. Y. Acad. Sci., Ser. II*, 1954, 14, 29-34.
7. ———. *Factor Analysis: An Introduction and Manual for the Psychologist and Social Scientist*. New York: Harper, 1952.
8. ———. The Principal Invariant Personality Factors Established in Objective Tests. Adv. Public. No. 1, 1953, Lab. of Person. Assess. and Group Behavior. Urbana: University of Illinois.
9. ———. A Universal Index for Psychological Factors. *Ibid*. No. 3, 1954.
10. ———. The O-A Personality Factor Batteries. Champaign, Ill., Instit. Person. and Ability Testing, 1954.
11. ———, SAUNDERS, D. R., & STICE, G. F. The 16 P. F. Questionnaire. Champaign, Ill., Instit. Person. and Ability Testing, 1950.
12. ———, & BAGGALEY, A. R. The Salient Variable Similarity Index -s-for Factor Matching. Adv. Public. No. 4, April, 1954, Lab. of Person. Assess. and Group Behavior. Urbana: University of Illinois.

13. ———, & Cross, P. Comparison of the Ergic and Self-Sentiment Structures Found in Dynamic Traits by R- and P-techniques. *J. Pers.*, 1952, 21, No. 2, 250-70.

14. ———, Blewett, D., & Beloff, J. The Inheritance of Personality: A Multiple Variance Analysis of Nature-Nurture Ratios for Personality Factors in Q-data. *Amer. J. hum. Genet.*, 1955.

14a. ———, & Baggaley, A. R. The Theory and Practice of Structured Personality Measurements. *Psychol. Monogr.* (In press.)

15. Coombs, C. H. Mathematical Models in Psychological Scaling. *J. Amer. statist. Ass.*, 1951, 46, 480-89.

16. Eysenck, H. J. *The Structure of Human Personality*. London: Methuen, 1953.

17. French, J. W. *The Description of Personality Measurements in Terms of Rotated Factors*. Princeton: Educ. Test Service, 1953.

18. Guilford, J. P. An Analysis of the Factors in a Typical Test of Introversion-Extraversion. *J. abnorm. soc. Psychol.*, 1934, 28, 377-99.

19. Kelly, E. L., & Fiske, D. W. *The Prediction of Performance in Clinical Psychology*. Ann Arbor: University of Michigan Press, 1951.

20. Kretschmer, E. *Körperbau und Charakter*. Berlin: Springer, 1950.

21. Maslow, A. H. Dominance Feeling, Behavior and Status. *Psychol. Rev.*, 1937, 44, 404-29.

22. McClelland, D. C., & Liberman, A. M. The Effect of Need for Achievement on Recognition of Need-Related Words. *J. Pers.*, 1949, 18, 236-51.

23. Mead, M. *Growing Up in New Guinea*. New York: Morrow, 1930.

24. Saunders, D. R. The "Ruled Surface Regression" as a Starting Point in the Investigation of "Differential Predictability." Princeton Educ. Test Service, 1952.

25. Thomson, G. H. *The Geometry of Mental Measurement*. London: University of London Press, 1954.

26. Thurstone, L. L., & Chave, E. J. *The Measurement of Attitudes*. Chicago: University of Chicago Press, 1930.

27. ———. *Multiple Factor Analysis*. Chicago: University of Chicago Press, 1947.

28. Wittenborn, J. R., Mandler, G., & Waterhouse, I. K. Symptom Patterns in Youthful Mental Hospital Patients. *J. clin. Psychol.*, 1951, 7, 323-27.

perception, motives and personality

a clinical perspective

GEORGE S. KLEIN, Ph.D.

GEORGE S. KLEIN, PH.D.

Dr. Klein is associate professor of psychology and director of the Clinical Laboratory of the Research Center for Mental Health, New York University. He was Senior Psychologist at the Perception Laboratory of the Menninger Foundation. A graduate of Columbia University in 1942 with the Ph.D., and a diplomate in clinical psychology, Dr. Klein is a national leader in the field of perception, and an authority on the function of perception in personality. He is author of many scientific journal articles, and coeditor of the book, *Theoretical Models and Personality Theory*. He has also contributed an important chapter to Blake and Ramsey's *Perception: An Approach to Personality*.

Stating that the many concentrated man-hours of study which the issue of motivated perception has inspired were generated by clinicians, personality theorists and social psychologists, Dr. Klein gives a terse developmental history of the perception-motivation approach to personality. He points out that perceptual theories, which had been protected by a tradition of psychophysical methodology, were, to a great extent, first attacked by the work of Murphy, Goldstein and Allport. The attack was further inspired by psychoanalytic principles, by the clinical diagnostic work with tests by Rapaport and Schafer, and by the work of Bartlett and Sherif in the area of social psychology.

Klein believes that there has been too much emphasis of relatively simple, perceptual problems at the expense of the more complex, cognitive processes. These latter, of course, involve not only the perceptual processes, but numerous motivational factors as well. From this point of view, Klein has reviewed and analyzed much of the salient work in the field of perception; he has organized and refined many of these concepts and has integrated them with his own thinking to provide an interesting and stimulating approach to understanding personality.

ISSUES AND PARADOXES IN PERCEPTION-MOTIVATION
RESEARCH

Issues of motivated perception have probably attracted more concentrated man-hours of study in recent years than most other segments of the psychologist's interest. This momentum has been generated mainly by the clinician and personality theorist on the one hand and the social psychologist on the other. Loudly proclaiming perception's vulnerability to the claims of sets, expectancies, needs, values, and social norms, interlopers from these once distant lands have invaded perceptual theories comfortably settled in a tradition of psychophysical correlation, a tradition that had cushioned even the earlier impact of Gestalt theory's broader perspective to field events and context. With or without Gestalt theory, it remained more or less unmoved by the parallel activities of personologists and motivation theorists.

To a great extent the invasion was inspired by the organismic emphases of Murphy [67], Goldstein [29], and Allport [1], and by the pioneering studies of Murphy and his students [57, 82, 75]. But it drew its encouragement mainly from the revelations of the

I am greatly indebted to Dr. Robert R. Holt and Dr. David Rapaport for their many stimulating and invaluable comments on this paper.

psychoanalytic couch regarding the penetration of drive into all levels of behavior. The perceptual function seemed to be a crucial outpost of contact between world and personal strivings. Here the major pulls and pushes of living might appear in bold relief and under conditions of controlled observation.

From the standpoint of personality theory, perceptual responses seemed to be the measurable events long-needed to test conceptions of typological theories and of alleged organismic and adjustive strategies. The pioneering use of so-called intelligence tests in clinical diagnosis by Rapaport [79] and Schafer [83] gave powerful impetus to this trend by piercing the wall that had cut off psychometrics and "differential psychology" from theories of cognitive processes and personality structure. By tracing the outlines of character integration through responses to purely cognitive tasks, Rapaport and Schafer vastly encouraged the belief that thought functions in general—and therefore why not perception in particular?—could clarify the personal nexus of integrated activity which previously had been discussed largely outside the traditions of experimental psychology. Proponents of the more avowed "projective tests" had, of course, long proclaimed such links but had in the main developed their procedures within the confines of a "service" outlook and with cavalier disregard for theory which isolated them from the main currents of experimental activity. Personality investigations now became focused not merely on contents (attitudes, values, etc.), but on the *formal qualities of thought*.

It will be important as this discussion develops to bear in mind a distinction between two trends in this convergence upon the perception laboratory: One group of approaches, the motivational, had their sources basically in instinct and drive theory (tension-release theories of forces that discharge themselves on particular objects or events). Other approaches were based on the problem of adaptive style or forms of adjustment [103, 45]. These approaches do not pose the same problems and require different types of evidence, though each involves premises regarding directional forces that determine the course and outcomes of behavior.

From social psychology the migration to the perception laboratory started with Bartlett's studies [5] but gathered momentum with Sherif's studies of social norms, which suggested that the genesis and impact of values and social frameworks could be traced through such (allegedly) simple phenomena as the autokinetic response *[86]*. One can imagine the hopes this produced in social psychologists bogged down in the jungle of complicated social events and casting an envious eye at the simplified (if, from the standpoint of social issues, trivial) world of their experimental colleagues! Not only did the perception laboratory seem to promise controllable methods, controllable variables, and altogether an emotionally less hectic setting but, more than this, perceptual phenomena seemed to be *the* crucial ones to demonstrate how major social forces obtained *psychological* status and exerted their impact. It promised to show the grooves into which socialization guides behavior—how they are learned, and how they are *unlearned*. It seemed also to elevate the status of social psychology by implying that the study of social influences provides the basis of a sound individual psychology. The controlled setting of the perceptual laboratory, rather than the complex mire of social events, seemed to offer an equally effective—perhaps more effective —strategy for studying the social.

Within the confines of more restricted perceptual theory itself there were faint stirrings to support these possibilities of widespread linkages between perception and other regions of an individual's activity; e.g., psychophysiological findings which indicated hypothalamic innervations even of peripheral sensory structures; evidence from the Hamburg laboratory of tonic components in perceptual response (Werner), and dramatic demonstrations by Ames which brought into relief the priority of *achievement* over the "stimulus" in perceptual behavior *[3]*. Thus, there were a certain number on hand—a minority—within the specialized camp of perceptual research to greet the newcomers.

Where do matters stand some fifteen years later? For all of their value in energizing perceptual research and proliferating the range of novel questions, the net result has for the most part been to demonstrate biases brought to the field by personologists and motivation theorists. To accommodate conviction, the definition of perception itself has widened and loosened to leave ample room for "verifying" the primacy of motive in perceptual response. From the first enthusiasms of these demonstrations emerged the well-known generalization that that which looms large in value looms large perceptually. In this view, hypothesis, need value (the term for the directing agents vary but share the same premise) are allegedly involved in all perceptions in the very processes that mediate experiences of shape, size, distance and so on. Closer inspection shows that the evidence itself is less clear-cut than the claims: with respect to the involvement of perceptual activity, judgment, apperceptive elaboration, memory—all seem hopelessly enmeshed in the phenomena studied, defying a searching probe as to *where* precisely in the cognitive act the alleged forces exert their alleged effects. On the face of it, all these studies do seem to have brought current thinking to a point far removed from perception conceived as a camera or fact-registering mechanism, and even far removed from the early emphasis of Gestalt theory on the coercive correspondence of the patterned forms of brain field activity to configuration in the physical environment. But, in much of this work of the early forties there was an insidious and disconcerting solipsism, though it was not noticed in the burst of first enthusiasm. The drift of the work would have one believe that perception is the most labile of functions, at the whim and mercy of wish and need. Not much attention was given to the *limits* of this malleability. Where noted they were given an embarrassed nod and relegated to secondary interest, as for instance in Bruner and Goodman's early distinction between "autochthonous" and "behavioral" determinants of perception [11]. In this view it would be more precise to say that the organism is fated to misperceive than to perceive. The projective hypothesis seemed to have carried the day.

Some important voices protested. Wallach [93] doubted that purported distortions by motive—"autisms"—were *perceptual* effects in the strict sense. In order for selective distortion to occur —if it were indeed guided by a pregnant need or value, *something* —a stimulus—must be in *some* stage of organization, it must have *some* form for a selective force to operate efficiently on it. Thus, the effects were actually *post*-perceptual elaborations, not indications of influences upon perceptual process formation itself. Indeed, Wallach pointed out, fidelity would seem to be a condition for survival since it is hardly conceivable that the organism could operate unless the actual structures of environment—the physical field—were coercive to some extent.

Perhaps the most effective blast at the projective hypothesis in perception theory has been offered by Gibson [25, 27]. He notes, first of all, that the experimental conditions and phenomena in these studies are certainly not prototypic of all studies in perception; hence, generalizations from them can at best be limited to certain but not all aspects of perception. The experiments of the motivation theorists aim, he points out, to demonstrate the impact of meanings and values upon response, and perhaps individual differences and personal consistencies in these respects. As a result, such experiments deliberately maximize the non-correspondence of perception to stimulation in order to highlight this interest in motives. What these experiments therefore completely bypass are questions concerning *efficiency and "correctness"* of perception, which is and always was the central concern of the psychophysical experiment. The latter, in contrast, is designed to maximize the correspondence of perception to stimulation and is subject to the same limitations of generalization. It is treacherous to generalize from either of these types of studies to all perception, a point also emphasized in Brunswik's plea for a representative design in experimentation [15].

But the crucial matter, in Gibson's view, is not simply overgeneralization from a restricted experimental inquiry. He insists that an adequate understanding of the projective aspects of experience must be founded on a theory of *effective* perceptions; the first problem in perception is not its errors but its success. It is only from such a theory that one can evolve a systematic view of the processes contributing to error and distortion. "We know that patterns, pictures and symbols may be conceptualized, stereotyped, and distorted by conceptual customs . . . What we do not sufficiently understand is, for instance, how a face is perceived as such, or is perceived as the face of an acquaintance, or is perceived as the face of a hostile man . . . In other words, what do we discriminate and identify in these complex stimulus-situations which when conditions are favorable, yields a *correct* perception. This ought to be the primary line of inquiry, but instead it is almost completely neglected." [25, pp. 95–6] This point applies even to a full understanding of specific "projective tests."

This very important matter of strategy will be discussed further later. It is worth pointing out in passing, however, that Gibson's criticism of the stacked deck in motivational studies of perception is apt only for a group of studies which overgeneralize in the manner he describes: studies which confine themselves to impoverished stimuli (e.g., "ambiguous" stimuli, brief exposures, "open-ended tasks") and to tasks that put no premium on highly "accurate," specific discriminative response. It does not touch those studies which have yielded evidence of stylistic consistency in perceptual response [103, 49], nor the findings of such studies as Poetzl's [72] and Fisher's [20] which disclosed that even highly efficient discriminations are not free of the participation of "unadaptive" drive influences. The latter studies are especially effective in showing that distortion and autism are *not* the only marks of influence of motives in perception.

In order to prepare the ground for an attempt to survey some of the critical variables in motivation-perception relationships, it is necessary to examine the polar viewpoints in the controversy. It is not possible here to review all variations in these viewpoints, but a schematized review may highlight critical issues. This may be worth the risk of creating oversimplified amalgams of current points of view.

MOTIVATION-CENTERED APPROACHES

Most such studies address themselves to the "interaction" of motive and perceptual processes. Examples include demonstrations of "autistic" distortion, elaborations and selective sensitivity, as in "perceptual defense." This literature has been critically reviewed by a number of investigators from the standpoint of perceptual theory [37, 88, 60] and there is little point in repeating their work. As observed earlier, criticisms have disclosed the equivocality of these studies as to locus of the alleged interaction—whether it involves process formation (in the sense of Gestalt theory) or merely preperceptual or postperceptual processes. On the other hand little attention has been paid to the inadequacy of such studies from the standpoint of motivation theory itself, and a few remarks on this matter are appropriate.

Many of these approaches have been developed in designs that assume a linear relation between motive and perceptual effect, an assumption both unlikely in theory and inefficient in its predictive power. In part the fault has resided in a basic unclarity about the motives that are working in the experimental situation. Little regard is given to the complexity and range of motives in a *single* situation—motives other than the immediately specific one induced by an experimental instruction. I have in mind a range of pres-

sures extending from more or less conscious motives concerned
with self-esteem, achievement and failure, to silent, "unadaptive"
but no less profound claims from sexual and aggressive sources
that may also be tripped off in a situation. Few if any studies
have taken into account the entire motivational field or tried to
link experimental effects to *levels* of participating motives. It has
even been rare for an experimenter to evaluate the relevance or
irrelevance of a task to the dominant motives produced by an experimental instruction or a consciously self-imposed task. It seems
naïve to assume that a given perceptual outcome represents the
workings of a *single* motive, or that all tasks are equally prone to
influence by the same motive. Demonstration of this point is
provided by Poetzl's long-neglected studies [72] and their brilliant replication and confirmation by Fisher [20]. These studies
will be referred to repeatedly throughout this paper. One general
point deserves mention here. Poetzl and Fisher clearly show that
the motivational aura of an experiment ranges far beyond the
seemingly controlled and explicit claims of the experimental instructions or even the motivational components of the subject's
"ego investment," e.g., to do well, to avoid failure, etc. Tracing
from the selective reports of a subject to tachistoscopically exposed
picture details the later emergence of the picture details in the
subject's dreams, Fisher found that the experimental occasion itself had had profound personal significance. Peering through the
darkness to catch a glimpse of a momentarily appearing stimulus
had, for one subject, for instance, a voyeuristic meaning. Also to
most subjects the experimenter himself took on important symbolic significance.

Studies of the effects of specific motivational states have not
only oversimplified the motivational context, but also until recently they have neglected the importance of enduring structures
or constants in personality organization. The role of such enduring
"motive structures" has proven an especially important consideration for the problem of the limits of certain perceptual "distortions" [49].

Another significant feature in motivation-centered studies of
perception has been their narrow perspective in the matter of
"effects" or "influences" exerted by the motive. Except for the
Poetzl and Fisher investigations the whole issue of "effects" has
been squeezed through the eyelet of "error" measures and ver-

balized communications, and the sought-after effects have been limited to conditions where the subject was avowedly carrying out a purposeful, adaptive task, conforming according to his best knowledge with the experimenter's instruction. But such purposeful perceiving is not prototypic of all occasions or states of consciousness in which a person perceives and therefore where a motive-organized percept may guide behavior. Motivationally colored percepts may appear in the convolutions of a dream, in reverie states, in daydreams and "twilight" states, and the intrusion of motive upon percept seems to be more profound in these states than in adaptive discriminative behavior. In general, most studies have been confined to situations in which the *central* motive is one that steers S toward a disciplined adaptive response, usually a discrimination. If one conceives of the experimental circumstances as including a fringe of silent, if irrelevant, motives, if he further conceives of occasions and states of consciousness to range along a continuum from purposeful perceiving to dreams, and finally if he conceives of a variety of response levels from the conscious communications of the subject to nonverbal interoceptive events, then the matter of looking for the "effects of motive on percept" is broadened to its proper perspective.

Evaluations of effects have usually been based upon single-level responses that are often trivial to the motive concerned. For instance, perceptual defense studies have confined themselves exclusively to *absence* of response; evidence of the impact of the motive has rarely been sought on different response levels that are perhaps simultaneously activated upon exposure to a critical stimulus event.

Perhaps the most impressive oversight in motivation-centered studies is their failure to resolve a paradox created by their own demonstrations: With autism, perceptual defense, and other testimony to the corruptibility of perception, how is it possible that perception is as effective as it *can* be and usually is? Even in the Bruner-Goodman study *[11]*, the distortions were actually quite small even though the subjects were children, and one wonders if they would have any *practical* significance in the adaptive circumstances of everyday life. This is seen in the difficulties encountered in replicating claims of purported instances of autistic effect; it turns out that a *simple* motivational hypothesis is insufficient. Perception seems not to be at the whim of *every* motive, or at most at the whim of a particular one under special circumstances of stimulation, as the soberly watered-down conclusion by Bruner and Rodrigues *[13]* has stated. A host of qualifying conditions *in the stimulus situation* have to be stated. It is easy to see why Gibson could conclude that it takes impoverishment in the stimulus situation to highlight such "autistic" influences of motives—that, at least under conditions where a subject is oriented toward an adaptive, purposeful discrimination, it enters only either through ambiguity of instruction or insufficient discriminable cues—that it enters when there is little else to go by in the information provided.

There is impressive evidence that actions based on perception are efficiently co-ordinated with the attributes of objects to which action is directed. Perception can do its job of discrimination remarkably well. It creates workable notions of *what* things are to accord with what one wants, of *where* things are to be seen when he wants them.

Michotte's ingenious and systematic studies *[63, 64, 65]* have cogently demonstrated that even such higher-order experiences as impressions of *causality, permanence,* and *transiency* of an object, of surfaces conceived as *"picture"* or *"real,"* are difficult to explain simply on the basis of secondary projections of ideas or as secondary interpretations of processes conditioned by experience. They seem to be direct outcomes of complicated arrangements of movements, events and object surfaces in the physical field; experiences in response to such configurations have the directness and immediate "sensory quality" of the *phi* phenomenon.

For instance, kinetic configurations of objects yield definite and unequivocal impressions of *leading, pursuit,* and *propulsion* and other features of mechanical causality. Co-ordination—at the perceptual level—to the properties of surfaces and events and movements between objects in the world of things apparently can reach remarkably high levels of intricacy, possibilities that have been obscured by a philosophical assumption derived from Hume which emphasizes learning as the only basis for complex experiences and its consequent derogation of the possibilities of integrations occurring at the *perceptual* level itself. Heider *[35]* has shown that the structure of *events,* definable solely in terms of temporal sequence and movements, call forth highly uniform percepts of predictable cause, attribution, and affect. In Heider's study "projection" is quite definitely confined to symbolic embellishments of basic phenomenal co-ordinations that are perceptually given. Thus, two geometric figures which move in a certain relation to each other may invariably call forth a causal attribution of "A is hitting B"; A may be variously termed a "cruel father" or a "bully," etc., and B "a helpless son" or a "weakling"; but in both the action-invariants of the figures are quite stable. A study of the perception of emotion by Michotte [64] impressively makes the same point, the more so since on the issue of how emotion is recognized the projective hypothesis is all too easily assumed and is still unchallenged by many clinicians. Impressions of loving, fear, hostility, etc., often can be elicited as direct outcomes of kinetic invariants in movement patterns. Quite clearly, the Michotte and Heider investigations point up the adjustive significance of perception as involving intricate co-ordinations with definable attributions of object and event qualities.

Finally, the extremely important studies of Iwo Kohler [52, 53] further point up the remarkable capacity of the perceptual apparatus to achieve at the perceptual level complex co-ordinations of phenomenal properties with invariant properties of the "real" object world. Extending Stratton's earlier studies of prolonged reversals of the visual field, Kohler investigated the effects of prolonged wearing of distorting lenses—over a period of days and weeks—upon spatial orientation. Kohler biased optical stimulation in several ways. Wearing lenses that produced an upside-down reversal, his subjects soon achieved highly effective motor facility. But far more significant was his finding that in time phenomenal reversal developed—the world *"looked"* right-side-up. Kohler has shown, in short, that a persistent abnormality of optical stimulation leads in the end to reduction in the world's *phenomenal* abnormality.

"The habituation that results is not simply a matter of appropriate motor response, of manipulation, and locomotion; the actual *appearance* of the world changes in time, and then it changes all over again in the opposite direction when the optical device is removed from in front of the eyes." [28] Thus, perception seems to be modifiable, but more crucial than this, perception is very much a matter of co-ordination with a field of *invariances* in the real world, which it eventually achieves, or "reproduces" in experience regardless of the initial "distortions" or "biases" of proximal stimulation.

A crucial lesson in the Kohler experiment is the distinction it implies between *medium* and *object [cf. Heider, 32]*—that despite changes in the medium (proximal stimulation), repeated contact with the real world of invariances results in a refined co-ordination. The learning that occurs does not alter the ultimate appearance of the real world; the learning involves a shift in correspondence between stimulus and experience. True, sharply altered optical stimulation changes perception, but it does not lead to a permanent disruption of correspondence. Optical distortion induces a *shift* in the correspondence between stimulation and experience, not a disruption of the correspondence itself. The proof is the shift to abnormality again—in precisely the way demanded by the kind of changes that occurred. In short, the studies prove the modifiability of the *medium*, but *not of the distal invariances* with which experience is co-ordinated.

Kohler's work poses difficulties for the thoroughgoing "functionalist" position as stated by Ames *[3]* and his students. Theirs is the view that what one sees and experiences perceptually are products of the purposeful transactions that have developed between person and objects. *Where* something is depends entirely upon *what* it is and the purposeful relationship that exists between it and the subject. The meaningful world is built out of transactions —a learning theory of perception. On the face of it the Kohler results would seem to encourage this point of view; but at the same time, the essential point of co-ordination with distal invariances *despite a labile medium* finds no place in the Ames theory. Actually a perceptual system that undeviatingly follows the trajectory of purpose should produce uniqueness of experience rather than generality, because of the variety of "transactions," intricacy and individuality of purposes that occur in different personalities. Such an unbending functional theory fails because it does not accord any determining status to object organization independent of the experiencing subject.

THE PSYCHOPHYSICAL SOLUTION

In the face of these and other considerations the emphasis given by Gibson *[28]* and Hochberg *[38]* to psychophysical co-ordinations seems at first glance to be a needed counterpoise to the imbalances of what has sometimes been called motivational imperialism. According to Gibson the essential tie between real world and experience is a "correspondence between certain mathematical properties of the retinal image and certain phenomenal variables of the visual world—not only the qualities of color and so-called location but also qualities of the curvature and density and proportions and motions of things. These mathematical properties of the stimulus, if they can be specified, are the key to the deepest problems of perception." *[28]*

The chief novelty of this point of view is the staunch conviction that behind every quality of experience is a discoverable variable of stimulation. "This means not only that the sensory qualities, so-called, have stimuli, but that all the qualities of surfaces, edges, slopes, and shapes have stimuli, and that all the qualities of motion, action, and causality have stimuli, and that all the qualities of persons, groups, institutions, words, and symbols have stimuli. . . ." *[25, pp. 104–5]* The main problem in analyzing a perception therefore is to discover the stimulus, not merely to measure response, and the failure to keep this problem in focus has led to an overemphasis on response in motivational studies.

The relevant stimulus variables may be complex (e.g., ratios, patterns, reciprocals), but they are no less measurable than variations of intensity along a single dimension (e.g., brightness), and indeed Gibson *[28]* and Hochberg *[38]* have recently proposed a program of "global psychophysics" with implications of an entirely different methodology of psychophysics in order to provide for such "higher-order" variables. An example of this approach is Gibson's explanation of size and shape constancy in stimulus terms. The "adequate" stimulus for an experience of constancy is an *invariant*—a reciprocal relation among proximal conditions on the retina as between the retinal stimuli for size and distance. In general, the psychophysics of space perception would come down to a search for *invariants* both on the distal and proximal (retinal) sides. Invariants of three-dimensional experience are present in retinal images as "specific high-order variables of stimulation."

This approach is fundamental, says Gibson, even to the understanding of the perceptual bases of projective test responses. Even the Rorschach is determined by stimulation—of a special sort—which involves, in Gibson's view, "a game of controlled misperception." "The Rorschach ink-blots contain gradients of texture, shading, and color, including moderate gradients of varying definition, and steep or sharp gradients, the latter tending to produce margins. In this respect it is like an ordinary photograph, but the essential characteristic of the ink-blot is that these are *not* the specific gradients and margins which yield the surfaces and edges of objects in a photograph. The edges and surfaces which emerge in experience are ambiguous or equivocal. There are stimuli for corners, curves, indentations, protuberances, and interspaces in the ink-blots but these stimuli are mutually discrepant or conflicting. Since the spatial properties are not consistent, the objects are not consistent and what is seen can be almost anything. The orthodox description in the ink-blots is to say that they are 'unstructured,' borrowing a term from Gestalt theory, but this is a poor word since it has never been clear whether the physical stimulation lacks structure or whether it is only the perception which is unstructured. Or, for that matter, exactly what the term 'structure' means." [25, *p.* 97]

Despite the priority he gives to the problem of discrimination and its bases in stimulation, Gibson is impressed by the data on motivation-inspired studies and the findings of projective tests since the manner in which they pose a problem—allowing a wide latitude of "acceptable" response—is much more akin to the loose standards that govern much of our normal attitudes in "looking" at things. Only rarely are the stringent demands for precision of the psychophysical laboratory met with in real life. Most of the time behavior is not governed by necessities of accurate discrimination. Behavior is often satisfied with much less: it can often be effective within a wide range of tolerances of departure from the stimuli; i.e., on the basis of "schemata" or stereotypes. When, further, the central portions of a field of stimulation are unclear, then, and only then, according to Gibson, does projection work. To provide for both "tendencies" in behavior—actions based on precise discriminative responses and actions based on schemata—he proposes that there are two kinds of perception—schematic and literal. Both, it should be added, are consistent with his point of view that stimulation is prior to meaning, since even in schematic perception, stimuli are involved, but the "effective" stimuli in schematic perception are representatives of objects, whereas in "literal" perception experience is directly co-ordinated with measurable relations—invariances—in the stimulus field.

It is at this point that Gibson's corrective emphasis becomes overemphasis. His dichotomy is at best a classification, not a theory of processes, and one may reasonably suspect that it is a classification based on his desire to preserve intact his personal preference for a certain type of experiment, and it is hence artifactual. The dichotomy seems to be the product of the methods and conditions that he prefers to use for studying perception.

It is uneconomical to assume a dichotomy in the actual processes of perception. For one thing, when Gibson asserts in his crusade for the stimulus that perception does not often occur under "optimal conditions" of discrimination, he must mean in part "optimal conditions of *motivation*." Even where stimulation is not "impoverished," literal perception is the product of a certain intentional state; under others, "schematic" perception may be the outcome. Furthermore, he fails to take into account that, if one changes a person's state of awareness from the usual one of the typical antiseptic psychophysical experiment to the altered state of consciousness induced, for instance, by mescaline, the neat psychophysical correlates are undone. Under such "non-optimal" conditions, as in the mescaline state, it is not a matter of not responding to stimuli but of new stimulus organizations coming to the fore to participate in the percept.

Also, what Gibson calls a schematic impression—experiences that depend on the evaluations that a man places on things—comes about not only when stimulation is impoverished, but, also, whenever certain and not other properties of objects develop significance for a person. This is not to say that physical stimuli *per se* are any less important than he makes them out to be, but simply that there is more than one invariance that is *potentially* perceivable in an object or event-manifold. Different purposes—intentions—in relation to objects make certain properties of objects more or less salient. In short, Gibson's point of view makes no provision for the selection of what in the stimulus should be responded to. Since he is working with only one condition of motivation, his answers are specific only to that condition. In criticizing the motivation-centered theorists for their seeming assumption that the stimulus is a matter of accidental occurrence, he overlooks the problem of the selective force of motives that produce dispositions for discriminating what is in the stimulus.

The central fact in Gibson's approach seems to be that it conceives perception to proceed along a fixed course, assuming that certain invariances are salient in a particular perceptual situation. But what makes for the saliency? Is this solely a matter of physical stimulation and to be explained wholly by an analysis of the distribution of energies on sensory surfaces? Is there not also another field of forces—intentions—which establish conditions of saliency?

The problem of what governs saliency is perhaps overlooked by Gibson because he seems to take for granted that the psychophysical correspondences he obtains are not only the necessary but also the sufficient conditions for a given experience. He seems to reason that if a proximal invariance, as for instance a textural gradient, is highly specific for an experience of slant, this correlation exhausts the basis for the experience of depth. He ignores the possibility, emphasized by Boring [8], Brunswik [15] and Heider [32], that a variety of proximal conditions may serve interchangeably as media for the representation of the distal invariants. The distinction between thing-quality and the medium of thing-quality, and the possibility that a variety of medial conditions, "ordinal stimuli," in Gibson's terms, can convey thing-qualities, permits more flexibility in perception than Gibson allows for. But to provide adequately for the co-ordination of experience to thing-qualities and for the interchangeability of medial events or cues in conveying such qualities of objects requires much respect for the selective activity of the organism in the perceptual process. The essence of this activity, as we will try to see in more detail later, is *intended* co-ordinations—whether conscious or not—with thing-qualities.

Perhaps the core of all these difficulties in Gibson's viewpoint is the slight regard he gives to what perception accomplishes. In emphasizing retinal conditions as the principal bases of perceptual experience he seems to assume that they are identical with the actual object-qualities toward which purposeful perceiving aims. But one does not discriminate *gradients*; he discriminates *size* and *shape*; the gradients only mediate the latter; they are cues for these thing-qualities but are not identical with them. There are instances, as Heider points out in his analysis of action forms, where medial qualities themselves can become the *object* of perception. For instance, there are certain conditions where movements are the medium for interpretations of actions between objects; under other conditions, the movements themselves can be the object of perception. When medial and thing-qualities are distinguished, for the question of focus or intention in perceiving necessarily arises, the importance of a stimulus event as the aim itself of discrimination or merely as a cue or medial quality is not given by the stimulus arrangement itself.

The phenomena that Gibson has called two different kinds of perception seem on close inspection to have important similarities. First of all, all perceptions, "schematic" or "literal," share the property of being anchored in a field of motives and intentions. Secondly, both "kinds" of perception also involve central (i.e., relevant or irrelevant to adaptation) and peripheral (adaptively irrelevant) stimulus organizations. Furthermore, they involve processes of *mediation* whereby object-events are conveyed by proximal stimulus conditions. In this view, it is possible for projective or schematic perception to become literal. This could mean nothing more than that the setting has changed on the motivational side, not that a different set of perceptual processes have come into play.

That even Gibson's results depend upon stacking the cards motivationally in the experimental situation is suggested by Wallach's important demonstrations of memory effects on perception [97]. Proceeding from Gibson's finding of the importance of textural gradients for perceived slant and three-dimensional perception, Wallach has shown that, in order for a textural gradient to become an *effective* stimulus for perceived slant, a particular set must be induced. The effective operation of texture gradients presumes that the subject has recognized the object; i.e., he appreciates its meaning. When the texture gradients do not appear in a context that gives them meaning, they are much less effective as a basis for perception of slant. The importance of set is further underscored by the fact that, once a meaningful context is given, then textural gradient does indeed operate as an effective stimulus for slant, where previously, with the set absent, it did not.

It is not intended here that one get the impression that Gibson's emphasis on proximal stimulus conditions is wrong, but only that he overgeneralizes its importance because of a methodological artifact created by his efforts to highlight its importance. His studies invariably construct a *motivational "reduction-screen"* in which a single motivational condition—to discriminate correctly—is allowed to work, and he trusts his data only when he can safely assume that he has achieved this "optimal condition." Gibson has demonstrated correlations between object and proximal invariances and co-ordinations *under such conditions*, and no more. He has not provided a basis for determining *what* in the object will dominate experience. For any headway to be made in this problem, the range of motives in a situation—the motivational aura—must be appreciated by the experimenter. There is another problem in this equation—the issue of interchangeable mediation, the fact that thing-qualities may be formed out of a variety of media. The conditions of mediation determine dominance too. We will return to this issue in a later section.

The heart of the matter is how one construes the "stimulus." The conditions that convert a distal thing-quality into a "stimulus" include whatever it is that makes it worth discriminating—an intention, as well as the conditions of mediation. It may seem paradoxical at first glance but it is probably defensible to say that Gibson's "effective stimuli" are also responses in more ways than he is aware. His critical stimulus for slant, a textural gradient, is a *discriminable aspect* in a total field of stimulation. What makes this rather than another quality of an object field the focus for perception is partly a matter of expectancy or set—the *product* of an intention created by instruction. In short one must assume that the stimulus—the instigator of response—also includes intention. As Krech puts it, "motivation is neither superimposed from above nor injected from below, but is an attribute of the total field situation *[55, p. 121]*. . . . Instead of giving a *partial* description of the experimental situation, we must seek for as *complete a description as feasible*. No matter what experiment we are doing, we must seek to describe the so-called 'internal' *and* external stimuli, or the so-called physical *and* social. And this holds, I repeat, whether we are doing a rat experiment, a perception experiment in a darkroom, or a Rorschach study." *[55, p. 136]*

A DESCRIPTIVE MODEL OF A PERCEPTUAL SITUATION

Another look at the viewpoints reviewed and consideration of the gaps in theory they purport to fill and the phenomena they emphasize indicates that each seems apt and useful. This is somewhat surprising considering that they often present themselves as in fundamental opposition to each other. One is led to suspect that the theories highlight different aspects of the perceptual process, that disagreements between them are directed to oversights of the others, and that emphases subtly turn to overemphases through experimental designs that relegate to the background central variables of other points of view. The upshot is a curious situation in which vigorous points of view, often solidly enough anchored to measurable phenomena, move in parallel fashion over the same terrain, each encouraged by the seeming success of its tools to go its own way with little concern for others. The psychophysicist continues to be impressed by the subtle couplings of stimulus events and experience at higher and higher levels of complexity, and finds little reason to be impressed by demonstrations of malleability; personologists see more and more evidence of response consistency and therefore little reason to be impressed by an imperious object structure; the motivation theorist is quick to see in deviations of response the pressures of motive and drive. Each considers he is touching the essentials of perception, like the blind men and the elephant.

Only when one tries to assess a particular major viewpoint for *essential* validity do paradoxes emerge to pull up short any attempt to define perceiving from a single viewpoint. It has been seen that efforts to create a single conception of the whole process from the two polar viewpoints create the question: With autism, perceptual defense, projective hypotheses testifying to the corruptibility of perception, why does one see so well? But perhaps such paradoxes are the creations of total definitions of the elephant from the limited vantage points of restricted data.

To define the totality it would be wise first to make certain that the main outlines of the corpus have been sampled. To this end, it will be helpful to attempt a total overview of the circumstances of perceiving, to try simply to survey the classes of phenomena that are seemingly involved in a circumstance where perception occurs. Putting the facts of perception into a comprehensive schema may show whether indeed there are points of irreconcilability between the viewpoints described earlier, or whether each can fit logically into place with another.

This discussion will be limited to the events of an experimental situation in which a subject's response is a *discrimination*. This is of course not the prototype of all situations in which perception occurs, nor is it even for all experimental situations, but it is extremely common and indeed the paradigm for most experiments that have sought to demonstrate motivational distortions of perception.

In this overview of a perceptual situation, the perspective is the total cognitive act, since perceptual processes are only a phase of a larger response. In this, the present view follows Michotte who says [66]:

Perception should be regarded as a phase of action in the activity of the individual both motor and intellectual . . . When seen from this point of view the role of perception is evidently not in the presentation of objects of this or that color, for completely isolated objects remain devoid of meaning and thus of interest. It influences behavior only insofar as it has a signification that is given to it by the relations that unite it to other objects, relations in space and time, relations of causality and of finality, etc. The problem of meaning thus takes precedence, in the long run, over the problem of form."

In the laboratory as in life, to discuss a person's perception is to describe his participation in a segment of his world.

PERCEPTION AND COGNITION DISTINGUISHED

In taking this broader perspective, it seems valuable nonetheless to preserve a distinct meaning for perception. The basis for the significance at which cognition aims has to be sought first in the very process of perceiving before taking the apparently easy recourse to learning and past achievements in accounting for cognitive products. The word perception has borne the weight of many meanings, and this lack of precision has created difficulties in isolating the critical variables involved in purported influences of motivational forces on perception. Many claims of influences upon perception *per se* seem more likely to involve judgment, apperception, and not the process formations (e.g., contours, gradients) ordinarily implied when one speaks of a percept.

Perceptual formation implies first and foremost that physical events have achieved some measure of representation. By distinguishing perception from other phases of the cognitive act, one disciplines himself to inspect the stimulus configurations that contribute to the process; he is better prepared thereby to classify the effects of motives in behavior. Where a matter like a so-called "perceptual defense" is concerned, for instance, the issue partly turns upon the locus of the motivational influence—whether it is in the formation of the percept itself, or in some elaboration of the percept, or in the report process itself. The distinction then has value if it sharpens awareness to different parts of the total field of participating influences in tracing the antecedents of a behavioral outcome.

In this view, then, perceptual processes are the means through which qualities of things obtain representability. They yield object-qualities (conceived as properties of surfaces—as, for instance, "hardness" and "softness," as well as *relations* between objects and events; e.g., the properties of actions). As Heider puts it, "Perceiving is experienced as an entering of objective fact into the life space of the person." [36] A question about perception always implies: what is the stimulus configuration to which the perception is co-ordinated?

Following Heider [33], four aspects of the perceptual process have been distinguished, as shown in Figure 1. The object and event variables to which percepts are coupled—thing-qualities in this discussion—are sometimes called the "distal environment," to convey the idea that they do not present themselves directly on sensory surfaces but are conveyed to organism via a medium. On the side of the environment, then, there are independent thing-qualities (including actions and relations among events) and their physical representation or mediation. The thing-qualities of objects are independently definable stable units; it is this quality of invariance which makes them potentially perceivable. On the side of the organism there is further mediation consisting of transformations of the physical impingements out of which the thing-qualities are reconstructed.

Figure 1

SCHEMATIC RELATION BETWEEN THE PERCEPTUAL SYSTEM AND ENVIRONMENT
(From Heider, F. Die Leistung des Wahrnehmungssystems. Z. *Psychol.* 1930,
114, 371–94).

ENVIRONMENT	PERCEPTUAL SYSTEM
Th - M	M^1 - Th^1

Th —the relevant environment (we call it often "the world of things,"
    but people, events, etc., belong to it also).
M —the mediating events, the stimuli which impinge on the organ-
    ism directly.
M^1 —the processes in the organism correlated to the stimuli, ranging
    from purely neural events to psychological ones that can be
    experienced to a certain degree, e.g., as reduction color.
Th^1—experiences which refer to the "things" of the environment.

Brunswik uses an essentially similar model in defining perception as "a relatively stabilized connection between focal variables"
[16, p. 19]: between an initial focus—external thing-quality, which
can be an object, situation, event, etc., and a terminal focus, the
representation of this object in the life space. Between the two
foci lie two regions of mediation: in the case of the environment
physical structures and processes; e.g., the sheaf of light rays passing
through the air of a room in vision, which physically represent
visual thing-qualities; within the organism there are medial structures and events (e.g., the properties of sensory surfaces, cortical
properties, impulses) or processes through which the eventual reconstruction is brought about. Thus, *physical* impingements become *psychological* impingements via a separate set of mediational
processes out of which the terminal focus or *represented* thing-
quality develops. As will be seen later, sometimes the relation of
raw material to thing-qualities is definable in part by the balance
among intentions that develop toward different parts of the environment. In this sense the organization of the properties of things
is a layered affair.

To emphasize the co-ordinations that develop between external
stimulus configurations and phenomenal experience does not mean
that perception reduces to a study of "accuracy" or "correctness."

Accuracy is essentially a matter of appropriateness to a set of arbitrary external standards. If one is reminded that reality testing is mainly geared to efficient resolutions, ultimately to promote more efficient drive satisfactions, then the conditions for "accuracy" and the definition of accuracy itself become relative matters based on valuations of possibilities. The crux of the matter is not whether a perceptual outcome meets an experimenter's standards, but what features of the situation are critical for the perceptual event, and how they coerce outcomes; in short, the issue is processes, not standards.

Focus on the role of stimulus configuration in a motivational theory derives from an interest in effectiveness, not necessarily accuracy. It changes questions regarding perception into the form: What qualities in an object are reacted to, in terms of what intentions, in what state of awareness of the subject and toward what outcomes in experience?

A BRIEF SURVEY OF THE MODEL

Attention should now be given to the experimental situation. Because the context of perceptual formations and their effects is complex, it will be useful to sketch broadly the main classes of relevant variables in preparation for more detailed consideration later on. The model is pictured in Figure 2. It is probably not quite correct to speak of these as variables in the strict sense but as classes of phenomena. Some have received only limited attention in laboratory studies and will probably require more definition before they can be dignified as variables. The arrangement shown in Figure 2 also implies something more than a classification: it suggests a sequence of events. According to this model, it is correct to speak of the main happenings in an experiment not as one but as several trains of thought that are simultaneously active.

Figure 2, then, pictures a hypothetical sequence following roughly a line from preperceptual or preparatory processes to behavioral outcomes. It begins with the *intentional field* of the experiment—its motivational context. This is conceived as a hierarchy, at the center of which is an intention—induced by an instruction—to single out a particular quality (in this case hue). In real life such discriminations are usually part of a more inclusive

Figure 2

ADAPTIVE STATE IN PSYCHOPHYSICAL EXPERIMENT : STRONG EXECUTIVE INTENTION

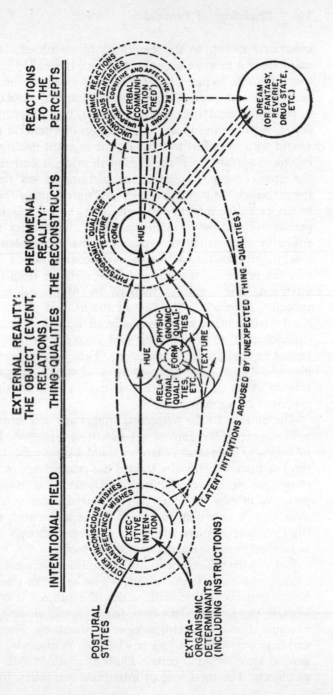

behavioral intent, to do something to an object, to control or manipulate it in some respect, and hence it is called here an *executive intention*. When a subject intends an object he develops an orientation—an expectancy or anticipation to a particular property in the object field. One assumes further, that other intentions are active, varying from those on the fringes of attention that are consonant with the effort to focus on the relevant quality (e.g., wanting to co-operate, to make a good showing, a curious interest in the proceedings) to dispositions pictured as on the outermost fringes which for various reasons are "nonadaptive" and irrelevant to the executive intention at hand (e.g., sexual interest in the experimenter, aggressive intentions, etc.). The latter may be provoked by the setting, the apparatus, the experimenter, etc. The total intentional field is shown in concentric dotted lines to indicate the peripheral motives and their distance from the center of attention. One conceives then of an intentional hierarchy: the executive intention is the part of the field of potentially greatest clarity, while other purposes shade off into the shadows of semiconsciousness, to preconscious and unconscious motives (the latter not exemplified in the diagram). Thus the diagram pictures the possibility of a more complex array of intentions provoked into activity in an experiment than is usually implied simply by the experimenter's instruction.

The motives in the outermost fringes are in a sense unadaptive with respect to the aims of the executive intention. Relevancy of intention to the executive motive is not a simple dichotomous matter. For instance, curiosity toward the proceedings or the desire to co-operate are relevant, although unspoken, because they are not points of inquiry. But they may be linked to an unconscious voyeuristic wish or a wish to seduce the experimenter, which, under the circumstances, are adaptively irrelevant, though of course not as intensely so as the nagging of a sore tooth.

Just as with the executive intention, the outermost fringes of activated intentions (e.g., "wishes") also establish claims upon the object and event field with which the subject is confronted. A wish, to use Lewin's definition, has a source, an aim, and a point of application. An intention aims at something when it is active, and here perception plays a crucial role. Wishes and intentions in general are directed at certain kinds of relations with certain kinds of objects. The total field of intentions comprises, to use another term of Lewin's, tension systems. Via the invariances of thing-qualities which achieve perceptual representability, the tensions of wishes are partly reduced.

Since intentional foci are hierarchically arranged in terms of a central (dominant) and peripheral array, the question comes up of how the dominance of the executive intention is preserved. There is of course the usually carefully wrought instruction provided by the experimenter, efforts to reduce anxiety, etc., which reinforce this focus. In addition, there is a critical set of events whose role in the preservation of an executive intention has often been overlooked: perceptual postures. There are patterns of muscular orientations that accompany the activation of an executive intention. They include the favored upright position, the preference for foveal vs. peripheral fixation in vision, tonic distributions over the body, etc.

All intentions—even the wishes in the peripheral field—create preperceptual anticipations with respect to a range of object properties. A particular experimental setup will have physical shapes, surfaces, volumes, colors, tactile qualities, forms, etc. If actions are concerned, there will also be movements of various speeds. All of these are potential foci of discrimination—thing-qualities. In this physical configuration the component thing-qualities are organized into part-to-whole units, both within and between objects. An object in this sense is no single thing-quality but represents a hierarchical array of units—invariances—*independently* definable in physical terms.

In this physical hierarchy the physical event that is potentially relevant to executive intentions is bound to other invariant qualities, and occupies a position within a part-whole stratum that is defined by the physical organization. This physical saliency may not correspond to the prominence given it by an executive intention, a fact of importance in evaluating the interplay of motive and thing-quality. The physical patterning of thing-qualities will make certain kinds of discriminations much easier than others; e.g., it is easier to see the shape of objects than the shape of the empty spaces between them. Thus, so far as physical saliency is concerned in the total organization of an object, the hue of a face may not be as vital to the definition of the face as form. Therefore, an adequate description of the object confronting a subject would include not only its phenomenal reconstruction but also its own macrophysical structure, describing the part-whole dependencies quite independently of their phenomenal representation. Such inherent physical arrangements make a difference in arrangements that can develop in the phenomenal field. The second part of Figure 2 pictures this hypothetical physical hierarchy in which the intentionally salient property, hue, has a secondary status to form in the physical stratum.

The sequence of events depends upon another set of events—not pictured in the diagram. These are events of the physical medium upon which thing-qualities are imposed and whose adequacy or lack thereof for conveying the object's organization will limit the fidelity and variety of impingements that reach the sensory surfaces. At this latter juncture a new set of events, processes of proximal mediation, develops within the perceptual system, also assumed and not shown in the diagram. Here again the adequacy of these mediational processes and events creates limiting conditions to representability of thing-qualities and to the influence of motive. In this schema any physical invariance is potentially a registerable thing-quality, given optimal conditions of mediation. These then form the raw material for the construction of the subjective field of thing-qualities.

The third portion of the diagram shows the reconstructed object field. It consists of a hierarchy of phenomenally represented thing-qualities. A relatively chaotic experience would result if physical object-saliences—the part-to-whole arrangement of invariances in the physical object—were exclusively to determine this hierarchy. The perceiver is saved from this by the directive and selective effects of intentions which guide and focus attention, so that the laboratory wall, the odd table to the left of the subject's line of sight are suppressed into a "background," and a particular thing-quality —shown here in the diagram as hue—is central, hue being the subject of most concern. The perceptual reconstructions form an array in terms of those that are close to the subject's attention—qualities centrally relevant to the executive intention—to other qualities that are potentially capable of being brought into awareness to those in the outermost fringes that are registered but incapable of being brought into focus. Thus, the hierarchy pictured as the "phenomenal reality" parallels in part the strata of the *intentional* field, but only in part, for the physical organization of the field defines the limits to the transpositions that can occur in the field of attention, and also to the separable co-ordinations that can occur between specific motives and specific thing-qualities. The diagram refers to the field of reconstructed thing-qualities as "phenomenal reality"—structures formed from the impingements of the object-field via medial events in the perceptual apparatus. By the term, phenomenal, is meant the thing-qualities that have gained representability—the registrations that have occurred. It does not imply the perhaps more usual meaning given to it, that which is available or potentially available in consciousness. This distinction between registrations in and outside awareness is an important assumption in the scheme, as will be seen.

The third part of Figure 2 shows, then, the part-whole arrangement of the perceptual field and its structure, which is a blend and a compromise between the physical hierarchy of object qualities and the intentional field. Some of these qualities may never attain conscious status, especially those formations which become linked with the aims of unconscious wishes, which by means of defense and other controls (also assumed but not shown in the diagram) remain distant from awareness. Thus the images or memories aroused by an unconscious voyeurism may find an apt representation in a particular form of the object. The latter may be a peripheral thing-quality in the phenomenal object-field of Figure 2. This possibility alludes also to another assumption made by the model, one which will demand much more attention later on. It is assumed that perceptual formations can develop outside of conscious awareness. Not all units of the physical object-structure achieve registration, i.e., perceptual structure. And not all that are registered are necessarily available to conscious report. Yet one speaks even of these relationships within and between object-qualities as perceived in the sense that representations have occurred. The diagram conveys the idea of an array of registered qualities—percepts—ranging from those that are focal to executive intentions and hence available to conscious report, to "distant" registration at the outermost fringes of awareness, which may be wholly unavailable to immediate verbal report. The arrows show some hypothetical co-ordinations that may develop between peripheral intentions and the fringes of the field of reconstructed thing-qualities.

The central point about motivated perception in this scheme is that it involves simultaneous *co-ordinations* in depth between the hierarchies of intention and object qualities, the latter a stratified array in the perceptual field partly defined by the central and peripheral components of the intentional field. In this scheme, all perception is motivated and motives play a central role in the "purest" psychophysical experiment.

The expression, "co-ordination," can be understood only with proper regard for two parameters: (1) the central and peripheral foci produced by the multiple intentions that make up the aura of an experimental situation; and (2) the physical part-whole manifold of thing-qualities within and between objects, hierarchically organized, containing the "intended" units. Thus, the co-ordination of an object with an executive intention does not exhaust the possible co-ordinations that can simultaneously develop between the peripheral arrays; nor does it eliminate the possibility that several intentions may share in the qualities of a particular percept. The model provides for the possibility that different intentions may share in the qualities of a particular percept. The model provides for the possibility that it is precisely those thing-qualities that are potentially relevant to active peripheral wishes that stand the greatest chance of becoming perceptually structured. Thus the blackness of a light-tight compartment of a tachistoscope may be totally irrelevant to an executive intention; but it may achieve the status of a peripherally registered thing-quality that will find its place in a field of active connotations—latent wishes—through the relevance the quality of blackness may have to the aims of the latent wish.

Within this context of events in the experimental situation, the realm of possible effects in action and behavior of motives and percept co-ordinations turns out to be a much more complex set of possibilities than is usually envisaged. Since disparate claims upon object-formations sometimes are involved, any complete analysis of the interplay of motive and perception poses questions regarding the central and peripheral intentional foci in the situation, the locus of the motive in question within this hierarchy, the conditions of physical and proximal (psychological) mediation of thing-qualities, and the field of actual registrations. Figure 2 also shows the possibility that the registrations that develop in the phenomenal field, and the phenomena of the reporting process, may excite new intentions and images and memories that are not at first present. These too then would participate in the perceptual situation. A proper evaluation of the effects of motives must take into account the balance of all these relationships. In addition to all this, one must provide for the fact that reactions to percepts in behavior and action can occur on a *variety of levels* and that the penetration of a motive into cognitive activity can potentially occur on *all* of these levels if in different forms, and in different states of awareness. The fourth segment of Figure 2 expresses these possibilities.

In the usual experimental situation the discrimination is *communicated*, either *verbally* or through some other motor response. In either instance the response is a communication to the experimenter. But such communications do not exhaust the behavioral reactions to co-ordinations of motive and thing-quality. For instance, autonomic reactions may be a behavioral consequence of certain co-ordinations between *peripheral* intentions and *peripherally* registered thing-qualities, or such co-ordinations may appear in the guise of unconscious fantasies. It is also possible, as shall be seen later, that co-ordinations among the peripheral participants in the perceptual registrations may even penetrate to conscious report upon the central thing-qualities of the experiment in the form of unspoken cognitive and affective impressions.

One would expect certain imbalances in the participating forces to produce distinctive effects both in the phenomenal reconstruction and in the behavioral reactions to these formations. For instance, where an executive intention is strong, it would be expected that the co-ordination with appropriate thing-qualities, so far as verbal communication is concerned, will be relatively unhindered by the participation of intentions in the fringes of the motive field. However, co-ordination of fringe wishes with thing-qualities, especially if the latter are high in the physical stratum of organization, may also be represented in conscious report, if less strikingly than on nonconscious levels of behavior or in other cognitive states, e.g., dreams.

Where an executive intention is weak, as for instance through the deliberately vague instruction given on a Rorschach Test, peripheral intentions activated by the test situation may intrude even upon the conscious verbal reports of the subjects. The pictured scheme allows for the possibility that reduced postural supports can make it difficult to carry through an executive intention (e.g., if the subject were to make a discriminative response in a prone position). Under each circumstance, distinctive "distortions," reflecting the peripheral co-ordinations, may appear more easily in the verbally communicated discriminations.

The scheme also allows one to picture the possibilities under various other conditions of imbalance; e.g., when executive intentions are strong but the object field is *impoverished*, as when the mediating conditions of thing-qualities are insufficient. In such circumstances the balance of peripheral and executive intentions in the final cognitive outcome would well be upset in favor of domination by unadaptive intentions, and create a favorable condition for outright projections to appear in the verbally communicated reports. The scheme provides for the possibility that the capture of representations and the warping of discriminations are magnified when the events that preserve the domination of an executive intention in an experiment are relaxed.

Finally, the possibility of "delayed" behavioral outcomes, of motive-percept co-ordination, is recognized by the descriptive scheme. The "effects" of the interactions may not be exhausted in the behavioral reactions observed in the immediate experimental situation. The effects may be delayed. The multiple participation of motives in thing-qualities in the experiment proper may be revealed in the constructions of a later dream, in a fantasy, or in some other altered state of consciousness where executive intentions with respect to the object-field no longer dominate, thereby allowing the emergence of such peripheral co-ordinations into awareness.

In the sections that follow the implications of the four main segments of the descriptive model shall be explored in more detail.

THE INTENTIONAL FIELD OF AN EXPERIMENT: EXECUTIVE AND "FRINGE" INTENTIONS

Now some comments need to be made about the "intentional field" that develops in the ordinary experimental situation. Instructions to the subject orient him to particular object qualities; and discrimination then becomes the "satisfying" outcome of perceptual activity.

Usually the subject's task involves little in the way of urgent or private motives and wishes. On the face of it, the task, even in most motivation-centered experiments, sets a problem in "reality testing," but the reality testing is to be performed for its own sake, justified on no other basis than the person's acceptance of an instruction to be "accurate" or as precise as possible. There is no urgent investment in the object; the latter is neither a crucially sought after prize, nor a barrier to effective action nor the attaining of some other object. Usually the stimuli are presented under conditions that the subject could never dream of accepting were he not either indulgent of the experimenter, awed by him, or paid. The usual discrimination task is simply a temporary collision with an object in the game of co-operating with the experimenter.

The tasks usually require the subject to discriminate, to be accurate, to match percepts with external standards, to maintain an analytic attitude, to maintain immunity to distraction and preoccupation, to operate solely on the level which the experimenter's instructions conveys; not to wonder what it's all really about, but to pay attention only to what the experimenter directs him to ("Use no tricks, please!"), not to get bored ("Only a few minutes more"); in short, to perceive on the experimenter's terms. Furthermore, the subject is usually barred from knowing what his answer, the consequences of his response, really means. Thus the factor of feedback, so critical in real life when precise discriminations occur for reality testing, is denied him. Under such conditions it is remarkable how accurate a subject really can be. And this accuracy testifies to the kind and intensity of motivation which the experimenter is able to induce. It is a type of motivation that in real life is evoked only when circumstances are significant enough to warrant it, when a person has designs upon objects, of mastery, domination, and control. It may be called an *executive intention*.

Let there be no misunderstanding. The results yielded by such a setting are not being minimized, even though they are not prototypic of the ways that an executive intention operates in real life under conditions where manipulations and action upon an object have far more crucial significance. Experimental studies which are conducted under "optimal conditions" for provoking executive intentions yield valuable information about the *potentialities* that exist in people for high or low order adaptive discriminations.

In order to appreciate more fully the nature of executive intentions, which in the laboratory are assisted through co-operation with the experimenter, it is useful to see the role they usually play in the actions of real life. Executive intentions turn one toward an object, in order to discriminate a particular unit-property in preparation for effective action upon it. When one looks at a chair he is not, except when orientation is of a general kind, *simply* interested in the chair. He can look at the texture of the chair, the verticality of it, its style and comfort. It may be important for him to know if the edges are sharp rather than curved so that he won't nick his trousers as he walks past it. Such discriminations are adaptive in the sense that they result in acts of relationship toward the object. Such an executive intention establishes a focus: one doesn't pay attention to all qualities of an object at any one time, but to one particular unit-property of it. Another way of expressing this is to say that executive intentions bring an object into the center or forefront of the field for purposes of "effective" prediction and action upon it. In a sense such executive intentions also imply delay of "action" for purposes of efficient discrimination, of control in preparation for action.

If one speaks of the "effects" of this class of motives upon perception, he must say that they bring about an "efficient coordination" with a thing-quality in an object field. Executive intentions aim to represent some aspects of objects so as to permit predictable statements about them for purposes of action. Thus, while it *is* meaningful to speak of the role of such motives in perception, it is clear that, to the extent that these motives are really fulfilled, the effects promote *efficiency*, not inefficiency or autism. It is too often assumed that motives are necessarily distorting in their effects.

But such one-sided emphasis upon executive intentions does not exhaust the participation of motive in perception. Certainly it does not alone account for the perceptual consequences when other motives of an "involved ego" are provoked, e.g., having fun, esthetically evaluating (what does one "see" under such a motive, or when seeking deeper meanings of existence beyond experience?). The picture of perception that emerges when reality testing is confined to such a one-sided notion of participating motives is bound to be limited. (And let it be remembered that this priority of executive intentions, paramount in traditional psychophysical tasks, is the salient motive even in motivation-inspired experiments which purport to show autistic influences on, say, size estimation.)

Executive intentions are active against a background of other, more irrelevant and even (for the immediate purpose) unadaptive intentions that are at the fringe of the situation. What is the evidence that executive intentions are not the only motive force in an experiment? To begin with, Wallach's recent investigations indicate that perceptual registration can elicit or activate perceptual cues—"perceptual memories"—that in turn affect the ongoing process of perception [97, 98]. This should at least point up the possibility that perceptual activity may activate traces (meanings, connotations) on a much wider scale than those immediately relevant to a particular act of discrimination.

The most direct evidence comes from Fisher's studies [20] which show that even in an experimental situation an aura of "transference motives" envelops a subject's participation in the experiment. These can operate insidiously and silently in setting up "claims" upon the object-field, counterintentions and competing intentions for thing-qualities of the object-field. One thing that stands forth in Fisher's work is that the experimenter's explicit instructions in the task do not exhaust the motivational context of the experiment. The significance of the setting, of the experimenter himself, the apparatus, the task, all activate motives (memories) at other levels. Fisher's experiments, like Poetzl before him, included instructions for the subjects to describe and draw what they saw following brief exposures (1/200 sec.). Then, if a subject brought in a dream the next morning, he was asked to free-associate to elements of the dream and also to draw scenes from it. From this material, employing psychoanalytic techniques of dream interpretation, aided by detailed clinical information about the subjects, the motives and wishes of the dream were reconstructed and the protocols and drawings carefully analyzed for instances where elements of the experimental situation (the stimulus slide material as well as other conditions of the experiment) had actually "registered"; i.e., had achieved structural representation or form and been worked into the contents and themes of the dreams. First, all dreams so obtained seemed to reflect wishes and motives activated unconsciously in the experimental situation itself. Thus, one woman subject, a patient, had a dream in which the experimenter took on the role of one who could rectify a fantasied mutilation of her body. Secondly, numerous elements of the stimulus picture—portions reported or not in the original responses, as well as the experimenter himself—appeared in the dream fabric, taking on special meanings that conformed to the underlying contents of the dream. One of the stimulus slides showed three tall pieces of sandstone eroded into kinglike forms. The same subject, in whom the fantasy of a castration appeared in other clinical evidence, reported only the *upper* portions of the slide. It is likely, says Fisher, that the experimental instructions (to look and describe) stirred up exhibitionistic wishes. The immediate response of one male subject, also a patient, to exposure of the slide depicted three girls, clad in shorts and bras, taking a picture. From knowledge of the major conflict areas of the patient, gleaned from the clinical history, Fisher had good reason to conclude that the cameralike appearance of the experimental apparatus exposing a picture on the screen was involved in the provocation of exhibitionistic wishes in the experimental setting. The dream of the subject following the experimental session was also actually concerned with watching and exposure, and elements of the stimulus slides contributed concrete details to the development of this theme in the dream.

From these observations it is possible to say that, if intentions of the executive variety set up an anticipatory framework for focusing the subject on certain and not other attributes of the field (e.g., only upon the tachistoscopically exposed picture), so is it possible to speak also of intentions created by "more silent" motives (wishes) which also compete for the total field of perceptual registrations. Executive intentions are salient, but they are so against a background of other equally insistent, even though silent, motives. There is a center and a periphery to the motivational field, determined by the adaptive relevance of the various components. Intentions are involved in perception beyond the immediately adaptive ones that require discrimination for control and mastery.

It is not surprising that the irrelevant fringe of motives has rarely elicited the experimenter's interest, for they are silent participants, while executive intentions are easy to capture phenomenally. More important, however, is the fact that intentions that have nonadaptive origins require that one understand the *individual subject* in order to see the particular interplay of motives that give the situation its significance for him. It requires a broadening of the experimenter's interest to include the larger organization within which behavior is charted—the individual's personality. Perceptual theory itself cannot provide such a perspective; only personality theory, guided by a careful assessment of each S's personality, can be wholly effective. That is why viewpoints associated with what perception *can* accomplish in tasks of discrimination result in biased views of what is *possible* in any single occasion of perceiving. A complete theory of perception entails an awareness of what the perceptual process is *able* to do and at the same time an appreciation of the strategies of the total organism and where it is trying to go.

It is necessary to pause a moment to inspect the nature of the demands made by wishes upon perception. First of all, a force that involves wanting or wishing something is different from the actions that are involved in doing something in order to obtain it. The activity of a wish involves a disposition directed toward a certain relationship with a certain kind of object or class of objects. In this desired relationship *representations* of thing-qualities are involved; i.e., previously formed surrogates of the environment are, to use Lewin's expression, in a state of tension. In this sense, a wish can be a motive for action, but it is not to be identified with any particular action. The manifestations of wish in *behavior* vary with certain conditions that define the context of its arousal; e.g., relevancy (dominance by executive intention), acceptability of the wish (its positive or negative significance in the system of defenses), and availability of the objects involved. The critical consideration for perception is that the invariant feature of a wish is not the actions that may bring about the object, but the representations of thing-qualities that are active.

One form by which a wish may manifest itself in action, behavior, is in the activity of thought. If thing-qualities are always the "points of application" of wishes, then wishes can be in part achieved, their tensions partly reduced, by the appearance of the perceptual counterparts of the critical thing-qualities. In this sense, perception plays an irreplaceable role in the activity of wishes, producing an "identity in thought" of the thing-qualities involved in a wish.

Freud [22] pointed out that an essential component of the satisfaction of need is a particular perception which leaves an image (content) that remains thenceforward associated with the memory trace of excitation produced by the need. As a result of this link, the next time the need is aroused, efforts will be made to recathect the memory image of the percept and re-evoke the original satisfaction. An impulse of this kind is a wish; reappearance of the perception is a partial fulfillment of the wish, partial in the sense that the object is attained in thought. In this view, autism or hallucinations would reflect conditions in which a wish has taken the shortest path to fulfillment, a path leading directly from excitation produced by the need to a complete cathexis of the perception. The main point in all this is that, in a wish, representations of particular thing-qualities are active; these create sets or expectancies which, if not countered by executive intentions, result in the cathexis of particular object properties (invariances) in the same manner as executive intentions; or, where there is impoverished stimulation or where the object-organization places no check upon the "resonating" process of object and wish, the tension of a wish can result in an actual hallucination.

It has been seen that many of the intentions in the motivational aura of an experiment are allied with wishes pressing for discharge, i.e., seeking out perceptual representations of thing-qualities relevant to them. Executive intentions can mobilize perception to its full discriminative potentiality in the arousal of anticipations and expectancies; but silent activations of unadaptive wishes can also arise, as has been seen, from implications beyond the surface adaptation specifically stated or required by instructions, by the apparatus, and from the manner and conceived importance of the experimenter himself (e.g., as an authoritative figure), etc. The motives of an experimental situation seem, then, to be in a hierarchical arrangement, some near the surface and linked to a specific adaptive purpose, and others more closely tied to deeper drives and untrammeled by the claims of an adaptive purpose.

The effects of this dialectical push and pull of intention, executive and fringe, in cognitive outcomes appear through immediate distortions, either of the conscious percept or of the cathexis of other peripheral thing-qualities in the stimulus field, that may not be immediately evident but which may be noted in later occasions. If experimental conditions are those that produce the dominance of an executive intention, the opportunity is diminished for more peripheral active intentions to project themselves in behavior. But a thing-quality may *simultaneously* be shared by intentions of different levels. A cigar may be a cigar and simultaneously a symbolic penis. It is possible for an object to gratify a routine hunger and an unconscious fellatio fantasy. A perceptual formation may find relevance to the dispositions of a wish and to an executive intention. As Poetzl first emphasized, in perception there occurs a wide range of peripheral registrations that are "irrelevant" to an adaptive purposeful act of perception, and these provide a fertile ground for the partial discharge of the more silent non-adaptive intentions.

To the extent that this fringe context is *not* kept at bay by the executive intentions of the moment, it is possible to trace claims made by such wishes in the perceptual and cognitive outcomes, both in the immediate discriminative response and later on in other contexts such as dreams or drug states. Reality-oriented perception is motivated perception based on an appreciation of an objective possibility, and the participation of nonadaptive wishes in the purposive behaviors that develop in such circumstances may be minimal or only subtle. Under certain conditions, wish fulfillment may take place either when there is no question of meeting the demands of an executive intention, as in dreams, or in circumstances where *intense* wishes can override other adaptive claims as in a hallucinatory revival of percepts of need-gratifying objects. These conditions of cognitive state and intensity of motive are of great importance in speaking of the *"effects"* of motivation. It is obvious in this picture of the motivational context that motivational claims cannot be confined to conditions of "impoverished" stimulation. Wishes and intentions can also participate actively in well delineated object-fields. Only the consequences and forms of this participation change with different intentions. Fringe intentions may warp the clean-cut influence of an executive intention and distort a registration to its own aims, and these effects may be seen in the "conscious" responses of the subject in the experiment, or their capture of the immediate stimulus field may be revealed in other states of awareness. It now seems very doubtful that the "effects" of the motives operating in an experimental situation—especially those of the nonadaptive fringe—are exhausted by *immediate* responses in the situation; rather the effects may often occur later, especially in other states of awareness, as in dreams.

If the motivational aura is a central fact in an experimental situation, what are the determining forces that preserve the *dominance* of certain executive intentions over other motives in the experimental situation? The critical factor in determining the balance of motivational intensity in a situation seems to me to be a set of variables, relatively overlooked in discussions of perception, which I choose to call *perceptual postures*—the postures of executive perceiving.

POSTURAL SUPPORTS OF EXECUTIVE INTENTIONS

If the motivational aura is as pervasive as it has been pictured, what insures the dominance of an executive intention over other more silent claims upon objects? For the single-motive assumption of classical experimentation this constitutes no problem; what preserves the central focus required for discrimination is simply the instruction, insured by the subject's co-operation. But it has been seen that there are wishes which claim a share in the formation and perpetuation of percepts and in the behavioral effects of these percepts.

Perhaps a clue is given by the way a person "prepares" himself for a stimulus when he aims for an accurate or efficient discrimination. If he is observed closely as he "sets" himself to disengage one aspect of the stimulus from another, it may be noted that his body seems to relate itself in a typical manner toward the object-field. He braces himself (the most congenial position for discrimination is evidently the upright position); he turns his eyes directly upon the object; he tries to bring the relevant field into his focus. Subtler measurements would perhaps show that a pattern of muscle tensions is involved in this attitude of "alertness" [cf. Malmo 61]. Possibly long evolution has evolved a series of local properties that aid such focused efforts. For instance, the eye, even in focused attention, is never still; and this very fact, preventing quick fatigue, perhaps insures more prolonged scrutiny of an object than would otherwise be possible. Saccadic eye movements, without loss of the object, are perhaps a high-order achievement of evolution that aids detailed discrimination. Also, the significance of the upright position in aiding efficient discrimination has often been overlooked though its importance is suggested by Witkin [102] and Werner and Wapner [100]. The "preference" for a vertical rather than prone position, a foveal rather than peripheral focus, etc., are conditions not to be taken for granted; they may be the very bases of effective discrimination. In short, active discrimination seems to involve large-scale and local muscular supports. Whether such "muscular sets" *are* themselves the manifestation of the discriminative act, or whether perception is itself a "tonic state" *[100, 101]*, are issues that need not be argued here. It is enough to point to their importance as preperceptual events and as conditions that implement an executive intention.[1]

Now if all this is so, it should be possible to reduce experimentally the dominance or "autonomy" of executive intentions by upsetting the efficacy of such postural supports, and thereby to establish conditions favorable to projection or for the freer play of nonadaptive intentions in cognitive behavior. All conditions that would eliminate or render less effective the postures necessary for discriminative executive perception should encourage the intrusion of wishes that may be peripherally and irrelevantly activated in the perceptual situation. The types of regressive participation in objects that can be reasonably linked to wish-dominated (projective) perception should be much more evident when executive intentions are reduced and the postural supports for sustaining the latter are either absent, made difficult, or eliminated.

That the disciplined discriminations in executive intentions may become more difficult in the absence of supportive postural conditions brings to mind the importance of the couch in the associative process of an analytic therapy hour. One of Freud's great intuitive insights was that the supine position is conducive to fluid associations and the emergence of drive-organized contents, and generally to the invasion by primary process into the logical matrix of conscious thought. Whatever Freud's personal reasons may have been (apparently he did not especially relish the strain of face-to-face confrontation several hours a day, and the effort involved in concealing communications conveyed by his own facial reactions), the significance of the supine position extends beyond this. There is a tendency nowadays to discount the importance of the couch in analysis on the grounds that it is simply a ritual or con-

[1] The value of conceiving executive intentions as distinct from the pattern of postural supports, of treating them as operationally separate until empirical analysis dictates otherwise, is that under certain circumstances one may have a strong discriminative set *without* the postural supports necessary for effecting it. Thus, sensitivity to object-qualities, to gradients, to cues of perspective and figure-ground distinctions may be crucially supported by such preparatory activity of the musculature.

vention, and not crucial to the analytic process; but the significance of the upright position for logically ordered thought may be
involved. Of course, the supine position does not inevitably produce associative fluidity. Often, inhibition is exaggerated on the
couch; but it is also common that muscular tensions are very much
in evidence in such instances, which seem consistent with the tight-
ness, constriction and withholding of communications. [81]

Man's evolution to the preferred upright position probably had
enormous consequences for his perceptual potentialities and his
discriminative capacity in relation to objects around him. It may
well be that spatial perception depends much more on the vertical
orientation than is appreciated. In making possible new discriminative sets it perhaps also made possible man's developing many
more intentions and claims upon objects than he could have without it.

In a significant paper, Irwin Strauss speculates about these possibilities [91, p. 7]:

In getting up, in reaching the upright posture, man must oppose
the forces of gravity. It seems to be his nature to oppose with natural
means nature in its impersonal, fundamental aspects. However, gravity
is never fully overcome; upright posture always maintains its character
of counteraction. It calls for our activity and intention. . . . Awakeness and the force of gravity are mutually interdependent. While
awakeness is necessary for upright posture, that is, for counteracting
gravity, gravity *determines waking.*

Again, concerning upright posture [91, p. 32]:

It lifts us from the ground, puts us opposite things, and confronts
us with each other . . . it is true that sleep and rest, lying down and
lying with someone are essential functions; it is no less true that man
is built for upright posture in gait, that upright posture, which is as
original as any drive, determines his mode of being-in-the-world.

The importance of postural conditions to the disciplined momentum of waking thought was brought home to this writer in experiences he had under the influence of mescaline. At a certain stage
in the experience while trying to "rest" on a couch, a kaleidoscopic
array of disturbing images flooded awareness. The inclination was
immediately to stand up and walk about, at which the array of
picture images clicked off, and attention was again focused and
guided by anticipations secured by normal gait and movement. A

significant series of studies by Malmo and his associates *[61]* has actually succeeded in recording patterns of tension distribution over the body in acts of attention and focused discriminative effort. Recent studies by Russian investigators within the Pavlovian framework lend further importance to the critical nature of preperceptual muscular preparations of the organism in discriminative behavior *[109]*.

An interesting experiment bearing upon the importance of postural conditions in perception was carried out recently at the Chillicothe VA Hospital on the autokinetic phenomenon. Subjects were asked to report the movement of a stationary point from a sitting position and a prone position. It was found that the locus of the illusory movement changed according to the position of the subject. For instance, when the subject sat upright in a dark room he experienced the *light* as moving; when he was lying prone (on a low table set on rollers) it seemed to him that *he* was moving rather than the light. The possible mechanism involved is far from clear, but the experiment does illustrate, at the very least, how perceptual alterations can occur simply with the change of bodily position in space.

Wilhelm Reich some years ago proposed that the "defensive armor" of hysterics and other character structures are partly represented in stabilized forms of muscular tensions *[81]*. Reich's contribution here goes a step beyond these remarks in suggesting that, not only are *specific* discriminative acts accompanied or "prepared for" by muscular orientations, but also such orientations may become structuralized, acting in effect as protective outposts which buffer and cushion the flux of stimuli that impinge upon a person. This suggests the intriguing possibility that there may be differences among people in the typical forms of such muscular preparations upon taking an executive intention given by a laboratory instruction. For instance, the hysteric's "muscular armor" perhaps produces a condition of reactivity to stimuli that would affect discriminative perception. It is possible, pursuing Reich's thought a step further, that the postural processes subserving defense may have the general function of making possible delays and detours of thought that facilitate discriminative response. There are hysterics whose repressive tendency operates in such a fashion as to prevent detailed perceptual registrations, in order not to see what unconsciously they fear they may see. Muscular orientations could well subserve such an orientation of "not penetrating to reality." On the other hand repression may work, not through such preparatory avoidance but *post*perceptually, in the form of an overdeveloped hypersensitivity which sees much in a stimulus field "efficiently and quickly" in order the more effectively and efficiently to "repress" the particularly noxious connotations. The relations of postural preparations in discriminative perceiving to defensive and control functions are problems that promise considerable empirical yields.

The thesis here, then, is that nonadaptive wishes are more likely to exert direct influence upon the perceptual process if the ordinary postures of the perceiver are relaxed. In certain states of awareness when these are bypassed, as in a dream, and executive intentions are relaxed, the possibility of perceptual transformation of objects to conform to pressures of nonadaptive wishes is more possible. The relaxation of executive intentions may result in the activation of memory schemata related to implicit or fringe motives that may then dominate conscious response. Moreover, the effects of motives upon conscious adaptive and purposeful cognitive behavior may also be intimately contingent upon relationships between posture and intention. Such relationships of intentions and varieties of postures are as yet largely unexplored.

CO-ORDINATION WITH THE OBJECT

The happenings described thus far are preperceptual; they are preparatory phases of the cognitive act. But executive intentions —supported or not by perceptual postures—as well as other component intentions of the motivational aura must realize themselves upon properties of objects. No matter what the intention, its "aim" implicates some formation or structure independent of the intention. Far from freeing inquiry from concern with objects and with the nature of object structure, therefore, to speak of motivated perception requires giving detailed attention to these very matters. A theory of motives in perceiving *is* a theory of the organism's participation in objects, of the coupling of motive with unit properties of objects, of co-ordinations between the pressures of intentions on the one hand and proximal registrations of "stimuli" on the other.

Before one can understand the influence and impact of the "capturing" force of intentions he must have an idea of the possibilities of capture in the structures of objects themselves. By possibilities of capture is meant attributes of an object's organization which present themselves for co-ordination with intentions and wishes, for it is these attributes that are meant when one says a person is in touch with significant aspects of his environment.

When one speaks of "looking" at an object, what does he mean? In the first place he does not simply mean that he sees a surface, nor a figure-ground difference, though both are involved. As remarked earlier, one looks at whatever it is that is *intended* by his interest in looking. Of course, in a psychophysical experiment where threshold sensitivities are measured, such intentions could indeed refer to a figure-ground difference or a textural difference. More often than not, however, such structural units are the means for conveying other thing-qualities that are usually more interesting, e.g., the shape of an object or its location. However, there is to be seen in this example a critical characteristic of the impingements issuing from objects that form upon sensory surfaces: they comprise formations—units—which stand in respect to each other as *central* (the relevant foci of intention) or *peripheral* (irrelevant), and as *thing-quality* (the foci of intentions) or *medium* (the means by which the thing-qualities are conveyed). As will be seen, multiplicity of intentions in the field implies that the central or peripheral, and the thing or medial status of a perceptual formation are a relative matter. Behavioral outcomes, including adaptive behaviors and the trains of thought and action that may later occur in other cognitive states such as dreams, reflect a balance in these respects and the co-ordinations that have occurred with various levels of intentions.

The relevant elements of an object for perception are its thing-qualities—invariance, earlier defined as some critical attribute that cannot be altered without changing its unit character, some property that retains some measure of independence of changes in the elements composing it. In this sense of "object" there is no *single* property that is definitive. This is partly why Boring is led to conclude that the central task of perceptual analysis is "to discover the stimulus" [7] for the effective stimulus is not a particular object but a *property* of an object.

The *perception* of a thing-quality involves correlated invariances and on the side of the object such invariants are physical arrangements that are themselves mediated to the organism. For instance, sphericity is such an invariant; it can be realized through an infinite variety of elements. On the perceptual side such invariances are the reconstructs, formed out of invariant relations among the events in the perceptual medium. What are potentially registerable, then, are physically definable invariances of objects. The realm of physical invariances is more extensive than the region of perceptual reconstructions, though it is possible that evolution has not exhausted the possibilities of new sensibilities in these respects [cf. *Murphy 69*].

Unit-properties or thing-qualities are to be found not only in the surfaces of things (colors, shapes, textures), but also in physiognomic qualities, etc. They can be formed of static *relations* among objects or of temporal successions of events (actions). They can consist of causal sequences, e.g., "A hitting B" or "A leading B," in which *attributions* of agent and consequent are given by kinetic arrangements, as in the phenomena of Michotte's studies. As units, all are potentially perceivable, and can be "intended."

The unit-properties of things fall into a classification of *thing-modalities* roughly consisting of *surface properties, movements, conditional relations,* and *causal units.* This classification is not hard and fast; thus, surface properties may themselves exist in a conditional relationship: the pink hue of a face may differ from that of a pink square. The thing-quality in such instances is a relational event in the visual pattern. The pliability of an object is perceived in terms of whether or not the object's shape is determined by its support. In general, conditional relations are unit-properties—invariants—formed either of static arrangements of surface properties (relations of size and location that yield the property of distance) or of movements comprising actions. Units formed of conditional relations also usually imply attributions of something "belonging" to something else, or something as an agent "causing" something else. Often such causal units are formed and mediated by relations existing among a succession of events. Thus, causal units within and between objects and movements are given by conditional relations. The relations induce an *attribution* (of A belonging to B or A hitting B) which is physically defina-

ble. As units, they too are potentially perceivable or registerable
thing-qualities. Thus, in the co-ordinations that develop between
intention and objects (thing-qualities) are to be included in the
realm of potentially registerable thing-qualities such causal units
as are comprised of actions and events. In the meaning of "object" that has been described it is possible to speak even of personalities as objects (the perceived qualities may be called "traits"),
but this introduces a set of parameters too complex to consider
here. Heider has been the outstanding pioneer in this conception
of personality as a "perceivable object."

"Object," then, is said to be conceived in this broad sense: first of
all, as an array of unit-properties; or secondly, as composed of
relations which signify qualities such as causality, permanence,
persistence, affects, intentions, etc.

In the organizations existing within and among objects, component unit-properties—the potential thing-qualities of perception
—stand in a part-to-whole arrangement to each other, though as
units each retains a definable independence in some structural
respect from the elements that comprise them or of other units of
which they may be also constituted. Thus the unit-properties that
make up an object always exist in some hierarchical arrangement,
the description of which defines the object. There is a dependence, for instance, among the unit-properties of a book. If one
pulls the corner of the book, the rest of the book goes with it,
but not necessarily does another book adjoining it on a shelf.
Also, the unit-properties within an object are not of equal
rank; each is invariant in regard to units of lower order, and the
strength or weakness of such component dependencies of this
stratum of invariances defines the physically organized character
of an object.

The hierarchical nature of an object-organization is important
in understanding the workings of the multiple intentions in a
perceptual situation: first, the many invariances of which an object consists are all potential foci of these intentions; second, the
part-whole cohesion of the organization establishes limits upon
the transposition of the units that can occur in the perceptually
reconstructed object-field under the influence of motives.

This leads to the point that the hierarchy of qualities (invariances) that is the physical object is paralleled by a hierarchy
of properties in the field of perceptual registrations. As has been

seen, the intentional field is arranged in a central and peripheral array—from those that dominate attention (the executive intention) to those on the outermost wings of consciousness. It is to be expected that the phenomenal outcomes of perceiving—the perceptually registered *thing*-qualities of objects—would at least in part parallel this array. To the central and peripheral intentions correspond central and peripheral unit-properties among the registered thing-qualities. This means that the selection of a unit-property that occurs under the pressure of an intention or a wish will often not be precisely limited to a thing-quality most relevant to it but may also implicate an invariance which is salient because of its relational strength in the *physical* hierarchy. Of course, the physical constraints of the object hierarchy, the cohesiveness of its part-whole character, will set limits on the transpositions of its component invariances in the hierarchy formed by attention. The most dominant physical property of a chair may be its solidity, an invariant that resists change through a wide range of variations in texture, another unit-quality but one lower in the stratum. If the *intended* saliency is the chair's texture itself, it is to be expected that the saliency of texture will be restricted by the importance of *solidity* in organization of the chair; and solidity will perhaps by that fact be nearer the center of the *phenomenal* hierarchy than would be the case if it were not physically dominant. This should make a difference in the effects of the phenomenally central percept on behavior; e.g., it may influence how texture itself is seen and this influence may be detected in S's report.

To reiterate, thing-qualities in the phenomenal realm are reconstructs. To say that something has been perceptually registered is to say that a unit has developed, an invariant. And to the extent that physical units have been represented or reconstructed in some formation they have achieved subjective status. Where excitations or impingements do not develop into such units no perceptual *registration* has occurred. Thus, the saccadic movements of the eye as it "looks" at a square produce successive impingements on the retina and in a pattern that actually is quite markedly different from the physical source; but the unit formed, the perceptual registration, is neither the individual excitations (the variant impulses) that comprise the successive events, nor the succession itself, nor a path that the excitations follow; the registration is a particular shape of invariant. It is this restriction of perception to the registration of units that leads one to expect that the quantity of impingements or excitations upon the sensory surface far outnumber the actual number of registrations that occur, although it will be seen that such registrations are themselves in turn far greater in number than are "required" for a task at hand.

So far the discussion has concerned the thing-qualities that are the potential foci of intentions. It has been noted that thing-qualities are hierarchically arranged in their own physical environment, and the phenomenal rearrangement occurs according to the central and peripheral intentions that are active in a situation. It is important also to appreciate that the phenomenal reconstruction is never based on direct contact with thing-qualities and that the unit-property which is intended and grasped is conveyed, or again in Heider's words, it is mediated. Like the physical hierarchy of thing-qualities the properties of media are important too to an understanding of the possibilities and limits of the participation of motives in perceiving.

The medium of an object-quality, like the object-quality itself, consists first of all of physical events in the environment that are co-ordinated in turn, in the event perception occurs, with medial events in the perceptual apparatus (cf. Figure 1). Certain parts of the environment have the significance of media through which we perceive something else. One sees and hears things through air, through empty space, through smoke, "through a glass darkly."

It is through such physical events serving as media, usually wave-events, that thing-qualities "impose" their form on the environment. Events which serve as media have qualities distinctly different from the organizations of thing-qualities, and Heider has described these differences in detail in two monumental papers *[32, 33]*. For present purposes, three qualities of media stand out in importance. In the first place, the organization of medial events that convey a thing-quality is in a sense borrowed; the arrangement is a "spurious" or arbitrary one, to use Heider's words *[32]*, and not intrinsic to the medial events themselves. The medial order that corresponds to a thing has an aggregate or composite character, and the component events themselves can potentially convey various organizations of thing-qualities. In the second place, connected with this vicarious relation of thing-quality to medial event is the lack of univocality between *particular* medial events and a particular thing-quality. Thus the same thing-quality may be conveyed through a variety of media: to a considerable extent medial events are interchangeable with respect to the formation of spurious units that convey a thing-quality. Finally, a distinguishing characteristic of certain medial events is that they may themselves be unit-properties within a definable hierarchy of qualities which temporarily may *serve* as media. What may on one occasion be a thing-quality and a potential focus for perception may on another occasion be a medium for a different thing-quality which is in focus.

So far as perceptual activity is concerned, it is the "spurious units" of extraorganismic mediae events that impinge upon the sensory surfaces. Further, there must be intraorganismic events in the perceiving structures that are directly correlated with those of the environmental medium. If the thing-quality *and* physical medium be components of the stimulus situation, then it must be assumed that the *proximal events* in the perceptual apparatus which constitute the medium for reconstruction of the distal event are also part of the "stimulus." Out of these intraorganismic events the thing-qualities are reconstructed. Such reconstruction can occur in depth, ranging from thing-qualities immediately relevant to the dominant intention to peripheral thing-qualities having no such relevance or having a relevance only as the aims of peripheral motives in the intentional field. In this descriptive picture is being bypassed the problem of a theory that would account for *how* the reconstruction via mediation is possible. Again, the purpose here is simply to describe the classes of occurrences that must be assumed in an experiment on discrimination, a survey of pertinent variables.

It is important to distinguish the main varieties of intraorganismic mediation. There are, first of all, the properties of the perceiving apparatus itself. These condition the varieties of events that can participate in the reconstruction of thing-qualities. Thus, the potentiality for figure-ground distinctions or gradient functions resides in such inherent characteristics of structures. Astigmatism is a feature of proximal mediation just as the dust on glass or the smoke filling the room describes features of the physical medium. Each adds "noise" to the signal and prevents accurate phenomenal reconstruction of the thing-quality being viewed. Then there are the impulses or excitatory events, activities of the structures which themselves have no phenomenal status in the sense of formation or representation. The function of these events is purely mediation; such elements are rarely experienced as such, nor do they themselves usually acquire the status of formations—percepts.

Finally, there is a class of medial events consisting of proximally formed units that themselves correspond to distal thing-qualities which temporarily acquire a medial function. These are *registered* units. In the case of these events the mediating function of a unit may be partly imparted to it by the nature of the intentional field. As Heider points out in describing the perception of actions, the same pattern can be seen as A chasing B, or as B leading A, two events of entirely different social meanings. For instance, units formed out of *actions* often involve attributions. A primary consideration in the structure of such units is how the component events are anchored in a context of lower to higher dependencies, consisting of attributions of origin and cause and effect. Such attributions can go on in a hierarchy of layers—part-whole dependencies. Where in the hierarchy fixation will dwell and what the component unit will convey in such causal sequences is determined partly by the dominant and peripheral intentions that are active with respect to an object-field. In order to determine whether a particular pattern arrangement will result in one or another impression of object-quality, it is necessary to consider the total realm of possible representations of the unit-quality and of the conditions of mediation which make one or another form of proximal mediation more or less salient. This is partially determined by the dominant intention, as well as by the structural conditions of mediation in the perceptual apparatus.

These and other distinctions between thing and medium must be appreciated in any thorough appraisal of the co-ordinations that develop between intentions and objects. In the first place, it makes a big difference in assigning a perceptual experience to its correct *locus* in the total field of thing-medium correspondences. For instance, an illusion does not necessarily reflect a deficiency in the perceptual apparatus; it can be traced to certain qualities of the physical medium. Occasionally one incorrectly confuses medial events of the physical environment with properties of his own perceptual equipment, as when a man looking through a fine haze rubs his eyes under the misapprehension that the blurring is taking place *here*, not there, or a person in a dark room who has been handed a flashlight with a red filter may conclude that the room is "red" when he flashes the light. Again, faint illumination impoverishes the *physical* medium and therefore proximal stimulation. On the other hand, deficient experience can often be traced to structural conditions of the *perceptual medial field*. Klein and Krech [50] showed how properties of the cortical conducting medium differ in brain-injured and non-brain-injured, and can result in qualitatively distinct features of perceptual experience. To the extent that a medium is limited in its capacity to serve as such, it is important to know this inadequacy in accounting for "distortions." These considerations bring into dramatic relief the great accomplishment of perception—that despite the vicarious character of the mediational fields both on the physical side and in the perceptual apparatus, the reconstruction of thing-qualities can be accomplished with fidelity. It is not remarkable that illusions occur (either as the result of properties of physical mediation alone or of the perceptual medium alone) but that they do not occur more often.

The thing-medium distinction takes on further importance especially in percepts involving *attributions*; e.g., of one unit's "belonging" to another, of A's being touched by B, etc. In thing-qualities of a conditional relation, type units are themselves the media of a core-relation. For example, meaning is perceived through letters and reading. As noted, an event which has the function of a medium has attributes different from those of the same event when it is a thing-quality. A man looks through the glass window at the buildings beyond. The glass has no interest for him other than that it helps or hinders his seeing the objects behind it. The glass may be dirty; if he says that the building he is looking at has a "fuzzy" outline, he has wrongly attributed a quality of the medium to the relevant thing-quality. Many perceptual experiences involve attributions of medium- and thing-status to perceived units. As will be seen later, it is in influencing such attributions that motives can *directly* alter the unit-character of a perception.

It has been noted that the differentiated nature of the physical object itself and the adequacy of physical and perceptual mediation both make a difference in the multiplicity of registrations that may comprise the phenomenally reconstructed field under the guidance of intentions. Also affecting the phenomenal hierarchy are those perceived units which have interchangeable status as medium and as thing-quality. Any invariant quality can potentially be a thing-quality, the focus of an intention; but perceptual registrations may include a variety of formations which themselves are irrelevant to the dominant focus upon another thing-quality. This is the case when a unit is medium for a thing-quality in the part-whole hierarchy of an object. Thus, slant may be conveyed by a textural gradient or by the tilt of a line, and where slant is the *relevant* thing-quality of an executive intention these formations serve as its media. Were the textural gradient itself the invariant that is in focus, then one could try to specify *its* medial conditions. To say that a medial quality can become an object, that for example, a textural gradient, even though a cue for depth or slant, can also be perceived in its own right, only reiterates a quality of all invariants: in the case of texture, that it is possible under certain conditions to perceive a retinal image of texture that will remain *invariant* under a certain range of transformations, including depth itself.

That such interchangeability of medial properties is possible with size and distance relationships has been demonstrated by Boring *[7]*. Not all medial events can become percepts but many can because of their unit-character invariance. It is this latter quality that makes it possible for them to be separately registered even though retaining a medial status with respect to the *dominant* thing-quality. Some of the more common unit formations that serve as media are figure-ground and contour gradients; they also include "higher-order" patterns, e.g., ratios, that Gibson has termed "ordinal stimuli." The fact that the medial unit has registered, that it has a perceptual, if peripheral, status, adds to the number of *potential* object-qualities available for co-ordination with the activity of intentions in the field. As will be seen later, such peripherally registered events are an important reservoir upon which peripherally active intentions can draw to discharge aims.

Returning to the main theme, the relevance of objects to the region of intentions, dominant and fringe, that operate in a perceptual situation, it is important to note that, if an executive intention is aroused with respect to a thing-quality, and if the conditions of the physical and proximal medium make possible its registration, it is reconstructed in a patterned proximal arrangement. But objects have other perceivable properties too and these also are represented in the medial events. They may be irrelevant to the central intention but, if they are representable in a medium, it is also possible that they, as well as the central one, may be registered. A critical question arises here: Are these "irrelevant" thing-qualities *actually* registered? It has been seen that the Poetzl and Fisher studies indicate that many such "irrelevant" object-properties are indeed actually registered. Even though not conscious, and even though not affecting what the subject is directly reporting on, they acquire structure. The assumption that there is a field of perceived qualities outside awareness does not find easy acceptance in current theories of perception, and yet this is where the implications of the intentional field point. The problem of unconscious perception arises and this issue will be discussed now.

CENTRAL AND PERIPHERAL REGISTRATION IN THE PERCEPTUAL FIELD

It has been seen that an adequate appraisal of an experimental situation must recognize the activity of stimuli outside the reaches of the immediate steering influence of an executive intention, or of a particular set of thing-properties and their proximal representations. The possibility of multiple activations of motives in an experiment has repeatedly been alluded to as has also the necessity of assuming that objects and events are layered organizations of thing-qualities which may be simultaneously appropriate to the aims of various active intentions. These assumptions carry the further implication that the actual range of perceptual registrations that occur in an experiment is much broader than is required to meet the explicit requirements of instruction. To proceed a step forward in an understanding of the multiple coordinations that may occur between intentions and objects in an experiment, one must consider more closely some of the issues raised by this suggestion that peripheral as well as central registration is possible.

Seeing encompasses more than is consciously intended. For instance, when one notices as he writes that the point of his pen is sluggish, he does so because he wants to write; under such circumstances it does not come to his "attention" that the pen is also black. The latter is not "important" at the moment. Later, in some other connection, this incidental information about the pen may emerge to awareness in a completely different context. It seems clear that much of what one perceives is not the direct outcome of an executive intention alone, but an incidental outcome as well. Thus it is possible to speak of a periphery and a center in the visual field (not to be confused with the anatomical fovea and periphery on the retina). It would seem that the perceptual system works as if it picks up a great deal, concerns itself with a little and acts upon still less. If, then, more is perceptually registered than is actually "seen" or consciously looked at, one can not be justified in identifying the qualities of *conscious* experience and the distal invariants involved with the totality of what is registered.[2] Further, whatever is registered, even though "irrelevant" to conscious intention, may nevertheless *persist* and retain independent status. In an experiment, then, registration is perhaps much more inclusive than an adaptive discriminative selection requires. Linked to this assumption in the descriptive scheme are two other assumptions: that such peripheral registrations provide a source of discharge of active, though not dominant, motives, and further that co-ordination with fringe motives is perhaps what gives permanence or persistence to these perceptual registrations, i.e., creates memory residues.

The evidence for these assumptions has admittedly not been fully developed. With respect to the matter of simultaneous arousal of surface and depth intentions there will be comments other than the discussion in the previous sections. Suffice it to mention here again that the results of Fisher and Poetzl give strong experimental evidence of a pervasive motivational aura. In addition to this they provide numerous examples to show that one takes in visually much more than he uses for immediate

[2] Freud's distinction between the functions of consciousness and perception is of interest in this connection: "We know that perception by our sense organs has the result of directing a cathexis of attention to the paths along which the incoming sensory excitation is spreading: the qualitative excitation of the *Pcpt.* system acts as a regulator of the discharge of the mobile quantity in the psychical apparatus. We can attribute the same function to the overlying sense-organ of the *Cs.* system." [22, *p. 616*]

executive purposes, and that he is conscious of even less. For instance, for one of Fisher's subjects the click of the projector's shutter during the experiment seemed clearly represented in a dream as the shot of a bullet [20]. Registration, as these studies verify, is far more efficient than has been thought to be the case.

The possibility of peripheral registrations, of thing-qualities attaining perceptual status independently of immediate relevance to an executive intention, has received relatively little attention in perceptual theories. And yet a legitimate question for perceptual theory is involved here. It is sometimes said that memories are never lost, but one might also ask which of the infinity of impingements upon the sensory surfaces become memories. Do they all? One walks along a road and a whole series of partial impressions crosses his field. These may have some retinal reality or registration. But can they be spoken of as preconsciously perceived, that is, converted to the status of memories? Indeed, has one any right to assume that they are registered at all? That they persist? If so, if some are and some are not, what are the rules of elimination? While such a wide range of registration is amply attested to by the Poetzl and Fisher studies and by clinical observation, the conditions of such registration and their persistence are not yet well understood.

Questions concerning central and peripheral registrations might be phrased in terms of the figure-ground distinction of Gestalt theory: are background forms perceived and are these structurally independent of figural formations? What are the conditions for the persistence of such registered background forms? How do they become "memories"? Is this peripheral field of "preconsciously" perceived thing-qualities active in the discharge of peripheral intentions? These imply critical issues upon which hinge basic conceptions of the possible ways in which motives influence perception, and the manner in which it is possible for effective perceiving to occur at the same time that imperious claims are made by motives upon objects without regard for the immediate adaptive demand for effective perception.

Gestalt psychology has much to say about the relation between figure and ground but there is little room in it for the assumptions made here. Kohler, for instance, seems to hold that background has no form, and as such no psychological existence since figure is the only form that is in awareness [54]. Forms may provoke retinal excitations but if they are not included in the *chosen* Gestalt (figure) they are not perceived. If background forms have any effect it is not as independent structures but as providing a context of assimilation, contrast and intensification effects upon the central figure only. The classical Gestalt laws of figure and form apply to formations that have been termed *central* in the stimulus field, i.e., in awareness. The theory *does* provide for what Kohler has termed "silent organizations" (e.g., frames of reference which govern figure formation), but it does not support the idea of separate, independent registration of forms not in central focus. An illustration of the nonindependence of background forms is Kohler's classic example of the forms traced by the contours of land and sea masses in a map. In the usual map, land masses are shown in vivid colors, water masses in pale blue. In the map of Europe the Italian "boot" stands forth as figure. Now, if one reverses the color values of water and land, he is surprised by the "new forms" that emerge. They are definitely unfamiliar, indicating that they had not previously been "perceived." It would seem that "superfluous" registrations of background forms do not occur.

As Ehrenzweig has pointed out [19], the assumptions made by painters stand in contrast to this conclusion. Also, psychoanalytic theory and practice. Painters devote painstaking care to hidden form combinations. But if the spectator won't see them anyway and they have no visual existence, why bother over them? Quite commonly in artistic productions the hidden form combinations are superimposed across the boundaries of readily recognizable objects; e.g., the human figures of a painting by Poussin may describe a rectangular arrangement, or the light masses may describe a definable shape. The painter seems also to take meticulous pains to keep these forms in the background, as if to assume that they may gain in emotional impact by that very fact, and that the peripheral status of a form gives it certain *positive* properties that it might lose if it were in awareness. If "background" forms are influential in this manner, they must have, at least potentially, visual existence, even if their existence is the product of perceptions outside of awareness.

The oversight in Gestalt theory of the possible significance of peripheral registrations is apparently due to (a) its neglect of the possibility that perception in its actual occurrence is a developmental process—that is to say, it is a temporally extended event in which the outcome in experience is seemingly immediate, but not actually so—and (b) its neglect of the distinction between medium and thing. For instance, proximal events are mediators of thing-qualities. Were these proximal events directly perceived they would have the status of "sensations," and this possibility is denied in Gestalt theory. They may be components of the final percept (the "immediate" percept of Gestalt theory), but are only the media for it and not identical with it. They have a unit-character that is essentially independent of the thing-property they mediate. Implied here is the possibility that such intermediate events *leading up to* the final percept may be separately registered and achieve independent status perceptually.

The problem of what becomes perceptually formed—what gains status as a percept—is not as obvious as it may seem. In the apparent immediacy of vision, one overlooks the fact that what is given is essentially a *construction*. A saccadic scanning occurs in focusing upon an object. The resulting perception is the outcome of movement. Now while Gestalt theory recognizes the importance of such saccadic build-ups, it does not accord them any phenomenal significance as registered events—unit formations—independent of the final formation. Only the experience given in the immediate perception is phenomenally real. Very likely the individual excitations in fixation do not have perceptual registration. But there is a real question whether formations, involving contours and gradients on the retina, which are known from Gibson's studies to be critical to experiences of slant and perspective, gain perceptual registration. The basic question is when in the immediate workings of the eye—at what stage of the integrative activity of perceiving—does an impingement become a registration, and a registration become a conscious percept, or memory?

The artist continually explores "latent" form properties of objects. His is a continued scrutiny of the multilayered hierarchy of unit-properties in objects, i.e., of form properties which under ordinary circumstances have only "medial" status and are rarely the *direct* aim of conscious purposeful vision. This seems, indeed, to be the main reason for the often noted liberation of the artist from the usual thing-constancies. The artist learns to perceive against the normal principles that govern figure-ground, good form, continuation, closure, etc. He destroys in order to discover new forms. He breaks through constancies in order to focus on those *invariances* or properties that are latent in the constant object. For him what in ordinary vision has the status of a medial formation becomes a thing-quality. To discover perspective as a thing-quality means that he must become "aware" of objects *in* transformation with perspective. In exploring the property of perspective as an independent thing-quality—a relation in this case —he asks in effect through what transpositions of objects perspective does remain invariant.

To ordinary people the superimposed hidden patterns that are accessible to the painter even when he attends to more figural forms emerge only under exceptional circumstances. Ehrenzweig cites an excellent example [19]: On a slow car drive through a mist it may be difficult to guess what the objects are on the way. Only isolated pieces and contours may appear. Gradually, however, these all may add up to a very peculiar and unfamiliar combination that has a particular connotation. Then the mist clears and one sees what *is* in fact there. Immediately the former projection vanishes. One might with effort project the vanished image into the now completely revealed object but it takes an act of disciplined concentration to do so. The artist, however, sees such invisible form combinations all the time.

It would appear that the peripheral or background nature of a form acquires for it certain *positive* properties that it no longer has when in awareness. It may be that these properties are analogous to those of dream images. Thus in dreams, forms are fluid and fuse easily; they do not tend toward the precision, simplicity and singleness of meaning of adaptive conscious vision. Superimposition is possible. Conscious forms have a "bump-erasing" function; peripheral forms may not be as disciplined in this respect. It may be that the well-known Gestalt laws of good continuation, closure, etc., hold for the perceptions of figural but not for peripheral forms. The ambiguity of peripheral forms may perhaps make it possible for symbolic formations to develop that resonate with the aims of "irrelevant" intentions, and for forms to take on attributes that they might not easily have were they in central focus. This raises the further possibility that fringe forms may influence central or figural forms, not in the usual sense of contrast or assimilation (merely as emphasizing or de-emphasizing figural form), but in a more indirect way in their resonances with inadaptive intentions and affects. This further broadens the possibilities of where "effects" of motives may be observed: behavioral effects may originate in the interplay of latent intentions and peripheral perceptual registrations, exerting indirect effects upon conscious forms.

This possibility arises when inquiry is made into the reasons for the artist's insatiable search for form. He seems not to do it simply because of a detached interest in form *per se* but quite the reverse. More likely, form plays an important role in the discharge of motives and wishes which, in a deeper sense, define the impetus for his wanting to paint at all. Form for him may bind the pressure of a wish; if so, his is a constant search for the apt form that would serve as a temporarily relieving focus of discharge.

The essential point here is that peripheral (i.e., superimposed, background) forms in a painting may often be important because of what they *symbolize*.

It often happens that the unconscious symbolism of perceived background forms influences subtle aspects of our perception of the figure. Background forms may lend themselves easily to symbolic use because they are not bound up in particular meanings of executive intentions.

Clinical observations present many demonstrations of preconscious perception, and the assumption of preconscious registrations has indeed achieved something of axiomatic status in psychoanalytic theory. What *has* escaped notice is the question of the range and content of registrations of preconscious forms, the conditions under which they persist and obtain separate status, and the further use to which they are put after the suppression, *in the ongoing activity of thought*. Take for instance the fact of a temporary elision in a perceptual field—as in a hysterical scotoma —a "repression" involving a preconscious recognition of a painfully significant object. It is usual to take for granted the possibility of such preconscious perception and suppression and to explain a good deal of conscious behavior in terms of it. But inquiry rarely goes further than this: for instance, what has happened to the percept itself? Assuming that an object was recognized preconsciously, what is its subsequent fate as a *percept*? Is it eliminated? Does it completely fade? The problem has been recognized in connection with the participation of day residues in dreams. Thus, such "peripheral" registrations resonating with significant motives and wishes may initiate the process that flowers later as a dream. But why certain day residues and not others? What does the preconscious percept acquire in cathectic charge that gives it permanence and persistence? Some preconscious percepts do, apparently, acquire such status, but under what terms and conditions? Freud pointed out that certain preconscious perceptions are at an advantage in this respect: they are recent and hence unencumbered by associations, they are briefly given (that is, they are not hypercathected and therefore do not have the *single* concrete meaning of an adaptive, hypercathected percept) *[22]*. If the property of fluidity and that of the interchangeability of medial forms be added, then the possibility appears that peripheral forms have a unique value in the discharge of latent wishes.

If it be assumed that many more registrations occur than enter consciousness, and if such registrations persist, obviously there are processes other than "repression" (in the psychoanalytic sense) that eliminate them from awareness. But what is their relation to *repression* in the usual sense? Do such peripheral formations —the outcomes simply of the way the visual apparatus works rather than "repression"—have a value in the discharge of latent wishes? Analytic theory has not exploited the importance of the peripheral formations implied in the distinction between center and periphery. It has dealt with repressed contents only.

The issue of perception outside awareness has arisen in recent years in the experimental literature, largely in alleged experimental demonstrations of "perceptual defense" *[56, 62, 73]*. These are essentially demonstrations in the laboratory of preconscious recognition and suppression phenomena long and often before reported by clinicians. But they are the closest approximations, aside from the Poetzl and Fisher investigations, to experimental demonstrations of perceptions outside awareness (*cf.* especially Lazarus and McCleary, *[56]*). There are many difficulties of experimental design and overgeneralization in these studies *[60, 38]*, but even assuming the claims made regarding unconscious recognition, these studies raise again the critical question which oddly enough they have not made explicit: What has happened to the alleged preconscious percept? Does it remain active?

This discussion has emphasized the importance of the fringe

of perceptual registrations outside awareness and its significance for the discharge of active intentions. Further, it has been postulated that the very fact that hypercathexis is absent gives to such peripheral percepts qualities that make them especially amenable to the discharge of nonadaptive motives or intentions. These considerations have brought to the forefront certain basic problems in perception itself: What phases in the perceptual reconstruction of an object- or event-pattern gain independent perceptual registration? What are the conditions that determine the persistence of a percept? What selective principles guide registration and conversion to trace-structures? Finally, what are the vicissitudes of such perceptual registrations in the discharge of motives?

These questions point again to the basic issue of what in an object's structure potentially comprises this perceptual fringe. It has been seen in earlier discussion that it is possible to conceive the thing-qualities of an object or an action, and the relations among them as hierarchically arranged, from those whose salience comes from an executive intention in awareness to those that are outside attention—"latent" object properties that are not "used." If these fringe unit-properties are registered, they are grist for the workings of nonadaptive wishes and intentions. Also an object has been spoken of as consisting of many potential foci for perception (whether preconscious or central).

Another relevant consideration from the pictured conception of a hierarchic object-field is the interchangeability of status of medial- and thing-units. There is an inventory of invariances that are more or less serviceable for the mediation of still higher-order invariances in an object organization. What is medium for the fulfillment of one intention may have a *thing-quality* for the discharge of nonadaptive intention on the fringes of the motive-field. It has been seen that a variety of proximal formations can serve interchangeably as medium-end thing-qualities. They include contours, gradients (e.g., texture, shading), color, movement, rhythm, mass (e.g., volume and density), and temporal units—such things as are involved in attributions of causality. While ordinarily they are part components of larger whole-qualities, as units they have invariant properties; and hence they can also be perceived; i.e., they can register. It is by manipulating "medial forms" such as those in the background of a picture that artists can create effects upon forms centrally focused in a picture. When such background forms are linked further to an emotional symbol, the effects are intensified. Gradients, edges and surfaces may be peripherally perceived in the same manner as superimposed form patterns of a painting and they may acquire relevance to fringe intentions of the motivational field.[3]

All of these considerations broaden the range of possible and expected effects of motives upon perception. They underscore the point that such effects are not a simple matter of a motive of one level having an effect on the perception of a *particular* thing-property. The issue, rather, involves relationships of peripheral or surface qualities of a thing—its medial and unit-property characteristics—to central and fringe motives that are active at the moment of response. It is obvious that any complete inventory of the effects of motives on perception in an experimental situation must take into account these multiple possibilities.

It follows also from what has been said that all ways of minimizing the intensity of executive intentions, such as diffusion of focus (drug states), eliminations of postural supports for discrimination, prolonged fixations, etc., may result in the reduction of dominance of the central field and an increase in the domination of

---

[3] The possibility of medial qualities being preconsciously perceived and acquiring an active peripheral status is not directly supported by evidence, but studies employing reduction screens suggest this possibility. It is possible to so reduce the complexity of cues as to make the subject dependent upon but a *few parameters* of the stimulus. Thus he comes to use whatever is "available" proximally. This fact has misled some investigators to assume that such a correlation between a proximal invariance and distal invariance is both the necessary and sufficient condition for a given constancy. As Boring points out in criticism of Gibson:

". . . it seems to me that Gibson is in error in thinking that stimulus-controlled phenomenal size becomes indeterminate when stimulus-controlled distance, under reduction, becomes indeterminate." [8, *p.* 247]

Seen size does not become independent of stimulation with the elimination of the possibility of such proximal representation: another pattern of proximal events is simply substituted as the "key" cue.

In Boring's view, "what you perceive can be thought of as an invariant." [8, *p. 246*] The critical fact seems to be that an object consists, in a sense, of an inventory of invariances which are potentially discriminable under various degrees and kinds of *reduction*. "The invariances tell us what the organism can do under attitudinal training to perceive its own physiological basis, the data out of which it can, after much evolution, create an extremely useful apprehension of the world that it accepts as its reality." [7, *p. 147*]

central response by peripheral percepts and resonated nonadaptive wishes. Also, peripheral registrations may be recoverable only through alterations in consciousness which reduce the selective activity of executive intentions; e.g., hypnotic, hypnogogic and reverie states, dreams, prolonged fixations, fatigue, drug states, etc.

THE CAPTURED OBJECT: A SUMMARY OF "SELECTIVE" INFLUENCES OF MOTIVES IN PERCEPTION

Perception has been regarded as a phase of a more inclusive aggregate of processes termed "cognition," processes that are always implicated whenever there is a stake in an object and when the qualities of this object are "intended." The original query, How do motives affect perception? must be confronted within this larger context.

As has been seen, no situation that engages cognition, even the laboratory context, is free from the workings of intentions; but whether the impact of motives can be observed anywhere in the *perceptual* process itself is a distinct matter, not to be confused with the easy-to-accept assumption that cognition *in general* is so influenced. It is possible to grant the pervasiveness of motives and still maintain, as many have, that perception is essentially "autochthonous." In this view, perception serves upon what is relevant to intention, but the biases of motives do not complicate its workings. The perceptual process does not itself judge or condemn; its "selectivity," it is often said, is wholly a matter of its own properties, not those of a motive. Its detachment could be likened to that of a parimutuel machine, recording the bets, assaying the odds and winnings, but favoring no bettor.

Further, the same argument runs, it is misleading to judge from evidence of motivational participation in a cognitive *product*; i.e., in a report or an action or a communication that perception was *specifically* implicated. Not only perception but other cognitive events are represented in cognitive products and these must be separately assessed for their responsiveness to the claims of motives. And if perception is so closely geared to other processes that one must assume that *all* are responsive, is it not a mistake to assume that the contributing processes reflect *equally* the momentum of motives, or even of the *same* motive? From the perspective of the total cognitive act, it may be that the steering impact of intentions is *generally* more critical in *preperceptual* events and at various *reaction* levels *to* the percept than in perception itself.

It is difficult to hold to this diehard avowal of the independence of perception from motives if one looks at the more salient qualities of the perceptual experience itself. One of these is the intimate contact with *meanings* which so vividly identifies an experience as a perception rather than as a memory or judgment. When one perceives a chair, the experience is of a contact with an objective fact. This holds for any of the chair's particulars that may be sought out—its texture, its shape, its color, and, for that matter, also its physiognomic or "expressive" qualities. The chair "enters" into our life; one participates in certain of its aspects. One does not know something *about* the chair—he knows it directly; nor are "facts" of the chair, its thing-qualities, *experienced* as deductions or inferences. The thing-qualities of perception are not segregated in awareness from the thing-qualities of "objective fact." As Nuttin puts it [70], to perceive consciously is "to be open" to things. In short, intimacy of contact with object-meanings seems to be the most salient identifying mark of a percept. This being the case, it is not absurd to expect that intentions, which after all concern the search for meanings in the environment and endow it with significance and value, will participate *somewhere* in the formative processes of perception. The impetus toward meaning in perception is at least consistent with what would be expected of a motivationally steered process. This is why Brentano and Act psychology required the term, "intending," in the very definition of perception; for them, "intending" a quality is inherent in every perception and is the basis of the "selectivity" that is inevitable in perception.

If the loci of effects must be distinguished, it is equally necessary to recognize that effects will be multiple and that they will appear at different levels at the different loci, issuing from a variety of simultaneously active motives. In previous pages the multiplicity of claims that typically occurs even in a laboratory experiment has been described. Every moment of life is a dialectic of intentions, shifting in relative importance, pulling in different ways, establishing restraints on thought and action and imparting qualities of relevance and irrelevance to objects and to different properties of the same object. As has been seen, motivational participation cannot be reduced to the activity of a single level of intentions. Intentions, both peripheral and central, establish a field of expentancies. As Tolman puts it, they create an "affect" and "incentive-demand" setting *[92]*. The actual state of affairs seems to be that of a simultaneously active array of intentions coordinating with a stratified arrangement of potentially perceivable properties—invariances—in the physical organization of objects. The activated motivational field constitutes, in a sense, an attraction field of activated ideas (memories) which draw into their orbit perceptual registrations. Any active motive has within its orbit a range of object-properties—thing-qualities appropriate to it. Furthermore, such claims are not necessarily muted by the fact that one may be "unaware" of them. Awareness can determine only adaptive relevance; it is not itself critical to the development of percepts. Investments in object-qualities develop from the activity of intentions and the object-quality units they implicate. And a good portion of this may occur outside awareness. Clearly, there is little basis for expecting all activity of the intentional field to be summarized in a single effect.

In evaluating the *forms* of motivational influence, it is necessary to look beyond "error" or "accuracy" scores which so often constrict analyses. As has been seen, accuracy is not itself a process but an evaluation of products, an evaluation usually on the experimenter's terms, *not* the subject's—some arbitrarily conceded standard of what *should* be adaptive. Often such "error" scores can be misleading if the error is presumed to arise in the perceptual process itself. For instance, an "error" may reflect inadequacies of physical mediation rather than anomaly in the perceptual process.

An example of how the error concept can mislead is the once-common interpretation of "illusions" as "errors of perception." It is not difficult to demonstrate that many so-called illusions are not errors of perception but, to the contrary, reflections of effective responsiveness of the perceptual process to a certain set of field conditions *[cf. Wallach's demonstration of the kinetic depth effect, 96]*. On the other hand, absence of an illusion under certain conditions where the "distortion" is to be normally expected may indicate pathology of the perceptual process. Thus, in certain types of brain injury some of the well-known perceptual illusions may be minimal.

Clearly, the regions of participation of motives in cognitions and the range of their effects turn out to be a much more complex set of possibilities than the apparent cohesiveness of a response would at first glance suggest. The real issues concern the conditions that determine capture by one or another intention and perception, the conditions that determine the phenomenal outcomes of simultaneous claims made on an object-field by multiple intentions. The questions are best asked not in terms of production of error but rather in terms of what distal qualities of an object are reacted to, what intentions and states of awareness, and toward what outcomes in "appearances" and behavior.

In this accounting of conditions that determine limits and forms of participation by motives at each of the several phases of the ongoing cognitive process, the issue of whether phenomenal constructions correspond to distal organization is, of course, relevant: "errors" and "distortions" in this respect are certainly of great interest. But the question of "error" here is not the same as in evaluating products against an arbitrary standard of adequacy, since these errors involve an analysis of distal and phenomenal correspondences and the relevant processes involved.

As has been seen, the interplay of intentions and cognition can be investigated at various loci. "Effect" of motive implies that imbalances produced by intentions have had consequences in the hierarchy of central and peripheral intentions, in the organization of proximal mediation, and in the arrangement of reconstructed thing-qualities (the phenomenal field), in the actions and communications that follow, and in the observable behaviors of altered states of awareness.

Various possibilities have been pictured in Figure 2. In this schema, antecedent and consequent are a purely relative matter. While the preperceptual events are a necessary context for perceptual activity, they are also "consequent" events in the sense that they reflect conditions of expectancy and disposition.

It is possible, then, to speak of the effects of intentions upon preperceptual events. Included among the preperceptual events are the postural conditions that determine the efficiency of executive intentions and the degree to which these preserve their saliency in the cognitive process. Clearly, imbalances at this phase (e.g., reduced postural supports, making executive intentions difficult to maintain, or intense latent or peripheral intentions) can crucially affect the course of events at subsequent stages.

In the sequence of events shown in Figure 2, the phenomenal field is a basis for action upon the stimulus itself, and in part it is the outcome of action [cf. *Piaget 71*]. It is assumed that the motivational effects at these two points can well be different. The phenomenal field is an antecedent condition—neither the sole determiner of action nor identical with it. In this schema it is quite proper to note the effects of motives on the phenomenally reconstructed field and at the same time to recognize that the prediction of effects in *actions* does not depend *solely* upon the constructions of the phenomenal field. An example is the "movement" response on the Rorschach. To distinguish the perceptual components from the associative, one would need to know whether the *phenomenal* formations involved are similar to those that would develop if the eye confronted the distal invariances of an *actually* moving object.

With respect to formation of percepts, i.e., the structure of the reconstructed field of objects, the critical issue is the extent to which phenomenal reconstructions reflect peripheral and central intentions and how these compare with the macrophysical structure of the distal object. It is at least conceivable that the directive influence of motives will be evident in the phenomenally reconstructed field of thing-qualities. In assessing the "effects" of motives on perceptual formation, an exceedingly important possibility is that such influences are reflected through *mediating* processes, e.g., in the development of the proximal units which establish limits to what can be reconstructed in the distal aggregate of thing-qualities. Here, in the field of proximal mediations, the arrangements in the object field and the saliencies established by the intentional field are both blended into a phenomenal organization.

Turning to the motivational effects upon reaction *to* the perceptual formations, the critical questions concern the manner in which percepts are translated into acts of *communication*, or *discharge* (e.g., in fantasy or imagery), or into some *manipulative* action upon the object-field. The possibility that perception may terminate at several such levels of reaction simultaneously has been shown.

It has been common practice in need-perception studies to infer from "distortions" of response that perceptual organization itself was implicated by the warping influence of a need. Closer inspection usually shows that these effects more likely concern only *behavioral reactions* to the percept (the fourth main portion of Figure 2); e.g., communications to the experimenter in word and action. All that such studies demonstrate *directly* is selectivity in report processes or in measurable behavioral reaction. It is not certain that perceptual formation itself—the phenomenal field—has been modified. More likely the report reflects several levels of reactions. Take, for instance, the "effects" termed "perceptual defense." Here delayed-recognition threshold *may* mean that phenomenal organization has been modified, or that some level of communication with the experimenter has been affected, or both. In the present scheme, a distinction between behavioral effects and perceptual formations is vital. The formations of the phenomenal field, while inseparably linked to *some form and level* of reaction is not to be identified with them. Thus, level of report and communication is crucial in evaluating consequences of the motivational aura in cognition.

The effects of motivational participation may be seen not only at various levels of response during the laboratory situation, but in later circumstances and in altered *states of awareness*, as in dreams, daydreams, reverie states, etc., when executive intentions of conscious, purposeful thought are no longer active. Rapaport in a significant discussion of this matter has spoken of such states of awareness as "structures" [79]. For consideration here, they may be considered as conditions which establish the potentiality (or lack of it) for certain co-ordinations to develop between motive and phenomenal field, and the impact of these co-ordinations upon ongoing trains of thought and action. Thus, an adequate accounting of the ways in which such links between the phenomenal field and different strata of motives influence thought, action, and communication must also take account of the quality of awareness since the latter establishes varying contexts for the influences that perceptions can have upon action and thought.

The Balance of Forces in the Cognitive Process

In this paper, some of the conditions in the field of intentions and in the structure of objects that allow and restrict the intrusion of motives in cognitive behavior have been summarized. In accounting for the outcomes of intentions it is necessary to inspect the imbalances that exist among the principal classes of events shown in Figure 2.

As indicated earlier, a strong, executive intention *unsupported* by appropriate postural factors would reduce the efficiency with which an intentionally salient thing-quality in the phenomenal field is registered; at the same time, it would allow co-ordinations of peripheral intentions with object-properties which might not otherwise occur, these perhaps influencing in turn the phenomenal character of the more relevant thing-quality itself. It is also possible to have a strong, executive intention but an impoverished object-field, impoverished either in the sense of a weakly integrated thing-quality or inadequate mediations—in the physical or proximal field, or both. These conditions, too, may increase the possibility of peripheral intentions' making their way into the various levels of thought and action. Furthermore, it is possible to have a weak executive intention (as established, for instance, by the typical Rorschach instruction) and an object-field that is equivocal in the sense described earlier. Again, in responses to Rorschach cards, this, too, would permit peripheral trains of intentions to dominate phenomenal formations as well as communications which follow upon these percepts. The response picture on the Rorschach would change considerably if, instead of equivocal intentions, a *strong* one were induced (e.g., if one were to ask the subject to discriminate only a particular shape or form, or that he take an "accuracy" set). Some other possible imbalances that can occur have been indicated in earlier pages. Figure 2 makes it abundantly clear that it is possible to stack the deck in a number of ways that would reduce or increase the possibility of motivational intrusions upon cognitive organization.

In all of the events pictured in Figure 2, little mention was made of *personality constants* in cognitive functioning, processes variously connoted by such terms as cognitive style, stabilized regulative mechanisms, character defenses, and the like—forms of control which have been hypothesized to account for the integration and distinctive self-consistency that distinguishes a person's behavior. The importance for cognition of such quasi-stable structures, or system-principles as Angyal [4] has termed them, has been treated in detail elsewhere [41, 45]. Various studies have effectively demonstrated the necessity of taking them into account in refining predictions of cognitive behavior.[4] There is not time to examine in detail the influence of such constants at each phase of the cognitive process. Systematic investigation of their influence is still in an early stage and does not yet allow any firm conclusions as to whether their effect is most extensive upon preperceptual events or upon the phenomenal field or in processes of communication and action.

There is evidence to support the possibility that certain forms of regulatory constants, or cognitive attitudes, exert influence upon phenomenal organization itself, and that they result in individual differences by determining the potentialities for certain and not other proximal organizations to develop, hence making it easy or not for different types of discrimination to occur. There are reports of significant individual differences in the ease with which certain unit formations characteristically appear, e.g., in propensities for closure, contrast gradients, etc. The regulative principles of this type of study are concerned with individual differences in proximal variables which are commonly the subject of psychophysical measurement. Studies by Holzman [40], Postman and Bruner [74], Smith [90], Johansson [43], and others seem to be yielding increasingly impressive indications that reliable variations among individuals are to be expected in parameters of proximal organization, and that higher-order regulatory principles determine in part the personal constants of individual differences seen at these levels.

---

[4] A number of studies have attempted to define personality constants in cognitive terms; e.g., "cognitive attitudes" of leveling and sharpening, focusing, tolerance and intolerance for instability, broad and narrow equivalence-range tendencies, flexible-control and constricted control [40, 85, 23, 49]. Witkin [103] has demonstrated two cognitive styles which he terms "field dependence" and "field independence," and Else Frenkel-Brunswik has proposed another basis of self-consistency in cognitive behavior in her distinction between tolerance and intolerance for ambiguity [21].

The class of regulatory constants involved in these studies is perhaps an order of control different from "defenses." Studies have attempted to show how processes of "repression," "isolation," etc., affect cognitive performance. However, it is possible that defenses are specifically linked to *particular* drives and drive derivatives, e.g., reaction formations with aggressive drives. In this sense, their regulatory function may be quite different from controls whose directive influence is independent of particular forms of need and need gratification.

This distinction between defenses and other forms of regulatory constants of personality has been discussed elsewhere *[49]*. In terms of a further exploration of the implications of this distinction for cognition, it will suffice here to mention that these two classes of regulatory constants may be variously effective at different loci of the cognitive process. Thus, certain principles of control may directly influence phenomenal organization, affecting in part the proximal mediation of distal thing-properties while other regulatory constants may exert influence at other reaction levels. For instance, defensive regulations may influence associative processes, judgment and motor behavior, delaying or determining action and controlling the approaches to objects via actual motor co-ordinations. There is much to be clarified in theory and experiment concerning the nature and properties of such regulatory constants. The viewpoint traced in this chapter allows for the possibility that the perceptual apparatus is equipped to reflect certain kinds of over-all personality principles and not others; that not all phases of a perceptual cognitive relationship will perhaps reveal *equally* the workings of a defense or a "cognitive attitude." Also essential to the descriptive scheme outlined here is that not only particular intentions with clear-cut relevance to *particular* objects participate in cognition, but a variety of highly generalized regulative principles —perhaps best regarded as forms of motivational energy too—also participate. For present purposes, the complexities of personality constants in cognitive behavior have been bypassed in favor of issues concerning the structure of the perceptual process itself: the "local system" properties of perception and conditions within it which predispose it or not to bend to motivational pressures. It is such qualities of perception to which an eventual theory of personality constants in cognition must accommodate itself if it is to generate profitable predictions about cognitive phenomena.

* * * * *

Some of the more salient features of a perceptual situation which seem to be essential to a more precise understanding of the selective effects of motives in the cognitive process have been surveyed. While it was impossible to avoid theory and the filling in of gaps with speculation, these were intended to be incidental to a descriptive and classificatory aim: to arrange in proper juxtaposition the classes of phenomena, some commonly overlooked, which are critically involved in responses that people give when they are asked to mobilize their efforts for effective discrimination, as in a psychophysical experiment. The terrain which has been covered is extensive and it is recognized that the variables regarded here as especially important require more detailed definition and systematic investigation to clarify their specific and relative importance.

BIBLIOGRAPHY

1. ALLPORT, G. W. *Personality: A Psychological Interpretation.* New York: Holt, 1937.
2. ————. *The Nature of Personality: Selected Papers.* Cambridge: Addison-Wesley Press, 1950.
3. AMES, A., JR. Nature and Origin of Perception: Preliminary laboratory manual for use with demonstrations disclosing phenomena which increase our understanding of the nature of perception. Mimeographed. Hanover, N. H.: Institute for Associated Research, 1946-47.
4. ANGYAL, A. *Foundations for a Science of Personality.* New York: The Commonwealth Fund, 1941.
5. BARTLETT, F. C. *Remembering: A Study in Experimental and Social Psychology.* Cambridge, England: Cambridge University Press, 1932.
6. BLUM, G. S. An Experimental Reunion of Psychoanalytic Theory with Perceptual Defense and Vigilance. *J. abnorm. soc. Psychol.*, 1954, 49, 94-98.
7. BORING, E. G. Visual Perception as Invariance. *Psychol. Rev.*, 1952, 59, 141-48.
8. ————. The Gibsonian Visual Field. *Psychol. Rev.*, 1952, 59, 246-47.
9. BRENMAN, M., GILL, M., & KNIGHT, R. P. Spontaneous Fluctuations in Depth of Hypnosis and Their Implications for Ego-Function. *Int. J. Psychoanal.*, 1952, 33, 22-33.

10. BRUNER, J. S.   One Kind of Perception: A Reply to Professor Luchins. *Psychol. Rev.*, 1951, 58, 306-12.

11. ————, & GOODMAN, C.   Value and Need as Organizing Factors in Perception. *J. abnorm. soc. Psychol.*, 1947, 42, 33-44.

12. ————, & POSTMAN, L.   Symbolic Value as an Organizing Factor in Perception. *J. soc. Psychol.*, 1948, 27, 203-8.

13. ————, & RODRIGUES, J. S., JR.   Some Determinants of Apparent Size. *J. abnorm. soc. Psychol.*, 1953, 48, 17-24.

14. BRUNSWIK, E.   Psychology in Terms of Objects, in *Proc. 25th Ann. Celeb. Inaug. Grad. Stud.*, University of Southern California, 1936, ed. H. W. Hill, 122-26.

15. ————.   *Systematic and Representative Design of Psychological Experiments.* Berkeley: University of California Press, 1947.

16. ————.   The Conceptual Framework of Psychology. *International Encyclopedia of Unified Science*, Vol. 1, No. 10. Chicago: University of Chicago Press, 1952.

17. CARTER, L. F., & SCHOOLER, K.   Value, Need and Other Factors in Perception. *Psychol. Rev.*, 1949, 56, 200-07.

18. CHEIN, I.   Review of Miller, J. G., *Unconsciousness*, New York: Wiley, 1942. *J. gen. Psychol.*, 1943, 29, 165-85.

19. EHRENZWEIG, A.   *The Psychoanalysis of Artistic Vision and Hearing.* New York: Julian Press, 1953.

20. FISHER, C.   Dreams and Perception. The Role of Preconscious and Primary Modes of Perception in Dream Formation. *J. Amer. psychoanal. Assn.*, 1954, 2, 389-445.

21. FRENKEL-BRUNSWIK, E.   *Personality Theory and Perception.* New York: Ronald Press, 1951, 356-419.

22. FREUD, S.   The Psychology of the Dream Processes, in *The Interpretation of Dreams*, Chap. 7 (The standard edition of the complete psychological works of Sigmund Freud). Translated by J. Strachey. London: Hogarth Press, 1953.

23. GARDNER, R. W.   Cognitive Styles in Categorizing Behavior. *J. Pers.*, 1953, 22, 214-33.

24. GIBSON, J. J.   *The Perception of the Visual World.* Boston: Houghton Mifflin, 1950.

25. ————.   Theories of Perception, in *Current Trends in Psychological Theory*, ed. W. Dennis. Pittsburgh: University of Pittsburgh Press, 1951, 85-110.

26. ————.   The Visual Field and the Visual World: A Reply to Professor Boring. *Psychol. Rev.*, 1952, 59, 149-51.

27. ————.   Social Perception and the Psychology of Perceptual Learning, in *Group Relations at the Crossroads*, eds. M. Sherif & M. O. Wilson. New York: Harper, 1953, 120-38.

28. ———. Ordinal Stimulation and the Possibility of a Global Psychophysics. Symposium on Recent Trends in Perceptive Theory. 14th International Congress of Psychology, Montreal, June, 1954.

29. GOLDSTEIN, K. *The Organism.* New York: American Book Company, 1939.

30. GUTTMANN, E., & MACLAY, W. S. Mescaline and Depersonalization. *J. Neurol. and Psychopath.*, 1936, 16, 193-212.

31. HARTMANN, H. Ego Psychology and the Problem of Adaptation, in *Organization and Pathology of Thought*, ed. D. Rapaport. New York: Columbia University Press, 1951, 362-96.

32. HEIDER, F. Thing and Medium. *Symposion.* Translated by F. and G. Heider, from F. Heider: Ding und medium (Verlag der Philosophischen Akademie), Erlangen I, 1927, 109-57.

33. ———. The Function of the Perceptual System. Translated by F. Heider, from F. Heider: Die Leistung des Wahrnehmungssystems, Z. f. Psychol., 1930, 114, 371-94.

34. ———. Environmental Determinants in Psychological Theories. *Psychol. Rev.*, 1939, 46, 383-410.

35. ———, & SIMMEL, M. A Study of Apparent Behavior. *Amer. J. Psychol.*, 1944, 57, 243-59.

36. ———. The Psychology of Interpersonal Relations. (Unpublished manuscript.)

37. HELSON, H. Perception and Personality—A Critique of Recent Experimental Literature. *USAF Air University School of Aviation Medicine Project Report* (Project #21-0202-0007, Report #1), July, 1953.

38. HOCHBERG, J. E. Psychophysics and Stereotypy in Social Perception. The University of Oklahoma. Third Conference in Social Psychology: Emerging Problems in Social Psychology, March 16-20, 1954.

39. HOLWAY, A. H., & BORING, E. G. Determinants of Apparent Visual Size with Distant Variant. *Amer. J. Psychol.*, 1941, 54, 21-37.

40. HOLZMAN, P. S. The Relation of Assimilation Tendencies in Visual, Auditory, and Kinesthetic Time-Error to Cognitive Attitudes of Leveling and Sharpening. *J. Pers.*, 1954, 22, 375-94.

41. ———, & KLEIN, G. S. Cognitive System-Principles of Leveling and Sharpening: Individual Differences in Assimilation Effects in Visual Time-Error. *J. Psychol.*, 1954, 37, 105-22.

42. ITTLESON, A. *Perception: A Transactional Approach.* New York: Doubleday, 1954.

43. JOHANSSON, G., DUREMAN, I., & SÄLDE, H.   Motion Perception and Personality. *Acta psychol.*, 1955, 11, 289-96.

44. KLEIN, G. S., & SCHLESINGER, H. J.   Where Is the Perceiver in Perceptual Theory? *J. Pers.*, 1949, 18, 32-47.

45. ————.   The Personal World Through Perception, in *Perception: An Approach to Personality*, eds. R. R. Blake and G. V. Ramsey. New York: Ronald Press, 1950. Pp. 328-55.

46. ————, & SCHLESINGER, H. J.   Perceptual Attitudes toward Instability. Prediction of Apparent Movement Experiences from Rorschach Responses. *J. Pers.*, 1951, 19, 289-302.

47. ————, SCHLESINGER, H. J., & MEISTER, D. E.   The Effects of Personal Values on Perception: An Experimental Critique. *Psychol. Rev.*, 1951, 58, 96-112.

48. ————, HOLZMAN, P. S., & LASKIN, D.   The Perception Project: Progress Report for 1953-54. *Bull. Menninger Clin.*, 1954, 18, 260-66.

49. ————.   Need and Regulation, in *Nebraska Symposium on Motivation*, ed. M. R. Jones. Lincoln: University of Nebraska Press, 1954, 224-74.

50. ————, & KRECH, D.   Cortical Conductivity in the Brain-Injured. *J. Pers.*, 1949, 18, 32-47.

51. KLUVER, H.   Mechanisms of Hallucinations, Chap. 10, in *Studies in Personality*. New York: McGraw-Hill, 1942.

52. KOHLER, I.   Rehabituation in Perception. Translated by H. Gleitman from I. Kohler: Ungerwohnung in Wahrnehmungsbereich. *Die Pyramide*, 1953, 5, 6, & 7.

53. ————.   *Über aufbau und Wardlungen der Wahrnehmungswelt.* Vienna: Rudolf M. Rohrer, 1951.

54. KÖHLER, W.   *Gestalt Psychology*. New York: Liveright, 1947.

55. KRECH, D.   Cognition and Motivation in Psychological Theory, in *Current Trends in Psychological Theory*, ed. W. Dennis. Pittsburgh: University of Pittsburgh Press, 1951, 135-36.

56. LAZARUS, R. S., & McCLEARY, R. A.   Autonomic Discrimination without Awareness: A Study of Subception. *Psychol. Rev.*, 1951, 58, 113-22.

57. LEVINE, R., CHEIN, I., & MURPHY, G.   The Relation of the Intensity of a Need to the Amount of Perceptual Distortion: A Preliminary Report. *J. Psychol.*, 1942, 13, 283-93.

58. LEWIN, K.   Behavior and Development as a Function of the Total Situation, in *Manual of Child Psychology* (2nd edition), ed. L. Carmichael. New York: Wiley, 1946.

59. LOWENSTEIN, O., & LOEWENFELD, I. E.   Disintegration of Central Autonomic Regulation during Fatigue and Its Reintegra-

tion by Psychosensory Controlling Mechanisms. I. Disintegration. II. Reintegration. *J. nerv. ment. Dis.*, 1952, 115, 1-21,
121-45.

60. LUCHINS, A. S.   An Evaluation of Some Current Criticisms of
Gestalt Psychological Work on Perception. *Psychol. Rev.*, 1951,
58, 69-95.

61. MALMO, R. B., SHAGASS, C., BELANGER, D. J., & SMITH, A.
Motor Control in Psychiatric Patients under Experimental
Stress. *J. abnorm. soc. Psychol.*, 1951, 46, 539-47.

62. McGINNIES, E.   Emotionality and Perceptual Defense. *Psychol.
Rev.*, 1949, 56, 244-51.

63. MICHOTTE, A.   *La perception de la causalité*. Louvain: L'In-
stitut Supérieur de Philosophie, 1946.

64. ———.   The Emotions Regarded as Functional Connections,
in *Feelings and Emotions*, ed. M. I. Reymert. New York:
McGraw-Hill, 1950, 114-26.

65. ———.   La perception de la fonction "outil." *Essays in Psychology Dedicated to David Katz*. Almquist: Uppsala, 1951,
193-213.

66. ———.   In *A History of Psychology in Autobiography*, eds.
E. G. Boring, H. S. Langfeld, N. Werner, & R. M. Yerkes.
Worcester: Clark University Press, 1952.

67. MURPHY, G.   *Personality: A Biosocial Approach to Origins
and Structure*. New York: Harper, 1947.

68. ———, & HOCHBERG, J.   Perceptual Development: Some
Tentative Hypotheses. *Psychol. Rev.*, 1951, 58, 332-49.

69. ———.   Human Potentialities. *J. soc. Issues*, 1953, No. 7
(supplement series).

70. NUTTIN, J.   *Psychoanalysis and Personality*. New York: Sheed
& Ward, 1953.

71. PIAGET, J.   *The Origins of Intelligence in Children*. Translated by Margaret Cook. New York: International Universities
Press, 1952.

72. POETZL, O.   Experimentell erregte Traumbilder in ihren Bezie-
hungen zum indirekten Sehen. *Z. f. Neurol. & Psychiatr.*, 1917,
37, 278-349.

73. POSTMAN, L., BRUNER, J. S., & McGINNIES, E.   Personal Values
as Selective Factors in Perception. *J. abnorm. soc. Psychol.*,
1948, 43, 142-54.

74. ———, & BRUNER, J. S.   Hypothesis and the Principle of
Closure: The Effect of Frequency and Recency. *J. Psychol.*,
1952, 33, 113-25.

75. PROSHANSKY, H., & MURPHY, G.   The Effects of Reward and Punishment on Perception. *J. Psychol.*, 1942, 13, 295-305.

76. RAPAPORT, D. *Emotions and Memory.* Baltimore: Williams & Wilkins, 1942. (2nd edition, New York: International Universities Press, 1950.)

77. ———. *Organization and Pathology of Thought.* New York: Columbia University Press, 1951.

78. ———, SCHAFER, R., & GILL, M. *Diagnostic Psychological Testing*, Vols. 1 and 2. Chicago: Year Book Publishers, 1945-46.

79. ———. Toward a Theory of Thinking, in *The Organization and Pathology of Thought*, ed. D. Rapaport. New York: Columbia University Press, 1951.

80. ———. Cognition, Cognitive Organization, and Consciousness. Symposium on Cognitive Theory, University of Colorado, Boulder, 1955.

81. REICH, W. *Character-Analysis.* New York: Orgone Press, 1949.

82. SCHAFER, R., & MURPHY, G. The Role of Autism in Figure-Ground Relationship. *J. exp. Psychol.*, 1943, 32, 335-43.

83. ———. *Psychoanalytic Interpretation in Rorschach Testing.* New York: Grune & Stratton, 1954.

84. SCHILDER, P. *Mind: Perception and Thought in Their Constructive Aspects.* New York: Columbia University Press, 1942.

85. SCHLESINGER, H. J. Cognitive Attitudes in Relation to Susceptibility to Interference. *J. Pers.*, 1954, 22, 354-74.

86. SHERIF, M. *The Psychology of Social Norms.* New York: Harper, 1936.

87. SINGER, J. L. Personal and Environmental Determinants of Perception in a Size Constancy Experiment. *J. exp. Psychol.*, 1952, 43, No. 6.

88. SMITH, B. Social Psychology. *Amer. Rev. Psychol.*, 1952, 3, 175-204.

89. SMITH, G. J. W. *Psychological Studies in Twin Differences* (with reference to after-image and eidetic phenomena as well as more general personality characteristics). London: Gleerup, 1949.

90. ———. *Interpretations of Behavior Sequences.* London: Gleerup, 1952.

91. STRAUS, E. W. The Upright Posture. *Psychiat. Quart.*, 1952, 26, 529-61.

92. TOLMAN, E. C. Performance Vectors and the Unconscious. *Proceedings 14th International Congress of Psychology*, Montreal, June, 1954, 31-40.

93. WALLACH, H. Some Considerations Concerning the Relation between Perception and Cognition. *J. Pers.*, 1949, 18, 6-13.

94. ———, & AUSTIN, P. Recognition and the Localization of Visual Traces. *Amer. J. Psychol.*, 1954, 67, 338-40.

95. ———, & GALLOWAY, A. Constancy of Colored Objects in Colored Illumination. *J. exp. Psychol.*, 1946, 36, 119-26.

96. ———, & O'CONNELL, D. N. The Kinetic Depth Effect. *J. exp. Psychol.*, 1953, 45, 205-17.

97. ———. Memory Effects in Perception. Symposium on Recent Trends in Perception Theory, 14th International Congress of Psychology, Montreal, June, 1954.

98. ———, O'CONNELL, D. W., & NEISSER, U. The Memory Effect of Visual Perception of Three-Dimensional Form. *J. exp. Psychol.*, 1953, 45, 360-68.

99. WAPNER, S., & WITKIN, H. A. The Role of Visual Factors in the Maintenance of Body Balance. *Amer. J. Psychol.*, 1950, 63, 385-408.

100. WERNER, H., & WAPNER, S. Sensory-Tonic Field Theory of Perception. *J. Pers.*, 1949, 18, 88-107.

101. ———, & WAPNER, S. Towards a General Theory of Perception. *Psychol. Rev.*, 1952, 59, 324-38.

102. WITKIN, H. A. Perception of Body Position and of the Position of the Visual Field. *Psychol. Monogr.*, 1949, 63, 1-46.

103. ———. *Personality through Perception*. New York: Harper, 1953.

104. WITTREICH, W. J. Aniseikonia and Distortion of the Self-Image. *Abs. Am. J. Psychol.*, 1943, 8, 357.

105. ———. A Preliminary Investigation into Certain Aspects of Perception, Including the Honi Phenomenon, in *Human Behavior from the Transactional Point of View*, ed. F. P. Kilpatrick. Hanover: Hanover Institute for Associated Research, 1951.

106. ———. The Honi Phenomenon: A Case of Selective Perceptual Distortion. *J. abnorm. soc. Psychol.*, 1952, 47, 705-12.

107. ———, & RADCLIFFE, K. B., JR. The Influence of Simulated Mutilation upon the Perception of the Human Figure. *Naval Medical Research Institute Research Report* (*Project NM 004 008.04.02*), 1954, 12, 241-50.

108. WOODWORTH, R. S. Reinforcement in Perception. *Amer. J. Psychol.*, 1947, 60, 119-22.

109. ZAPOROZHETS, A. V. Development of Voluntary Movements. Communication, 14th International Congress of Psychology, Montreal, June, 1954.

the cross-cultural approach

to the study of personality

MARGARET MEAD, Ph.D., D.Sc.

MARGARET MEAD, PH.D., D.SC.

Associate curator of ethnology of the American Museum of Natural History, and recognized throughout the nation as one of the foremost leaders in the field of cultural anthropology, Dr. Mead received her Ph.D. degree from Columbia University in 1929 and, since that time, has gained international fame for her contributions to the field of anthropology and associated areas, being especially recognized for her work in the development of the relationship between personality and culture. Dr. Mead has contributed to many professional journals, has submitted chapters to several of the best-known texts in the social sciences, and has written a number of books, among which are her well-known *Coming of Age in Samoa*, and *Growing Up in New Guinea*.

Emphasizing that the cross-cultural approach to the study of personality is based in the discipline of cultural anthropology, but that the approach also involves the extensive use of the theoretical findings and methodological devices of a number of other disciplines, Dr. Mead points out that the first contribution of a cross-cultural approach to understanding personality lies in helping the student to recognize those aspects of human personality which are given by our biological humanity and would be present in the absence of any learning, those which are to be attributed primarily to our common humanity, and those which may be related to the particular culture within which an individual has been reared or to which he has emigrated and adapted.

Dr. Mead sees human personality as taking different forms because of the threefold processes of rapid social change, urbanization, and drastic technological change. Present-day man is moving in an unpredictable world without guidelines, and an urgent task on which the various approaches to the study of personality might combine is the fuller understanding of the new atmosphere within which personality is formed.

INTRODUCTION

The cross-cultural approach to the study of personality is based in the discipline of cultural anthropology, but involves also the extensive use of the theoretical findings and methodological devices of a number of other disciplines—human, especially child, development, dynamic psychiatry, learning theory, clinical psychology, studies of constitution-temperament, Gestalt psychology, and most recently, ethology, cybernetics, and electrocephalography [35, 38, 72, 82, 85]. All of these fields deal with studies either of individuals or of selected groups of individuals within our own cultural limits, sometimes within the limits of one European tradition, perhaps including its transplanted forms—as Freudian psychology in Austria, Germany, Britain, France, and the United States, or Gestalt psychology in Germany and the United States, or electrocephalography in France, Germany, Britain, and the United States. As human beings are never found in a cultureless state—with the controversial exception of "wild children" occasionally reported to have been found, without traces of learned human behavior, wandering in forests—all studies of personality within our own cultural limits include, sometimes explicitly but more often only implicitly, a great many pieces of learned behavior as if they were universally human and, in many cases, even inevitable or given by our genes, instead of learned from other members of society. From such simple matters as feeling tone and the localization of blushing on the body or the type of gesture which indicates assent or dissent, through such matters as the localization of the future—in front of us rather than behind our backs—our own traditional way of thinking and feeling, with its attendant images, formulations, and patterns, is taken for granted.

The first contribution of a cross-cultural approach is therefore to assist other students of personality to unravel these various threads so that it will be possible to tell which aspects of human personality are given by our biological humanity and would be present in the absence of any learning—provided the infant could manage to survive; which are to be attributed primarily to our common humanity—for example, the significance of our long-dependent infancy—and so may also be expected to be represented in some form in every human culture; and which aspects of personality may be expected to be related to the particular culture within which an individual has been reared or to which he has emigrated and adapted. Such an analysis can never be an "either-or" matter. For example, the human capacity to count can be attributed to the complexity of the human nervous system; some counting, although it may be a sort of cluster estimation of the number of bananas on a bunch [37] rather than serial counting, may be found in every known culture. But the use made of counting—whether in a calendar, in reckoning history, or predicting the future, in the handling of economic events, or the development of ceremonial—and the units of counting—five based on one hand, ten on two hands, four on a four-footed animal [22], twenty on both hands and both feet, etc.—will vary from one historically given tradition to another. And we shall not expect to find either an excessive interest in accuracy which involves complex counting or the types of mysticism and mental aberration which attribute mystical importance to numbers in other than very rudimentary form except in those cultures in which the use of numbers has been historically developed. Whether we are considering the way in which human beings relate themselves to their own bodies, to other human beings, to the physical world around them, or to the universe, we find that each and all of these are culturally modified and patterned. It is from the culture within which one is reared that one learns how to organize one's emotions—whether, for example, love and hate are believed to be so compatible that a man will expect also to hate, or possibly even to kill, that which he loves most; or whether they are felt to be so incompatible that, in order to love, a child is taught that all hate, all resentment, or even doubt must be kept firmly out of mind. From the culture one learns which parent is to be treated with more respect, whether grandparents are to be respected as the parents of one's respected parent, or, for example, if it is possible for grandfather and grandchild to conspire together to laugh at the person who is the child of the one and the father of the other. In some cultures, a man will be applauded by certain classes or possibly even by the whole population if he permits human love to override all other considerations—the attitude taken by the American public to Edward VIII's abdication of the English throne—while in others, as in traditional Bali, for example, a high-caste would be expected to kill a wife who had dishonored him only formally and by accident, knowing she was innocent and yet unable to save her.

The child from its earliest days of life, and very probably prenatally also, begins to learn this culture pattern which is exemplified by every act of those with whom it comes in contact. Technically the word "culture," as used by anthropologists, is an abstraction which applies to the entire body of learned behavior, from the humblest and most private act—the way in which an ox is fed, a sheep sheared, a young girl taught to handle her body modestly when she bathes, which foods may be served together and to whom—up through the elaborations of art, literature, music, and philosophy of which each people have been so proud. Sometimes parts of these cultural patterns are shared by many peoples, as the Christian religion is shared by peoples in many parts of the world; and historical periods, used by historians, are a way of identifying the similarities between the cultures of peoples who share in the same traditions. Madariaga [49] pointed up the contrast between the tradition shared by several peoples at the same period and the continuities within a single national tradition through history, when he wrote his discussion of *Hamlet*, in which he claimed that as the sixteenth century had been the age of Spain, he as a twentieth-century Spaniard had better tools for interpreting Shakespeare than did the nineteenth-century English critics. Here Madariaga claims as an analytical tool his own embodiment

206   *Psychology of Personality*

of his own culture, linking him by cultural links with the sixteenth century throughout Europe. In technical anthropological work also the anthropologist learns to be conscious of his own culture, its special preoccupations and limitations; as he must always use it to interpret other cultures, in the end translating other languages into his own, empathizing the postures, gestures, and body images of others with his own body, grasping the patterned perceptions of others because he has himself learned to perceive the world around him in patterned ways. When cross-cultural analysis deals with relatively impersonal matters which do not implicate the emotional organization of the observer, it is possible to be "objective" in the sense that the anthropologist can learn to care about the analysis of basketry or pottery as such, without any particular commitment to coiled or twined basketry, hand-made or wheel-made pots. He can discipline himself to the rigorous scientific standards which make it possible for him to exclude "bias," his hope or fear that some piece of evidence will support one theory rather than another, and adopt an impersonally constructed and cross-culturally valid set of categories of measurement for purposes of comparison.

In the study of personality, however, the anthropologist has to use skills that are closer to those of the physician and the artist, and the test of the validity of his material has to be constructed so as to include the culturally patterned personality of the observer within the statement of his results. So we would not expect that an American, a Spanish, and a Chinese anthropologist, respectively, would ever perceive the same things, especially when statements of emphasis and value are involved, when all three look at the culture of the Zuni Indians [9, 46]. But we may reasonably expect that it will be possible to give an account of the culture of Zuni Indians which will be accurate enough to cross-check with developing psychological theories, provided we know the culture, the particular theoretical background, and the idiosyncratic personality structure of the observer. Redfield's study [78] and Lewis' recent restudy of a Mexican village [45] are a vivid demonstration of the differences in the accounts which will be given by two anthropologists, working with different sets of tools, at different periods of history, and with a different temperamental interest—Redfield in harmony, Lewis in dysfunction.

One of the troublesome problems in discussing the way in

which the personality of each child reared within a society and of each immigrant who becomes a permanent member of it reflects the whole culture of that society, is the question of what we mean by the word "whole." In a recent critique of the study of the personality of members of modern nations, Dr. John Bennett [11] claims that when one studies the *whole* culture, the endeavor becomes so broad as to be meaningless. Yet when the embryologist discusses the growth of some particular part of the embryo, he can only do this in relation to the whole, both in time and in space; each minute bit of tissue must be seen in spatial relationships to each other bit, and in relation to the stage which it has reached. When we speak of relating the personality of each individual born within a culture to the "whole culture" we are referring to such a patterned relationship. The peasant will not learn the habits of the nobleman, but the habits of each will include a recognition that they live in a society in which peasant and nobleman both participate. Even the practices of an alien group, such as gypsies, will include a recognition that they also live within a society in most of whose practices they do *not* share. Membership in a large nation or a small one is something that affects all members of that society in some way, as the Pole transmits pride, the Czech caution, and the Norwegian independence to the children who are reared to carry on the tradition. Such basic cultural values will appear in routine modern practices, as when Polish children are reported to return to a clinic line to receive a second injection as a way of demonstrating their courage.

So when we speak of the cross-cultural study of personality, the way in which the learning person learns one version of the whole culture—whether this be the version suited to a genius or an imbecile, to prince, peasant, merchant, skilled mechanic, conservative landowner, or radical labor leader, a priest in the Catholic Church, or the leader of a small Protestant sect, a modern obstetrician trained in a large medical school, or a local midwife skilled only in gathering herbs in the forest—nevertheless, all will share in one culture pattern and, if our observations are full enough on any one of them, we should be able to abstract the main pattern of the whole. So in a recent comparison [73] between test results given by French working-class children in southern France in 1948, and the hypotheses about French culture developed in ignorance of these unpublished and unanalyzed test results by anthropolo-

ists *[75]*, the test results are found to conform to the hypotheses
with a high degree of correspondence; but there are certain differences, which may plausibly be attributed to various characteristics
of French working-class culture—a lesser use of historically elaborated symbols, more recognition of possible paternal violence—
than was found in the performance of individuals of predominantly middle and upper class background.

It is for this reason that I prefer to reserve the term *culture* for
the entire learned behavior of a group, and not to speak of sub-
cultures, but rather of class, age, sex, occupational, or regional
versions of the whole culture. Our model for cultural learning is
the rearing of the child within the family, which itself is a member of a larger group, the band, the tribe, the region, the nation,
the members of which are bound together within a functioning
society. By studying, in great detail, the differences in personality
which so develop, in interaction between the individual and other
human beings who already share that culture, we can specify the
significant regularities in the learned aspects of the personality
structure which can be referred to the culture which these individuals share. These regularities can then be compared with the regularities in the cultural character of members of other cultures,
and related to other variables—for example, whether the society is
organized on a hierarchical or equalitarian basis, whether the religious system is monotheistic or has many gods, whether it is a society based primarily on status, like a Medieval European society,
or contract, like the Western European world since the industrial
revolutions, etc. Other types of variables may also be taken into
account, such as constitution, climate, nutrition, disease, population, variety of terrain which is included within the cultural
bounds, continuity or discontinuity of the land held, e.g., the
British Commonwealth as compared with the United States or the
USSR.

Psychologically, the ways in which children are reared, the order
and emphasis of bodily experience, the types of prescribed interaction with other human beings of different ages, both sexes, and
specified relationships, the types of sanctions used to induce or
prevent behavior, the implication of certain zones of the body and
of certain modes peculiar to certain zones—intake rather than introjection, passive-looking rather than active-grasping—all of these
may be related to the discovered regularities in the character of

one people, reared under one set of institutions, as compared with the cultural character of another people.

At this point it may be useful to introduce a few definitions. The term *culture* will be used to apply to the totality of learned behavior shared by any specified group who may, loosely, be called a society, that is, who feel themselves to belong to a social unit which has political meaning and continuity. So we may speak of the culture of Eastern European Jews, although they lived in several different national *states*, because they related themselves to each other in an Eastern European Jewry, which was felt by them to be a society, although not a state. The variations in a culture found in different classes or at different periods, I shall refer to as *versions* of that culture.

Where a group of peoples share cultures which show significant historical contacts and relationships, whether or not they are contiguous, this will be spoken of as a *culture area*. So Spain, Portugal, and Latin America form, from the point of view of a large number of shared traits, an Iberian culture area; but the countries of Latin America, Central America, and North America, from the point of view of a different set of traits, also share in a culture area of the Americas. If one wishes to compare Christian beliefs held by recent converts in the Malay jungle, Greenland Eskimos, Baptists in Tennessee, Chilean Catholics, and a Lebanese Christian sect, one may say they are all Christians, or they all share in certain aspects of historical Christianity, but they belong to different cultures, although the adjective "Christian" may be applied to each of them.

By *personality* I shall mean the total pattern of an individual's behavior which may be referred to his constitution-temperament, the culture or cultures within which he has been reared and has lived, and his particular series of life experiences.

In these pages the concern will be with the regularities of individual personality, acquired through learning in the culture or cultures in which a given individual has grown up, and these regularities we will refer to as *cultural character*. Thus a puny feeble-minded child with an IQ of 50, an eldest child of wealthy Protestant parents in the northeastern part of the United States, an average intelligent, exceedingly brawny only child born to Jewish artisans in the Midwest, and a brilliant, slender child, youngest of ten, born to a Catholic farmer in California—although they would differ in intelligence, in physique, in experience, in religion and in values—would all have American cultural characters. These characters would be representative of the versions of the national character current in their homes and communities, of the ways that individuals of their physiques, sensitivities, and degree of intelligence, with their particular set of experiences, e.g., of being eldest, only, or youngest, moving often, having been in a railway wreck, etc., were integrated into individual patterns.

By *constitution-temperament* I shall refer to those qualities of mind and body whose form is determined at birth, either by the genes or by the prenatal, intrauterine maternal environment. As interaction between hereditary components and the environment begins from the moment of conception and proceeds in a complex and decisive fashion during fetal life, it becomes a matter of convenience whether we introduce cultural factors into the analysis before or after birth. There is mounting evidence of the extent to which prenatal events may affect the developing child, derived from studies of the mother's health, detailed measurements of the relationship between maternal states and amount of fetal activity, the crucial effect of certain diseases occurring at certain points in development, and a recent new examination of maternal impressions [76]. Nevertheless, although all of these are functions of the society and its culture into which the individual is being born— as societal and cultural factors operate in choice of food, incidence of infectious diseases and type of maternal tension—how much such fetal responses may be described as regularly related to the culture is a matter for further examination.

There is suggestive evidence that among certain primitive peoples fetal movements are not as conspicuous—even when the mother wears no clothing—as they are among modern fully clothed women, but this again might be a function of nutrition rather than a more direct expression of cultural expectations. Alternatively, an example of the expression of cultural expectation would be a correspondence—not referable to nutrition—between the adult belief that the uterine infant "sleeps" quietly until the moment of delivery when the child turns over, and the absence of fetal movement [54]. Among the same people menstrual pain as such is not recognized, but is referred either to digestive disturbances or to the rheumatic response of the menstruating girl to sitting in a badly constructed seclusion hut, on damp, cold ground. If the women of a group do not expect or recognize fetal movement, and so refer what fetal movement occurs to some other internal factor, it may well be that an interaction system is lacking in which the mother, to use our idiom, "feels life" and responds with active delight to it, which in turn may affect the prenatal activity of the infant, and have repercussions in postnatal life. Or, to consider the possibilities from another point of view, the modern woman, whose activity is both more constricted and less integrated with her own body, may not provide to the uterine infant the situation within which to adjust unobtrusively. Sitting in a chair reading a newspaper may be not only a better circumstance in which to observe the uterine "kicking," but also a position in which the infant is more likely to kick.

A third type of interaction may occur if the mother carries her child in an unusual way, which may arouse anxiety in the members of her family and village, which may provoke them to take special measures to hasten delivery and to protect the mother from various sorts of further danger once she has been pronounced vulnerable, which may in turn affect her diet or her type of activity—as she may be forbidden to pursue her customary activities of food gathering, fishing, etc. A comparable type of situation occurs in our modern culture when, if a physician is alarmed over the ability of a mother to carry her baby to term, she is kept in bed for many months. Such a cultural premium on producing a particular infant, while it may occur in certain families or classes, or even for every woman in some societies, is by no means a universal attitude.

Just as the evidence is not yet sufficient to state that systematic relationships, having identifiable expression in the subsequent development of the child, can be pointed out between culture and prenatal life, so also the whole question of constitution-temperament is unresolved. By *constitution* I shall mean those properties of the individual physique for which the ground plan is given by the genes. To what extent prenatal environment, nutrition, and life experience in different cultures—including traumatization, and immunizing and strengthening experiences at different critical periods of growth—alter constitution in ways which are nonetheless predictable and remain systematically related to the hereditary form, we do not know.

Psychiatrists have contributed notable instances and systematic research on some of these interrelationships. In their study of obese children [13], Bruch and Touraine were able to isolate regularities in the attitudes and behavior of mothers of only sons brought to a clinic because of obesity. These mothers were first-generation immigrants to the United States; they had been personally ambitious and foiled in their ambitions, resented their children who were seen as a deprivation, lived in very constricted and neat quarters where the children were allowed little freedom to play or move about, and compensated for these negative attitudes by stuffing the children with food. Here original potentialities for obesity in the boys—for not all only sons of disappointed ambitious immigrant women become obese—special character twists in the mothers, combined with situation—being an only child, in a city of apartment dwellers with little space—had a result which would appear in any routine constitutional assay of the boys in question. In turn their obesity would set off another set of repercussions, in their inability to participate in sports, in the attitudes of school friends toward them, and these might again set off various counterresponses in the organisms of the boys. As most studies of constitution, in which any significant relationship has been found between "constitutional" type and personality factors, have included the proportions of the soft parts of the body to each other as an essential element in assessing constitution, such instances of interaction in a culturally specific environmental setting become very significant. It is probable that any advance in studies which attribute a determinative role in personality to "constitution" awaits more definitive studies of growth, so that the limits of this type of interaction between "native constitution" and culture and situation may be determined.

There are also various smaller problems, such as whether individuals with a recognizable constitution will make certain predictable selections within the culture in which they are reared, will make certain sorts of career choices, commit certain kinds of crimes, break down, if they do break down, in certain predictable ways. The bulk of work on constitution has been done on such selections *within* a culture. The further suggestion has been made that certain cultures can be shown to be related to the choices of certain constitutional types, on the assumption that not only is there a hereditary disposition to a certain type of body, which predisposes an individual to certain behaviors within a culture, but that also whole populations may be shown to tend toward one constitutional type, to which certain emphases in their history may be attributed. A study by Willemse [90] of constitution and delinquency in South Africa has been derided for coming to the conclusion that boys with a given type of extramuscular build are more given to committing crimes of violence in the country. Actually, within any given culture in which attitudes toward violence, self-control, bullying, self-defense, etc., are well defined, the possibility that boys with a certain constitution—itself partly the result of their interaction with the environment—may end up in certain occupations, commit certain types of crime, or marry certain types of woman, makes fewer unproved assumptions than would be necessary to show that men of the same build—if they occur in a position of numerical or political preponderance—will always shape the culture to certain emphases because constitution and other aspects of personality are *inalienably* associated.

In using the term *constitution-temperament*, I am emphasizing the present state of uncertainty about what aspects of inherited behavior are definitely associated with identifiable differences in body form—especially those differences which can be determined by measurement, fluoroscope and X-ray, and the various complex photographic methods for recording proportions. It is most unlikely that the term constitution, which applies to a patterning of indices, will ever correlate significantly with any list of single traits such as reaction time, which was the type of assumption made by Allport and Vernon [1] in their classic attempt to measure such relationships. Rather, the relationship will be one of matched patterns, in which the "temperament"—inborn tendency to certain types of behavior—and the "constitution"—inborn patterning of physical form—will be found to have very complex relationships to each other.

If it becomes possible to make a genuine cross-cultural study of this problem—as it would be if we studied identical twins reared apart in different cultures—we may begin to get some evidence on the degree of linkage that can be assigned to constitution-temperament. There is an alternative possibility that so-called temperamental factors may be functions of the innate structure of an individual's central nervous system and/or other systems of the body, particularly the endocrine system, and that the observed congruences between certain constitutions and certain temperaments may be themselves culturally produced. All individuals with certain types of congruence between constitution and temperament will then manifest the same type of personality within a given culture, and thus set a style to which individuals with the same constitution and different temperaments, or the same temperament and different constitutions, will attempt to conform; the first by alterations in occupational choice or interpersonal style, the second by introducing postural, sartorial, and cosmetic modifications of physical appearance. Examples of such modification of appearance can be seen in the efforts made by fat young men who aspire to being poets to look soulful, or delicate-boned, meagerly fleshed young men to look like go-getters by affecting padded shoulders, square-toed shoes, and a hearty handshake. It is also quite possible that whole cultures may have been dominated by some such combination of expected temperament and expected constitution, and that the various adjustments that individuals born without one or the other may have had to make, may have become themselves part of the culture pattern—as a type of nun's coif which holds the chin tightly in place, or the judge's costume which does not leave the massiveness of the head and the age of the judge to "nature" but supplies a wig. There are so many conspicuous congruences of this sort that explanations of periods, cultures, and even of culture areas in these terms, have been perennially tempting—of which Charles Morris' attempt to associate constitution and culture [77] is a recent conspicuous example.

Another approach to the identification of inborn capacities is by means of electrocephalographic studies of brain functioning in individuals whose behavior in certain other respects has been identified. Grey Walter at Bristol, England, has begun work on the way in which different brains respond to different types of stimuli, on the response to pattern, and the extent to which personality traits shown in the real world—such as ductility or originality—have analogues in the patterned interrelationships of brain waves [86, 88]. A related approach—although it begs the question of innateness with the use of the term *invariant*—is that of Chapple, Arensberg, Saslow, and others, in which the individual's style of response in verbal intercommunication can be recorded by a trained observer on an Interaction Chronograph, and the resulting patterns reduced to mathematical formulas [16, 17]. By this method the predicted behavior of an individual, who has been tested in an interview which is stylized in form and free in content, can be matched with the behavior of successful and unsuccessful individuals functioning in a specific role in the society—for example, as salesgirl at a bargain counter, information desk clerk, traffic policeman, member of a submarine crew—so that the characteristic, invariant behavior of the individual may be used to select for the particular job. Studies of individuals who occupy and so set the style of certain roles in society can be used to particularize further the job or role requirements in terms which can always be made to refer to measurable aspects of personality, such as the capacity to sustain non-response, the capacity to deal with interruption, etc.

Such role relationships will differ from one cultural setting to another. The various interlocking and compensatory devices—for example, by which men, from whom one type of response is demanded all day, select wives or find mistresses who reinforce, counterpoint, or neutralize these demands—may be found to have taken various characteristic cultural forms through time. For example, in eastern European Jewish culture the well-to-do man sought out a son-in-law of intellectual promise who also represented the type of intellectual which he himself would like to have been, and within this relationship of choice great intimacy was expected. This can be contrasted with cultures like that of England, where the eldest son was his landed father's heir regardless of temperamental compatibility, and a certain social distance was expected between a man and his heir, regardless of whether they were or were not father and son.

The word *character* is used here to refer to those aspects of the personality which an individual with a given constitution-temperament, exposed to an idiosyncratic series of situations within a given culture, develops in the course of his interaction with the other individuals who make up his environment. Each human individual develops a unique *character*, a large component of which can be referred to the culture within which he is reared—this shared set of regularities I shall call *cultural character*. It is important to recognize that *cultural character*, or the form of learned behavior embodied in the character structure of an individual which is found to be held in common by all members of a given culture is not a set of uniformities, but a set of regularities which may in fact appear to be extremely diverse or contradictory, but which nevertheless will be found upon examination to be systematically related to each other [57]. So the same culture may produce the spendthrift and the miser, the skeptic and the burner of books. The sensuous court and the ascetic monastery may occur together, while in another culture there may be such neglect of the flesh that neither sensuousness nor rigid asceticism is relevant to its emphases. These contrasts and emphases may be distributed in many different ways—by sex, class, region, age, occupation, sect, cult—but the cultural character of each individual reared within the culture, or immigrant to it, will reflect the whole. Any abstract statement about the cultural character of a people has to be reduced to such a bare skeleton statement that it will have less specific content than a similar abstract statement about a class or region, and less still than a comparable statement about a single individual. Where it takes many volumes to do justice to the biography of an El Greco or a Leonardo, a series of carefully worked-out abstract statements occupying a few dozen pages may deal comprehensively with the way in which El Greco or Leonardo shared the cultural character of all the other members of contemporary Seville or Florence.

In the same way the shared characteristics of the human face may be depicted by a simple diagrammatic representation which differentiates the human face, for example, from the face of an anthropoid ape or the face of a sheep; but to paint adequately the face of any given human being, which carries not only his particular anatomical and physiological make-up, but also his experience as a human being who has lived all his life in a given society in a particular way, requires many hours of laborious brushwork, and a much higher degree of skill.

Many students of the humanities are troubled when they approach statements about the *cultural character* of a modern nation, because they feel that the statement is so meager, so much less than that given by any one of the thousands of works of literature and art which form the content of the culture. On the other hand, psychologists are troubled for the opposite reason, because the statements still seem to them to be much broader and deeper than our present tools warrant, and they are wary of statements which cannot be made in terms of how many, how often, how long, etc. So the statement, "For the English people the King is a symbol of unchallengeable position without direct political authority, on the basis of which the image of the goodness of the father can be formed," seems to them to say too much, while to the student of the British monarchy it will seem to say too little. When Wolfenstein and Leites *[93]* make an intensive study of the plots of British movies over a specified period, and outline and count the ways in which the handling of the father's character supports this statement, the psychologists are a little better satisfied.

Cultural character may be studied in a cross section of the adults of a given society sharing a common culture. When this is done, the most useful descriptions which have been developed so far hark back to assumptions about the way in which this character was formed by the interaction between growing child and other human beings within the culturally regular child-rearing and educational systems. So it is possible to say of a people that they have a preference for symmetrical relationships between adults, and are stimulated to assertive behavior when an opponent is a little stronger, but inhibited in assertive behavior if an opponent is considerably weaker. This statement, which can be made both about English character and about American character, has then to be qualified further by the statement that the English act— when they see themselves as stronger than the opponent—by giving him a *handicap* of some sort which will bring him up to equality, while the Americans act—when they see themselves as weaker than the opponent—by treating the difference in strength between themselves and their opponents as justifying strong assertion on their part. These two related but contrasting forms of behavior in turn have to be referred to situations in the childhood experience of English and American children. In the former, the father acts and the child is a spectator, so that the father speaks from strength, modulating his strength to the child's weakness, and this becomes the child's model for action. In America the child speaks to his father's spectatorship, and his own acting from weakness to strength becomes his model for action. Without some such reference to childhood learning the statements about symmetrical behavior remain descriptive and static *[4, 7, 56, 61, 72]*.

Any statement about character implicates the way it was learned. So the actual study of how children learn particular cultures seems a better approach than the reconstruction of this learning from the verbalizations and behavior of adults. Furthermore, if the process of learning during growth is made a focus of study, all types of learning, however specialized they may be in different

234 Psychology of Personality

cultures, can be referred to the laws of biological development, with the recognition that there must be continual theoretical interaction between students of biological development and students of culture. Assumptions about prehension and the stage and form in which the use of the human thumb develops, based on American observations [25], must be corrected by studies of alternative forms of grasping, such as the emphasis on the ulnar side of the hand in Bali [71], and on the midfingers of the hand among the Manus.[1] But, however often statements about growth have to be modified and expanded to accommodate new information, all the present evidence suggests that human growth will be found to have certain regularities as the helpless newborn infant learns to co-ordinate his responses within his environment. Indeed it is to these common features of the growth process and the functioning of the human nervous system in particular that we owe the possibility of making statements about cultural character.

It may be useful to mention briefly some of the ways in which the term *cultural character* may *not* be used. It is not *modal* character, neither a real nor an artificial type summation of the most frequently occurring traits when such traits are measured on some standard scale. Thus a real *modal* character for the United States might be an individual who chewed gum. A statement about *cultural character*, which would include gum-chewing and non-gum-chewing Americans, would be a specification of the high degree of tolerance for material which is taken in—into the mouth, or through the eyes and ears into the mind, or through temporary hire or purchase into one's life—and as easily discarded. The actual statistics on how many people chew gum or tobacco and spit it out, or how many people are content to read billboards as they motor without finishing the written matter, is a statement of quite another order which requires highly sophisticated and expensive forms of market research. Still less is *cultural character* a way of stating *average* behavior. The average American can be derived from large numbers of statistics about income, type of clothing, car ownership, type of job, amount of education, preference for steak and ice cream. Similar averages also can be constructed by subjecting a proper sample to attitude scales; so the average American, in addition to having a specified amount of money, may also

[1] Unpublished field work, American Museum of Natural History Admiralty Island Expedition, 1953–54.

be specified in respect to such matters as belief in God and the future life, relative importance of hard work or luck in acquiring wealth, or a preference for magazines or books, and so on. This average American would be a construct from a large number of statistical samplings on separate items, assembled into a synthesis which need not be an exact description of any single American. Cultural character statements, on the other hand, if made correctly, should be statements about every single American, although any given individual may illustrate the particular statement by reacting negatively or positively, extensively or slightly, in the area being covered.

Nor is the statement of cultural character a statement of an *ideal* type. The ideal American not only does not chew gum, but also is not superficial; he retains the speed of intake which makes Americans so often content with the partial ingestion of gummy substances or billboard messages, but, by virtue of greater speed or longer hours or a lifelong habit of improving his reading speed, he takes in everything around him and makes good use of it. The gum-chewing complex includes the knowledge that such behavior is not ideal, and this very knowledge contributes to the relaxation, the permitted slouch, the covert disposal, and many other subsidiary aspects of the gum-chewing habit. Within the regularities of the cultural character, in a statement about any given version, the systematically related types of behavior which are distinctive of classes, ages, and occupations may be found implicitly or explicitly represented: as "girls sit like this, not like boys"; or in a society with changing manners, "girls sit like this now, just like boys"; "domestic servants go on the street in their working clothes, not like nurses and waitresses who wear their own clothes to work"; "kept women take the dog out in house coats, but respectable married women dress for the street." When a respectable married woman does go out on the street in a housecoat, her behavior will be articulately or inarticulately referred to this image of the woman in a housecoat, and possible embarrassment at meeting a friend, or refusal to smile at someone who smiles at her baby, may be the result. Contrasts between behaviors will in this way be related to the ideal, as both the kept woman and the respectable married woman have an ideal of marriage and respectability, which is part of their shared set of values, to which one conforms and the other does not.

It may also be useful to relate cultural character to cultural *stereotype*—either that held by a people of themselves or those held of them by others. The stereotype differs from the ideal in a number of ways, for not only does it include a set of negatively valued traits—so a people may see themselves as spendthrift or stingy, ill-mannered abroad, slow and out-of-date, etc.—but also it almost always contains an element of caricature. As the caricaturist selects only a few of a possible totality of traits to emphasize, and however faithful he may be in individual details, produces a caricature in his final drawing, so also the stereotype—in terms of the purposes for which it is developed, as vaudeville show, radio, TV, newspaper cartoon, etc.—is related to narrow and special emphases. Almost always the spectatorship of other tribes or nations is included in the stereotype which a people hold of themselves, thus introducing another set of distortions. So the stereotype of the Englishman contains French, German and Italian responses to the Englishman at a given period. The stereotype of the Scot has been developed on a Scot-English antithesis—the Scot is seen as thrifty, planful, extremely, and probably illegitimately, oversuccessful abroad, overweeningly proud of being a Scot instead of an Englishman, born with a divine right to perfectibility. This image is shared by Englishmen and Scots, and is constantly put in play between them. It is not a cross-culturally relevant statement about Scots, of an order which could be generalized so that every other people in the world could be described in comparable terms. Such a cross-cultural statement would have to be of the order, "The Scot has handled the problem of relative superiority and inferiority of his membership in a society shorn of former political autonomy (a problem which faces many peoples) by concentrating on his moral superiority to the group who are more numerous than he and politically dominant over him, and has disciplined this sense of moral superiority by describing it as a potentiality of being born a Scot which will only be attained by hard and unremitting attention and industry of a sort of which the contrasted, politically dominant, majority group are represented as being incapable."

A disciplined anthropological statement does not subsume the particular culture contrast problems of two or more nations or periods, but attempts to describe, in terms which are comparative within a known and recognized universe, such as "all European nations," "all industrialized nations," "all the cultures of the New World," "all Catholic nations," "all primitive people," always with the added provision—as far as we have reliable information on the subject. Thus in the stereotype of the American, which the American shares with other peoples with whom he comes in contact, the American chews gum. This for Americans is a negatively tinged trait, becoming violently negative when used by foreigners who are respected, as an expectation element in their treatment of Americans whose class or occupational status has always been defined partly by their *not* chewing gum. It may be positively tinged for the children, or the working classes, or the aboriginal peoples of other countries with whom Americans come in contact, and this positive tinge itself then becomes an intractable element in the relationship between Americans—who are a little ashamed of gum-chewing as an outstanding stereotyped trait—and a people who have such poor judgment as unambivalently to admire gum and gum-chewing.

At the same time the individual elements which occur in such limited culture-bound stereotypes are almost always accurate, in the sense that they represent regularities which are continually manifested in the interaction process out of which they have been distilled. The pride of the Spaniards, the brashness of the Americans, the assertiveness of the Jews, the stinginess of the Scots, the sensuous emphasis on food and drink of the French, the pedantry of the Germans, the arrogant assumption of strength of the Englishmen, are all—within given contexts—traits which strike other people who encounter them, in their contacts with these peoples, and their appreciation of others' recognition of these traits becomes part of their own self-image. So when Americans go out of their way to observe the manners or learn the language of a foreign custom, they do this against a background of knowledge of the stereotype that "most Americans are brash, rude, inconsiderate of other people abroad in their insistence on other people speaking English and giving them fried eggs for breakfast." Or, when a Jew is very quiet and unassertive, as many Jews are, his unassertiveness contains in it the knowledge that most people, usually including himself, think that Jews are assertive.

While the science of national character has developed as a special division of culture and personality studies, there has been a continuous attack on its premises as being identical to a reaffirmation of negative stereotypes which social psychologists have devoted considerable time to exploding. Much of this difficulty can be cleared up if it is realized that the elements which make up such stereotypes are accurate but incomplete descriptions of national character in particular *cross-cultural* contexts. When, for example, a Netherlander writes a book called *The English: Are They Human?* [79], what he says about the English will contain elements of accurate observation, to the extent that it is the way the English strike the Netherlands observer; and these elements will also be regularly related to actual traits of English character; but the selection, arrangement, and emphasis will be particularly related to Netherlands culture. However much the trained anthropologist may learn to allow for his own cultural position as an ingredient in his analysis, the only certain way to offset it is to have observations made from the same theoretical position by members of several cultures, including representatives of the culture which is being studied [72]. If an element like extreme carefulness with material things—characteristic of traditional New England—is examined from the point of view of members of other parts of the United States who consider this behavior as stinginess, from that of the Italian peasant who regards it as intelligible but relates it to a quite different type of traditional poverty and a different style of saving, from that of a people who have no use for saving at all, and from the standpoint of the New Englander who thinks his behavior is well described by such words as "thrift" and "frugality"; then the emphases due to the cultural positions of the various observers will be compensated for, and a final statement will emerge which is more accurate, because it has been mediated by the disciplined cultural awareness of each observer, and more objective, because these cultural positions have been used. The kind of "objectivity" which attempts, without this process, to develop cross-culturally valid categories of analysis of members of different cultures has so far been proved to be so loaded with unanalyzed hidden cultural bias as to be unusable.[2]

2 The closest attempt to produce a "culture free" test that I know of is Kilton Stewart's Ring Puzzle Test, in which mazes, patterns of holes in a graded series of metal plates, can be solved by fitting a broken ring in and out of them. This test has met one of the very difficult problems in cross-cultural testing, that of motivation; for many peoples have been found who are uninterested in speed, in accuracy or competitive success [42]. The Stewart Ring Puzzle Test is to a high degree self-motivating; the ring is caught (trapped)

METHODS OF CROSS-CULTURAL ANALYSIS

We may now turn to the question of what sorts of models or methods of cross-cultural analysis make it feasible to relate descriptions of members of one culture to descriptions of members of another, and so to discuss the cultural component in the personality of any individual, or the cultural regularities in the personalities of all the individuals in a given culture, or, finally, the cultural contribution in any given culture to personality as a whole.

Let us take, for example, four women who present themselves to agencies designed to help immigrants to the United States bring over relatives. Although all four are members of large living families containing both parents and siblings of both sexes, one woman is interested in bringing over her father, but shows less interest in her mother's fate; the second emphasizes a younger sister; the third, her mother; the fourth, both parents. If these four women come from the same European culture, their choices may be assumed, until the matter is explored further, to be related to their personal relationships to these particular members of their respective families, and to be expressive of their own personality organization in such matters as relative dependence or independence of parents, development of types of responsibility, solution of the Oedipal conflict in childhood, and so on. But if these four women come from different cultures, then it is necessary to know something of the pattern of parent-child and of sibling relationships in each; e.g., the strength of the cross-sex tie in Poland, of the sibling tie among the Czechs, of the tie between women of the same family in Italy, and the emphasis upon "the parents" in

---

somewhere in the metal sheet, and the individual becomes committed to getting it out at the other end. So far this test has stood up in cross-cultural situations with one recent contretemps. The ring and plate are supposed to be strong enough so that the subject must follow the exact path and cannot twist either one out of shape; but in recent experimentation with adolescents on Monserrat in the British West Indies, Dr. Rhoda Métraux found that the people exerted such force that the rings were bent, and that here a more fragile type of ring, which would involve protectiveness of the material, rather than a strong but not quite invincible metal, was what was needed. Solving a maze, although an excellent learning test in many ways, and one that has been used extensively in animal experiments, thus, even in this simple form, has cross-cultural complications. When we come to such complicated problems as the patterning of aggression, the difficulty of cross-cultural measures is even greater [3].

Germany. Not until these cultural regularities are allowed for—which have become part of the personalities of these four women —can one draw any conclusions about an individually significant element in the choice made by each. Only after it is ascertained whether a petitioner is responding in the way which is culturally expectable for a member of her sex, age, class, and religion, or deviantly—as, for example, if a Czech shows no interest in sibling ties, or an Italian woman rejects relatives of her own sex—can the importance for the particular personality of this individual be properly evaluated. A Spaniard who is a Roman Catholic, an Italian who drinks wine with his meals, a middle-class American who takes a bath every day—these are the behaviors which, within a culture, we classify as "normal," "natural," i.e., culturally expectable, and which, with sufficient knowledge, we can treat in the same way across cultural lines.

But when we turn from such externals as membership in a historical church or deeply established dietetic or hygienic habits, to the question of character—of the way in which love and hate, fear, shame, doubt, and responsibility are patterned—we need more precise methods of comparison. In making these comparisons, we make two assumptions:

1. There is a psychic unity of mankind—that so far no evidence has been adduced to show any differences in the comparative ability of members of different "races" to learn and to function effectively in any culture where they are not treated with selective positive or negative discrimination because of physical distinguishability from other members of the society. This includes the assumption that in groups of equal size the range of variation will be—for purposes of cultural learning, functioning, and creating— the same; each group will contain—if large enough—approximately the same proportions of gifted and ungifted, brilliant and plodding, excitable and unexcitable individuals. To the extent that the brain and the whole central nervous system and the endocrine glands are involved in such human learning, functioning, and creating, these are also assumed to be comparable in the aspects which are relevant. (Brain size, for example, does vary, but has not been shown to be relevantly related to mental functioning.) Differential susceptibility to disease, for example, which is often found between races—if not referable to differences in experience

and so in immunization—might nevertheless be practically significant as an aspect of survival in a particular environment, but would
not affect the assumption of the psychic unity of mankind. A
Polynesian is believed to have a lower resistance to malaria than
a Melanesian, and his chances of survival in a malaria-infested
environment are poorer; but if he does survive, he will, as far as
we know now, develop and function in the same way as a member
of a different race with a greater immunity. In fact, this lack of
resistance to malaria, which can be assumed to be a function of
the stock to which the Polynesian belongs, may unfit him less for
functioning in an alien environment than the learned intolerance
of a strange environment of a Balinese.

2. Human growth follows the same general course in every
society. It is assumed that the individual develops a character *as
he grows*, that his maturational sequence determines the form of
his responses to experience, and that the incidence of the same
experience at different stages of growth will have different char-
acterological consequences. So, being cup-fed from birth, and
being weaned at one year, or at three years, are assumed to be
different experiences, and this difference can be regularly related
to the stage of growth. The newborn will never have experienced
the breast at all; the year-old child is robbed of a satisfaction of
which it has a highly integrated experience combined with an
ability to recognize mother, breasts, and the relationship between
these and hunger; the three-year-old, although having had a longer
habituation to the expected gratification, is also able to seek other
gratifications more easily—he can run about freely, may be part of
a play group, and so on. Studies of growth have mainly been
made on European and American children, but so far the only
comparative work done has confirmed the broad outlines [71].

We can then combine a general growth model [26] which shows
the different types of maturational sequences, the expected limits
for the development of any such ability as walking or talking, with
the model derived from psychoanalytic theory—based on both
adult and child analysis—which associates each stage of growth
with certain zonal-modal primacies and emphases and with certain
tasks for the developing individuality [19]. From these sources we
get a model which specifies the infant's degree of dependence,
motility, high variability at birth—a variability higher than that

of any other living creature in range of response style, etc.—the primacy of the oral *zone*, the mouth; of a *mode*, that of inception; a primary *task*, the establishment of trust; and the later expression of the conflicts of this early period in a sense of *sin*. This period of oral inception—if we use this maturational model—is followed by a period where the emphasis is on the attainment of motor control—of the sphinctors and the musculature—in which the anal zone is primary, the modes of holding and releasing are emphasized, and the task is to attain autonomy. Successes and failures in accomplishing the tasks appropriate to this stage of maturation are accompanied by pride and shame, both of which have bodily counterparts in a response of the vascular system by flushing (with pride) or blushing (with shame), and characteristic postural responses affecting the posture of the head and neck muscles.

If instead of following a maturational sequence, we wish to follow development in a *zone*, then the later developments of oral behavior—use of language, speech making, erotic involvement of the lips—may be pursued as they are elaborated either in a whole culture or in an individual version of that culture. Or, instead, we may follow out a *mode*, and consider inception as it occurs—in the woman as a prelude to conception, in all listening, in passive looking and taking in the world, etc.

The implications of a stage of maturation, of a zone, of a mode, of a life task and of the emotions associated with each life task, may then be followed out as different cultures have elaborated or neglected them *[72]*. So it may be shown that some cultures treat the infant from birth as if it were already capable of autonomy and self-control, muting as much as possible the recognition of a period when such autonomy is impossible. Other societies may extend this period far beyond the limits which would seem to be given in biological maturation—carrying and breast-feeding children until they are four or five years old, or selecting such treatment for youngest, only, or favorite children and so providing them with a contrasting experience which differentiates them from other children in the society. A stage may be anticipated—holding a child upright before it can stand, walking it with adequate support long before it can walk, addressing it as if it were capable of understanding and responding; or a stage may be prolonged—carrying a child that is able to walk, feeding a child after it can control its hands, dressing it after it is able to cope with buttons and buckles. One stage may be selected for emphasis and most learning experiences may be crowded into it—so respect for property may be taught so thoroughly between the time a child can reach and can walk that nothing has to be done about it again. Or, in contrast, respect for different sorts of property may be taught in different ways over many years—the infant may be taught to respect the eyes of another; the two-year-old, the body; the three-year-old, possessions; the four-year-old, the name; the ten-year-old, the reputation; and so on.

In the same way, we can explore and specify the way different cultures emphasize a particular zone: contrasting one culture which places predominant emphasis on the importance of eating, speech making, poetry, all oral arts; with another which may emphasize a different zone, for example, care of property, exchange, thrift, gift exchange, exercises involving control skills, and so on.

Alternatively, we may explore in the same way the emphasis on a mode. So the Arapesh [54, 62] primarily emphasize the mode of passive intake—accepting objects of manufacture from others, attempting little themselves, hunting by "looking until game appears," with the initiative attributed to the game, or waiting in a village until a dream tells them that a quarry has fallen into a trap. In contrast, the Manus [53, 62] emphasized activity—forcing other peoples to give them the manufactured objects which they wanted, by providing goods (fish) and services (transportation) which the other people could not refuse, and by acting, although they themselves owned no property except that which they could make from objects traded from others, as if it were they who took hold of and grasped any situation.

If the ego tasks identified for each maturational stage are examined in the same way, then it is possible to find cultures which rely—as a major sanction for evoking acceptable social behavior—on a sense of sin which has been developed in early infancy during the infant's stormy rages, with their assumed concomitance of destructive annihilating fantasies about parents and nurses [30, 68]. Other cultures, instead, tend to use primarily the tasks of the second period—that in which autonomy is attained—and bring up children to fear the censure of those who are despised, the extreme position from which shame develops, or, at the other end of a scale which is equally appropriate for this age, to seek the praise of those whose opinion is respected, that is, to learn to act in order to be proud of having so acted [64].

The human growth-modal-zonal model can be used cross-culturally primarily by extension and elaboration. For example, Balinese flexibility can be seen as an elaboration of a type of fetal and neonatal flexibility which in most cultures is ignored and tends to disappear [71]; or the extreme visual responsiveness of the Chinese can be related to the way in which Chinese parents and nurses distract the child from handling nearby objects by shifting its attention to looking at distant or unreachable objects [15]. Using this model, it is assumed that, because the model deals with the completely biologically given, every culture can be stated within it, even though the most formal presentations have been based on the trunk and major zones, with arms, legs, and skin treated as extensions of the zones. This particular emphasis is probably culturally determined, but it takes very little rearrangement of the diagrammatic representation of the model—and none of the basic theory—to include the limbs and skin as well as the head and trunk, and so produce a model on which every human society can be fitted.

The emphasis here has been principally upon the model provided by psychoanalytic insights into the importance of modes and zones, which has been majorly developed by Erik Erikson [19] on the basis of both clinical and cultural materials, and upon the combination of this model with developmental psychology on the one hand, and with cross-cultural studies of different types of sanctions—sin, shame and pride, and guilt—on the other [64]. In recent publications, Erikson [20] has expanded this conceptual scheme with further emphasis on the life tasks appropriate to each stage of development through puberty; and in recent anthropological work on contemporary cultures it has been found useful to view individual cultures as relying more or less heavily on the learning appropriate to a given stage [72].

There is, however, another way of using psychoanalytic insights, by focusing primarily upon the defenses and counterdefenses as they become standardized in different cultures. So we find cultures which emphasize one of the three types of fear outlined by Anna Freud in *The Ego and the Mechanisms of Defense* [24]—fear of own impulses, of which Britain [32] and Arapesh [54, 63] are good examples; fear of the punitive effects of one's own conscience, of which Germany *[74]*, Japan *[28, 10]*, and Old Manus *[52, 21]* are good examples; and fear of external threat and danger, of which the Iatmul of the Sepik River *[2, 55, 62]* are an example, and which is a type which is coming to be increasingly common in America *[19, 60, 62, 81, 93]*—or, finally, a fourth type, exemplified by the Balinese, in which fear is communicated directly from adult to infant by bodily contact *[8, 64]* without involvement of more complex learned reactions to the standards of the society. When these various types of fear and the defenses which the individual learns to erect against them are analyzed—especially with reference to the situations the study of which has been found to be rewarding, such as weaning, toilet training, sibling rivalry, and the Oedipal conflict with the parents—cultures are found to have very different and highly characteristic types of defenses and counterdefenses. The work of Martha Wolfenstein and Nathan Leites *[44, 91, 92, 93]* has made extensive use of this method of analysis, as has that of Geoffrey Gorer *[28, 29, 31, 33]*. So, in an analysis of films regarded as fantasy solutions of such conflicts, Wolfenstein and Leites have shown *[93, 94]* how Americans handle their inadmissible impulses by projecting them on external figures who can be overcome after they have attempted to frame the hero by making false accusations against him. In contrast, in English films belief in the ability to control one's own impulses is exemplified in the theme of the good father who does control his impulses and who provides support for women and children in controlling theirs. In French films, distantiation and recognition of the inevitability of disappointment in impulse gratification are stressed in the tragic results of fathers seeking inappropriate gratification for themselves.

A third model is provided by the structure of the human family *[7, 59, 62, 72]*, by the circumstances of differences in age, sex, and size in the family, and by the universality of the family in all known human cultures. Here the basic given positions are that each child is of the same or opposite sex, same or different constitution-temperament, and younger and smaller than the parent; and that siblings fall into this same pattern—same or opposite sex, younger or older, bigger or smaller, same or different constitution-temperament from each other child. Within this universal family situation, there are other biological universals. The child is breast-fed, involving a complementary relationship to its mother—the mother gives, the child takes, the child's mouth is a receiving vessel, the mother's breast an actively dispensing one. Even where this pattern is modified—as among the Manus by the mother handling her breast as if it were a piece of plumbing through which an exchange with the child takes place, thus minimizing the complementary pattern, or when a bottle is substituted which the child can hold in its own hands—the essential complementary character remains.

The succoring, "giving" behavior of the mother is met by behavior of a different, complementary order—the depending, "taking in" behavior of the child. This essentially complementary aspect of feeding and being fed pervades the whole of the relationship of the infant and small child to members of the family, large and small, as it is carried, kept warm, clothed, bathed, comforted, explained to, and taught by those who are responsible for initiating and carrying out these activities. A large number of modifications can be introduced. So the mother may see herself as feeding the baby when her breasts irk her by their fullness, or as feeding the baby when it cries, or as feeding the baby when it is time to feed the baby (thus attempting to negate the complementary nature of the relationship as a direct interpersonal act by letting a schedule or clock intervene); or she may see the baby as compelling her to feed it, transforming the reality situation in which she has the milk, the mobility, and the maturity to control the situation into one in which control is attributed to the child—as among the Iatmul [62].

In the same way, the one who is responsible for carrying the child may treat it as an appendage and ignore the child which, safe in shawl or blanket or backboard, simply adjusts as best it can; or may provide the child with a stance from which it can maintain a life which is relatively independent of the activities of the carrying person; or may subordinate other activities to the task of carrying—often signaled by carrying a baby in the right arm, making what is a minor enterprise in many societies into a major one; or may even transform the whole carrying activity into one in which the baby is seen as a passenger in a compliant human vehicle which takes it where it wants to go [67]. However, whether the culturally stylized aspects of the carrying relationship follow the lines which are biologically given by the size and strength and relative maturity of adult and infant, or whether the most elaborate social devices of denial or reversal are developed, every child-rearing system in the world has to deal with the inability of the infant to transport itself and with the need for some form of transportation, in which complementary aspects are always present. A people may develop folk tales about giant babies born with iron teeth, or about infants who, after thirty years of gestation, are born so strong that the parents are unable to sever the umbilical cord and the giant infant has to do it himself—but the biological facts remain firm and incontrovertible, providing a basis on which variations may be related again to the common conditions of our humanity.

By classifying the relevant types of behavior which occur within this family model—complementary when behavior A is responded to with behavior B, symmetrical when A evokes A, reciprocal when through some device it is possible to alternate between A to B and B to A—it is possible to examine any pattern of parent-child interaction, and to arrange these behaviors in a series. So in the English upper- and middle-class system, aspects of the system can be represented by the diagrammatic statement:

Parents	Children
(Succorance	(Dependence
(	(
(Dominance	(Submission
(	(
(Exhibitionism	(Spectatorship

In contrast, the American middle-class pattern would be stated:

Parents	Children
(Succorance	(Dependence
(	(
(Dominance (slight)	(Submission (slight)
(	(
(Spectatorship	(Exhibitionism

It can then be shown that the behaviors at each end of the series of pairs are linked together, so that in one culture dominance is associated with exhibitionism, while in the other dominance is associated with spectatorship. This method of end-linkage analysis, developed by Gregory Bateson [2, 4, 7, 72], provides a flexible model which makes it possible to fit the peculiar aspects of any culture together with the constants in the family pattern which occur in every culture.

This model is less implicated by the biologically given than is Erikson's zonal-modal one, because it recognizes that, while all parents must come to terms with the weakness, immaturity, and dependency of the human infant, they may couch these terms in many different ways in different cultures. For example, the strength of paternal authority can be so great that whether father is tall or short is irrelevant; or the relative meagerness or bountifulness of a woman's supply of milk may lack significance because the baby is fed cow's milk ordered from the dairy. If a mother wishes to act as if the cry of a three-weeks-old baby forced her to stand to attention as if she were a private responding to the voice of a drill sergeant, where the penalty for disobedience is court martial, she can do so; when she does, the baby learns something which, although originally incompatible with its biologically given position of relative weakness, can in time become part of a system which will make it possible for a person who speaks from weakness to speak with vociferous expectation of accession to his demands.

End-linkage analysis permits the incorporation of degrees of historically variant behavior into what is still essentially a universal, biologically based model. So for the Balinese, end-linkage analysis substitutes for the variables *dominance* and *submission*—essential for the analysis of European and American cultures—the variables *elevation* and *support*. And parents, subjects (of sovereigns), and worshipers (of gods) provide support to infants, rajahs, and gods [7, 8]. Or among the East European Jews, it is important to distinguish the extent to which parents, men of standing, the rich, the learned, and the well provide benefice to children, the obscure, the poor, the ignorant, and the sick, who respond with deference [39, 40]. Or in Manus, parents, dependents, and "wards" underwrote the activities of children, entrepreneurs, and Ghostly Guardians, who responded with a heightened activity level—so that the acts of a member of one group promoted the strength of the other. A man fished to demonstrate his Sir

Ghost's approval of him, and in turn his Sir Ghost prospered him because he had fished.[3]

Small differences in the patterning of responses between parents and children and their correlative behaviors—as between teacher and pupil, employer and employee, gods and worshipers, sovereigns and subjects, audience and performer—may be delineated in this way. So, for example, a crucial difference between the behavior of Americans and Englishmen—the former acting from weakness, and exhibitionistic when weak, or weak when exhibitionistic, the latter acting from strength, and joining exhibitionism and strength together—can be referred to the difference in the way, in the two cultures, in which parents—especially fathers—respond to their children's lesser strength. In Britain the father provides the model for *later* behavior; in America he is the audience for *present* behavior while the child is still relatively small and weak [61].

A fourth model, which makes it possible to compare the most diverse cultural developments through the mediation of a biological model, is provided by Edith Cobb's analysis of cosmic sense [18]. This formulation stresses that just as in breathing and metabolism there is a continual interchange between the organism and the environment of chemical elements necessary to life, so between the organism and the environment as perceived by the senses there is an analogous relationship. The perception of the outer world must be assimilated and used, and products of the assimilation and use must be returned again to the environment. The culture provides the growing child with a medium within which this perceptual interchange takes place, as objects are perceived, named, sung about, played with, drawn, used figuratively in poetry and oratory, dreamt about, and are otherwise involved in culturally patterned activities which provide the child, and later the adult, with ways of perceiving the universe of which he is a part. Play, art, religion, and philosophy [48] may all be cross-related through this scheme. When cultures are analyzed in these terms we find that, within any culture, the growing child—and so the adult personality—may be provided with the richest or the most meager materials for its imagination to play upon, and various sorts of disorders of personality and unexpected appearances of genius [43] may be related to an

[3] Unpublished field work, American Museum of Natural History Admiralty Island Expedition, 1953–54.

imbalance between the perceptual capacities of an individual for this cosmic interchange and the materials on which his culture permits him to feed [66]. Where the culture is relatively homogeneous, and class, or wealth, or caste, or rank differences are not great, any gifted child is able to draw on all the available resources and the chances of his imaginative hunger and thirst exceeding his possible fare are much less than in societies where, because of great discrepancies in these factors, children may encounter a stimulation —as in hearing music which no one around them is able to reproduce—which produces extraordinary manifestations, in genius or in crime, as the case may be. At present we know of no culture which does not have some elaborated system of relationship between man and the universe, although there are a few partially reported tribes of South America of whom this can only barely be said [37]. To date, however, wherever full accounts have been collected by recorders who have understood the language—including the possibilities of languages of plastic and graphic representation and of posture and gesture as well as of words—every known people has been found to deal, and that with considerable elaboration, with the natural world around them; naming parts of it, peopling it with spirits or forces of various sorts, incorporating parts of it in dance or song, enriching their language with words derived from the movement of water, the strength of the wind, the growth of plants, the movements of the sun and moon. By relating these contrasting cultural forms to a common biological need for perceptual balance of the organism within the environment, only less essential to human beings than breathing and taking nourishment, these very complex activities—within which those faculties which we are accustomed to think of as "the highest" manifest themselves— can be brought within the same scheme which seeks to explain the cultural component in personality by the way in which human beings with common biological capacities perceptually relate themselves, through historically developed cultures, to their own bodies, to other human beings, and to the universe [12].

So far I have dealt only with ways of analyzing and cross-comparing in which regularities in the character structure of all the personalities who develop within a given culture may be systematically shown to be related to a universal biological base which each culture has elaborated. All Americans, for example, will show in some way our basic attitude toward strength and weakness, which associates action and initiative with the weaker position, toward autonomy and control, toward a God who helps those who help themselves, and toward a physical world, once found empty and then patterned by man *[29, 60]*. All English people will show in some way a basic attitude toward strength and weakness, which associates action and initiative with strength, toward a God whose gentleness includes a willingness to be a junior partner in men's affairs, and toward a physical world which embodies the previous efforts of man to tame and till, shape and model the world around him *[58]*.

Still another useful model can be found in learning theory, where by using types of learning which have been isolated in experiments on animals—especially psychological experiments on rats —formal types of learning may be isolated, such as rote learning, instrumental avoidance, etc., and cultural procedures may be analyzed to show varying combinations and emphases. In contradiction to the other models which have been discussed—Erikson's zonal-modal-task model, defenses and counterdefenses, end-linkage and cosmic-sense—which are all based on living human materials, the model based on learning theory *[5]* is more formal, and it is necessary to introduce a large number of operations before the experimental behavior of rats in an unnatural situation can be compared to the behavior of human beings in a "natural" situation. Some attempts to do this have been unfortunate—as, for instance, the attempt to describe the life situations which a child encounters as a maze; this is strictly inapplicable except in those instances where psychologists or educators wish to arrogate to themselves the Godlike position of the animal experimenter who constructs the maze to give information about his hypothesis, but where the experimenter is only related to the rats themselves in that he must take into account their limitations as experimental animals.

In this respect, learning theory is only a little less unsatisfactory than cybernetic models, in which machines, constructed to perform humanly desirable operations by nonhuman methods, are used not only as analogies *[82]*, which is helpful, but also with attempts at point-for-point reference to human behavior *[36]*, which is not. The anthropologist, like the clinician, has repeatedly found that, useful as these animal and mechanical models are as devices for sharpening formulations, in the end it is more satisfactory to rely on the "living model"—the human being, human family, or human group studied in its natural habitat, where the unanalyzed variables are not omitted because the student has not yet isolated them, but are rather carried along with the data, embedded in it, correcting for many possible errors, either at the time, or at later periods when the data are reworked by improved hypotheses [80, 69].

CULTURAL INFLUENCES UPON INDIVIDUALITY

So far we have dealt with ways in which the cultural regularities in the character structure of all the individuals sharing a single culture may be identified and integrated theoretically with our knowledge of human biological and psychological mechanisms. Our ability to do this is increased by each advance in knowledge of regularities in human growth and constitution, in the psychological processes such as self-identification, defense and counterdefense against unbearable or socially disapproved impulses, in the limitations on human endurance of strain, and in the potentialities, many of them as yet untapped, which cultural and individual elaborations of the cosmic sense imply. Reciprocally, each new culture which is well studied from an ethnopsychological point of view widens our ability to distinguish between the biologically given and the culturally created.

We may now turn to another aspect of the problem: the extent to which individuality is dependent upon the form of the culture which an individual embodies. A failure to distinguish clearly this relationship has resulted in enormous confusions between psychologists and psychiatrists on the one hand, and anthropologists on the other. Anthropologists, working within their special responsibilities and competences, have described—for any given culture—the regularities in dress, manner, speech, ethical beliefs and religious practices which characterize an entire population. They have, until very recently, lacked any special tools for the delineation of individual intrapsychic differences, although they have seldom omitted considerable mention of the differences between individuals. As modern personality and culture work has developed, it has been a recognized task of the anthropologist to describe differences among individuals as a function of the culture within which they have been reared. So Ruth Benedict [9] and Ruth Bunzel [14] worked on the problem of the individual in Zuni, on the extent to which extra intensity was denigrated and punished, and the implications for the individual of such punishment. In Samoa [51] it was found that the mechanisms of child rearing, in which children were part of large households without strongly developed ties to their individual parents, seemed—when checked against the unusual household in which there were only parents and children—to be important in developing a type of character structure in which individuals were less highly differentiated than under contrasting conditions which permitted stronger parental identification. Samoan conditions contrasted with the Manus [52], where small children were found to identify heavily with their fathers, and a correspondence was found between the status and resulting self-assurance of the father at the time his son was five to eight years old and the ultimate style of the son's interpersonal behavior as dominant, neutral, or retiring. Kardiner and Linton [41], on the basis of Linton's ethnological field material, attempted to delineate what might be the relationship between the attributed personalities of eldest children among the Tanala and the personalities of non-inheriting younger sons. Geoffrey Gorer, in his study on the Lepchas [27], which included actual work with and knowledge of a large number of individuals, traced complicated relationships between family situation and personality expression. In more recent work in contemporary cultures, the way in which the large expansive pre-Revolutionary upper-class Russian family or self-contained Russian village gave free play to a large number of contrasting types, among whom the child was free to choose and whose presence gave extra definition to the type chosen, can be contrasted with post-Revolutionary cultural practice in the Soviet Union, in which the official attempt is to align every institution of child rearing back of one character type —optimistic, cheerful, persistent, realistic, unflinchingly industrious, and goal-oriented [30, 65]. A recent preliminary study of Irish orientations toward family life, conducted among Irish-Americans, has suggested the importance for the Irish of having as teaching models in the schools celibate men and women who are highly respected [50], which contrasts with the different role of the celibate religious orders in Sicily.

The inclusion in a description of the character-forming processes inherent in any culture of mechanisms which serve to differentiate boys from girls, eldest from youngest, children of one class from children of another, the favored from the less favored—all regular extensions to a study of culture—serve to illustrate the way in which culture contributes to the amount and style of individuality which will be found in a society. Thus extreme emphasis on precocity will develop one sort of individuality, extreme playing down of precocity—as in Samoa [51] where the best student must wait for the worst—something very different.

But these mechanisms are ways in which situations, themselves culturally based, create differences by sex, class, rank, and so on, which, if no such processes were present, would not exist in this form at all. So cultural processes may result in the creation of apparent evennesses and uniformities—as in Samoa; or where rank, or sex, or order of birth are of great importance, in the creation of extraordinary differences in the developed personality which, it is assumed, are entirely cultural, i.e., the apparent differences in assurance and certainty of two brothers which could have been reversed if nothing had been altered except their order of birth. If all the attributes of individuality of a person are considered from this point of view, it will be seen what a large proportion of the ways in which one person differs from another are cultural creations, through mechanisms of differential parental care and differential education. This possibility of culture is perhaps most sharply highlighted in a culture which eliminates sex differences which are important in other societies, or in one which has created a sex-typed character structure which seems to go against deep biological trends—as when initiative is placed in the hands of the woman, or the man is made the more cherishing parent [54, 62].

Cultures not only may, or may not, contain mechanisms for differentiating individuals from each other in this way, endowing them with quite strikingly different personalities—so that they will walk, talk, think, act differently in respect to the roles to which they have been reared; but in addition those characteristics which are seen as *individualizing* are also a function of culture. The grossest forms of physical difference, difference in sex and age, extreme differences in physique and intellectual endowment, in emotional excitability, and in those peculiarly felicitous combinations of traits which we call "genius" are recognized in every society; but the attention given to any detail within one of these categories varies enormously. Height in our own culture is very important, determining eligibility for the armed services, the police, and a variety of other occupations; it may be used to differentiate between elite and non-elite branches of the armed services, get a boy a scholarship all the way through college, prevent a girl from becoming an airplane hostess. In many other cultures, height is of far less significance. Complexion, especially in areas where racial mixture is visible and socially significant, may become an important attribute which in turn will determine thousands of outcomes in a person's life situation—as in the extreme sensitivity within the American Negro group to variations in skin color and hair form [89]. Small life history events, in themselves probably without any implications for personality—such as being born in a caul, which endowed one with second sight; or being born with the umbilical cord around one's neck, which among the Mundugumor [54] gave one the right, open to no one not so born, to be an artist; or birth out of wedlock; birth in some foreign country during one's mother's accidental sojourn there; possession of one remote Jewish ancestor in Nazi Germany; all such small events may be given tremendous cultural significance, and may become pivotal in the development of individual personality.

Equally differentiated, as between cultures, are the areas within which personality is permitted expression. Dress, cosmetics, ornamentation, may be an area in which the vagaries of individual taste and symbolism may be given tremendously free range; or the finest detail of haircut, ornament, and dress may be specified in usage or ordinance, by age, sex, class, occupation, and so on. The prescribed style may be to reduce every sort of individual difference in appearance as much as possible, so that beards will be trimmed to a fine point obtainable by all, or the use of wigs will be encouraged so that everyone's hair will have the same exuberance, or even, as in the present American situation, individuals with deviant or deformed features will be encouraged to seek plastic surgery to repair the deviation. Flaunted idiosyncracy, such as that permitted to aristocrats, intellectuals, or artists, represents another cultural extreme. The unsophisticated traveler going from one culture to another often mistakes these contrasts in explicit exhibitionistic individuality or conformity for a difference greater than it actually is. Such a traveler, accustomed to identifying individuality by differences in facial expression and finding that the facial expression of some other group of people shows no recognizable variation of the sort he has previously associated with individuality, may assume that the new group has no individuality. Only if both groups have weighted the same kind of physical appearance as expressive of individuality, and then one group has penalized, while the other has encouraged, a display along these lines, can we begin to take such a contrast as indicative.

We may turn now from a consideration of status-oriented, role-oriented, and life-situation differences in personality, and of the elaborations of contrasts among these in different cultures, to a consideration of other types of difference of more usual interest to psychologists—differences in intelligence, memory, imagery, and so on. Here again we find that aspects of psychology, conventionally thought of as a matter of individual differences, may be themselves a function of the culture. Take methods of learning, for example. The differences in ability to learn by rote, by meaningful association, by abstraction, etc. *[5]*, may be institutionalized so that in a given culture one form of learning, as compared with another, may be the accepted form. To the extent that a capacity to learn in one way rather than another is innate, different individuals will be penalized and rewarded and individualized as successes or failures in these different cultures. What is true of learning is also true of imagery. Certain cultures rely more on visual, others on auditory imagery. In turn this will affect, for example, the individual with very vivid visual images who may be a prophet in one society and a disregarded deviant in another. Auditory images may threaten the sanity of an individual who is highly auditory in a visually oriented society, but will place him well within the normal range in one which relies more on hearing. A tendency to "remember" past events by reconstituting them as dramas, complete with conversations and circumstantial details which never occurred, makes the individual simply an ordinarily articulate member of the group in Iatmul, but an untrustworthy, despised liar among the Manus, where actual reproduction of an event, as perceived within a completely shared frame of reference, is the cultural requirement. So while all cultures must use in their elaborations human potentialities which are accessible to all normal human beings *[70]*—for example, all normal human beings are capable of some rote memory, some memory based on meaningful association, some abstraction and generalization—there is so great a range of possibilities for emphasizing or de-emphasizing wide sectors of human abilities as to have enormous reflections in the differences among the individuals who must learn one cultural system rather than another. A striking recent example of a change in such a cultural emphasis is the reported Soviet attempt *[34]* to penalize visual imagery in favor of a type of hand-eye-word reality orientation recommended by a behaviorist model in the 1920's, whose ideal was the person who could take the clock apart and describe what he was doing as he did it.

The way in which certain events, impulses, and processes of the body are kept "conscious," that is, within ready access of the "self," differs from one culture to another. These types of magical thinking or thinking by formal analogy, which are regarded as normally part of the primary process in our culture, may be regular parts of a shared secondary process in another society, while disallowed adjustments to reality sequences may be kept unconscious *[66, 84]*. Such cultural differences will also have profound repercussions in the sorts of individual differences which can be institutionalized. The man with readiest access to processes which in others are unconscious may be both an artist and, to a degree, an outcast in one society, but he may be a conformist priest in another. The general approach to the forbidden may result in a preference for the police records as in England where the vicariously enjoying reader can indulge himself, sure that the criminal has already been brought to justice; or, as in the United States, the emphasis may be far greater on "getting away with it." This widespread tendency in turn will be a factor in shaping the personality both of the future criminal and the future law-abiding man, of the writer of crime detection stories and the readers for whom he writes.

If a catalogue were made of the ways in which culture permits the individual expression of superiority or inferiority—with respect to sex, status, role, type of mind, type of imagination, and gift—it might well seem so overwhelming that one might ask whether there is any such thing as individuality at all, except as mediated by culture. In one sense the answer would have to be in the negative, if an assumption of the complete absence of culture were to be included in the question. Without language, without society, without models in the behavior of other human beings, without criteria for distinguishing his inner world from his outer world, without the rich and elaborate results of other men's observation, experimentation, construction, and creation, the most innately gifted person—capable of becoming in other circumstances an Einstein or a Leonardo—might be merely the wariest wild creature in the forest and the most likely to survive, or perhaps the least wary and the least likely to survive. But we do not need to concern ourselves with such an extreme model. If we recognize that all human cultures have already implicated a very large part of man's innate capacity—his ability to observe, reflect, innovate, reject, rearrange his environment, to order and classify his experiences, to imagine that which he has not seen and formally embody this vision in ways which can be communicated to his fellows— and if we recognize also that all cultures are systems of approximation, which teach most of the tradition to most of the children most of the time with varying degrees of success from culture to culture, then the possibility of the expression of individuality becomes greater. Both Lawrence Frank *[23]* and Sapir *[83]* have emphasized the extent to which each individual, by means of his private and idiosyncratic version of his culture, becomes, through the very omissions and distortions involved in this private world, a potential innovator and creator. These possibilities of individual innovation and change become relevant in those periods of history in which the traditional transmission system breaks down, when what the parents and elders, the institutions, and the rituals teach is no longer what the children learn. The familiar features of such periods—the breakdown of artistic styles, the appearance of large numbers of religious cults and panaceas, the outbreaks of protest and rebellion—all testify, at the sociological level, to the accumulation of individual variations from the norm of cultural character on which the continuation of that society has been postulated.

In the earlier discussion of the use of models, the importation into personality theory of thinking based on animal experiments was questioned because of the artificiality of the situation, the absence in human life of a figure comparable to the experimenter, and the disallowance of unrecognized variables. There is, however, another type of model from the nonhuman field that, like the work of field anthropologist and clinician, draws on living models in natural settings, supplemented by experiment, which promises to be highly stimulating to cultural theory. This is the field of ethology, particularly the work of Lorenz *[47]* and Tinbergen *[87]*. Attention to their detailed specification of the sequences of inter-bird, inter-animal, or inter-fish behavior—as between parents and offspring, peers, or mates—has refocused our attention on some important cultural processes of urbanization and culture contact. Comparisons of the behavior of wild birds and barnyard fowl reveal a significant loss of elaborate rituals of intercommunication as the domesticated bird comes to respond to simpler sets of signals in parental care, enmity, or mating. This contrast between the wild species, with its very complex hereditary patterns and pre-figurative learning (capacity for imprinting), and the simplified or vulgarized patterns of the barnyard, is analogous to the differences which can be found between populations which embody homogeneous and highly stylized cultural forms—notably primitive peoples in the savage state, peasants long attached to the same land, and aristocrats carefully reared to their exact rank—and populations which have been recently urbanized, have migrated to a new environment, or have been subjected to very rapid technological or ideological change. In the former case, in the homogeneous societies, we find a great elaboration of patterns which are deeply shared by the entire group, and high degrees of redundancy, as the same emphases appear in word, tone, gesture, in etiquette and religious ritual, in parent-child and mate-to-mate relationships, just as elements of the nesting pattern reappear as part of the courtship ritual of wild ducks. The position of each individual of a given temperament and life history is likely to be so accurately specified that relationships among persons assume some of the economy and aesthetically pleasing qualities of a ballet; the nonessential and incongruent have been pruned away and the essential is both efflorescent and harmonious.

Costume provides us with another simple demonstration of this point. Traditional costumes have a beauty which is usually lacking in the hastily assembled, only partially comprehended ensembles worn by people in stages of transition from one form of life to another—where pajama tops become shirts, undershirts, full dress; where women who have only worn cotton field dresses appear incongruously in shorts, peasant girls in French heels, stately ladies with their hair done up in bath towels. The effect lies partly in the lack of traditional relationships among the articles of wearing apparel which are derived from several discrepant sources, partly in the lack of the appropriate posture and gesture of the wearer, and partly in the presence—as audience and critics—of persons who wear the same objects "correctly," that is, within a pattern made harmonious by use.

What is true of dress is equally true of speech and manners, and of the expectations which people have of each other as neighbors, friends, buyer and seller, employer and employee, lovers, spouses, parents. As each partner to a paired relationship finds that the cues he gives are meaningless and that he is equally powerless to pick up the cues which he is being given, the interpersonal behavior becomes stripped and diagrammatic, and only the crudest cues are used. In such situations "pidgin" languages develop. The story of the origin of the word "pidgin"—as what the English speaker thought the Chinese speaker was saying when the Chinese speaker thought he was saying "business"—aptly sums up the lower level of the re-established communication, itself often a caricature of real communication that serves to prevent rather than to encourage any exchange of ideas [6]. Such situations lead to the development of various kinds of devices—the running use of funny stories, the salesman's patter, the adolescent's line—synthetic artificial products which lack the depth of more traditional and redundant types of communication.

As in speech, so in other forms of communication there will be a shift of level. Instead of placing another person instantly by caste or class, religion or occupation, as can be done in slowly changing traditional cultures where dress, speech, and demeanor *all* give the clues, single and possibly unreliable clues, such as clothes alone, may be used to provide much more superficial statements. Where the older established system of cues has been lost, we find the situation of girls who accept advances from men in uniform simply because they look like members of their own social class—in uniform—and who react with horror when they see the same men out of uniform—a mistake which would never be made in a society where accent and posture fit the clothes so perfectly that any one item gives an adequate clue to the whole, and disguise is virtually impossible. In changing urban situations, absolute standards of manners and morals, which have highly concrete manifestations in any stable society, have to become more flexible. A man does not know whether a girl's consent to stay out after midnight or to go for a drive without a chaperone does or does not mean that she is sexually accessible. It is no longer possible to convey to a hall porter or night clerk in a hotel that one is weary simply by tone of voice. People even find it difficult to convey quickly to others that they are really very angry, as some people expect the voice to get hotter as fury rises while others expect it to get colder. Rape, virtually impossible where rules and cues are well known, becomes more frequent as men and women mistake the context of a situation until it is too late to draw back.

Human personality, in these settings which are becoming increasingly characteristic of the majority of the world's peoples of the mid-twentieth century, is taking quite a different form. Because of the threefold processes of rapid social change, urbanization, and drastic technological change, few adults live in the world in which they were reared, or receive from their children responses like those which they once accorded their parents. Interpersonal behavior can be trusted less and less to one's automatic, learned sense of what is the right thing to do. More and more one must learn to be alert, aware, and watchful—if one cares for precision of interpersonal responses—or to be content with a shallow *lingua franca* of interrelationships which reveal little and simply get one safely through an encounter. As less social behavior can be spontaneous and unthinking, left to the safety of habit so deep that it is called "instinct" in everyday speech, certain other things disappear from human life—the sense of intimacy with the natural world and the physical environment, a sense of intimacy with others which comes from a background of a contemporary relationship of a hundred comparable roles, sung in song and story, implicit in every word and gesture. Memory, that essential of any sense of the self, is transformed by habits of superficial matching of often irrelevant details in the history of two essentially disparate life histories. Friendships and love affairs, grounded only in the present, tend to disappear apparently without leaving a trace. Like the domestic fowl, urbanized man, in a period of rapid social change, seems to lack the depth and grace of wild birds, or exotic native peoples, or peasants with wonderful faces.

A very present task on which the various approaches to the study of personality might well combine is the fuller understanding of this new atmosphere within which personality is formed and to which very few of our social practices are attuned. Psychoanalysis and other forms of psychotherapy may be said to be responses to the disorganization of personality which results when individuals leave a stable culture and attempt to adapt to some new and conflicting standard. Within the heightened self-awareness which results from the cultural contrast, the therapist can assist the patient to reassess those standards and types of behavior which are proving unserviceable and self-defeating. The social case-worker is trained to mediate between individuals reared within one set of institutions and the new and unfamiliar institutions within which they must learn to adjust. Certain religious movements develop to capitalize on the sense of loss which an individual, reared in a more stable culture, experiences in the modern world. Totalitarian regimes flourish on the same sort of nostalgia for law and order. But all of these moves, whether for good or evil, only deal with particular consequences of our present type of culture, rather than seeking completely new educational and medical procedures which are germane to it. We need better ways to utilize the strengths of what has variously been called *tentativeness [19]*, *situationalism [60, 62]*, *other directedness [81]*, to develop a type of person who moves with as much strength and grace in an unpredictable world as his ancestors once moved in a predictable world, now without ruts and tramlines, used to sure progress through trackless space, like the airplane—symbol of our mid-twentieth-century world.

BIBLIOGRAPHY

1. ALLPORT, G., & VERNON, P. E. *Studies in Expressive Movement*. New York: Macmillan, 1933.
2. BATESON, G. *Naven*. Cambridge: Cambridge University Press, 1936.
3. ———. The Frustration-Aggression Hypothesis. *Psychol. Rev.*, 1941, 48, No. 4, 350-55. Reprinted in *Readings in Social Psychology*, eds. T. M. Newcomb, E. L. Hartley, *et al*. New York: Henry Holt, 1947, 267-69.
4. ———. Morale and National Character, in *Civilian Morale*, ed. G. Watson. Boston: Houghton Mifflin, 1942, 71-91.
5. ———. Social Planning and the Concept of Deutero Learn-

ing, in *Science, Philosophy and Religion,* Second Symposium, eds. L. Bryson & L. Finkelstein. New York: Conference on Science, Philosophy and Religion, 1942, 81-97. Reprinted in *Readings in Social Psychology,* eds. T. M. Newcomb, E. L. Hartley, *et al.* New York: Henry Holt, 1947, 121-28.

6. ———. Pidgin English and Cross-Cultural Communication. *Trans. N. Y. Acad. Sci.,* 1944, Series 2, 6, No. 4, 137-41.

7. ———. Bali: The Value System of a Steady State, in *Social Structure: Studies Presented to A. R. Radcliffe-Brown,* ed. M. Fortes. Oxford: Clarendon Press, 1949, 35-53.

8. ———, & MEAD, M. *Balinese Character: A Photographic Analysis.* New York: Special Publications of the New York Academy of Sciences, II, 1942.

9. BENEDICT, R. *Patterns of Culture.* Boston: Houghton Mifflin, 1934.

10. ———. *The Chrysanthemum and the Sword.* Boston: Houghton Mifflin, 1946.

11. BENNETT, J. W. Review of *The Study of Culture at a Distance,* eds. M. Mead & R. Metraux. *Amer. J. Sociol.,* 1954, 60, No. 1, 91-94.

12. BOORSTIN, D. Lecture delivered at the American Civilization Conference, Brown University, 1950.

13. BRUCH, H. & TOURAINE, G. Obesity in Childhood. V. The Family Frame in Obese Children. *Psychosom. Med.,* 1940, 2, No. 2, 141-206.

14. BUNZEL, R. *The Pueblo Potter.* (*Columbia University Contributions to Anthropology,* Vol. 7.) New York, 1929.

15. ———. Explorations in Chinese Culture. Dittoed. Columbia University Research in Contemporary Cultures, 1950.

16. CHAPPLE, E. D. The Interaction Chronograph: Its Evaluation and Present Application. *Personnel,* 1949, 25, No. 4, 295-307.

17. ———, & ARENSBERG, C. Measuring Human Reactions: An Introduction to the Study of the Interaction of Individuals. *Genet. Psychol. Monogr.,* 1940, 22, No. 1, 3-147.

18. COBB, E. The Ecology of Imagination in Childhood. (Unpublished manuscript.)

19. ERIKSON, E. H. *Childhood and Society.* New York: W. W. Norton, 1950.

20. ———. Growth and Crises of the Healthy Personality, in *Symposium on the Healthy Personality,* ed. M. J. E. Senn. New York: Josiah Macy, Jr., Foundation, 1950, 91-146.

21. FORTUNE, R. F. *Manus Religion.* Philadelphia: American Philosophical Society, 1935.

22. ———. *Arapesh*. (Publications of the American Ethnological Society, Vol. 19.) New York: Augustin, 1942.

23. FRANK, L. K.   Cultural Coercion and Individual Distortion, in *Society as the Patient*. New Brunswick: Rutgers University Press, 1948, 166-92.

24. FREUD, A.   *The Ego and the Mechanisms of Defense*. Translated by C. Baines. New York: International Universities Press, 1946.

25. GESELL, A., *et al*.   *An Atlas of Infant Behavior*. New Haven: Yale University Press, 1934.

26. ———, & ARMATRUDA, C. S.   *Embryology of Behavior*. New York: Harper, 1945.

27. GORER, G.   *Himalayan Village*. London: Michael Joseph, 1938.

28. ———.   Themes in Japanese Culture. *Trans. N. Y. Acad. Sci.*, 1943, Series 2, 3, No. 5, 106-24. Reprinted in *Science News*, 1946, No. 1, 26-51.

29. ———.   *The American People*. New York: W. W. Norton, 1948. *The Americans*. London: Pearn, Pollinger & Highan, 1948.

30. ———.   Some Aspects of the Psychology of the People of Great Russia. *American Slavic and East European Review*, 1949, 8, No. 3, 155-66.

31. ———.   The Concept of National Character. *Science News*, 1950, No. 18, 105-22. Harmondsworth, Middlesex: Penguin Books, 1950.

32. ———.   *Exploring English Character*. London: Cresset, 1955. New York: Criterion, 1955.

33. ———, & RICKMAN, J.   *The People of Great Russia*. London: Cresset, 1949. New York: Chanticleer Press, 1950.

34. HAIMSON, L.   The Soviet Conception of Action in Theory and Practice. (In preparation.)

35. HALLOWELL, A. I.   Culture, Personality, and Society, in *Anthropology Today*, ed. A. L. Kroeber. Chicago: University of Chicago Press, 1953, 597-620.

36. HENRY, J.   Anthropology, Education, and Communication Theory, in *Education and Anthropology*, ed. G. *Spindler*. Stanford: Stanford University Press, 1955.

37. HOLMBERG, A. R.   *Nomads of the Long Bow*. Washington: Smithsonian Institution, Institute of Social Anthropology, Publication No. 10, 1950.

38. HONIGMANN, J. J.   *Culture and Personality*. New York: Harper, 1954.

39. JOFFE, N. F.   The Dynamics of Benefice among East European Jews. *Social Forces*, 1949, 27, No. 3, 238-47.

40. ————. Non-Reciprocity among East European Jews, in *The Study of Culture at a Distance*, eds. M. Mead & R. Metraux. Chicago: University of Chicago Press, 1953, 386-89.

41. KARDINER, A. *The Individual and His Society*. New York: Columbia University Press, 1939.

42. KLINEBERG, O. *Race Differences*. New York: Harper, 1935.

43. KRETSCHMER, E. *Physique and Character*. Translated from the 2nd revised and enlarged edition by W. J. H. Sprott. New York: Harcourt, Brace, 1926.

44. LEITES, N. *A Study of Bolshevism*. Glencoe, Ill.: Free Press, 1953.

45. LEWIS, O. *Life in a Mexican Village: Tepoztlan Restudied*. Urbana: University of Illinois Press, 1951.

46. LI, A-C. Zuni: Some Observations and Queries. *Amer. Anthrop.*, 1937, 39, No. 1, 62-76.

47. LORENZ, K. The Comparative Method in Studying Innate Behavior Patterns, in *Physiological Mechanisms in Animal Behavior*, eds. J. F. Danielli & R. Brown. (Proceedings of the Society for Experimental Biology, No. 4.) Cambridge: Cambridge University Press, 1950.

48. LOWENFELD, M. The World Picture of Children: A Method of Recording and Studying Them. *Brit. J. med. Psychol.*, 1939, 18, Part 1, 65-101.

49. MADARIAGA, S. DE. *On Hamlet*. London: Hollis & Clark, 1948.

50. MARK, L. Some Hypotheses Concerning Tendencies towards Centrifugality among Immigrant Irish Families. (Master's thesis, Columbia University, New York, 1954.)

51. MEAD, M. *Coming of Age in Samoa*. New York: Morrow, 1928.

52. ————. *Growing Up in New Guinea*. New York: Morrow, 1930.

53. ————. Melanesian Middlemen. *Natural History*, 1930, 30, No. 2, 115-30.

54. ————. *Sex and Temperament in Three Primitive Societies*. New York: Morrow, 1935. London: George Routledge, 1935. *Sexo y Temperamento*, translated by Ines Malino. Buenos Aires: Editorial Abril, 1947. *Kvinnlegt, Manligt, Mansligt*, translated by Gulli Hogbom. Stockholm: Tidens Forlag, 1948.

55. ————. Administrative Contributions to Democratic Character Formation at the Adolescent Level. *J. nat. Ass. Deans Wom.*, 1941, 4, No. 2, 51-57.

56. ————. *And Keep Your Power Dry*. New York: Morrow, 1942.

57. ————. Educative Effects of Social Environment As Disclosed by Studies of Primitive Societies, in *Environment and Education*,

A *Symposium.* (Human Development Series, Vol. 1, No. 54.) Chicago: University of Chicago Press, 1942, 48-61.

58. ———. A GI View of Britain. *New York Times Magazine,* March 19, 1944, 18-19, 34.

59. ———. The Cultural Approach to Personality, in *Encyclopedia of Personality,* ed. P. L. Harriman. New York: Philosophical Library, 1946, 477-87.

60. ———. The American People, in *The World's Peoples and How They Live.* London: Odhams Press, 1946, 143-63.

61. ———. A Case History in Cross-National Communications, in *The Communication of Ideas,* ed. L. Bryson. New York: Harper, 1948, 209-29.

62. ———. *Male and Female.* New York: Morrow, 1949.

63. ———. The Mountain Arapesh. V. The Record of Unabelin, with Rorschach Analyses. *Anthropological Papers, American Museum of Natural History,* 1949, 41, Part 3, 289-390.

64. ———. Some Anthropological Considerations Concerning Guilt, in *Feelings and Emotions, The Mooseheart Symposium,* ed. M. L. Reymert. New York: McGraw-Hill, 1950, 362-73.

65. ———. *Soviet Attitudes toward Authority.* New York: McGraw-Hill, 1951.

66. ———. Some Relationships between Social Anthropology and Psychiatry, in *Dynamic Psychiatry,* eds. F. Alexander & H. Ross. Chicago: University of Chicago Press, 1952, 401-48.

67. ———. Research on Primitive Children, in *Manual of Child Psychology,* ed. L. Carmichael, 2nd ed. New York: John Wiley, 1954, 735-80.

68. ———. The Swaddling Hypothesis: Its Reception. *Amer. Anthrop.,* 1954, 56, No. 3, 395-409.

69. ———. Robert K. Lamb—1904-52. *Hum. Org.,* 1954, 12, No. 4, 33-37.

70. ———. Untitled paper in *The Psychobiological Development of the Child,* Vol. 1, eds. J. M. Tanner & B. Inhelder. World Health Organization. (In press.)

71. ———, & MACGREGOR, F. C. *Growth and Culture, A Photographic Study of Balinese Childhood.* New York: Putnam, 1951.

72. ———, & METRAUX, R. (eds.) *The Study of Culture at a Distance.* Chicago: University of Chicago Press, 1953.

73. MEADOW, L. A Study of Dyadic Relationships in the French Family. (Unpublished paper read before the 62nd Annual Meeting of the American Psychological Association, New York, September 5, 1954.)

74. MÉTRAUX, R. Parents and Children: An Analysis of German

Child Care and Youth Guidance Literature, in *Childhood in Contemporary Cultures*, eds. M. Mead & M. Wolfenstein. Chicago: University of Chicago Press, 1955.

75. ———, & MEAD, M. *Themes in French Culture, A Preface to a Study of French Community.* (Hoover Institute Studies.) Stanford: Stanford University Press, 1954.

76. MONTAGU, M. F. A. Constitutional and Prenatal Factors in Infant and Child Health, in *Symposium on the Healthy Personality*, ed. M. J. E. Senn. New York: Josiah Macy, Jr., Foundation, 1950, 148-210.

77. MORRIS, C. W. *Paths of Life: Preface to a World Religion.* New York: Harper, 1942.

78. REDFIELD, R. *Tepoztlan—A Mexican Village.* Chicago: University of Chicago Press, 1930.

79. RENIER, G. J. *The English: Are They Human?* New York: J. Cape & H. Smith, 1931.

80. Report of the Committee on Food Habits. *Manual for the Study of Food Habits.* National Research Council, Bulletin No. 11, Washington, D. C., 1945. (See also for bibliography of cultural studies of food habits.)

81. RIESMAN, D. *The Lonely Crowd.* New Haven: Yale University Press, 1950.

82. RUESCH, J., & BATESON, G. *Communication, The Social Matrix of Psychiatry.* New York: W. W. Norton, 1951.

83. SAPIR, E. *Selected Writings of Edward Sapir*, ed. D. Mandelbaum. Berkeley: University of California Press, 1950.

84. STEWART, K. *Pygmies and Dream Giants.* New York: W. W. Norton, 1954.

85. TANNER, J. M., & INHELDER, B. *The Psychobiological Development of the Child.* Transactions I of the 1953 Conference, World Health Organization, London: Tavistock Press, 1956.

86. ———, & INHELDER, B. *Ibid.* Transactions II of the 1954 Conference, London: Tavistock Press, 1956.

87. TINBERGEN, N. *The Study of Instinct.* Oxford: Clarendon Press, 1951.

88. WALTER, W. G. *The Living Brain.* New York: W. W. Norton, 1953.

89. WARNER, W. L., JUNKER, B. H., & ADAMS, W. A. *Color and Human Nature.* Washington, D. C.: American Council on Education, 1941.

90. WILLEMSE, W. A. *Constitution—Types in Delinquency.* New York: Harcourt, Brace, 1932.

91. Wolfenstein, M. The Emergence of Fun Morality. *J. Soc. Issues,* 1951, 7, No. 4, 15-25.
92. ———. *Children's Humor: A Psychological Analysis.* Glencoe, Ill.: Free Press, 1954.
93. ———, & Leites, N. *Movies: A Psychological Analysis.* Glencoe, Ill.: Free Press, 1950.
94. ———, & Leites, N. Plot and Character in Selected French Films: An Analysis of Fantasy, in *Themes in French Culture,* by R. Métraux & M. Mead. (Hoover Institute Studies.) Stanford: Stanford University Press, 1954.

the approach of the authoritarian personality

NEVITT SANFORD, Ph.D.

NEVITT SANFORD, PH.D.

Dr. Sanford is professor of psychology at the University of California, Berkeley and Coordinator of the Mary Conover Mellon Fund for the Advancement of Education, at Vassar College. A graduate of Harvard University with the Ph.D. degree, he has worked with children and adults, in both research and clinical settings, in various institutions in this country. Dr. Sanford is well-known for his work in the field of personality theory, and was co-director, with T. W. Adorno, of the project that produced the classic study, *The Authoritarian Personality*.

Dr. Sanford and his coworkers in *The Authoritarian Personality* studies have regarded their work as a contribution to the knowledge of personality in general and not, as many have seen the work, as mere studies in prejudice. These studies were an effort to focus on the problems of social discrimination an approach that combined psychoanalytic theory of personality, clinical methods for the diagnosis of personality, and modern social-psychological devices for opinion and attitude measurement. The authors of the study, however, believe the title for their book was an unhappy choice inasmuch as the work deals more specifically with potential fascism than with actual authoritarianism.

In the present work, Dr. Sanford is concerned with criticism which has been directed toward *The Authoritarian Personality*. Readily admitting the "psychoanalytic bias" which many reviewers found in the original work, he still believes that the current trend toward unification in theory does find needed expression in this work. Much of the criticism directed toward the work was based on the critics' expecting far more from the study than the authors intended or expected. The chief hope of the authors is that the method of approach exemplified in *The Authoritarian Personality* studics may be employed in the discovery and elucidation of other patterns of personality.

INTRODUCTION

That "The Authoritarian Personality" should have a place in a book on theories of personality is a little surprising and very pleasing. It is surprising because the volume published under this title has been regarded by its authors primarily as an empirical study, one which yielded results that were susceptible to interpretation according to diverse points of view. It is pleasing to see this work included in this book because the authors of *The Authoritarian Personality* have always chosen to regard it as a contribution to the knowledge of personality in general, and not merely as a study in prejudice. It is true that the volume was published as one of a series called *Studies in Prejudice*, and it has most often been mentioned in connection with the problem of social discrimination. Actually, we came to conceive of a central structure in personality which had a determining role not only in overt prejudice but in various areas of behavior: social attitudes, political behavior, role taking in groups, and so on. It is this conception or, better, this aspect of the work, which has turned out to be most significant.

It is important to note at the outset that *The Authoritarian Personality*, the book, and the authoritarian personality, the concept, are two different things. Authoritarian personality is the name for a "type" of personality or a personality syndrome that is, supposedly, fairly common in the world today. Different writers conceive of the "type" or syndrome somewhat differently, and the work of describing the organization that exists in fact is far from having been completed. Experience has shown that *The Authoritarian Personality* was not a very happy title for the book. It will be obvious to anyone who reads the volume that it has to do mainly with potential fascism, and that the title was not thought of until after the writing was virtually finished. This title was supposed to convey the idea that the main concern was with a pattern of personality organization, and to indicate the similarity of the work to that of Fromm [25] and of Maslow [38] who had written about the "authoritarian character." But the title has led to misunderstandings. For example, since authoritarian personality has become almost a household term, it is not infrequently asked why, in such a large study of this personality type, a more systematic method of study was not used or why more of the common manifestations of this type in action were not covered. The answer, of course, is that we were not studying the authoritarian personality; we set out to study anti-Semitism, arrived eventually at the conception of potential fascism in the personality, and finally chose *The Authoritarian Personality* as a connotative title.

The Authoritarian Personality has no systematic position such as that presented by factor theory, psychoanalysis, field theory or even culture-personality theory; but it is not eclectic either. The "psychoanalytic bias" which so many reviewers have found in our work is readily admitted; yet it does seem fair to say that the current trend toward unification in theory finds expression in this work.

Unification is expressed in the backgrounds of the authors and in the very fact of their collaboration. European sociology and American social psychology, nonpsychoanalytic dynamic theory of personality, field theory, neo-Freudian theory, training in experimental, statistical and clinical methods were, in addition to classical psychoanalysis, well represented in the backgrounds of the research workers; and the study was a more or less deliberate attempt to bring to bear upon a single phenomenon, anti-Semitism, a diversity of skills and points of view. Yet there was never any serious problem concerning "agreement on fundamentals," if, indeed, any necessity for such agreement was ever felt. The common orientation to psychoanalysis and the common interest in social phenomena seem to have been enough to hold the work together.

Classical psychoanalysis has, however, shown no eagerness to clasp the work to its bosom. And there is good reason for this because more support was received from psychoanalysis than was given it. Even though psychoanalysis was fundamental to the whole endeavor and the research is replete with confirmations of psychoanalytic hypotheses (in the sense that things came out as if those hypotheses were true), the work as a whole could not be assimilated into the classical psychoanalytic system. This is because the bulk of the research had to do with matters about which psychoanalysis has had little or nothing to say, that is, the everyday behavior of large samples of normal people.

There is no purely psychoanalytic theory of anti-Semitism; attempts to produce one have yielded something that was not essentially different from the psychoanalytic theory of a great many other things. This is due to the fact that one cannot go directly from depth psychology to complex social behavior. Between the unconscious impulse or complex and the overt act or openly expressed attitude, a great many other factors of personality and of the contemporary social environment intervene. It is precisely at this point that most attempts at theory-making, in the work under consideration, have been directed.

In order to explain complex social behavior it is necessary to weigh the contributions of unconscious impulse, unconscious defense, preconscious response readiness, rational deliberation, social stimuli of the moment and the perceptions of these, and to formulate the interactions among these different kinds of variables. Thus it is that most of the theoretical work on the authoritarian personality belongs to what, from the point of view of psychoanalysis, may be called ego psychology. Our major concern has been with the ways in which the ego manages or fails to manage the impulse life, the way it strives to make sense for itself of the complex social world. There has been concern too with what might be called "other-directed psychoanalysis," if one might use this term to describe modern attempts to formulate the roles of peer groups, social institutions, the contemporary social environment generally, in determining central personality structures.

But this concern with what, from the classical psychoanalytic point of view, would have to be called the superficial does not mean that there has been an inclination to leave "the basic" strictly alone. The study of relatively large numbers of normal people by clinical procedures, procedures designed to produce the kind of material upon which psychoanalytic theories were originally based, constitutes a severe test of certain psychoanalytic propositions. The questions of what is "normal" and what is human nature begin to loom very large.

One is led to wonder whether certain patterns of character development which classical psychoanalysis has treated as universal in the species are not, instead, products of certain patterns of social organization or even social pathology. This question may be asked about certain aspects of superego development in authoritarian personalities. Similarly, this is not the first time that workers using modern clinical methods with normal people have been struck by how much "pathology" there is in the normal. One finds in normal people the kinds of disturbed childhood environments, infantile fixations, unconscious complexes, mechanisms of defense, that have commonly been regarded as indices of psychopathology. This means that there has had to be a new accent on those positive adjustive devices by which the normal person, with a normal amount of morbidity, keeps functioning. It turns out that the differentiation between the adequately functioning person and the neurotically handicapped one is more subtle than has often been thought. This is another reason for a special accent upon ego psychology.

However, there has been no watering down of psychoanalysis in *The Authoritarian Personality*. Its excursions into ego psychology and its accent upon determinants of behavior other than depth-psychological ones are in no sense substitutions for the older psychoanalytic propositions. As indicated above, the concern was largely with areas of the person and of behavior to which classical psychoanalysis does not apply. When it comes to areas where psychoanalysis does apply, such as in the understanding of neurosis itself or in the treatment of psychosis, classical psychoanalysis is given its due. The real watering down of psychoanalysis in recent years must be attributed to those psychoanalysts and psychoanalytically oriented psychologists who have sought to apply to everyday behavior concepts and theories originally designed to explain the operation of deep unconscious processes in neurosis and psychosis. This has meant that some of these concepts and theories have been stretched to a point where they have become almost meaningless.

In the work under consideration, there has been no hesitation to modify classical psychoanalytic theory when this seemed called for by research findings. This was very rarely done because, first, at the level of personality with which the authors were working, there was rarely any opportunity to apply a crucial test to any psychoanalytic proposition; and, second, as background, as general orientation, as a source of ideas for hypotheses to explain the phenomena observed, little fault was found with psychoanalysis.

It should be pointed out here that, in so far as a new theory has been concocted in *The Authoritarian Personality*, it has been of the low order or even *ad hoc* variety. Although in the beginning there was a general background of theory, with a certain sense of theoretical direction, it was found repeatedly that it was necessary to invent a particular theory to explain observed facts, and then to proceed to collect more facts to test that theory. It will be a long time before the very general, loosely cohering, theoretical approach embodied in *The Authoritarian Personality* can be made into a true theoretical system. I would suggest, however, that, when this is accomplished, there will then exist the long-sought "general theory of action."

One more point about theory. In the research there were encountered the most persistent problems of personology, e.g., the problems of personality organization, of "types," of levels of functioning, of genetic vs. contemporary determination of personality. The authors of *The Authoritarian Personality* hope that in these areas there has been a contribution not only to theory but also to knowledge of personality functioning.

Let us turn now to an outline of what these pages are intended to cover. I should like to begin with an account of how the research culminating in *The Authoritarian Personality* was started and how it was conducted. This story has not been fully told before. I offer it now as a means for correcting certain common misapprehensions and as a basis for some comment about current research practice in this country.

Then we may proceed immediately to a description of the major pattern of personality that emerged from the research. More particularly, we shall consider how the F (for potential fascist)-syndrome was arrived at, the details of its content, and the basic ideas underlying it. After considering some clinical studies of the F pattern, we shall discuss the attempts to reduce the pattern to its essential elements (factor analysis and cluster analysis), and this will lead to a consideration of the general theory of the syndrome and of personality "types." Here will be presented the types of authoritarian and nonauthoritarian personality structures suggested by our study, and this will be followed by empirical studies of differentiation within the extremes, and of similarities between the extremes, on the F scale.

Differentiating sharply between personality and behavior, there will be next an attempt to evaluate the roles of personality and of situational factors in determining overt prejudice, and more than this, an attempt to formulate the interaction of personality and situation in producing various phenomena of behavior. The general formulation will be exemplified by considering how authoritarianism in the personality is expressed in such social roles as parent, husband or wife, political leader, teacher, group member.

In discussing the origins of the F-syndrome it is necessary to accent, as was done in the research, the development of the individual in the setting of family life with particular reference to early events. The data to be presented consist mainly of what adult subjects had to say about their childhoods. But it is possible to make sense of these unreliable reports by considering them in relation to the general knowledge of development and, particularly, in relation to more recent studies, including studies on children — and so to evolve a more or less coherent theory. Recognizing, however, that the childhood experiences of the subjects must have depended in considerable part upon the total social situation in which their parents lived, and noting variations in the incidence of authoritarianism from one culture or subculture to another, it becomes clear that an account of the origins of authoritarian personality must include attention to broad historical and cultural forces. Although one cannot go so far beyond the limits of his own discipline without trepidation, these larger determinants must be considered.

In the summing up, there will be an attempt to evaluate the

researches on the authoritarian personality and to consider therapy, both individual and social.

The study of the authoritarian personality actually began in 1943 as a result of an anonymous donation made for a study of anti-Semitism.

This writer, together with Herbert Conrad and others, had been engaged in some studies of personality factors in relation to certain aspects of "war morale," using John Harding's morale scale [29] and, later, local scales of our own design having to do with optimism-pessimism with respect to the war [11, 12]. Scale scores were related to life history data, personality scale items, projective questions and a TAT story, particular attention being paid to extreme scorers. Interpretation from a psychoanalytic viewpoint was frequently employed. A study of anti-Semitism fitted in well with this pattern of research.

It seemed that the place to begin the study was with the construction of a suitable instrument for measuring anti-Semitism. Then scores on the scale could be related to questionnaire data bearing on personality and sociological factors, as had been done in the studies of morale mentioned above. By the early spring of 1944, the scale was ready for publication, together with a certain amount of validating data gathered by administering the scale, together with the general questionnaire, to several samples of college students [36]. The basic material of this paper and much of the thinking that went into it—mostly Daniel Levinson's work—appear in Chapter III of *The Authoritarian Personality*.

Meanwhile, also in the fall of 1943, this author had met Dr. Max Horkheimer, director of the Institute of Social Research, which had moved after Hitler's revolution from Frankfort to Columbia University. This institute had published in 1936 the well-known *Studien über Autorität und Familie*, which linked psychological dispositions with political leanings and contained some of Erich Fromm's early work on the sado-masochistic character. It was still pursuing theoretical and empirical studies of anti-Semitism and allied phenomena. Dr. Horkheimer, keenly interested in bringing to bear upon the theories being developed by his institute some of the quantitative methods of American social psychology, made some funds available to the anti-Semitism project. These funds made it possible for us to invite Dr. Else

Frenkel-Brunswik and Dr. Suzanne Reichard to join the project part-time and to begin the task of making clinical studies of subjects scoring at the extremes on the anti-Semitism scale.

There now followed a most exciting and creative period. All four staff members conducted interviews; and, in the conferences which followed these experiences with key subjects, it was difficult to get the floor, so great was the need to express ideas concerning the personality dynamics of the anti-Semite. Dr. Frenkel-Brunswik concentrated on the analysis of the interview material. Here her grasp of psychoanalytic theory, her broad experience with the analysis of qualitative material and her insistence upon conceptual clarity were richly rewarding. Dr. Reichard made a special study of the Rorschach responses, and Dr. Levinson continued to give a large part of his time to the development of questionnaire methods for getting at personality and ideology. Before the end of summer, 1944, the paper, "Some Personality Correlates of Anti-Semitism" *[22]*, was ready for publication, and Reichard had written up her study of Rorschach responses *[43]*.

Meanwhile Horkheimer had become director of the newly established Department of Scientific Research of the American Jewish Committee (A.J.C.). This department had been set up with the object of initiating and stimulating fundamental studies of prejudice, and it was natural that Horkheimer should wish to further the research in Berkeley which had already profited from his help and in which he firmly believed. The idea now was that T. W. Adorno, long-time member of the Institute of Social Research and close associate of Horkheimer, should participate actively in the research, sharing its direction, and that there should be continued exploration for personality correlates of anti-Semitism, using both more intensive clinical studies and quantitative studies with large samples.

The financial support of the A.J.C. would insure that the several senior researchers could devote more time to this work, that some assistants could be employed, and that continuity would be assured for at least three years. The A.J.C. were offering their support to *exploratory* researches which were to be carried forward by empirical methods. They never asked for, nor did they receive, any statement of a research design, nor were they offered more than a general idea of the kinds of findings that might be made. They knew only that approved quantitative methods were being used and that the thinking of the group was guided by psychoanalysis and by the broad social theories of Drs. Horkheimer and Adorno. They never indicated what they wanted us to do or what they hoped the research would find out.

Thus, the group members were always free to pursue hunches or to follow up whatever was suggested by a particular finding. Full advantage was taken of this. The proposition that anti-Semitism has a functional aspect, that is to say, is put in the service of the needs of the individual, was hardly a research hypothesis; it was, in this instance, an assumption, like the assumptions that "Behavior is goal-directed," or "The organism functions as a whole." To arrive at testable hypotheses in keeping with this general assumption required some doing as well as some thinking; as indicated above, the best hypotheses were for the most part conceived *after* data were collected rather than before; and then some, but not all, of these hypotheses were tested by further data collection.

From the beginning to the end, the research was loosely organized. Of the senior researchers only Dr. Levinson ever devoted full time to the project, and he for only three years. Dr. Adorno lived in Los Angeles and carried on his collaboration by correspondence and visits to Berkeley. When the grant from the A.J.C. was made, Dr. Frenkel-Brunswik began working half time on the project while continuing to carry out her duties at the Institute of Child Welfare. Late in 1944 she began her own study of prejudice in children, also with the support of the A.J.C., a study that was carried on concurrently with, and after the conclusion of, this project. In July 1945, I started working half time on the project. Previously I had been busy full time with the Psychology Department of the university, the Institute of Child Welfare and the Office of Strategic Services.

Just as the group enjoyed maximum freedom as far as relations with the A.J.C. were concerned, so each member enjoyed a great deal of autonomy within the group. The result was that in pursuit of particular ideas or interests there was a tendency to go off in various directions and to set up outposts in some fairly remote areas. Nevertheless, everyone shared the same theoretical outlook and there was always a central line of attack: the development of scales that would express in quantitative terms expanding conceptions of what prejudice involves, clinical study of individuals scoring at the extremes on these scales, and the subsequent re-vision of the scales. Further financial assistance was received from the Social Science Research Council, the Rosenberg Foundation, the Research Board of the University of California and the Graduate Division of Western Reserve University. That it was possible to produce a book, instead of writing a series of papers, was due not so much to any original "master plan" as to our shared underlying theory and the fact that our diverse investigations turned up similar results, or results that permitted the same general line of interpretation.

In this light it is a little odd, if not flattering, that this work should be evaluated according to the standards which ordinarily hold for researches, in well-tilled fields, which set out to provide a crucial test of some familiar hypothesis. Some critics write about *The Authoritarian Personality* as if it were the research project which we might well have begun along about the time we decided to write a book about the data already collected. This, of course, is not an excuse for mistakes made in handling data and in their interpretation. There is, however, a good answer to the rather surprising charges of Shils [58]. He assumes, first, that the group set out to do a large study of authoritarianism as it is conceived of today (he refers to the work as a "monumental research *into* [italics mine] *The Authoritarian Personality*"), and, second, that any truly knowledgeable person setting out to investigate this phenomenon in 1943–44 would have seen that "authoritarianism of the left" was just as important as "authoritarianism of the right"; that the insufficient attention given to the former must have been due, therefore, either to political naïveté or to political bias or, more likely, to both. It should be recalled here that the F scale, which the group and others in recent years have called a "measure of authoritarianism," was not designed until the late spring of 1945, and that what we had primarily in mind at the time was an aggregation of scale items that would predict anti-Semitism and ethnocentrism without mentioning the names of any minority groups. The difference between the way Shils and the group itself view this work is well illustrated by the fact that, whereas both refer to "pseudo-conservative" as an *ad hoc* conception, the group does so proudly while he does so contemptuously. The group has regarded this conception as a valuable fruit of the exploratory–empirical approach. Shils seems to think that it should have been arrived at intuitively or, better still, from consultation with political scientists and included in the original "design."

There is a place for the exploratory study. Consider, for example, *Explorations in Personality* [41]. Methodologically primitive according to present-day standards but a mine of suggestiveness for, up to now, about eighteen years. "Exploratory study" does not mean a self-conscious "preliminary study" or a casual, free-floating observational study; but a study that goes after facts, becomes involved with data, while permitting thinking about those data, or insights derived from them, to determine the next stage of data collection. It is a study in which curiosity about what lies over the next hill becomes the determining motive, and which is therefore willing to "travel light," not waiting for the proper development of base camps. Very probably, neither *Explorations in Personality* nor *The Authoritarian Personality* could have been produced without the kind of financial support—or a lack of such support—that gave real freedom to the investigator, nor could they have been produced had the investigators been wedded to the kind of methodology which such writers as Hyman and Sheatsley [32] regard as the ideal. The impression is strong today that research becomes more and more design-centered—rather than content-centered—more and more conventionalized. Somebody is always taking the joy out of it. As a friend said after looking over the Hyman and Sheatsley exercise, "These 'scientists' make me nervous." Yet, I do not wish to encourage any widespread revolt against the scientific superego of today, however externalized it may have become. Obviously, there are times when it is necessary to submit to this discipline, and the critique of Hyman and Sheatsley is so penetrating, so permeated with good will, that the temptation to submit is strong. However, what really must be watched in the methodological experts is their tendency to inject their own philosophy or theoretical biases under the guise of methodological orthodoxy. For example, Hyman and Sheatsley, in reproaching us for neglecting national norms in some of our interpretations of responses to scale items, presumably base their remarks purely on methodological principles; actually they are promoting social relativism, a point of view specifically rejected in the study. Methodological cobblers ought to stick to their lasts.

No one would argue that there is some kind of necessary affinity between originality—or whatever it takes to break new ground—and methodological laxity. Mistakes which our group made in the management of data were not due to any ideological objection to statistical or experimental rigor. They were due rather to ignorance, lack of skill, and, apparently, failure to secure the right advisors. Still, it is doubtful that greater methodological purity or rigor, or adherence to the advice of the most advanced experts—even Hyman or Sheatsley—would have made any crucial difference in the general results and conclusions of our work.

The Authoritarian Personality has been called by highly responsible critics "monumental," "a classic," "a milestone" in social research. This can be interpreted as a rather severe criticism of social psychology and personology. What have our people been doing then? It ought not to be so difficult to produce a work like *The Authoritarian Personality*. All that is really essential is a reasonably comprehensive theoretical framework, curiosity, and freedom—freedom from hampering research conventions, from the conventional expectations of sponsors and from the aspiration to produce a monumental work. Then one simply follows one's nose, so to speak. Instead of saying, "This experiment raises more questions than it answers," and then turning attention to something else, one proceeds to try to answer a few of those questions—and later questions raised by this new effort. If the pattern which emerges in the end has such coherence that it appears to have been put in at the beginning, so much the better. There is no good reason why work which proceeds in this way should not maintain high standards in sampling, in generalization, in the collection and analysis of data, but even so it is inevitable that much of it will have to be followed up and checked by more exacting methods. There is a difference between exploratory research as used here and the conventional hypothesis-testing research which is so common today. It is no criticism of the latter to say that there is need for more "explorations in personality."

THE F SCALE

Although the idea of constructing a scale for measuring potential fascism in the personality appeared at a relatively late stage in these explorations, it still came at a time when the focus of attention was upon anti-Semitism and prejudice. A Likert-type scale for measuring ethnocentrism (E) had been constructed and studied in relation to anti-Semitism (A-S). This scale, which embraced hostility to various intra- and extra-national outgroups as well as the tendency to overestimate and to glorify the ingroup, correlated so highly with anti-Semitism, .80, that it seemed reasonable to view this latter as, mainly, a manifestation of general ethnocentrism. Ethnocentrism, in the group's thinking, had become something very general indeed. Not only did it include generalized outgroup rejection and exaggerated ingroup loyalty but also such defects in thinking as stereotypy, rigidity, and rationalization; it was a way of looking at groups and group relations that was, in the long run at least, maladaptive; it had begun to take on the aspect of a fundamental psychological problem.

The high correlation between A-S and E meant that it would be possible to go on studying anti-Semitism without having to rely on the original A-S scale itself. This scale had evoked protests both from a local chapter of the Anti-Defamation League, who considered that the instrument spread anti-Semitism, and from the dean of a graduate school, who objected to "the pro-Semitic bias" in this research. From whatever point of view it was seen, this scale did tend to bring the matter of prejudice painfully into the open and it was used with reluctance, particularly in groups that included Jews. But the same considerations held for members of other minority groups. The real need was for an instrument that would measure prejudice without appearing to have this aim and without mentioning the name of any minority group.

The idea of the F scale was a product of thinking about the A-S and E scales. An effort was being made to abstract from the A-S and E scale items the kinds of psychological dispositions —fears, anxieties, values, impulses—being expressed, the thought being that a systematic covering of this ground might suggest additional E items. There were certain general themes in the item content: e.g., Jews were "extravagant," or "sensual" or "lazy" or "soft"; or Jews were mysterious, strange, foreign, basically different; or minority groups generally failed to come up to ordinary standards of middle-class morality. It was as if the subject, in agreeing with these scale items, was not so much considering Jews or other minority group members as expressing concern lest other people "get away" with tendencies which he himself had to inhibit, or anxiety lest he be the victim of strange forces beyond his control, or lest his moral values, already somewhat unstable, be undermined. And since, apparently, items expressing these kinds of preoccupation were agreed with consistently by some subjects regardless of the minority groups involved, would not these subjects agree with such items even though no minority group were mentioned at all? In short, why not have a scale that covered the psychological content of the A-S and E scales but did not appear to be concerned with the familiar phenomena of prejudice? Certainly this fitted in with Leo Loewenthal's memorable if somewhat exaggerated dictum: "Anti-Semitism has nothing to do with Jews."

It cannot really be claimed that this notion came as the result of a deliberate quest for an instrument that would be less awkward to administer to groups of varied ethnic backgrounds, although it came at a time when the need for such an instrument was keenly felt and this implication of the new notion was more or less immediately seen. Furthermore, this notion was conceived at a time when the group was prepared to exploit it to the full. Interviews with subjects scoring high on A-S and E had suggested many psychological characteristics of the highly prejudiced subjects, and whereas many of these characteristics had not yet found a place in the A-S or E scales there was no reason why they should not. And now, since attention was going to be directed to items expressing the general outlook of the highly prejudiced individual, it was possible to make use of the vast literature on Nazism and Fascism and, particularly, the ideas represented by Dr. Adorno and the Institute for Social Research. Finally, it was possible to make explicit a theoretical assumption which, actually, had been a guide to the group's thinking for some time.

The essence of this assumption was that some of the deeper needs of the personality were being expressed by agreement with prejudiced statements. If this were true, then these needs should express themselves in other ways as well. If, for example, a subject's tendency to attribute weakness to Jews sprang from his own underlying fear of weakness, that fear might also express itself in an over-accent upon his own strength and toughness. Thus, scale items having to do with the supposed weakness of Jews or of other people and items expressing exaggerated strength and toughness would correlate positively in a population of men because agreement with both kinds of items commonly sprang from the same underlying source, fear of weakness. All of us were accustomed to this kind of thinking in terms of levels of functioning in the personality; it had loomed large in earlier work of Frenkel-Brunswik [20] and of Sanford [52]. It is, of course, essentially psychoanalytic.

Given this way of looking at things, the task became one of imagining what personality needs were commonly expressed in overt prejudice, and then thinking of other surface manifestations of these same needs. The intention was, of course, to gain access to those other manifestations by means of scale items. Here it was possible to make good use of the existing literature on anti-Semitism and Fascism. Fromm [25], Erikson [16], Maslow [38], Chisholm [7], Reich [42], Stagner [59] were among the writers who influenced us the most, although heaviest reliance was on the group's own earlier explorations. The central personality trends which were expected to be most significant were those which emerged from the analysis of clinical material and those which, as hypothetical constructs, seemed best to explain the consistency of response to the A-S and E scales.

CONTENT OF THE F SCALE

For every item of the F scale there was a hypothesis or, more usually, several hypotheses stating the nature of its supposed connection with prejudice. And there were hypotheses concerning the relations of these items one to another, theorizing having led the group more and more toward the conceptualization of a *pattern* of personality that predisposed the individual to prejudice and fascism.

Here it seems worth while to go into some detail, for progress in an understanding of authoritarianism will come from the closest involvement with the subtle workings of this and similar trends in the personality.

Conventionalism

First consider the idea of *conventionalism*. It was observed in our conversations with anti-Semitic subjects that most of their accusations against Jews were couched in conventionally moralistic terms. This theme was also pronouned in the original A-S scale items. It may be recalled that Hitler made this same type of accusation when addressing middle-class audiences. Our thought here was that we were dealing not so much with bad experiences with Jews or with adaptation to a general climate of opinion as with a need to adhere strictly to conventional, middle-class values, a disposition to feel anxious at the sight of or the thought of any violation of these values—something that could be attributed to instability in the individual's own value system. It is important to note that conventionalism refers not merely to conformity with middle-class values but to *rigid* adherence to such values, to an *over*accent upon them and to responsiveness to contemporary *external* social pressure. Items expressive of this trend invited the subject to go *all-out* in his support of conventional values, e.g., "A person who has bad manners, habits, and breeding can hardly expect to get along with decent people."

Authoritarian Submission

Submission to authority, desire for a strong leader, subservience of the individual to the state, had for some time been put forward as important aspects of the Nazi creed. It was thus natural that these themes should be taken into account in a search for the correlates of prejudice. *Authoritarian submission*, as we termed the hypothetical generalized disposition of personality, was conceived of not as a balanced, realistic respect for valid authority but as an exaggerated, emotional need to submit. This seems well represented in the item: "Every person should have a deep faith in some supernatural force higher than himself to which he gives total allegiance and whose decisions he obeys without question." Here, as with conventionalism, the individual is assumed to be oriented toward external powers or agencies of control rather than under the direction of a conscience of his own.

Authoritarian Aggression

Authoritarian submission is closely related, conceptually, to *authoritarian aggression*. Both attitudes, according to theory, spring from underlying hostility toward ingroup authorities, originally the parents. The individual strives to keep this hostility in check by over-doing in the direction of respect, obedience, gratitude toward the ingroup authorities and by displacing the underlying hostility toward these authorities onto outgroups. This is the most essential connection between authoritarian submission and ethnocentrism. But it appears that the tendency to displace hostility is more general than that seen in the common forms of prejudice; the greatest variety of people and actions are likely to become the objects of condemnation. The connection of this hostility and its original source is seen in the fact that the kinds of things for which the individual would punish other peoples are the same as those for which he was punished or for which he feels in his heart he deserves to be punished. But he has identified himself with the ingroup authorities of his childhood, and found in the tendency to punish wrongdoing in others a safe, and fairly well-sanctioned, outlet for his aggression. The items chosen to represent authoritarian aggression offer the subject a chance to favor condemnation, total rejection, stern discipline or severe punishment as ways for dealing with a variety of people and forms of behavior; e.g., "Sex crimes, such as rape and attacks on children, deserve more than mere imprisonment; such criminals ought to be publicly whipped, or worse."

Anti-intraception

It was common to note in the interviews of more prejudiced subjects, and in some of the A-S and E scale items with which they heartily agreed, disapproval of a free emotional life, of the intellectual or theoretical, of the impractical. These were things they tended to attribute to their outgroups. And there was theory at hand to explain the relations of these attitudes to prejudice and to the personality trends just discussed. The individual who had been forced to repress hostility against his parents and others who appeared to be strong, and who was thus forced into submissiveness which impaired his self-respect, would naturally be required to maintain a narrow range of consciousness. Self-awareness might threaten his whole scheme of adjustment. He would be afraid of genuine feeling because his emotions might get out of control, afraid of thinking about human phenomena because he might, as it were, think the wrong thoughts. The term *anti-intraception* was borrowed from Murray *et al* [41]. It stands for a general attitude of impatience with and opposition to feelings, fantasies, speculations and other subjective or "tender-minded" phenomena. A sample item: "When a person has a problem or worry, it is best for him not to think about it, but to keep busy with more cheerful things."

Superstition and Stereotypy

The narrowness of consciousness just referred to appeared also to be a major source of both *superstition and stereotypy*, two tendencies which loomed large in our early clinical studies of highly prejudiced individuals. Superstitiousness indicates a tendency to shift responsibility from within the individual onto outside forces beyond one's control. It suggests a narrow area within which there is a conscious sense of self-determination, a broad area of unconscious forces which are projected onto the external world, to appear to the individual as mystical or fantastic determinants of his fate. Stereotypy is the tendency to think in rigid, oversimplified categories, in unambiguous terms of black and white, particularly in the realm of psychological or social matters. It was hypothesized that one reason why people, even those who are otherwise "intelligent," resort to primitive explanations of human events is that so many of the ideas and observations needed for an adequate account are not allowed to enter into the calculations: because they are affect-laden and potentially anxiety-producing they could not be included in the conscious scheme of things. The assumption here is, of course, that many of the common phenomena of prejudice were superstitions or stereotypes. The present task was to devise scale items that would express these tendencies without reference to minority groups, e.g., "It is entirely possible that this series of wars and conflicts will be ended once and for all by a world-destroying earthquake, flood, or other catastrophe."

Power and Toughness

As suggested above, the state of affairs in which the individual has to submit to powers or agencies with which he is not fully in sympathy leaves him with a nagging sense of weakness. Since to admit such weakness is to damage self-respect, every effort is made to deny it. These include the projection of weakness onto out-groups according to the formula "I am not weak, they are," and the use of the mechanism of overcompensation, according to which the individual seeks to present to the world an aspect of *power and toughness.* Accent on the strong-weak, dominant-submissive, leader-follower dimension in human relations is, of course, a familiar feature of the Nazi outlook. In our experience it appeared that the "power complex" contained elements that were essentially contradictory. Whereas the power-centered individual wants to have power, he is at the same time afraid to seize it and wield it. He also admires power in others and is inclined to submit to it, but is at the same time afraid of the weakness thus implied. A common solution for such a person is to align himself with power figures, thus gratifying both his need to have power and his need to submit. By submitting to power he can still somehow participate in it. The following is a sample of the items designed to represent this theme: "Too many people today are living in an unnatural, soft way; we should return to the fundamentals, to a more red-blooded, active way of life."

Destructiveness and Cynicism

Although authoritarian aggression provides a very broad channel for the expression of underlying hostile impulses, it seemed that this might not be enough for many of the prejudiced subjects. We supposed that they harbored, as a result of numerous externally imposed restrictions upon the satisfaction of their needs, a great deal of resentment and generalized hostility, and that this would come into the open when it could be justified or rationalized. *Destructiveness and cynicism* was the term for rationalized, ego-accepted aggression, not including authoritarian aggression. Cynicism was regarded as a form of rationalized aggression: one can the more freely be aggressive when he believes that everybody is doing it and, hence, if he wants to be aggressive he is disposed to

274 *Psychology of Personality*

believe that everybody is similarly motivated, e.g., that it is "human nature" to exploit and to make war on one's neighbors. It seemed a fairly safe assumption that such undifferentiated aggressiveness could be directed against minority groups with a minimum of external stimulation.

Projectivity

The mechanism just described is, of course, a form of projection. And it will have been noted that this unconscious defensive device has had an important place in our earlier related theory-making, particularly in the discussion of authoritarian aggression and of superstition. Indeed, projection has a crucial role in the whole theory of prejudice as a means for keeping the individual's psychological household in some sort of order. The most essential notion is that impulses which cannot be admitted to the conscious ego tend to be projected onto minority groups—convenient objects. In constructing the F scale, the concern was with a readiness to project, with *projectivity* as a general feature of the personality, considered independently of the object onto which the projection was made. Hence, the items expressive of this tendency were designed to tap any preoccupation with "evil forces" in the world, with plots and conspiracies, germs, sexual excesses.

Sex

Concern with *sex* seemed to deserve a certain amount of special consideration. Inhibitions in this sphere, and moral indignation with respect to the sexual behavior of other people, had been noted in the interviews with our prejudiced subjects; sexual immorality was one of the many violations of conventional values which they attributed to minority groups. Ego-alien sexuality was conceived then as a part of the picture of the typical prejudiced person, and included in the F scale were several items having to do with belief in the existence of "sex orgies" and with the punishment of violators of sex mores.

In summary, there were nine major personality variables which, by hypothesis, were dynamically related to overt prejudice.

1. *Conventionalism.* Rigid adherence to conventional middle-class values.

2. *Authoritarian Submission.* Submissive, uncritical attitude toward idealized moral authorities of the ingroup.

3. *Authoritarian Aggression.* Tendency to be on the lookout for, and to condemn, reject and punish people who violate conventional values.

4. *Anti-intraception.* Opposition to the subjective, the imaginative, the tender-minded.

5. *Superstition and Stereotypy.* The belief in mystical determinants of the individual's fate; the disposition to think in rigid categories.

6. *Power and Toughness.* Preoccupation with the dominance-submission, strong-weak, leader-follower dimension; identification with power figures; exaggerated assertion of strength and toughness.

7. *Destructiveness and Cynicism.* Generalized hostility, vilification of the human.

8. *Projectivity.* The disposition to believe that wild and dangerous things go on in the world, the projection outward of unconscious emotional impulses.

9. *Sex.* Ego-alien sexuality; exaggerated concern with sexual "goings on," and punitiveness toward violators of sex mores.

THEORY UNDERLYING THE F SCALE

In their theoretical work on the F scale the research group leaned heavily upon the concepts of superego, ego, and id. It was considered that these features of the personality have characteristic modes of functioning in the ethnocentric subject. As a first approximation, one might say that in the highly ethnocentric person the superego is strict, rigid and relatively externalized, the id is strong, primitive and ego-alien, while the ego is weak and can manage the superego-id conflicts only by resorting to rather desperate defenses. But this general formulation would hold for a very large segment of the population and, thus, it is necessary to look more closely at the functioning of these parts of the person in the authoritarian syndrome.

In considering the variables which entered into the theory underlying the F scale, it may be seen that the first three—Conventionalism, Authoritarian Submission, and Authoritarian Aggression

—all have to do with superego functioning. The accent is upon external reinforcements of strict superego demands, and upon punishment in the name of those authorities to whom the subject has submitted.

Anti-intraception, Superstition and Stereotypy, and Projectivity may be regarded as manifestations of a relatively weak ego. Anti-intraception involves the primitive defensive mechanisms of repression, denial, keeping things ego-alien. Superstition shows an inclination to shift responsibility onto the external world, as if the ego were giving up its attempts to predict and control, while Stereotypy is an attempt to deal with complex events by means of oversimplified categories. Projectivity is the consistent use of another relatively primitive mechanism of defense.

Power and Toughness is another manifestation of ego weakness, involving as it does an over-accent upon the conventionalized aspects of the ego, e.g., the emphasis on "will power"; but this variable, like Destructiveness and Cynicism, and Sex, also expresses with a minimum of indirectness the activity of id tendencies.

However, superego, ego and id can be separated in this fashion only arbitrarily. In actuality, the functioning of any one of these agencies depends at any moment upon the activities of the other two; and everyday behavior, expressed attitudes and values, are not readily classifiable as manifestations of superego, ego or id but are to be understood as expressions of the relationships among these agencies. This, at any rate, was the thinking that went into the F scale. Consider the item: "He is indeed contemptible who does not feel an undying love, gratitude, and respect for his parents." On the surface, this item expresses authoritarian aggression and authoritarian submission and, hence, might be classified as primarily a superego item. But the theory was that agreement with this extreme statement might well mask an underlying hostility toward the parents. To put this differently, it was hypothesized that unconscious hostility toward the parents was a distinguishing feature of the highly ethnocentric person, and the problem was to determine how this tendency might give itself away in an attitude scale. One answer was through signs of a reaction formation, this mechanism being a common one in the highly ethnocentric person. Thus the present item has to do with an interplay of superego, ego and id: an underlying unconscious, ego-alien tendency, coming mainly from the id, has led to anxiety of punishment (superego) which the ego seeks to ward off or reduce by transforming the forbidden tendency into its opposite. But this is not all. This is merely the authoritarian submission expressed in the item. "He is indeed contemptible" is authoritarian aggression. The ego must, so to speak, be doubly sure that punishment is avoided and it must see to it that the original id tendency finds some sort of gratification; hence, it joins forces with the punitive agency, imputes the "badness" to other people who may then be freely aggressed against in good conscience.

Or consider the item: "The wild sex life of the old Greeks and Romans was tame compared to some of the goings on in this country, even in places where people might least expect it." Here it is assumed that underlying sexual tendencies, inhibited because of a strict superego, have found through the ego's work some expression in fantasies, which, however, can be enjoyed or tolerated only when other people, and not the self, are the actors and when the fantasies are accompanied by moral indignation.

Now it is not suggested that the whole authoritarian personality structure is somehow embedded in each F scale item. But it is fair to say that theory of the kind just indicated lay behind the writing of each item, and that, according to this theory, the F pattern is a structure whose features are so closely interrelated that a clear expression of one permits quite reasonable inferences concerning the activity of the others. Perhaps the items just used are among the best for making this point, but all the F scale items should be viewed from this standpoint.

The F scale works as if the superego, ego, id theory were correct, and there is no doubt but that without this theory the scale would not have been constructed. On the other hand, it cannot be claimed that such results as have been obtained could not be explained as well in other terms.

CLINICAL STUDIES OF THE F PATTERN

In trying to understand the inner workings of the F-syndrome one is not, of course, limited to consideration of the F scale. The interviews and projective techniques which yielded the hypotheses underlying the F scale also yielded some of the most convincing evidence concerning the truth of those hypotheses. To consider an example, the interviews, like some questionnaire material, showed unmistakably that the tendency to glorify his parents was a distinguishing feature of the highly ethnocentric subject. And the interviews also gave evidence of ambivalence in this subject's relationship with his parents. It was usually not long after the statements of glorification that a note of complaint or self-pity began to creep into the interview. How might one demonstrate that overt glorification of the parents is functionally related to underlying hostility toward them? One way would be to use a projective technique to obtain an independent measure of the latter and see if the two vary together. Unfortunately, this is not simple. What are the TAT signs of repressed aggression? Certainly not the frequency and intensity of aggressive actions by heroes of the stories. These seem to be, for the most part, indications of aggression that is accepted by the ego; it is more pronounced in the low scorers than in the high scorers on the F scale. But Betty Aron [2] did conclude that there was more *ego-alien* aggression against the parents in the stories of high scorers, the indications being such things as the frequency with which parent figures were the victims of affliction or death and the frequency and intensity of aggression against parental figures on the part of characters with whom the storyteller was not identified. Thus, to arrive at diagnoses of deep-lying tendencies on the basis of the TAT requires *interpretation*. Although Aron's work goes a long way toward the objectification of such interpretation, and although it argues persuasively for a functional relationship between overt glorification and underlying hostility, it remains in need of independent validation.

The same considerations hold for the Projective Questions. The material elicited by this procedure is for the most part on the same level of personality as the F scale. Responses to the open-ended questions could easily be—and they sometimes were—translated into F scale items. Thus the Projective Questions yielded a large amount of material that confirmed independently the F scale findings on the difference between ethnocentric and non-ethnocentric subjects. But, more than this, the material from the Projective Questions called for interpretation, for the conceptualization of underlying trends that would explain the pattern of overt expression.

Two of the Projective Questions were as follows:

1. We all have times when we feel below par. What moods or feelings are the most unpleasant or disturbing to you?
2. There is hardly a person who hasn't said to himself: "If this keeps up I'll go nuts." What might drive a person nuts?

These two questions, like the six others used, brought out numerous differences between highs and lows on the E scale. The "lows" are disturbed by conscious conflict and guilt feelings, frustrations of love and dependence, consciousness of hostility toward loved objects, and they suppose that people are "driven nuts" by inner psychological states or by a dominating environment. The "highs," on the other hand, are more disturbed by violations of conventional values, by self or others or by a threatening or nonsupporting environment; they are also more disturbed by, and state that people are "driven nuts" by, what Levinson called "rumblings from below."

According to Levinson, "These responses refer to situations or bodily conditions which, by inference though not explicitly, tend to bring out ego-alien trends such as passivity, anxiety, and hostility." Examples, from the subjects' responses, are: "Quietness, boredom, inactivity"; "When at a party everything is quiet and dead as a morgue"; "Lack of work or anything to do, causing restlessness and lack of self-confidence." How does one know that such responses as these are signs that the subject is struggling with id tendencies, such as passivity and hostility, which might break into the open unless the anti-intraceptive defenses of keeping busy, having excitement, not thinking too much, are employed to the full? One does not *know*, of course, but this formulation seems to go a long way toward explaining why it is that the very same subjects who feel that they must keep busy are also most concerned about the dangers to mental health of "overwork," "too long hours," "mental fatigue," "undertaking too much." The very activities which ward off the bad impulses may, if persisted in too long, intensify those impulses and increase the danger of a breakthrough. The point to be emphasized is that, when one is working with a theory that postulates levels of personality, he need not suppose that his hypothetical "deeper tendencies" are, so to speak, things which he will one day get his hands on. Even in psychoanalytic practice these deeper tendencies are rarely revealed directly; they are the stuff of interpretations, not just those which the analyst offers the patient but those which he makes for himself. In other words, psychoanalysis, like the research reported in *The Authoritarian Personality*, makes maximum use of hypothetical constructs. The "correctness," or one might better say the usefulness, of the psychoanalytic formulation is gauged by its service in making sense of a great diversity of material and in predicting what a patient will do next. And it is the same in such research as this: does the formulation explain the relationships observed and does it permit the prediction of responses in particular types of situations? The truth of such formulations may rarely be demonstrated to the satisfaction of all, but one may hope to creep up on it.

The largest amount of clinical material in *The Authoritarian Personality* was derived from interviews, the analysis of which is reported in great detail in chapters by Else Frenkel-Brunswik, William Morrow and Maria Levinson. As critics have pointed out, the statistical relationships based on the analysis of interview material from the regular sample of subjects are seriously in need of cross-validation. Criticisms of the methodology in Frenkel-Brunswik's chapters have often been severe, but these are precisely the chapters that most people turn to for an elucidation of the inner working of the potentially fascist pattern, for here they find richness, complexity and comprehensiveness. There is a paradox here. The interviews were not conducted with any thought to their later quantitative analysis. They were going to be used for exploratory purposes and, later, as the basis for case studies that would exemplify some of the patterns that emerged from the other procedures. When it became apparent, however, that certain differences between "high" and "low" ethnocentric subjects appeared regularly in the interview material it seemed that comparisons in quantitative terms would be an aid to description. This, as it turned out, was asking for trouble, for what was essentially clinical work now became subject to the standards for criticism which hold for small sample statistical studies.

Morrow, in his study of prison inmates, used his interview material only for case studies and thus escaped such criticism as was directed toward Frenkel-Brunswik, while Levinson in her study of psychiatric clinic patients analyzed the regular intake interviewers in a way that was methodologically impeccable. The fact that all these approaches led to about the same conclusions concerning the structure and functioning of the F-syndrome probably has made more of an impression upon the authors than upon many readers, who have tended to take chapters or procedures or special studies one at a time and to ask whether they really showed what was claimed. Or perhaps the same general bias on the authors' part pervaded all of these investigations. At any rate, it was not suggested that the numerous findings concerning the dynamics of the F-syndrome did not need to be followed up by other workers.

The picture of potential fascism in the personality was considerably expanded by these clinical studies. All of the major variables of the F scale appeared in these studies. But there were many others besides. Although the procedure was to convert clinical findings into scale items whenever possible, many such findings were still to come in long after a place had been reached when it seemed wise to stop changing the F scale.

It may be well to mention briefly, on the basis of findings from the clinical procedures, some additional features of the potentially fascist pattern: relative inability to accept blame; a tendency to view interpersonal relations in terms of power and status rather than in terms of love and friendship; a manipulative attitude toward other people; the inability or the unwillingness to deal with the indefinite, the ambiguous or the merely probable; tendency to treat property as an extension of the self; tendency to see the real self and the ideal self as essentially the same, and signs of self-contempt underlying this self-overestimation; self-pity; rigidity in adjustment; constriction of fantasy; concreteness of thinking; less differentiated emotional experience; undifferentiated conception of the opposite sex; relative absence of a value for achievement for its own sake; ego-alien dependency; tendency in emotional crises to emphasize somatic rather than psychological complaints.

Perhaps some of these characteristics overlap, or might be reduced to, some of the variables of which the F scale took account. Perhaps not. What, indeed, *are* the essential or "basic" elements of the pattern under consideration? This is a question to be dealt with shortly. The chief point here is that the F scale does not pretend to cover all the facets of the potentially fascist pattern, and that with attention to the findings just described one could construct a second F scale that overlapped but little with the present one but performed in much the same way in relation to other measures. And this is to say nothing of the expansion of the F pattern in the hands of other workers.

STATISTICAL ANALYSIS OF THE F PATTERN

The question of what are the basic elements in authoritarianism calls, of course, for statistical analysis. The F scale in its final form comprised 30 items and had a split-half reliability of .90 in a sample of 517 college women. The average inter-item correlation was .13; the average item-total scale correlation .33. A factor analysis hardly seemed justified. No empirical support was found for the hypothetical clusters—authoritarian submission, anti-intraception, and so forth. Christie and Garcia [10], however, have discovered empirical clusters which do resemble rather closely the hypothetical ones. These workers performed a statistical analysis of the tetrachoric intercorrelations of F scale items for two samples matched for socioeconomic factors: the one comprising 57 male and female students at the University of California; the other, 57 male and female students at "Southwest City." The first sample yielded 7 clusters, the second, 8, all of which were very similar to those hypothesized. But there were difficulties. Some of the items fell into no clusters, and individual items generally fell into different clusters in the two samples. The authors suggest—probably correctly— that the latter phenomenon is largely due to the fact that the items are so vague that they quite frequently mean different things to different people, and, hence were organized differently in groups representing somewhat different cultures. This research seems to indicate that the discovery of "pure" attributes of general authoritarianism with the use of the present F scale items is probably impossible.

A suggestion for further work in this area would be that, in place of further analysis of the present F scale, one perform the analysis with an instrument three or four times as long. Perhaps the authors of *The Authoritarian Personality* did not place enough stress on the extreme condensation of the F scale. Concerned with predicting anti-Semitism by means of a conveniently brief instrument, and convinced that the best way to do this was through taking account of a large number of theoretically significant ideas, we frequently made a simple item serve several important hypotheses and consistently eliminated items that came too close to duplicating others. This is hardly the way to explore a broad area with a view to sorting out any pure elements that might lie there. A greatly lengthened F scale could easily be composed of discarded items, items suggested by later clinical findings, and items written by other workers in the course of constructing scales that correlate with F.

An indication of what is possible may be found in some work now being carried on by the Mellon Foundation project at Vassar College. A group of 441 college freshmen were administered both the F and the E scales. In addition, they responded to 677 true-false items from various personality tests. Of these true-false items, 178 had sufficient correlation with F and enough variance to comprise an experimental scale. Further item selection resulted in a 124-item scale which correlated .78 with F and .53 with E. (The correlation between E and F in this sample was .59. Cross-validation of the scale a year later with a new sample of 402 college freshmen gave a correlation with F of .74.)

(Incidentally, this work offers a comment on the familiar suggestion that since high scores on the F scale are obtained by agreeing with statements, the instrument measures not potential fascism but the tendency to agree with foolish statements. It may be, of course, that this latter tendency is indeed an important aspect of the potential for fascism. However, in the Vassar sample of 441 subjects, of 353 items unrelated to F, 56 per cent were marked "true" more often by high scorers on F than by low scorers, whereas 91 per cent of the 124 items in the new scale were scored in the "true" direction. Apparently, in this sample, a general tendency to agree does not distinguish subjects who score high on F).

Here is, at least, the possibility of developing an equivalent form of the F scale, something that may be of considerable practical value, particularly in work that requires a great deal of "before and after" testing. A new F scale is needed for other reasons. The present one is becoming too familiar to the present generation of college students, and, more than this, it contains too much "ideology." For example, it was possible for a group of New York City educators to condemn the instrument as a piece of subtle propaganda for Freudianism, Deweyism, and other "bad" things. The new items certainly have the merit of being ideologically neutral; they all come from such personality scales as the MMPI, the California Psychological Inventory, and the Maslow Scale for Dominance Feeling in Women.

In content, the 124 items range over a wide area. In one exposition of the new scale, where our concern was to show something of the breadth and complexity of authoritarianism, we had occasion to mention 28 variables each of which was exemplified by a few items. And since all of these items are relatively simple and unequivocal, in contrast to those of the original F scale, it was fairly easy to classify them under 11 headings. Most of the major psychological dispositions having a place in the original theory of the F scale are represented, with the exception of "Power and Toughness." Although a good many items of this latter type appear among the 677 used in this study, none was correlated with F in this sample of college women. Thus it is possible to conclude that "power and toughness" is not a feature of the F pattern in middle and upper-middle-class young women, however important it might be in men or in a large sample of the general population.

A factor analysis or cluster analysis of these 124 items would be very interesting. The task, though formidable, is not impossible, and its performance might proceed a long way toward the discovery of the more essential elements in the rapidly expanding F picture. It must be borne in mind that this 124-item scale is not the same thing as F, the correlation between the two being only .74. But this correlation could be raised, partly by further item selection and partly by finding new items that covered the content of F.

AUTHORITARIANISM AS A SYNDROME

There is a need to know, of course, not only the essential elements of F but how these elements are organized. Is F one very general factor that dominates a large number of minor ones, or a structure embracing a limited number of loosely cohering major variables, or an aggregation of truly independent factors? In *The Authoritarian Personality* there was an inclination to stress the conception of one very general factor and a variety of relatively minor ones. Individuals were thought to differ both with respect to the amount of this general factor and with respect to minor factors which entered significantly into the picture. The same view would seem to hold for the 124-item scale discussed above. That one general factor could account for much of the variation of items was indicated by the homogeneity coefficient [Kuder Richardson formula, 20] of .88 and by the fact that the distribution, which appeared to be normal, filled the possible range, 0–124, rather compactly.

Speaking of a general factor and of minor factors does not, however, imply thinking in terms of classical factor theory. The F pattern has repeatedly been referred to as a "syndrome." This conception came from Murray [41], who gives major credit to L. J. Henderson; it had a central place in the analysis of data in *Physique, Personality and Scholarship* [52], and the thinking here about the matter may not have matured very much since the publication of that work. *Syndrome* is a concept from clinical medicine; it refers to a complex of functionally related variables. In the ideal case, the variables are so related that a change in one will usually be accompanied by a change in the others. A syndrome might consist of factors that correlate zero in general population; in fact, it could exist in one and only one individual. Its existence, in such an instance, would be demonstrated when the experimental variation in one constituent leads to variation in the others. In other words, dynamic relationship and correlation in a population of individuals are two different things. Some syndromes are apparently fairly common among individuals in our society, and in these cases the dynamically related variables will be found to show some intercorrelation. The statistical conception of a general factor is not inappropriate here because a syndrome by definition has a unitary character, and one may explain correlations of the constituent variables with each other and with the total score on the basis of their common embeddedness in the total structure.

It is highly important to note, however, that the coherence of the variables in a syndrome may be quite loose. A variable which in one individual has a functional role in a given syndrome may in another individual be absent from that syndrome. The same variable may appear in different syndromes, its nature being modified by the character of the complex in which it is found. And, particularly important, syndromes themselves, though conceived as unitary structures, enjoy no true independence; their nature too will depend upon the still broader context of personality within which they have their being.

Thus it is that individuals may exhibit the same syndrome in about the same degree and yet differ among themselves in numerous significant ways. It is not proper to speak of an individual as "an authoritarian personality," thus implying that this is all one needs to know about him. No syndrome can ever totally embrace a person. Even when authoritarianism is pronounced, what emerges in behavior will depend upon what other syndromes are present. The closest one can come to speaking of a type of person is to note that in that person some broad and complex syndrome stands out above all the other known patterns. And one may speak of types of authoritarianism. Authoritarianism may vary from one individual to another according to which of the constituent variables are relatively pronounced, a matter which may depend upon what other factors are at work in the personality. Some of these variations in authoritarianism may be common in large populations.

It is perhaps in keeping with current trends in psychology that almost all the work on the F scale and on authoritarian personality trends has taken the direction of further inquiry *into* the syndrome rather than that of asking about broader contexts of personality within which the authoritarian pattern might have a place. The accent in the follow-up studies has been more upon the similarities of authoritarian personalities to one another than upon the differences among them, upon correlation within the F scale and with the F scale—rather than upon variables which might be related to authoritarianism in some subjects but not in others.

It had been thought that one of the most promising leads for further research contained in this work would concern the suggested "types" or subvarities of high and low authoritarianism. Evidently only two studies bear directly on this problem. Dombrose and Levinson [14] differentiated empirically between low-authoritarians who tended to favor "militant" programs of democratic action and low-authoritarians who tended to favor "pacifistic" programs. The former obtained lower scores on the ethnocentrism scale than did the latter.

Rokeach [45] found that he could distinguish low scorers on ethnocentrism who were markedly dogmatic from those who were less so. He had in his earlier study on the relations of rigidity and ethnocentrism noted that some of his low extremes exhibited a rigid approach to problem-solving which resembled that found more characteristically in his high extremes. These results seem quite consistent with what *The Authoritarian Personality* has to say about "The Rigid Low Scorer." Frenkel-Brunswik and her associates *[21]*, in their continuing study of prejudice in children, have added some empirical support for the distinction between a more constricted, conventional pattern of authoritarianism and a more psychopathic one.

It may be well to review briefly here the typology of authoritarianism and nonauthoritarianism which appears in *The Authoritarian Personality*. There is still hope that further research in this area may yet be stimulated. This typology is largely the work of Adorno, and is based upon clinical observation and analysis. It is a modification and extension of a typology of anti-Semites worked out and published by the Institute of Social Research *[33]*.

There are six distinguishable patterns among the High authoritarians and five among the Lows. It is to be emphasized that High authoritarianism is, in the view of this study, essentially *one* syndrome; what differentiates the "subsyndromes" is the emphasis on one or another of the variables that appear in the over-all structure. The patterns found among the Lows seem to be relatively more "independent." This is in keeping with the fact that the Highs were more alike as a group than were the Lows. Although potential fascism appears to be essentially one structure, there are a variety of ways in which it may, so to speak, be avoided.

HIGH-AUTHORITARIANISM

The varieties of high-authoritarianism were labeled, by Adorno, *Surface Resentment, Coventional, "Authoritarian," Tough Guy, Crank,* and *Manipulative*.

Surface Resentment

Surface Resentment is not on the same logical level as the other high patterns. It refers not so much to any deep-lying tendency in the personality as to a state of affairs in which the individual is provoked to prejudiced and authoritarian modes of behavior by externally imposed frustrations.

The Conventional

The Conventional pattern emphasizes conventional values and determination by external representatives of the superego. Individuals exhibiting this pattern would be very slow to engage in any of the more violent expressions of prejudice; they would be equally slow to oppose or to condemn such expressions if this meant "to be different."

The "Authoritarian"

The "Authoritarian" pattern is probably the purest instance of potential fascism as that picture emerged from the research. It is also very similar to Eric Fromm's conception of the "sado-masochistic character." The subject achieves his social adjustment by taking pleasure in obedience and subordination, while remaining ambivalent toward his authorities. Part of the repressed hatred of authority is turned into masochism and part is displaced onto outgroups.

The Tough Guy

The Tough Guy pattern, as might be expected, has the accent on "power and toughness" and "destructiveness and cynicism." One may find at a deeper level either the type of structure described by Erikson [16], in which a successful insurrection against the hated father is made possible through adherence to the gang leader or "older brother," or, the true psychopathic organization in which there is a basic disturbance in object relations and failure in superego formation, the individual being prepared to do anything to protect himself against what he perceives to be a hostile world.

The Crank

The outstanding feature of the Crank is "projectivity," with "superstition and stereotypy" also looming large. According to theory, individuals exhibiting this pattern have reacted to early frustrations by withdrawing into an inner world, one that has been built in considerable part upon denials of reality. They concentrate upon self-aggrandizement and the protection of their self-conception by projective formulas.

The Manipulative

In the Manipulative pattern "anti-intraception" is extreme. There is a marked deficiency of object-cathexis and of emotional ties. In the extreme case people become objects to be handled, administered, manipulated in accordance with the subject's theoretical or practical schemes.

LOW AUTHORITARIANISM

The patterns found among subjects low in potential fascism were labeled *Rigid, Protesting, Impulsive, Easygoing* and *Genuine Liberal.*

The Rigid

The Rigid Low appeared to have most in common with the over-all High pattern. The main idea here is that the absence of prejudice, instead of being based on concrete experience and integrated within the personality, is derived from some general external, ideological pattern. To quote Adorno, "The latter kind of low scorers are definitely disposed toward totalitarianism in their thinking; what is accidental up to a certain degree is the particular brand of ideological world formula that they chance to come into contact with. We encountered a few subjects who had been identified ideologically with some progressive movement, such as the struggle for minority rights, for a long time, but with whom such ideas contained features of compulsiveness, even of paranoid obsession, and who, with respect to many of our variables, especially rigidity and total thinking, could hardly be distinguished from some of our high extremes."

The Protesting

In the *Protesting* Low-authoritarian the decisive feature is opposition to whatever appears to be tyranny. The subject is out to protect the weak from the strong. One might say that he is still fixated at the level of the normal Oedipus Complex. Here, perhaps, belong those individuals who can lead or at least be effective in revolts but who can find nothing to do once the revolt has met with success.

The Impulsive

In the *Impulsive* Low-authoritarian unconventionality is the outstanding theme. Here the subject is able not only to be different but to sympathize with what is different, to look upon it as if it promised some new kind of gratification. For whatever reason, it appears that id impulses, with the exception of destructive ones, are allowed rather free expression. In some cases it seems that the rational ego is lined up with the id, in others that the individual is driven to gratify id impulses in order to gain proof that this may be done without catastrophic consequences.

The Easygoing

The *Easygoing* pattern is the opposite of the Manipulative high-authoritarian one. It is marked by imagination, capacity for enjoyment and a sense of humor that often assumes the form of self-irony. The subject in whom this pattern stands out is reluctant to make decisions or to commit himself and extremely unwilling to do violence to any person or thing. He seems to be governed by the idea of "live and let live." Theory concerning the etiology of this pattern puts the accent on the absence of traumatic experiences and upon pleasant relations with the mother and other females.

The Genuine Liberal

The *Genuine Liberal* is close to the psychoanalytic ideal, representing a balance of superego, ego and id. This pattern has features in common with those just described. As in the Impulsive pattern, there is relatively little repression, the subject sometimes having difficulty in controlling himself, but his emotionality is directed toward other people as individuals. As in the Protesting nonauthoritarian, there is identification with the underdog, but this is not compulsive or overcompensatory. And like the Easygoing type the Genuine Liberal is close to reality and relatively free of stereotypy, but he lacks the element of hesitation and indecision. Since his opinions and values are most essentially his own, in the sense of being integral to the personality, he stands rather in contrast to the Rigid Low scorer, although there may well be an element of rigidity in the firmness of his convictions. Perhaps the outstanding features of this pattern are ethical sensitivity and value for independence. The subject in whom it is highly developed cannot "keep silent" in the face of something wrong; he resists any interference with his personal convictions and beliefs, and he does not want to interfere with those of others.

There is a question as to the existence of a pattern of nonauthoritarianism in which liberal values and opposition to prejudice are aspects of a well internalized religious conscience. A major conclusion from our study of ethnocentrism in relation to religious attitudes and group memberships was that the "genuinely" religious, as opposed to conventionally religious, person tended to be low on ethnocentrism. According to the present typology a genuinely religious person might exhibit the Protesting or even the Genuine Liberal pattern. It might well be, however, that neither of these patterns does justice to the person in whom nonauthoritarianism is mainly the expression of a superego that insists upon values and standards of Christianity.

This typology deserves a great deal of study and empirical testing. As far as the present work goes, there is the most empirical support for the differentiation between the Conventional and the Tough Guy types of authoritarianism. The differences found by this study between the sample of authoritarian prison inmates and those of authoritarian college and professional people were quite obvious, though they were by no means great enough to obscure the common features.

Closely related to this matter of differentiation within the extremes is the question of possible similarities between one extreme and the other. This question has aroused very considerable interest in recent years. Other workers have been quick to grasp the significance of our conclusion that in authoritarianism one deals with a way of thinking, a way of looking at the world, that can vary independently of the content of ingroups or outgroups. This means that authoritarianism might cut across any existing dimension of political ideology, a matter that certainly invites investigation. Again, our data were collected in 1944–45; and by the time the book was published attention in the United States, scientific as well as popular, had shifted decidedly from fascism to communism. In the absence of empirical psychological studies that throw much light on the emotional appeal of communism, our book has been examined with this purpose in mind. Unfortunately, *The Authoritarian Personality* does not contain very much that is useful here. Obligated to study anti-Semitism in American subjects in 1944–45, the authors did not feel called upon to give communism any special attention. They did, to be sure, point up the problems arising out of the complexity of the right-left dimension in political ideology. Early in the research it was discovered that political-economic conservatism (PEC) is a relatively poor predictor of anti-Semitism. The correlation was .43 in the first 295 subjects. And, the correlation of conservatism with ethnocentrism and with potential fascism was, in all the various groups of subjects, around .50, on the average. We concluded that "It is clear that political ideologies do not fall neatly along a simple liberalism-conservatism dimension; that the relation between ethnocentrism and 'conservatism' is extremely complex." [1, p. 183] Attention was drawn to various subvarieties of rightist and leftist ideologies that could be found in the sample, and to the need for research in this area, while the search for other—more promising—predictors of anti-Semitism was continued.

In order to accent the complexity of the conservatism-ethnocentrism relationship and to dramatize the differences among conservatives—and to counteract, perhaps, the then widespread tendency to regard all conservatives as "bad"—a highly conservative young man was chosen as the subject of a case study that would exemplify the low extremes on ethnocentrism and potential fascism, and contrast with the case of another conservative young man who was at the opposite extreme on these dimensions. Nowadays it is possible that some researchers in this position would seek to find two political leftists to represent the "high" and the "low" authoritarian patterns. It would not be so easy to identify them if one selected on the basis of the E, F, and PEC scales by themselves, for extreme leftists almost always obtain extremely low scores on the F as well as on the E scale. (The low E-PEC correlation is due chiefly to the variability of the conservatives; apart from the genuine equalitarianism of the extreme leftists, these subjects are likely to have the particular kind of political sophistication that enables them to "see through" the test and to bring their responses into line with their over-all ideology of the moment.) As indicated above, it was clinical study that permitted the delineation of the *Rigid* low scorer and the noting of authoritarian trends in his make-up. Next in order of similarity to the high-authoritarian pattern was the *Protesting* low scorer, whose rather compulsive need to go against external authority, the father image, suggested that he was caught in the same dilemma as many of the high scorers, but was seeking a different kind of solution of the Oedipus Complex.

Meanwhile there has appeared a certain amount of quantitative work in this area. Rokeach *[46]* has reported similarity between the high and the low extremes on prejudice with respect to the tendency to favor "reification of thinking." Rokeach *[45]* also constructed a scale for measuring dogmatism and showed that this factor cut across the left-right continuum. This brings to mind Eysenck's *[17]* isolation of a "tough-mindedness" factor that also cuts across the conservative-radical dimension.

It is noteworthy that these similarities of extreme rightists and extreme leftists, and other similarities that have been mentioned, i.e., Rigidity and Stereotypy—and still others that might well be hypothesized, e.g., Anti-intraception and Manipulativeness—lie mainly in formal traits rather than in the contents of imagery or in broad motivational directions. This seems to be in keeping with the fact that, in the tendency to equate fascism and communism, the accent has been on similarities in method, and on the fact that means tend to be substituted for ends. Such considerations as these could easily lead to an overestimation of the similarities in the emotional appeals of fascism and communism in countries where the leftist parties are weak and despised. It used to be, before communism became established as a world power, that psychoanalysts quite regularly found in their bolshevist patients and acquaintances an intense Oedipus fixation, something that would stand rather in contrast to the *inverted* Oedipus situation which seemed to characterize potential fascists. It seems reasonable enough to suppose that an individual in whose personality the inverted Oedipus theme was central would find life in a state dominated by a communist bureaucracy to his liking or that he might be attracted by the power attributes of communism abroad or by the prospect of losing himself in a strong communist movement at home. As one surveys the scene in the United States today, he is struck by the similarities between the Communists and cultist anti-Communists, the more so since both insist on attacking liberals. But to neglect the differences between these two groups would be to miss something very interesting and significant. At the level of social and political action there are certainly marked differences, and it seems advisable to retain the hypothesis that these reflect differences at a deep level, in the type of resolution of the Oedipus Complex for example, instead of standing as superficial variations upon a common authoritarian theme. The need, of course, is for investigation of leftist zealots by methods as comprehensive as those that have been employed with potential fascists.

AUTHORITARIANISM AS A DETERMINANT OF BEHAVIOR

It is important to note that the authoritarian structure is a structure of *personality*, and that personality is by no means the same thing as behavior. Authoritarianism in personality is a matter of dispositions, readinesses, potentialities; whether or not it is expressed in behavior will depend upon numerous other factors including those of the social situation. It was for this reason that this research was regarded primarily as a study of *susceptibility*, in the individual, to fascist propaganda. Underscored was the view that it is on the level of behavior, mainly, that measures for combating or controlling prejudice will have to be undertaken, the understanding of personality offering nothing more than suggestions as to which measures might be effective with which subjects in which circumstances. Nevertheless, the concentration on personality was intense, the enthusiasm for it obvious; so it is not surprising or particularly unjust that reviewers should say that this study "neglected the social." It is, of course, wrong to characterize the work as a "personality approach" in contradistinction to other kinds of approach, as if there had been an attempt to explain in terms of personality factors the whole phenomenon of prejudice, or as if these various "approaches"—personological, sociological, economic, historical— were competing for the honor of sole determinant and that one or another would sooner or later win the day. The question is, what is the role of personality in prejudice? How does personality interact with various other kinds of factors in producing the manifest phenomenon?

That personality is of very great importance in prejudice is rather forcefully argued by the high correlations—around .70 on the average—between the F scale, on the one hand, and the A–S and E scales, on the other. Since much has been known about the social correlates of prejudice, and since economic interpretations have been predominant for a long time, these high correlations have been objects of the closest scrutiny. Every possible source of spuriousness has been explored. Today the important fact is that the correlation has stood up in numerous replications of this work. The E and F scales have by now been administered to numerous groups of the greatest variety in various parts of the United States, and in no case has the investigator failed to obtain a substantial correlation between the E and F scales. Thus one is spared the necessity of defending in detail a methodology employed ten years ago.

There is one point having to do mainly with the interpretation of the E–F correlation that seems interesting. Naturally, a correlation of .83 between a measure of "prejudice" (E) and a measure of "deep personality trends" (F) in a group of 154 middle-class women—to mention one sample—comes as something of a shock to the social scientist long accustomed to considering "prejudice" as mainly a function of contemporary social and economic factors. What seems a little odd is that reactions have taken the direction of questioning the methods by which such correlations were obtained rather than the more promising direction of questioning the validity of the E scale. The usual approach has been to regard E as a criterion measure and to inquire whether all the rules were followed in discovering personality correlates of it. But the important fact is that the E scale is itself a personality measure. True enough, when it is viewed as an ordinary measure of prejudice, the scale has much face validity, filled as it is with plainly negative beliefs and hostile attitudes respecting a variety of minority groups; but, seen in the light of the concepts and theory employed, it also has face validity as a measure of personality, filled as it is with unmistakable expressions of such tendencies as extrapunitiveness, conventionalism, and compartmentalization in thinking.

This explains why it is that this scale predicts external criteria such as rigidity in problem-solving or lack of progress in psychotherapy as well as, if not better than, the F scale. Since, in the thinking of this research, ethnocentricism and potential fascism are expressive of the same trends in a person, the E–F correlation is as easily regarded as a reliability coefficient as it is a validity coefficient. A reliability coefficient of .83—or .87, to mention the highest E–F correlation obtained—does not seem extraordinarily high. As for the validity of the E scale, its value as a predictor of such overt behavior as direct verbal or physical attacks upon members of minority groups remains something of a question. All that can be claimed for it is that it probably predicts as well as any other verbal instrument.

When F is correlated with other measures of prejudice, coefficients somewhat lower than those reported above are obtained. Thus, for example, Campbell and McCandless [6] report a correlation of .60 between the F scale and their own Xenophobia scale, and a correlation in the same sample, of 179 college students, of .73 between F and E. It has been suggested that this correlation between the personality measure and a completely independent measure of xenophobia might well represent the true degree of relationship between personality and prejudice. This conclusion would not be found disturbing. It must be pointed out, however, that xenophobia is not the same thing as ethnocentrism. The Campbell and McCandless instrument was limited to items referring to English, Japanese, Jews, Mexicans, Negroes; the E scale gave as much attention to "patriotism," or ingroup overestimation, and to a variety of minorities other than ethnic ones as it gave to Jews or Negroes. Before admitting that the difference in size between E–F correlations and correlations between F and other measures of prejudice is due to an element of spuriousness in results, one should require that this other measure cover the same ground as the E scale.

It does appear that E–F correlations in recent investigations have been running somewhat lower than those previously reported. It seems not unlikely that, when truly adequate sampling has been completed, the degree of relationship will have settled down in the neighborhood of .60, rather than .70. At the same time, however, one must reckon with a sort of "self-destroying prophecy." Prejudice has been the subject of an enormous amount of public discussion since 1944–45 when the data of this research were collected. The present study work has had a place in this discussion. Open expressions of prejudice have been increasingly frowned upon, so that one might well expect an increased discrepancy between verbal manifestation and underlying disposition. In any event, with respect to the overt phenomena of prejudice, one may well be content with the 25 to 35 per cent of the total variance which may safely be ascribed to personality.

But it is not merely as a predictor of prejudice that authoritarianism should be considered. As a central structure of personality, authoritarianism may be expected to influence behavior in a wide variety of situations; or, more correctly, as a system of response readiness more or less ingrained in the person, authoritarianism may be expected to express itself somehow in most of the individual's behavior.

Numerous investigations have been concerned with empirical correlates of the F scale; they have asked whether subjects scoring high on the F scale respond to some other test, or in some other situation in the way that authoritarian subjects might, by hypothesis, be expected to respond. Thus, for example, F. H. Sanford [49] studied 963 individuals, a representative sample of the population of greater Philadelphia, by means of a standard interview that included a short authoritarianism scale, and reported that subjects exhibiting more authoritarianism were less inclined to participate in political affairs, less likely to join community groups, less likely to become officers in the groups they did join, more reluctant to accept responsibility; and that they had characteristic ways of perceiving leaders, characteristic preferences among leaders and characteristic attitudes toward their fellow followers. Gump [28] showed that high scores on the F scale were closely associated with disapproval of President Truman's dismissal of General MacArthur, and Milton [40] has reported a correlation of .73 between F scale score and tendency to prefer "authoritarian" candidates for the United States presidency (e.g., MacArthur vs. Stevenson). But since the findings of these studies all rest upon self-reports, they were better regarded merely as indices of the same factors that the F scale measures rather than as measures of that instrument's validity.

In another group of studies the F scale has been used in connection with the currently widespread interest in the relations of personality and mental processes. Examples would be Rokeach's [44] finding that his more authoritarian subjects were more rigid in their approach to the solutions of arithmetical reasoning problems, Block and Block's [5] finding that their more authoritarian subjects showed a stronger tendency to establish norms in an experiment involving the autokinetic phenomenon and Fisher's [18] report that the visual memory image changed more, in the direction of simplicity and symmetry, in his more authoritarian subjects. These studies not only have the merit of having established correlations with measures that were entirely independent of the F scale but they seem to offer rather forcible arguments that authoritarianism is highly central to the personality.

Although the authoritarian syndrome as put forward here embodies a number of variables that seem to belong mainly in the area of cognitive functioning, e.g., stereotypy, projectivity, its major emphasis is upon factors in the realm of social relations: authoritarian submission, accent on power relations, and so forth. Accordingly, there has been some demand for evidence that F scale score is predictive of overt behavior in social situations. There is a certain irony in the fact that what was always of the least concern in this study has been the ground for some of the most persistent criticism of it. From a great deal of first-hand observation it was known that subjects high and subjects low on anti-Semitism differed in numerous very obvious ways in their overt social behavior. For example, the project's secretary, a good observer to be sure, could tell with considerable accuracy from a subject's telephone conversation about an appointment whether she was dealing with a "high" or "low," and if any doubt remained it was almost always dispelled by noting that subject's dress and manner when he or she appeared at the office.

The F scale was designed to be a convenient device for setting forth in crudely quantitative fashion some of the more important of the observed differences. So, the question, "Will the F scale differentiate groups of people who show authoritarian traits in their behavior from groups who do not show such traits?" is not one that has troubled the group very much. Still, one does not wish his attitude in this matter to be classed with that of Freud when he wrote that certain experimental confirmations of the repression hypothesis "could do no harm."

Science must from time to time prove the obvious, and it may be an error to treat lightly, for just a moment, the dangers of subjective bias and, particularly in the present case, of contamination of the observer. All this is leading up to a report of the fact that Eager and Smith *[15]* have now shown, in a manner that will be to everyone's satisfaction, that a short authoritarianism scale is a predictor of the actual behavior of camp counselors. Boys and girls at a summer camp were asked to guess which of a number of statements applied to which of the counselors. On the basis of the guesses the counselors were divided into two groups, a relatively authoritarian one and a relatively equalitarian one. It was found that the former had significantly higher F scale scores than did the latter.

An even more impressive validation study is that of McGee *[39]*, who secured very careful estimates of the authoritarianism of teachers, as shown in their performances throughout the school year, and found a correlation of .60 between these estimates and scores on the F scale obtained at the beginning of the year. However, the most gratifying evidence of the validity of this work has been the publication of Henry Dick's study of the German prisoners of war *[13]*. Here is an entirely independent research that reports numerous findings, respecting not only the general structure of the F-syndrome but the details of its workings, that are remarkably similar to those of the present study.

Also in the realm of social behavior, but apparently having most to do with factors of ego strength, particularly intraception, are demonstrations of relationships between the authoritarian pattern and unreceptiveness to psychotherapy *[Barron, 3]* and unwillingness to volunteer for psychological experiments *[Rosen, 48]*.

There is no doubt about it; the F scale really correlates with other measures. Is any other instrument as safe a bet for the M.A. candidate who wants a personality measure that differentiates subjects performing differently in an experimental situation? Apparently not. It is suggested that the reason for this is that personality is organized, and the F scale respects that organization. It is based upon some insight into, or at least preoccupation with, one area of organized functioning in the personality. It might be called a *psychological* scale. It taps central dispositions of personality by deliberately taking into account some of the ways in which such dispositions are related dynamically to diverse surface manifestations. Since it is of the very essence of personality organization that infinitely diverse performances are motivated in part by fewer more basic dispositions, and since the evidence is that the F scale has succeeded in getting hold of some of the latter, reports of many more empirical correlates of F should be expected.

Besides offering evidence for the validity of the F scale, the work described above contributes to the definition, and to an understanding, of the F pattern. The F scale was not intended to be, and it most certainly did not prove to be, a unidimensional scale. (The whole effort was directed to producing an instrument that would correlate with other indices of potential fascism and a concentration on purity of dimension might well have defeated this purpose.) We conceived of, and the evidence is that there exists in fact, a pattern of loosely cohering variables of personality.

It could be said of all the above studies that they improve the picture either by bringing in elements not observed by us (e.g., tendency to avoid social activities and membership in face-to-face groups), or by offering usable measures of factors noted clinically but not measured previously (e.g., the tendency to premature closure). Other work has taken the direction of studying in great detail certain particular attributes of the over-all pattern. Thus, misanthropy [Adelson and Sullivan, 1], rigidity [Gough and Sanford, 27], dogmatism and opinionation, [Rokeach, 45], and traditional family ideology [Levinson and Huffman, 35] have been more or less isolated and scaled. The unidimensionality of these scales is open to question, but they have been shown to have some validity. To give various other features of the authoritarian pattern this same kind of treatment would appear to be a worthy undertaking.

Further work on the relations of the personality syndrome to behavior might well be directed to the ways in which authoritarianism is expressed in some of the most common social roles—politician, parent, teacher, student, spouse, and the like—and inquire how authoritarianism of personality might be expressed in them. A few indications will have to suffice here.

The authoritarian political leader is a fairly familiar subject. Many of the ideas for the F scale were derived from consideration of the copious literature on the Nazi leadership. It seems that American demagogues exhibit pretty much the same pattern as the Nazis, as far as individual personality is concerned. Perhaps the point to emphasize now is that it takes a great deal more than authoritarian personality trends, however pronounced, to make a totalitarian leader: special abilities, the times, the receptivity of the people, should be mentioned, to say nothing of innumerable chance factors.

The authoritarian political follower was, of course, the primary concern of *The Authoritarian Personality*. In this regard the need for dissemination of knowledge is about as great as the need for knowledge itself. It is asked on every hand: "How do you explain the appeal of McCarthyism?" With all due respect to history, the international situation and the nature of the American political institutions, it might be suggested that what this country needs is a sort of *Reader's Digest* version of *The Authoritarian Personality*.

A number of good studies have related authoritarianism in personality to leadership and followship in general. F. H. Sanford [49], for example, in the study referred to earlier, educed evidence that subjects high on authoritarianism tended to prefer strongly directive leaders of status and power and to exhibit toward them an attitude of "bargaining dependency." There were also indications that the more authoritarian subjects tended not to accept responsibility; they do, however, "accept the leadership role but appear to regard a leadership position more as an opportunity to control people than as a mandate to serve them." Hollander [31], in a recent paper, reports that in a group of 268 Naval cadets, subjects high on authoritarianism tended not to be nominated by their peers for the hypothetical position of "student commander," the correlation being −.23.

It is necessary, of course, to distinguish between authoritarian behavior in leadership roles and authoritarianism in the personality; and it must be noted that the two do not necessarily go together. Conceivably, a person with strong authoritarian personality trends may, in an academic leadership position, bend over backward to keep things nice and democratic. Conversely, Lewin *et al.* [37] showed some time ago that a very democratic teacher may, without difficulty, deliberately create an autocratic social climate. Still, one would expect that, in general, those leadership roles in which authoritarian behavior is more or less required by the needs and expectations of the followers would tend to attract individuals in whose personalities authoritarianism loomed large, just as strongly authoritarian personalities might be expected sooner or later to put their own stamp upon the roles they chanced to assume.

The role of teacher is certainly one that serves well to elicit any authoritarianism in the personality. The strict adherence to sense-less rules, the disposition to treat minor infractions as if they were major ones, the device of punishing the whole class for the misbe-havior of one member—the picture is familiar. It is important to distinguish carefully between the responsible assumption of au-thority, which, though it may sometimes require stern measures, is always in the service of cultural goals that are shared by teacher and students, and authoritarianism, which springs from the needs —often the near panic—of the teacher alone. This has been done elsewhere [51].

It is important to note, too, the very large role of the situation in determining the authoritarian behavior of teachers. Consider the familiar situation in which the teacher is afraid of the principal, the principal of the superintendent, the superintendent of the school board, while the children are afraid of nobody. Some school setups are enough to bring out authoritarianism in almost anyone who has to stay within them. But there is no reason to doubt that those who are predisposed by virtue of personality will be the first to exhibit such behavior or will do so most vividly in the end.

Perhaps the authoritarian student is but a special case of the authoritarian follower. But the problem would seem to be one of particular interest and importance because of the role of authori-tarianism in resistance to learning and in determining the condi-tions under which learning occurs. It appears that when the sub-ject matter has to do with the concrete, the objective, the physical, and the teaching is straightforward and authoritative, the authori-tarian student may do very well. But when the concern is with human events and experiences, and the teaching is of the sort that is designed to change attitudes, then there is likely to be consider-able difficulty. Here it is not so much that the student is inclined to learn only by rote or to take things upon authority, but that he does not want to learn anything that would disturb the somewhat precarious adjustment that he has already made.

The difficulty for the educator lies in the fact that, when authori-tarian students are presented with a nondirective, flexible ap-proach in teaching and a free, unstructured environment, they are likely to leave the field. Goldberg and Stern [26], for example, found that ethnocentrism in freshmen at a liberal university was predictive of dropping out of school in the first quarter. On the other hand, directive teaching and a highly structured situation, which such students find congenial, are likely to intensify the very attitudes that one might like to change. Much work will have to be done in this area before one may know how to apply in the case of each student the right mixture of direction and permissiveness, of freedom and authority, of extraceptiveness and intraceptiveness in subject matter for the fullest possible realization of educational goals.

Concerning the role of the parent, apparently individuals with marked authoritarian personality trends adopt toward their children the same attitudes and practices that they characteristically adopt toward other people. Levinson and Huffman's Traditional Family Ideology Scale [35] contains items which express in a context of child training and family relations many of the same underlying attitudes and values that characterize the F-syndrome. The scale correlates .73 with the F scale. Kates and Diab [34], using the E and F scales in conjunction with the USC Parent Attitude Survey, found that in mothers ethnocentrism and authoritarianism were significantly related to dominant and possessive attitudes toward children, while in fathers authoritarianism was related to ignoring attitudes. One may, however, sound a note of optimism at this point. There is convincing evidence that an enormous change in child-training methods, a change in the direction of less authoritarianism, is taking place in this country. Even the highly authoritarian parent is open to suggestions where his children are concerned; there is enough involvement and enough uncertainty about what to do so that the authority of the mass media makes a very considerable impact.

The Levinson and Huffman scale also contains items expressive of that traditional pattern of husband-wife relationship in which the husband is supposed to be dominant, determined, adventurous, while the wife is submissive, timid, moralistically long-suffering. The high correlation of this scale with F confirms many observations contained in *The Authoritarian Personality*. Clinical experience shows that authoritarianism is an important factor in marital maladjustment. It is common for the authoritarian male with his overcompensatory insistence upon the manly virtues to seek a girl with the attributes of a clinging vine, and for the authoritarian woman to be attracted by a determined go-getter. Naturally the two have an affinity one for the other, but in marriage both are likely to be disappointed. Underneath the sweet façade of the clinging vine there is, too often, aggression and exploitiveness, while the go-getting features of her spouse are too often a mask for dependence and passivity. The case one most often sees in practice is that of the less authoritarian wife who is wondering what she can do about her more authoritarian husband. This is not to say there are not cases in which the authoritarianism of one partner is meshed with the masochism of the other in a relationship that is durable if not very happy. This whole area is much deserving of intensive study.

And the same might be said for various other social roles—physician, patient, counselor, counselee, employer, employee, military officers and enlisted men. The need is for research that combines sociological analysis—for example, of the requirements of the role and of the social system within which it has a place—with intensive studies of the individuals who take the roles. Where the focus of attention is upon behavior in the role, personality trends such as authoritarianism may be considered to be among the determining factors. Where the concern is with selection for the role, personality determinants will loom considerably larger. It may very well turn out that individuals with pronounced authoritarian personality trends are better suited than other people for certain roles that are necessary in a society such as this one. If personality itself is under study, then, of course, one must study behavior in various roles; here, sociological knowledge of the roles will help reveal those consistencies of behavior from which underlying personality structures are inferred.

But perhaps this is enough to support the argument with which the discussion of roles started, namely, that authoritarianism as a central structure in personality is sufficiently generalized so that it finds expression in virtually any of the individual's activities. To quote from a recent paper by Milton Rokeach [47], ". . . authoritarianism may well be observed within the context of any ideological orientation, and in areas of human endeavor relatively removed from the political or religious arena . . . authoritarianism can be recognized as a problem in such areas as science, art, literature and philosophy . . ."

Perhaps this discussion should not be closed without the comment that just as authoritarianism in personality helps to determine behavior in many varied situations, so there are situations which seem well-calculated to elicit authoritarian behavior. Thus Christie *[9]* has educed evidence that F scale scores of certain Army trainees increased as they became adjusted to military life. Eager and Smith *[15]*, in the study referred to earlier, observed that some camp counselors scored higher on F at the end of the season than they did at the beginning, as if insecurity or impatience, stimulated by some unexpectedly unruly children, had provoked authoritarian aggression.

This line of thought has been employed in an attempt to explain the behavior of the Regents of the University of California during the period of the oath controversy *[56, p.30]*:

As the struggle proceeded the Regents, of course, became more and more totalitarian in their actions. This, I think, is best understood in field-theoretical terms. They were in a position corresponding somewhat to that of a teacher before a rebellious and misunderstood class. The more things threatened to get out of hand the more rigid they became, and the more rigid they became the greater was the actual danger of a break-out somewhere, and so on. [But, be it noted, it was added that] the stronger the disposition [in the personality] the earlier did a Regent adopt a rigid attitude toward the rebellious faculty.

THE GENESIS OF AUTHORITARIANISM IN PERSONALITY

The major hypothesis guiding our investigations into the origins of authoritarianism was that such central structures of personality had their beginnings in experiences of early childhood. It must be granted, however, that the evidence on this was of a rather indirect sort: it was limited to what our subjects *said* about their childhoods. Naturally such retrospective accounts were distorted by the subjects' contemporary outlook. Nevertheless, it was possible to make reasonable inferences about what actually happened. Sometimes the reference was to more or less objective events or circumstances which the subject apparently had no reason to invent or magnify; sometimes, with knowledge of common modes of distortion, one could, so to speak, read between the lines and arrive at a reasonably convincing picture of the childhood in question. By taking the many differences between the reports of subjects scoring high and those scoring low on the F and E scales and considering these in the light of contemporary knowledge and theory of personality development, it was possible to put together a plausible account.

It may be helpful at this point to sketch very briefly the contrasting accounts of childhood by high- and low-authoritarian subjects. High-authoritarian men more often described their father as distant and stern, while the "lows" tended to describe him as relaxed and mild. High-authoritarian women characteristically saw the father of their childhoods as hard-working and serious, while low-scoring women more often perceived him as intellectual and easygoing. The mother of high-scoring subjects, both male and female, was more often said to be kind, self-sacrificing and submissive, while the mother of low-scoring subjects was more often described as warm, sociable and understanding. High-scoring men tended to accent the mother's moral restrictiveness, low-scoring men her intellectual and aesthetic interests. High-scoring women more often described their mothers as models of morality, restricting and fearsome, while low-scoring women were more often able to offer realistic criticism of their mothers.

In general, high scorers gave a less differentiated picture of their parents than did the lows. The tendency of the former was to offer a somewhat stereotyped and idealized picture at the beginning of the interview but to allow negative features to make their appearances when there was questioning about details; while the latter more often undertook an objective appraisal with good and bad features mentioned in their place.

When it came to the matter of the relations between the parents, the tendency of the high scorers was to deny any conflict, the lows usually describing some conflict in more or less realistic terms. High-scoring men usually described their homes as being dominated by the father; low-scoring men more often described homes in which there was general orientation toward the mother.

Discipline in the families of the more authoritarian men and women was characterized in their accounts by relatively harsh application of rules, in accordance with conventional values; and this discipline was commonly experienced as threatening or traumatic or even overwhelming. In the families of subjects low on authoritarianism, on the other hand, discipline was more often for the violation of principles, and the parents more often made an effort to explain the issues to the child, thus enabling him to assimilate the discipline.

In view of the more authoritarian subject's obvious inclination to put as good a face as possible upon his family and his childhood situation, we were inclined to assume that such negative features as appeared in his account were probably to be taken more or less at their face value; that is, to believe that the high-authoritarians came, for the most part, from homes in which a rather stern and distant father dominated a submissive and long-suffering but morally restrictive mother, and in which discipline was an attempt to apply conventionally approved rules rather than an effort to further general values in accordance with the perceived needs of the child.

This view of the matter seems to be in accordance with the findings of a recent quantitative study by Harris *et al.* [30]. These workers showed that the parents of prejudiced children tended in their answers to a questionnaire to emphasize obedience, strict control, the inculcation of fear and the like significantly more than did the parents of relatively unprejudiced children.

The real need here, of course, is for longitudinal studies in which developmental trends in children are observed against a background of actual events and practices in the home. The closest to this ideal so far would appear to be the work of Frenkel-Brunswik and her associates. These workers have measured prejudice in children as young as 10 years and have obtained information on family background, handling of discipline, and childhood events by means of visits to the home and extensive interviews with the parents: Frenkel-Brunswik writes *[21, p. 236]*:

A preliminary inspection of the data supports the assumption made in *The Authoritarian Personality* that warmer, closer and more affectionate interpersonal relationships prevail in the homes of the unprejudiced children; the conclusions concerning the importance of strictness, rigidity, punitiveness, rejection vs. acceptance of the child seem to be borne out by data from the children themselves . . .
In the home with the orientation toward rigid conformity, on the other hand, actual maintenance of discipline is often based upon the expectation of a quick learning of external, rigid and superficial rules which are bound to be beyond the comprehension of the child. Family relationships are characterized by fearful subservience to the demands

of the parents and by an early suppression of impulses not acceptable to the adults.

In this picture of parents and their discipline are very probably the major sources of the most essential features of the authoritarian personality syndrome, the superego's failure to become integrated with the ego, and certain crucial shortcomings in the ego's development. Discipline that is strict and rigid and, from the child's point of view, unjust or unreasonable may be submitted to, but it will not be genuinely accepted, in the sense that the child will eventually apply it to himself in the absence of external figures of authority. There also is good reason to believe that authoritarian discipline, of the sort described above, acts directly to prevent the best ego development. Where the child is not allowed to question anything, to participate in decisions affecting him, nor to feel that his own will counts for something, the stunting of the ego is a pretty direct consequence. It is for this reason that, when it comes to talking with parents about the prevention of authoritarianism and ethnocentrism in children, the recommendation is: "Treat the child with respect—especially after he is about two years old and begins to show signs of having a will of his own." This has nothing to do with permissiveness, nor does it work against the maintenance of high standards. Naturally the parent has to put certain things across; but, if he is to get acceptance and not mere submission, he must at least recognize that he is dealing with another human being.

GENERAL FORMULATION OF THE AUTHORITARIAN PERSONALITY SYNDROME

It seems worth while, now, to attempt a formulation in hypothetical terms of the over-all F pattern, a formulation that seems to order most of the statistical facts and clinical observations made, which may, it is hoped, serve as a guide to further research.

A very strict and punitive superego is behind the inability to admit blame or to bear guilt found in the F syndrome. It is this inability that makes it necessary for the subject to put blame onto others who may then be hated in the way that he would hate himself were he to become conscious of his own impulses. This superego is not integrated with the ego but stands much of the time in opposition to it. Indeed, the ego would get rid of it altogether if it could. And sometimes it almost succeeds. It is this state of affairs that permits one to speak of the superego in the F-syndrome as rigid. It either works in a total, all-out fashion, when one may observe strict adherence to conventional standards, strict obedience to the authorities of the moment accompanied by feelings of self-pity, or it works apparently not at all, as in a high school sorority initiation, or in the riots of sailors in San Francisco on V-J Day, or in children in an authoritarian classroom when the teacher is away. These examples show the great importance of external agencies, be they authority figures or the social groups of the moment. Wishing to be free of the punitive superego, the individual is always ready to exchange it for a suitable external agency of control; and if this external agency offers gratification of id needs at the same time, as in the crowd where anything goes because "everybody is doing it," or, as in the case of the authoritarian leader who says, "there is your enemy," then the way is open to generally regressive behavior.

The key notion here is the failure of the superego to become integrated with the ego. It is quite likely that the chief opponent of authoritarianism in the personality is an internalized superego that *is* genuinely integrated with the ego. Yet it must be admitted that something very similar to what has just been said about superego functioning in the F-syndrome has been put forward in psychoanalytic writings as a theory of superego functioning in general. Indeed, there is some justification for Fromm's [24] allegation that the Freudian superego is an "authoritarian superego." Insofar as the Freudian superego is limited to that which is built up through "identification with the aggressor," as described by Anna Freud [23] in particular, Fromm is quite right. But Freud had many other things to say about the superego, and probably never did arrive at a theory which satisfied him.

The interesting theoretical question here concerns the role of identification with the aggressor in the genesis of the superego in the authoritarian structure. On first view, this formulation seems made to order for what is known of the F-syndrome. The individual manages his ambivalent feelings toward his punitive parent by identifying himself with that parent, by actually internalizing the punitiveness, now receiving masochistic satisfaction through submission to parent figures and sadistic gratification through the punishment of others. The question here is whether, or to what extent, this "authoritarian superego" is truly *inside* the personality. There is much to be said for the view elsewhere [50] that the superego in the authoritarian pattern derives from infantile projections and introjections, that through failures in ego development it remains as an unconscious source of extreme anxiety, and that it is in order to escape this anxiety or in the hope of getting rid of its source that the individual must seek and have an authority.

The underlying drives that have loomed largest in these discussions, as they did in the research, are aggression, dependence, submission, passivity and homosexuality. Not only were these drives hypothesized in order to explain the interconnectedness of surface manifestations, but clinical studies also provided a mass of evidence that these were the crucial motivating forces in the more authoritarian subjects. Whether one speaks of id tendencies here depends upon his definition of that concept. One is inclined to say that these are id tendencies, for, though they have undoubtedly been in considerable part built up through experience, they are certainly primitive, impulsive, childish and alien to the ego. The important thing is that these drives were repressed in childhood, and hence were no longer accessible to the maturing effects of experience. It is for this reason that the subject acts as if any expression of dependence were the equivalent of a total descent into infantilism, as if any show of hostility against the parents were a giveaway of the wish to destroy them altogether. Given drives which are felt to have such potency, it is natural that anxiety should frequently be acute and that extreme measures for warding it off should have to be taken.

But subjects who are relatively free of authoritarianism also have to deal with aggression against parents, with dependence, passivity and homosexual trends. Indeed, there is nothing to indicate that these tendencies are less strong in them than in the more authoritarian subjects; the difference lies in the way these tendencies are managed. This is a matter of ego functioning. Because of the various failures in this department, such as the extreme narrowness of consciousness, rigidity of functioning, and use of primitive mechanisms of defense, that distinguish the more authoritarian subjects, there is justification for speaking of their greater ego weakness. But the weakness of the ego cannot be considered apart from the size of the task that it has to perform. There is in the authoritarian pattern the picture of an ego that is in constant danger of being over-whelmed either by emotional impulses from within or authorita-tive demands from without. In these circumstances it must devote itself to its last-ditch defenses, so to speak, being in no position to undertake any forward movements. When one asks what is cru-cially determining in this pattern, he finds himself accenting now the underlying impulses, now the demands and threats, now the ego weakness itself. However he looks at it, he perceives a single structure, the several features of which are mutually dependent.

THE HISTORICAL MATRIX OF AUTHORITARIANISM

The above accounts of the genesis of authoritarianism in the in-dividual personality put the emphasis upon early experiences in the family. Now it is necessary to ask what makes parents behave in the ways that apparently promote authoritarianism in their chil-dren? It will not do merely to say they are authoritarian themselves, thus pushing things back indefinitely into the past. One must con-sider that family life, within which personality develops, is con-stantly under the impact of various complex social and historical factors. In what times and places, under what general sociological conditions, or what conditions of cultural change, or stability, is the development of authoritarian personalities favored or discour-aged? This is a critically important matter about which there is very little exact knowledge.

Very much has, of course, been written about the importance of German institutions, or perhaps better, the breaking up of certain institutions—in the genesis of authoritarian and fascist personalities before and during the time of Hitler; but there is much here that remains mysterious. And it is not so easy to carry over knowledge of the German case so that it helps to explain the incidence of authoritarian personality in the United States. The kind of research that is called for is well exemplified in the work of Bjorklund and Israel [4], who relate modal personality and family structure to other aspects of the social process, such as growing industrialization and urbanization; and that being undertaken by the Institute for Social Research at Oslo in which authoritarianism, among other things, is being studied in seven different nations.

When it is said that authoritarian personality structure has its genesis in family life that, in its turn, goes forward under the influence of social conditions and processes, one means that the attitudes and practices of parents with respect to their children may be responses to stimuli of the moment. Such stimuli might arouse or set in motion such beliefs and policies as those found by Harris *et al.* *[30]* in the parents of prejudiced children. It is easy to imagine, for example, middle-class parents, who have climbed rapidly, and who have been made to feel insecure with respect to their new-found status, directing toward their children precisely that type of desperate, unreasonable control that has seemed to be most important in the genesis of the authoritarian syndrome. For that matter, one can understand such parental behavior resulting from a loss of status and of self-respect, as was so common in Germany in the aftermath of World War I.

Therapeutic Considerations

Authoritarianism, it appears, may be heavily influenced by the external field forces. This is of crucial importance to any consideration of what to do about the problem. It would be a sad state of affairs indeed if one were forced to conclude that the only thing that could be done was to give intensive psychotherapy to all people in whom authoritarianism in personality was highly developed. Actually, the stress upon personality *structure* has not been intended to suggest something fixed and solid and impregnable to influence from outside. Not only is authoritarianism in personality conceived of as more or less normally distributed; it is further believed that almost anyone is capable of having his authoritarianism evoked by sufficiently strong stimuli. The structure itself exists within a larger dynamic organization of personality, the whole of which is in some kind of interaction with the contemporary environment. Little enough, to be sure, is known about the conditions of change or of fixity in such a structure; but it is safe to assume that it is accessible to study by experimental methods. Christie *[8]*, for example, has shown that rigidity in problem solution—something which has appeared to be a factor in authoritarian personality structure—increases as a function of experimental frustration.

One may conceive of two opposite approaches to the problem of how to reduce authoritarianism and prejudice; and it may well be that progress will be made in the degree that these two approaches become integrated. The extreme of the one approach is individual psychotherapy; the extreme of the other would be attempts at manipulating the social situation without understanding of the people who live in it.

It should be remarked concerning individual psychotherapy, on authoritarianism of personality, not only that it is impractical but that it is very difficult. The person high on F rarely seeks, but rather resists the idea of psychotherapy; and once a start has been made, the technical problems are trying. One case [57] has been reported that is fairly representative of the psychopathic type of high scorer on F. Four years of therapy with this individual produced no satisfactory progress. To establish any kind of relationship that would involve him in the therapy was difficult enough; and, when a relationship was finally established, it was, as one might expect, an authoritarian one. With the therapist in the role of authority and this patient in the role of authoritarian follower, any progress in the analysis was exceedingly difficult; he would either act out his new role or else leave the situation altogether.

The study with a view to the ultimate control of situations that evoke or inhibit authoritarian behavior is perhaps somewhat more hopeful. Attention will have to be given to every type of social structure ranging from the small group to the society at large. This is a task in which all of the social sciences might well take part. Unless, however, these studies of the social complex take account of the potentialities and readinesses within the individuals involved, the major implication of *The Authoritarian Personality* will have been lost.

It may be hoped that knowledge gained from the intensive study of individuals can be combined with knowledge of group structure and functioning to form an integration of the opposing approaches mentioned above. What group structures, what institutional patterns, what cultural trends appeal to or serve to counteract authoritarian tendencies in personality?

At the present time, group psychotherapy and certain experiments in education seem to offer the best samples of the integration being urged. Freedman and Sweet [19] have recently offered evidence that patients with many features of the F pattern actually respond better in certain forms of group psychotherapy than they do in individual therapy. And many workers are exploring the possibilities of bringing into the classroom some of the techniques for involving the subject and for removing resistance that have been developed in connection with individual psychotherapy. This is a field of great promise as well as great difficulty.

It is not argued, of course, that such an approach is likely to be effective with extreme cases of authoritarianism. Obviously, however, most people are not extreme but "middle" on F, and one may suppose that they are prepared to move in either direction. For them, education in general seems to have some effect, as is indicated by the fact that scores on F and E tend to decrease as amount of education increases. There is evidence that experience with the psychological and social sciences is particularly effective. This is what knowledge of authoritarian personality trends would lead one to expect. Awareness of self and of one's relations to social processes works directly against authoritarianism; one might hope that educational offerings, having such awareness as their objective, will be enormously expanded, as they might easily be.

The preceding remarks have concerned authoritarianism in the adult personality. The prevention of authoritarianism in children is a different, and more hopeful, matter. As has been indicated, knowledge of the kind of child training that favors ego development and the internalization of standards is becoming very widespread in this country, particularly in the middle classes, and a movement toward nonauthoritarian principles and practices is being pushed along by the mass media of communication. The coming of age of another generation might mark an appreciable falling off in the amount of authoritarianism in this country.

CONCLUSION

The Authoritarian Personality was an effort to bring to bear upon the problem of social discrimination an approach that combined psychoanalytic theory of personality, clinical methods for the diagnosis of personality, and modern social-psychological devices for opinion and attitude measurement. The major contribution of the work was the empirical elucidation of the F or Authoritarian personality syndrome. It was shown that prejudice and other social attitudes and ideological trends were functionally related one to another and to this central structure. The conclusion was that these manifestations cannot be fully understood apart from the total personality of the individual who exhibits them. The elucidation of the F-syndrome involved not only the discovery of the major elements or factors that comprise it but the application of a variety of concepts for formulating the way in which personality is organized. Of particular importance was the conceptualization of levels of personality and of the conditions of communication among the levels. These, and other concepts from psychoanalytic, dynamic psychology, were not tested in any crucial way; but so consistent were the findings with them, that one could be left with little doubt as to their power and productivity.

Research that has used *The Authoritarian Personality* as its point of departure has tended, on the whole, to confirm the findings reported there. This research has both sharpened and expanded the picture of the content of the syndrome, and it has demonstrated the relations of this structure to behavior in a wide variety of situations. It has not, unfortunately, *deepened* knowledge of authoritarianism in personality. The accent has been upon quantitative studies of large groups of subjects and a few variables at a time. Such studies are important and economical; but sooner or later one must get back to the individual. A pressing need at this moment is for systematic, comprehensive and carefully conducted interviews with subjects representing the total range of scores on F, and for a method of analysis sufficiently rigorous to provide crucial checks on some of the very numerous propositions concerning the genesis and inner workings of the authoritarian personality syndrome. Such interviews, combined with a variety of projective techniques, would undoubtedly turn up additional variables and provide new insight into the dynamics of authoritarianism. Finally, one might hope that the method of approach exemplified in *The Authoritarian Personality* might be employed in the discovery and elucidation of other patterns of personality.

BIBLIOGRAPHY

1. ADELSON, J., & SULLIVAN, P.   Ethnocentrism and Misanthropy. *Amer. Psychologist*, 1952, 7, 330 (abstract).
2. ADORNO, T., FRENKEL-BRUNSWIK, E., LEVINSON, D., & SANFORD, R. N.   *The Authoritarian Personality*. New York: Harper, 1950.

3. BARRON, F. X. *Psychotherapy as a Special Case of Personal Interaction: Prediction of its Course.* (Doctoral thesis, University of California, Berkeley, 1950.)

4. BJORKLUND, E., & ISRAEL, J. The Authoritarian Ideology of Upbringing. Mimeographed. Sociologiska Institutionen, Uppsala, Sweden, 1951.

5. BLOCK, J. & BLOCK, J. An Investigation of the Relationship between Intolerance of Ambiguity and Ethnocentrism. *J. Pers.*, 1951, *19*, 303-11.

6. CAMPBELL, D. & McCANDLESS, B. Ethnocentrism, Xenophobia, and Personality. *Hum. Relat.*, 1951, *4*, 185-92.

7. CHISHOLM, G. B. The Reestablishment of Peacetime Society. *Psychiatry*, 1946, *9*, 3-21.

8. CHRISTIE, R. *The Effect of Frustration upon Rigidity in Problem Solution.* (Doctoral thesis, University of California, Berkeley, 1949.)

9. ————. Changes in Authoritarianism as Related to Situational Factors. *Amer. Psychologist*, 1952, *7*, 307-8 (abstract).

10. ————, & GARCIA, J. Subcultural Variation in Authoritarian Personality. *J. abnorm. soc. Psychol.*, 1951, *46*, 457-69.

11. CONRAD, H., & SANFORD, N. Scales for the Measure of War-Optimism: I. Military Optimism. II. Optimism on the Consequences of the War. *J. Psychol.*, 1943, *16*, 285-311.

12. ————, & SANFORD, N. Some Specific War Attitudes of College Students. *J. Psychol.*, 1944, *17*, 153-86.

13. DICKS, H. Personality Traits and National Socialist Ideology. *Hum. Relat.*, 1950, *3*, 111-54.

14. DOMBROSE, L. A., & LEVINSON, D. J. Ideological "Militancy" and "Pacifism" in Democratic Individuals. *J. soc. Psychol.*, 1950, *32*, 101-13.

15. EAGER, J., & SMITH, B. A Note on the Validity of Sanford's Authoritarian-Equalitarian Scale. *J. abnorm. soc. Psychol.*, 1952, *47*, 265-67.

16. ERIKSON, E. H. Hitler's Imagery and German Youth. *Psychiatry*, 1942, *5*, 475-93.

17. EYSENCK, H. Primary Social Attitudes As Related to Social Class and Political Party. *Brit. J. Sociol.*, 1951, *2*, 198-209.

18. FISHER, J. The Memory Process and Certain Psychosocial Attitudes with Special Reference to the Law of Prägnanz: I. Study of Non-Verbal Content. *J. Pers.*, 1951, *19*, 406-20.

19. FREEDMAN, M., & SWEET, B. A Theoretical Formulation of Some Features of Group Psychotherapy and Its Implications for Selection of Patients. *Int. J. group Psychother.*, 1954, *4*, 355-68.

20. FRENKEL-BRUNSWIK, E. Motivation and Behavior. *Genet. Psychol. Monogr.*, 1942, 26, 121-265.

21. ———. Further Explorations by a Contributor, in *Studies in the Scope and Method of The Authoritarian Personality*, eds. R. Christie & M. Jahoda. Glencoe, Ill.: Free Press, 1954.

22. ———, & SANFORD, N. Some Personality Correlates of Anti-Semitism. *J. Psychol.*, 1945, 20, 271-91.

23. FREUD, A. *The Ego and the Mechanisms of Defense.* New York: International Universities Press, 1946.

24. FROMM, E. *Man for Himself.* New York: Rinehart, 1947.

25. ———. *Escape from Freedom.* New York: Farrar & Rinehart, 1941.

26. GOLDBERG, S., & STERN, G. The Authoritarian Personality and Education. *Amer. Psychologist*, 1952, 7, 372-75 (abstract).

27. GOUGH, H., & SANFORD, N. Rigidity as a Psychological Variable. Mimeographed. University of California, Institute of Personality Assessment and Research, Berkeley, 1952.

28. GUMP, P. Anti-Democratic Trends and Student Reaction to President Truman's Dismissal of General MacArthur. (Unpublished paper.)

29. HARDING, J. A Scale for Measuring Civilian Morale. *J. Psychol.*, 1941, 12, 101-10.

30. HARRIS, D. B., GOUGH, H. G., & MARTIN, W. E. Children's Ethnic Attitudes: II. Relationship to Parental Beliefs Concerning Child Training. *Child Development*, 1950, 21, 169-81.

31. HOLLANDER, E. P. Authoritarianism and Leadership Choice in a Military Setting. *Amer. Psychologist*, 1953, 8, 368-69.

32. HYMAN, H., & SHEATSLEY, P. The Authoritarian Personality—a Methodological Critique, in *Studies in the Scope and Method of The Authoritarian Personality*, eds. R. Christie & M. Jahoda. Glencoe, Ill.: Free Press, 1954.

33. Institute of Social Research, ed. M. Horkheimer. *Studies in Philosophy and Social Science*, Vol. 9, 1941.

34. KATES, S., & DIAB, L. Authoritarian Ideology and Child-Rearing Attitudes. *Amer. Psychologist*, 1953, 8, 378 (abstract).

35. LEVINSON, D., & HUFFMAN, P. Studies in Personality and Ideology: Theory and Measurement of Traditional Family Ideology. Mimeographed. Harvard University, Cambridge, 1952.

36. ———, & SANFORD, N. A Scale for the Measurement of Anti-Semitism. *J. Psychol.*, 1944, 17, 339-70.

37. LEWIN, K., LIPPITT, R., & WHITE, R. Patterns of Aggressive Behavior in Experimentally Created Social Climates. *J. soc. Psychol.*, 1939, 10, 271-99.

38. MASLOW, A. H.   The Authoritarian Character Structure. *Ibid.*, 1932, 18, 401-11.

39. McGEE, H.   Measurement of Authoritarianism and Its Relation to Teachers' Classroom Behavior. (Ph.D. dissertation, University of California, Berkeley, 1954.)

40. MILTON, O.   Presidential Choice and Performance on a Scale of Authoritarianism. *Amer. Psychologist*, 1952, 7, 597-98 (abstract).

41. MURRAY, H. A., *et al. Explorations in Personality*. New York: Oxford University Press, 1938.

42. REICH, W.   *The Mass Psychology of Fascism*. New York: Orgone-Institute Press, 1946.

43. REICHARD, S.   Rorschach Study of the Prejudiced Personality. *Amer. J. Orthopsychiat.*, 1948, 18, 280-86.

44. ROKEACH, M.   Generalized Mental Rigidity as a Factor in Ethnocentrism. *J. abnorm. soc. Psychol.*, 1948, 43, 259-78.

45. ————.   Dogmatism and Opinionation on the Left and on the Right. *Amer. Psychologist*, 1952, 7, 310 (abstract).

46. ————.   Prejudice, Concreteness of Thinking, and Reification of Thinking. *J. abnorm. soc. Psychol.*, 1951, 46, 83-91.

47. ————.   The Nature and Meaning of Dogmatism. *Psychol. Rev.*, 1954, 61, 194-204.

48. ROSEN, E.   Differences between Volunteers and Non-Volunteers for Psychological Studies. *J. appl. Psychol.*, 1951, 35, 185-93.

49. SANFORD, F. H.   *Authoritarianism and Leadership*. Philadelphia: Stephenson Bros., 1950.

50. SANFORD, N.   The Dynamics of Identification. *Psychol. Rev.*, 1955, 62, 106-18.

51. ————.   Dominance *versus* Autocracy, and the Democratic Character. *Childhood Education*, November, 1946.

52. ————, ADKINS, M., COBB, E., & MILLER, B.   Physique, Personality and Scholarship. *Monogr. Soc. Res. Child Devel.*, 1943, 8, 1-705.

53. ————, CONRAD, H., & FRANK, K.   Psychological Determinants of Optimism Regarding the Consequences of the War. *J. Psychol.*, 1946, 22, 207-35.

54. ————, & CONRAD, H.   Some Personality Correlates of Morale. *J. abnorm. soc. Psychol.*, 1943, 38, 3-20.

55. ————, & CONRAD, H.   High and Low Morale as Exemplified in Two Cases. *Character and Personality*, 1944, 13, 207-27.

56. -————.   Individual and Social Change in a Community under Pressure: The Oath Controversy. *J. soc. Issues*, 1953, 9, 25-42.

57. ————.   Identification with the Enemy: A Case Study of an American Quisling. *J. Pers.*, 1946, 15, 53-58.

58. Shils, E.   Authoritarianism: "Right" and "Left," in *Studies in the Scope and Method of The Authoritarian Personality*, eds. R. Christie & M. Jahoda. Glencoe, Ill.: Free Press, 1954.

59. Stagner, R.   Fascist Attitudes: Their Determining Conditions. *J. soc. Psychol.*, 1936, 7, 438-54.

personality

an integrative view

DAVID C. McCLELLAND, Ph.D.

DAVID C. MCCLELLAND, PH.D.

Dr. McClelland, who received his Ph.D. degree from Yale in 1941, is now Professor of Psychology at Harvard University. Formerly, he was deputy director, Behavioral Sciences Division, Ford Foundation, and served on national and international committees in the field of psychology on many occasions. A frequent contributor of experimental and theoretical articles to psychological journals, Dr. McClelland has made significant contributions to the understanding of personality with his books, *Personality*, and *The Achievement Motive*.

In view of his background and contributions in both experimental and theoretical psychology, Dr. McClelland is the appropriate individual to undertake the difficult task of summarizing and integrating the approaches to understanding personality presented in this book. In summarizing the contributions of the other authors, he uses three main headings which correspond to variables and constructs which are thought by some to be basic in describing personality. These variables are motives (Sanford and Bellak), schemas (Mead), and traits (Cattell and Klein). According to McClelland, motivation is used to define the *why* of behavior; schema (ideas and values) is used to account for the *what*, or content-dimension of mind; and trait is used to describe *how* people adapt consistently to similar situations. He recognizes, of course, the tendency for some of the approaches to become increasingly concerned with more than the one basic variable employed, and considers this tendency in his integration of the theories.

Insisting that science should not be conceived primarily as an argument between people, but as an argument between people and nature, Dr. McClelland minimizes the inconsistencies which may appear in a theorist's approach: he feels that each theorist has made some contribution to a better or more economical description of the variety which is human personality. In reconciling these inconsistencies, and in integrating the three basic variables used to describe personality, McClelland has, in the process, set forth his own views of understanding personality.

AN INTEGRATIVE APPROACH

To provide any very useful summary or integration of the approaches to personality presented in this symposium is a difficult task. Their variety is great, and yet it is a healthy variety—healthy because it challenges us to consider all aspects of the subject, and because it would be quite wrong at this stage of development in psychology for anyone to assume that he has a corner on the truth about personality. Since the science of psychology is just beginning, it would be well to gain whatever insight may be possible from any approach which is seriously and conscientiously pursued. Nonetheless, the task of the summarizer is difficult and reminiscent of the fable of the three blind men and the elephant. One felt its ear and said it was very like a fan, another felt its tail and said it was very like a rope, and the third touched its side and said it was very like a wall. Now the situation requires some fourth blind man somehow able to construct a picture of a whole elephant from these three part-perceptions.

Actually, of course, the situation is not as bad as indicated here. In fact, it is rather easy to summarize the various contributions to this volume under three main headings corresponding to some basic variables or constructs previously argued as being necessary to describe personality adequately *[23]*. These variables are motives, traits, and schemas (e.g., ideas and values and traits). Dr. Sanford and Dr. Bellak, like most psychoanalytically-oriented thinkers, have been primarily concerned with motives; Dr. Mead has stressed the importance of ideas and values; and Dr. Cattell and Dr. Klein have been primarily interested in traits or modes of adjustment. This classification is by no means perfect (Dr. Klein, for example, has become increasingly concerned with the "schema" variable, with the organism's manner of reflecting what is objectively "out there"), but it will do for present purposes. Hence, it will be convenient to discuss the various approaches to personality under these three main headings: motives, schemas, and traits.

The order of discussion is to some extent arbitrary. Trait psychology is probably the best developed, at least in academic circles; and, since traits are easily recognizable aspects of personality, it might be well to begin with the known and proceed to the unknown, to start with traits and end with unconscious motives. This is the procedure followed previously *[23]*; but here, partly for the sake of variety, the procedure will be reversed, a developmental rather than a cross-sectional approach being taken. It is possible, of course, to argue that motives are laid down first in childhood, and that these are followed by schemas, and finally traits, although, of course, there is a considerable amount of overlapping. Nonetheless, the variables will be taken in that order.

MOTIVES

The concept of motivation has been adopted largely by psychologists to account for the *why* of human behavior. Why do people behave as they do; or, more specifically, why don't they behave as they should, or as they have in the past? These are the questions which, when one tries to answer them, give rise to the "motive" construct. It represents an attempt to get behind surface behavior to the roots of human action. Basic to the idea of root or cause is the notion that it may have different surface effects. For example, Else Frenkel-Brunswik *[14]* has pointed out that, while overt behavioral ratings on "exuberance" and "irritability" are negatively intercorrelated, both are positively correlated with clinical ratings of the drive for aggression. In other words, the same motive (e.g., aggressive drive) may have alternative behavioral manifestations leading to (or causing) irritability in some people and exuberance in others, or perhaps one trait and then the other in the same person on different days. Thus one may adopt the concept of motivation to account for the variability of surface behavior in terms of certain simpler causes or genotypes which lie behind and seem to activate and organize the great variety of phenotypical or surface behavior.

Current State of the Field

What is the present situation with regard to our knowledge of human motives? One may distinguish three general approaches to the problem. On the one hand there is psychoanalytic theory in all its richness and variety as it has been presented here by Dr. Bellak. The theory of motivation it presents is thorough, based on hundreds of thousands of hours of observation of certain types of behavior of certain types of people in therapeutic sessions, and is intended to present a complete picture of the variety of human strivings. Whatever one may feel about the limitations of the psychoanalytic view of motivation, one must certainly agree that it represents a vigorous attempt at an internally consistent and systematic theory. After Dr. Bellak's able exposition, there is no need to summarize its various characteristics here. Perhaps it will be sufficient to recall that the psychoanalytic view of motivation (a) bases motives on somatic, instinctual strivings, (b) traces motivational development through various "natural" stages, (c) stresses the crucial importance of the first six years of life in motive formation, (d) points to the child's relationship to his parents (as opposed to his peers, for example) as the major factor in determining the vicissitudes of motive expression and development, (e) deals extensively with motivational urges which are not conscious, and (f) limits the basic motives essentially to two or three—love, hate, and anxiety (which may be derived from the conflict of the first two). As to this last point, one can argue that, at the pragmatic level at least, psychoanalysis has been overly concerned with sex, aggression and anxiety in combinations and permutations so elaborate that they can even handle the dominance and submission drives of the authoritarian personality discussed by

Dr. Sanford. While one must acknowledge the importance of these motives, and even more the tremendous contribution that psychoanalysis has made to our understanding of them, one may also hope that some day our knowledge will extend in as much detail to other motives as well.

Other clinicians and personality theorists have attempted to deal with a much wider variety of motives, many of them rather unsystematically. In fact there is a group of psychologists who seem to feel that one must be prepared to talk about personality in terms of a very large number of motives—in fact, in terms of any set of motives which serves the useful, practical purpose of describing a particular person. Indeed, probably the bulk of practicing clinical psychologists belong to this group. They use whatever motivational constructs come in handy whether derived from psychoanalytic theory or from academic interest inventories. Allport [1] has given some theoretical support to this approach by arguing against thinking in terms of "a few motives common to all men," although it is difficult to see how one can have a science of personality unless he deals with a limited number of constructs. Murray [27] has moved toward bringing some order into this chaos by providing a fairly complete list of motives which at least has the advantage of attempting to produce some uniformity in the terminology psychologists use in describing motivation.

Other motivational psychologists have worked primarily with animals and in recent years have attempted to apply their findings at the human level [Dollard and Miller, 13]. These theorists start with the strong stimulation resulting from such primary biological tensions as hunger and pain and show how more complex drives may develop from the association of certain cues with such tension states. Similarly, cues which get associated with tension reduction serve as secondary or learned rewards. Finally, the absence of these reassuring cues, which have been associated with drive reduction in the past, arouses anxiety, itself a strong stimulus which will activate behavior until the cue appears which serves to reduce the anxiety caused by its absence. For example, the mother, according to Mowrer [26], becomes associated with the reduction of many primary needs for the young infant (hunger, thirst, discomfort, etc.), so much so, in fact, that her *absence* serves to produce anxiety (anticipation of tension states like hunger). Thus a need for mother develops in which she becomes a kind of reassuring sign or symbol which reduces the anxiety caused by her absence. In similar fashion, Brown [7] has derived the desire for money from the fact that it is associated with the reduction of various primary drives so that its absence will cue off anxiety, and its presence will serve to be rewarding in that it reduces this anxiety. This kind of theorizing is notable in that it is largely deductive in character and is based on illustrations and examples rather than on much concrete, empirical observation or experimentation with human beings. It has the further disadvantage of seeming to work only with one major learned motive, namely anxiety, when a great deal of empirical observation of human personality strongly suggests that anxiety is only one motive and perhaps in normal persons not even the most important one. Many people seem to be motivated more by hopes and pleasures than by fears and pains.

This, then, is a very brief summary of contemporary views of human motivation. Since it may suggest a certain disorder and a lack of solid accomplishment, what is to be done to straighten the situation out in a way which will make use of the contributions of these various theorists?

How and When Motives Are Formed

First, the origin of human motives ought to be considered. Suppose one accepts the psychoanalytic notion, which after all is based on a great deal of empirical observation, that motives are formed in the first years of life. He is then faced with the question of why this is so. Can any light be shed on this fact from a theoretical viewpoint? To do so requires at least a preliminary definition of what a motive is. If it be assumed, for reasons to be gone into later, that a motive involves a kind of preverbal affective association, the problem immediately becomes clearer as to why the early years are important. For one thing, affect or emotion seems to be easier to arouse in babies; at least they express it more obviously and it seems to involve more of the organism when it is aroused. For another thing, infancy offers opportunity for many strong associations to be formed through repetition. A great many things occur over and over again in an infant's life—e.g., eating, eliminating, sleeping—and many of them involve affective arousal so that we have both the affect and the opportunity necessary for forming strong affective associations.

Another central proposition of psychoanalysis is that character set in the first five years of life is extremely difficult to alter. Why should this be true? If one translates the term "character" into the type of affective associations just described, he can think of several possible reasons. For one thing, learning theory has assumed, since Jost *[19]*, that earlier associations are stronger and therefore more difficult to alter than later ones. For another, new learning, which is usually considered to be the cause for disruption of older learning, may in this instance not interfere so much because as a child grows older his new learning occurs in a perceptually quite different world in which he is larger, more able to manipulate his environment, etc. For example, he may have the type of mother who is quite anxious and upset by the way in which as an infant he soils himself and her. He may then acquire first a negative or punitive "mother image." Subsequently, however, he becomes toilet-trained, the primary source of his mother's disturbance is removed, and now she becomes pleasant and rewarding to him. Now he acquires a "positive mother image." Does it follow that the second "image" will *displace* the first through reproductive interference? Not necessarily. Reproductive interference occurs maximally if a new response is learned to an old stimulus, but here the stimulus has changed to a considerable extent. That is, the mother may still be the same person *objectively*, but subjectively she may look quite different to the child because he is bigger, perceives her against the background of a radically different apperceptive mass, etc. The rapid change in apperceptive mass in early childhood tends to produce a "layering" effect in which subsequent learning overlays but does not interfere with earlier learning because the change of context has altered the stimulus characteristics of the environment. Thus early learning may persist *along with* later learning.

Another important reason for the persistence of early learning is that much of it is inadequately represented symbolically. One of the chief advantages of symbols in learning is that they can be used to produce the conditions for unlearning and discrimination learning so readily. That is, the "layering effect" just described does not occur so often when the child is older because after he has acquired the use of language he can classify symbolically the situations in which his mother is angry and those in which she is pleased. Thus by the age of five he may be able to say to himself, "My mother is angry when I am too noisy; she is happy if I dress and feed myself." He develops an internally consistent image of his mother in which her responses are tied to certain discriminably different stimulus situations. The younger child does not have this advantage and cannot formulate so easily the conditions under which his mother is hostile or friendly. The result is that an earlier "archaic" image of the hostile mother may persist without modification by subsequent discriminations because the image was formed before the child could symbolize, and it remains inaccessible to the symbolization process with all the advantages that brings.

So much for the forming of motives and the reasons for the importance of the early period in life in producing persistent affective associations. Now, *how* are they formed? If it be assumed, as it has been so far, that motives are formed on the basis of affect, then it is necessary to have some understanding of the conditions which produce affect. American psychology has tended to stress, along with the psychoanalysts, the unpleasant or tension-producing aspects of early childhood. The child is conceived as making the best adjustment he can to the painful demands of various drives or drive stimuli. Elsewhere [24] it has been suggested that two important modifications ought to be made in this general picture. In the first place, the strength of the stimulus must also always be defined in terms of its discrepancy from the adaptation level of the organism. At the simplest level this means that, if one hand is adapted to cold water at a temperature of 15 degrees Centigrade, for example, it will feel strongly stimulated if placed in water of 33 degrees Centigrade whereas ordinarily such a temperature would appear neutral since it is near physiological zero. In its most general terms, this means that what stimuli will produce affect in a baby depends very much on what the baby is adapted to. The second and even more important modification in the usual conception of drives as intense stimuli is that some drives appear to be based on the pleasure resulting from small stimulus discrepancies over adaptation level in addition to those which are based on the negative affect resulting from larger discrepancies over adaptation level. Haber [15] has recently demonstrated, for example, that, if the hand is adapted to a water temperature at or about physiological zero, a stimulus change of one degree Centigrade in either direction is perceived as more pleasant than either no discrepancy or larger discrepancies. The importance of this finding in terms of what it potentially indicates about how motives are formed can hardly be exaggerated. It strongly suggests that there may be built into some or all of the sense modalities *optimum pleasure points* which serve to keep the organism restless or moving. Thus, if the child is adapted to one temperature, he might seek a slight variation in order to get pleasure; but, having found it, he would soon adapt at this level and might actually seek the earlier temperature to get pleasure again. In fact, the amount of deviation yielding most pleasure may vary from one adaptation level to another. In this way one might account for some of the "activity" drives and sensory pleasure drives that have always seemed to characterize the human organism even though there has never been an adequate theoretical basis for understanding how they came into existence.

It is in this way too that the important Freudian notion of developmental stages in pleasure zones on the surface of the body may be better understood; that is, the natural adaptation levels of various sensory modalities seem to be controlled largely in terms of internal mechanisms. There are, therefore, no logical reasons to prevent the assumption that these adaptation levels may shift for different portions of the body surface at different times in the life span as a function of hormonal or other internal changes. Thus, stimulation of the mouth region may produce pleasure in small discrepancies from a fairly high adaptation level during the first year of life; and then the adaptation level may shift downward, because of internal factors, so that the mouth becomes more "sensitive," and the same stimulation which previously yielded pleasure now represents a larger discrepancy from adaptation level, or pain. The baby may not seek to get mouth stimulation as persistently as previously and, at the same time, some other region of the body surface—e.g., the anal region—may be experiencing a shift in adaptation level control which makes it a greater source of pleasure. So far this is only a hypothesis which needs to be empirically checked, but it does provide a plausible explanation for Freudian assumptions about pleasure zones and their shifts with age. Incidentally, the same line of reasoning provides a basis for explaining some of the correlations that have been found between physique and other personality characteristics, since different types of body build should have different adaptation levels so that the amount and type of stimulation which will yield pleasure will differ from person to person. For example, the amount of stimulation from exercise which would yield pleasure for a heavily muscled mesomorph would probably be of a much higher order than that which would yield pleasure for the thinly muscled ectomorph. In this way one can account for the greater frequency of mesomorphs in organized athletics, not just because they are better at it, but because they enjoy it more.

According to this view, motives arise out of associations involving pleasure and pain. If positive or negative affect is produced by small or large discrepancies from adaptation level, then motives are associations which serve as cues for those changes in affect. Motives, then, are conceived as always being learned, learning actually entering into their formation in two different ways. In the first place, it may change the adaptation level so that what yields pleasure and pain will vary as the organism accumulates experience. Hebb [17] has shown, for example, that the very young chimpanzee is not at all frightened by the detached plaster cast of the head of an adult chimpanzee; but, as he grows older and presumably has learned what the total shape of a chimpanzee is, the same stimulus will produce a marked fear reaction. To the older chimpanzee, the detached head represents a marked discrepancy from what he has learned to expect. Hence it produces marked negative affect. But to the immature chimpanzee it means nothing in particular since the expectation of what a "complete" chimpanzee looks like has not as yet been formed. In no sense then must it be assumed that adult motives are tied to the simple sensory pleasures and pains of early infancy, nor need it be assumed, as Allport has [1], that, while motives are formed on the basis of such childhood experiences, they become functionally autonomous later. Rather one should assume that motives can be formed on the basis of affective changes at any time during the life span, and that the expectations on which they are based grow increasingly complex as the person matures. For what yields pleasure in children will produce boredom later as the adaptation level catches up with it.

Learning also enters into the formation of motives at the point of the connection made between certain cues and the resulting affective changes. To return to the chimpanzee example, if the plaster head produces a marked fear reaction, the cues surrounding the presentation of the head become associated with fear so that if they are presented again on a second occasion they will tend to evoke a partial redintegration of the innate fear response and certain new avoidance responses. If the chimpanzee is led into the room where the fear experience occurred, and the experimenter reaches for the cabinet in which the head is kept, he might expect withdrawal reactions from the chimpanzee. The details governing the formation of these motivational associations have been well worked out by the learning theorists. The only thing to stress again here is that the associations involve positive as well as negative affect. The organism seeks not only tension reduction or release from pain and anxiety, but mild changes in stimulation as well because they yield pleasure.

Measuring Motives

The question of how motives are formed being clarified to some extent, the more practical problem of how to measure motives in human adults may be considered. Here again one may be guided by the experience of the psychoanalysts. After all, theirs is largely a dynamic or motivational psychology based almost exclusively on a single method of measurement—e.g., content analysis of free associations produced in the therapeutic session. Perhaps it is the method of measurement—informal and intuitive though it often is, to be sure—which led to the best understanding of human motivation as yet available. It was this argument that led to an attempt to use more formally and systematically the psychoanalytic method of measuring motivation *[24]*.

First, short, standardized samples of "free" or imaginative associations were obtained by adapting Murray's Thematic Apperception Test procedures. Pictures were exposed briefly to subjects in groups who were asked to write four-minute stories for each of the pictures.

Second, efforts were made to arouse various motives experimentally to see what effects they would have on the thought content so sampled. After some experimentation with hunger and other motives, attention was concentrated on what came to be called the achievement motive (or n Achievement), which was aroused in the subjects by inducing experiences of success and failure on tests purporting to measure their intelligence or leadership qualities. When this motive was induced in a variety of such ways, certain changes were noted in the content of the stories the subjects were writing. After much trial and error, it was possible to define rather precisely the nature of this change. It involved increased references to "concern over a standard of excellence" on the part of characters in the story. That is, there were more statements such as "Joe wanted to pass the exam with a high mark," or "The inventors were hoping their machine would be a success," and fewer statements completely unrelated to the achievement area. A definition of achievement imagery thus was delineated. Whenever an instance of it was found in a story, it was taken as evidence that the person writing the story had himself some interest or concern in the achievement area. By totaling the number of such references present in a man's protocol, a single score could be obtained for him which was called his n Achievement score and which presumably reflected the strength of his achievement motive. There is neither the time nor the need to go into the details of the scoring procedure here since they have been fully described elsewhere [24]. Suffice it to say that this method of scoring, after all the refinements it has been through, has reached a point where it is fairly easy to learn and to apply and where high scorer reliability is possible.

The third step involved finding out whether a score derived in this fashion is related to anything of importance in the behavior of an individual. Two studies [24] will have to suffice to indicate how people with high achievement motivation differ from those with low achievement motivation. One deals with learning and the other with memory. In the former, Lowell had subjects perform for twenty minutes on a task which required them to rearrange some jumbled letters like "WTSE" to make a word. The "lows" performed at a more or less steady rate throughout the task, but the "highs" showed a marked and significant improvement in their speed of unscrambling words from the first to the last minute. In other words, they had learned to perform better in the course of the experiment, a fact which confirms the hypothesis that the achievement motive was being measured and that these people had a stronger desire to improve their performance relative to a standard of excellence. The memory experiment, performed by Atkinson *[5]*, was designed to shed some light on the well-known Zeigarnik effect, e.g., the better memory for incompleted than completed tasks. Atkinson found that subjects with high *n* Achievement did indeed recall incompleted tasks better but subjects with low *n* Achievement, on the contrary, showed better recall for completed tasks. One might argue again that subjects with high *n* Achievement were more concerned with doing well and therefore recalled the tasks which they had not been able to finish so that they could complete them, whereas those who were low in *n* Achievement might be conceived as somewhat lazier and as being more satisfied with what they had finished. Furthermore, Atkinson has been able to show that some of the conflicting results of different experimenters who have worked with this phenomenon are probably due to the fact that some of them have used volunteers whereas others have not. He has discovered that volunteers have higher *n* Achievement scores on the average, which means that those experimenters who used volunteers would be more likely to get the Zeigarnik effect than those experimenters who "drafted" an entire class which should include an equal number of "highs," who would show the effect, and "lows," who would show the opposite effect, so that the net effect either way might be pretty close to zero. It is clear on the basis of these and other studies that measurement of the achievement motive is of considerable utility in predicting behavior in a variety of situations.

Dr. Sanford has pointed out in his discussion of the authoritarian personality that certain motives appear to be the result of a certain type of interaction between the child and his parents. The origins of the achievement motive seem to be determined in a similar manner. Winterbottom *[cf. 24]* has shown that mothers who stress independence for their sons will tend to have sons with higher achievement motivation. She measured interest in independence by asking the mothers to fill out a questionnaire schedule concerning the ages at which they expected their child to learn his way around his part of the city, to make his own friends, to do well in school, and the like. Mothers who said they expected these things relatively early were the ones who had the sons with higher *n* Achievement. In passing, it might be noted that certain of the independence training items, namely those dealing with such matters as learning early to make his own money, cut up and eat his own food, put himself to bed, and the like, were *not* associated with higher achievement motivation. These items seem to involve care-taking activities on the part of the mother which she might want the child to learn so that she would not have to bother with him. This smacks more of the "authoritarian" parental approach and, in fact, Brown [8] has shown that lower achievement motivation tends to be associated with higher F scores, or authoritarianism. The mothers of those with high n Achievement, on the other hand, seemed to be genuinely interested in promoting the child's independent development for his own sake, tending to produce autonomous sons who strive to do well on their own and who, unlike the authoritarian, resist group pressures.

In the discussion so far, attention has been concentrated largely on the achievement motive simply because more is known about it than about any other motive; but the methods used to measure it and trace its relationships and origins could just as well be applied to any other human motive. The essentials for this method of approach are simply a method of collecting thought samples by having the subjects write brief imaginative stories, and a method of arousing the motive in question so that a careful, experimentally refined method of scoring for the motive can be developed. Preliminary work using this approach has been reported on the affiliation and sex drives [28, 10]. In the case of sex, special difficulties have arisen because sexual thoughts have turned out to be heavily laden with anxiety, as Freud argued years ago, so that one is forced to detect its presence, even in free-associative material, by scoring its various symbolic manifestations.

One might well ask at this point why this particular method of measuring human motivation is superior to other methods of measuring motivation—if indeed it turns out to be after this promising beginning. It was adopted because it had been used so successfully in clinical practice by the psychoanalysts and by Murray and his associates, and in this instance it was found to be of great practical utility. But why should this be so?

A good answer to this question involves reference to the other variables which appear necessary to a complete understanding of how personality functions. That is, if we may assume that behavior is determined by motives, by schemas, and by traits, it follows that, if the effects of schemas and traits are reduced to a minimum, behavior under such circumstances will be more likely to provide a pure measure of motives. And this seems to be the case when we are dealing with fantasy.

In fantasy the reality determinants which give rise to schemas as to what is "really" there are certainly reduced to a minimum. The subject was shown the picture cue for only ten or fifteen seconds for fear he might be led to try to describe the picture itself in a realistic fashion rather than create a story out of his own thoughts. As far as traits or habits are concerned, the task is for most subjects a relatively new one in which they have no idea what the correct response should be. Traits which are the result of past methods of performing should have little application to a situation in which the subject is asked to tell a creative or imaginative story unless, of course, he happens to be a creative writer.

Furthermore, the subjects usually do not know the reason for which the thought samples are being gathered and so they are not as likely to censor the material or alter it in a way which will present them in a particularly favorable light. The self-schema a person develops by the time he is an adult is an extremely important influence in determining any self-descriptive reports that a subject may make, particularly in the motivational area. That is, many people have formed a pretty good idea of what their motives are by the time they are adults, and, if asked, they may quite honestly report these impressions; but the fact is they may be quite unaware of what their real motives are. For example, if a subject rates his own achievement drive either directly or through a questionnaire technique, a score is obtained which correlates very slightly with the n Achievement score derived from associative material. The fact that one believes he has a high achievement drive is itself a psychological fact of some importance which indicates something about the person [11], but it does not necessarily reflect at all accurately the subject's real motivation in this area. Thus, by using fantasy, one escapes to some extent the contaminating influence of reality factors, traits, and the self-schema, all of which enter in to determine a particular bit of behavior [23].

It would be possible to list other advantages of measuring motivation in fantasy, such as the fact that in it anything is possible—even murder, rape, and arson; but possibly the overriding advantage, from the theoretical viewpoint discussed previously, is that fantasy may get at affective associations which were laid down at a preverbal or nonverbal level early in childhood. This is based on the assumption that a strong achievement motive is likely to develop in a boy if his mother stresses the fact that he should learn to do things by himself and for himself at a relatively early age. If this analysis is correct, she probably does not overstress success itself and the boy may never come to recognize that he has such a drive simply because it has never been verbalized for him. So the only way to cue off the associations which the motive involves is to do it indirectly by presenting certain pictures or visual stimuli which give rise to certain trains of thought in this area, provided the subject has had experiences which have given rise to such trains of thought in the past. In other words, if one assumes that motives are largely unverbalized affective associations, then he cannot expect to find them by direct questioning of the subject, but must measure them indirectly through their effects on associative trains of thought.

The Classification of Motives

The last question concerns the problem of what motives may be assumed to exist. Obviously, in one sense there are as many possible motives as there are individuals and situations in which affect occurs. Still it may be possible to discover a few motives like the achievement motive which will serve to describe most of the motivational activities of human beings. It is difficult, however, to know what these are. The best procedure for finding them would seem to be to follow the one adopted for the achievement motive in order to discover the motives which are of major importance in accounting for varieties of human behavior. When this is done, one certainly should not be surprised to discover that the motives the Freudians have stressed, namely love, aggression, and anxiety, will turn out to be of central importance. In another context [23], an attempt was made to estimate the areas in which one should look for motives of importance by considering the situation of the infant and the problems which he has to face universally in order to survive. Roughly speaking, there are four major types of learning situations which he faces; one involving protection or safety; another type involving affection; still another involving mastery problems; and, finally, one involving self-control, since in every society he must learn to regulate his sexual and aggressive impulses in some way or another. On the basis of this more or less rational analysis, one might expect to find a cluster of motives dealing with safety, another dealing with affiliation, a third with mastery or achievement, and a fourth with frustration reduction or the avoidance of the anxiety which arises from society's frustration of certain pleasure-seeking drives. This scheme has merit only to the extent that it suggests hypotheses as to what motives to study empirically by the methods outlined above. Others, of course, may find some other rational approach more valuable. Certainly there has been no lack of speculation on this point. The important point is that there is a need to begin working systematically and empirically with individual motives so that it will be possible to move toward the final goal, that of defining a limited number of motives through which the behavior of all men may be understood.

SCHEMAS

If the term *motive* is used to account for why man behaves as he does, the term *schema* may be used to account loosely for what his conceptions of the world are. A person lives in a particular geographical and social environment. Somehow or other he learns to orient himself in it and to develop certain schematic representations of it in his mind and memory. *Schema* was chosen to refer to these residues of experience largely because there is no other single term which will cover all the types of residue that serve to make up the contents of a man's mind. At the simplest sensory level, there is the term *adaptation level*, which refers to the stimulus intensity to which the sense modality is adapted or attuned; in perception, there are the "perceptual postures" referred to by Dr. Klein, which served to organize the visual field into up-down, right-left, etc.; and then, at the cognitive level, such terms as ideas, values, and role expectation, which may refer to a person's philosophy of life or simply to the ideas in terms of which he organizes his experience of the world. Schema refers to all of these concepts since there is reason to believe that the principles governing the formation of all of them are substantially the same.

Current State of the Field

Psychologists probably understand the schema variable less well than either the motivation or trait variables. At any rate, they have given little attention to it. Psychoanalysis, for example, which is so eloquent in the field of dynamics, has little or nothing to say about cognitive content, as such, as it is determined by the realistic characteristics of the social or geographical environment. It does concern itself with how ideas of truth, beauty or economic life may be determined or warped by motivational factors, but it does not concern itself directly with the ideas themselves or their cultural and environmental origins. Other psychologists have worked in this area largely with attitude scales or questionnaires dealing with specific issues of topical interest, such as attitudes toward the Negro, the United Nations, or whatnot. Here the emphasis has usually been not on the content of the attitude but on its directionality or strength. Thus, in the research on the authoritarian personality discussed by Dr. Sanford, the major interest was in the *degree* of anti-Semitism rather than on what the nature of the belief is and whether it is a key idea in terms of which persons tend to organize their experience or whether it can be derived from some more basic values. This is not the whole story, of course, and this research has moved beyond such a specific attitude to the basic organizing idea behind it—namely the authoritarian-submission perceptual dimension—but even here it is not clear to what extent this is a true cognitive dimension reflecting a reality state in the child's home and to what extent it is simply the projection of basic motivations. Probably the only psychologists who are consistently content-oriented are the clinical psychologists who have to be because part of their job is to discover whether patients are reality-oriented. One of the things meant by "reality-oriented" is that the person still tends to organize his experience "properly" in terms of certain basic time, place, and person dimensions or schemas; that is, he must know who he is, where he is, what time it is, etc. In the present volume, it has been Dr. Klein who has emphasized most strongly the need for remembering that perceptions or conceptions are based on *stimulus* characteristics as well as on motives. As an example, he has cited Michotte's work on the requiredness of perceiving as causation only certain sequences of stimulus events involving very precise relations of objects in time and space. One might even go further and raise the question as to whether causation is one of the basic ideas in terms of which the person tends to organize his experience. This is the kind of question with which psychologists have not been too much concerned, but it is the kind which ultimately will have to be answered if there is to be a genuine structural psychology indicating what the important schemas are.

The anthropologists, particularly those associated with Dr. Benedict and Dr. Mead, have been more interested in this problem inasmuch as they have tried to identify certain basic themes or values in a culture. It is only a simple step from such cultural values to the assumption that they are reflected in the thinking of the individual members of a culture and represent, therefore, for those individuals the way in which the world is schematized. As examples of what anthropologists mean by themes, consider the conclusion drawn by Wolfenstein and Leites [29] from a study of American, French, and British films that, in American films, when someone is falsely accused of a crime, he must save himself or be saved by some private detective work. He cannot rely on the police force to establish his innocence. In British films the reverse is often true; the police know best, and, though they may seem to be slow in arriving at the truth, one can always rely on them to do so in the end. This suggests that typical British and American individuals have different conceptions of the nature of authority and of the importance of the individual's taking initiative to clear himself of false appearances of guilt. To take another example, in French films the dramatic plot typically involves an aging man in conflict with a younger man over love of a young girl. The hero is definitely the older man whose tragedy is that he must renounce his love so that the girl may marry the younger man so that life may go on as it should. In American films, of course, it is the young man who is always the hero. Thus there is a clear contrast in the two cultures as to what some of the important elements in life are. Dr. Mead has given many other interesting examples of such themes; for example, the tendency among Americans to scan a great deal of material without really absorbing it—to chew without swallowing!

How and When Schemas Are Formed

With this brief introduction to the present status of knowledge about schemas, attention may now be turned to a more systematic treatment of the subject. First, how and when are schemas formed? As to *when*, there is no very precise answer since such an answer obviously depends on the type of schema under consideration. As far as certain perceptual schemas are concerned, such as the right-left and up-down orientations, these are undoubtedly learned very early in the child's life, probably even before any motives are formed. But the more complex values and ideas just mentioned probably develop much later, some at school age or even later in adult life. To begin at the beginning, consider the mass of stimulation to which the infant is exposed from birth on. Some of it is geographical in nature; e.g., the climate, the topography, the flora and fauna. Some of it is social; e.g., the family, and the larger society of which it is a part. Some of it is biological; e.g., the stimulation which comes from the muscles, tendons and inner organs as the body is moved into various positions or undergoes various internal changes. Each of these types of stimulation tends in time to get organized into certain basic schemas, dimensions, or ideas. It is said that the child orients himself perceptually and socially. The orientation process advances according to certain principles, which will be discussed subsequently, but the child does not have to do all the organizing by himself. Some of it is already done for him by the culture of which he is a member. Language, for example, is one of the chief ways in which the culture has organized some of the common, everyday experiences he will have. He may learn, for example, that he lives in a "flat" country where people live either on farms or in groups in villages. The very terms "flat," "village," and "farm" are ways of summarizing simply the experiences he will have in the region where he lives. In learning the language, he learns the way the culture has schematized these experiences previously. Furthermore, there are certain cultural institutions which are more or less formally charged with the responsibility of teaching him what the contents of cultural experience are. They include the family, various religious groups, and perhaps even a formally organized school. What is to be learned by the child may be explicitly formulated or implicitly conveyed by action and example. For example, on the implicit side, there is evidence *[Knapp and Goodrich, 22]* that the Protestant stress on the individual's responsibility for finding his own salvation has tended to emphasize certain values like self-reliance and independence which are required for success in science so that Protestants have tended to gravitate to scientific occupations, even though the *explicit* value placed on science is probably no greater in Protestant than Catholic circles. Or, to take another example, Child *et al. [9]* have shown that in the United States children's readers are typically written so that certain types of behavior (for instance, affiliation) are largely rewarded whereas certain others (for instance, aggression) are more punished than rewarded. In reading such material, the child unconsciously picks up the values which the culture has, even though neither the book nor the teacher using it consciously formulates for the child the general principles being illustrated. This is even more true of an unconsciously frequent theme like the one in these readers which show boys as independent, protective, and self-reliant while girls appear dependent, more apt to yield to frustration, etc. In other instances the instruction may be much more explicit; as, for example, when the child is taught the Boy Scout oath and learns that honesty, loyalty, tolerance, and the like are values which he should attempt to live by. Since so many of the individual's values come in an already organized form from the culture, it is important for the personality psychologist to study the themes or values in the culture in which the individual lives, because this is one of the best ways to get an idea of how the person organizes his experience. He does not, of course, reflect his culture perfectly, but he may reflect it to a greater extent even than he can consciously report, so that it becomes doubly important for the psychologist to know the themes in the culture from which he comes.

As regards the question of "how" these various types of stimulation get organized by the individual (as against the culture) into simpler schemas, two types of experimentation shed some light on the process. In the first place, there are Bartlett's *[6]* well-known experiments on memory for content in which he asks subjects to reproduce stories, read to them once or twice, after the passage of a period of time varying from one week to several years. He has noted that memory material tends to undergo various systematic changes. A good deal of the material is lost and the recollection becomes simpler and simpler or more schematic. Detail tends to be leveled out so that only a skeleton of the original plot remains, although sometimes an outstanding detail might be sharpened so that the whole story is focused upon it. It was Bartlett who stressed in particular the schematizing nature of memory, and he was also the first to point out in detail how it tended to get reduced to relatively simple, usually more familiar forms. From this point of view, one might regard the schematizing process as part of the economy of the organism's adjustment to a complex world. If all that the organism experienced were remembered exactly as it occurred without simplification and assimilation, it would be difficult to imagine how the adjustment process could take place efficiently. It would be as if the person had to consult the whole Library of Congress before making each response.

Another type of experimentation which sheds light on this process is that which has dealt with the concept of adaptation level or central tendency. Hollingworth [18] showed, for example, that, if subjects were asked to reproduce lines varying in length from 10 to 70 millimeters after having moved their pencils through grooves of similar length, the subjects were most accurate in their reproduction around the center of the series, or 35 millimeters. If, however, the range of stimuli to be reproduced was shifted to from 30 to 150 millimeters, once more they reproduced most accurately the line in the center of the series around 70 millimeters in length. The interesting point is that lines in the second series of 35 millimeters in length, which they had formerly been reproducing with most accuracy, were now being reproduced with considerably less accuracy than lines of 70 millimeters in length. In other words, shifting the experiences of the subject from one range of stimulation to another range of stimulation seemed somehow to have changed the subject's general conception of the length of the lines he was dealing with in a way which affected the accuracy of his reproductions. It is in this way that native Texans get a different idea of size and distance from the one people in Connecticut have.

The schematizing process can also be found in the social field where it most often goes under the name of stereotyping. Psychologists have known for a long time that individuals have a tendency to think of Negroes or Chinese or Germans as having a certain cluster of traits. Usually these psychologists have pointed out how inaccurate some of these stereotypes are. For instance, if Negroes are regarded as indolent, or Germans as authoritarian, they hasten to point out that not all, or perhaps not even a majority, of the persons in question have such characteristics. But aside from the inaccuracy of these stereotypes, it is obvious that they have a function in the economy of thinking in that they permit the individual to summarize and organize some otherwise quite complex impressions. Stereotyping, inaccurate as it often is, represents, nevertheless, a process without which thinking would be impossible.

Knowledge about the nature of schemas and the process by which they are formed has been summarized previously as follows [23, p. 54]:

1) Experience tends to get organized into something which is simpler than the original. This "something" may be called a schema, an idea, an expectation, or a value. 2) These schemas have been found to be of great importance at all levels of experience—sensation, perception, memory and thinking. 3) They are built up gradually and often without the subject's awareness. That is, the subject may not be able to verbalize the frame of reference in terms of which he is operating. 4) The way in which schemas are built up is not clearly understood, although Bartlett's work would suggest that they are determined in part by the serial order in which the experiences occur and in part by outstanding details. 5) Schemas are built up out of personal experiences but an important part of these personal experiences are social schemas or organizations of experience (e.g., cultural themes) which have already been worked out by the culture in which the person lives and which are communicated to him by members of that culture. 6) One of the most important social determinants of schemas is language, as it shapes the way the person perceives the physical and social world.

Measuring Schemas

In terms of the measurement problem, how is one to determine which schemas are important in a particular person's thinking?

This is an exceedingly difficult question to answer, even more difficult than in the case of motives, and really adequate methods for taking an inventory of the contents of a man's mind do not as yet exist. The direct approach would be to get a representative sample of the universe of a man's thoughts and then perform a content analysis on these thoughts which would serve to classify them under the fewest number of categories which would serve to account for them all. But even to describe the approach like this suggests its difficulties. How is one to get a representative sample of a man's thoughts? How does he know that it is representative? And what about the content analysis? Where does one get the relevant categories? Etc. As a kind of pilot study, the writer once attempted to follow this procedure with an individual college student to see if it could be done with any kind of meaningful results. The available material was, on the one hand, a full autobiographical statement which included a rather literate account of his philosophy of life and, on the other, a considerable amount of test data in which answers to individual questions were used rather than total scores.

The following ideas or concepts of this particular student, Karl, seemed to be of central importance *[23]*: (1) *Happiness of the individual is of primary importance and perhaps the ultimate goal of life.* For example, he subscribed to such sentiments as that knowledge is not so important in itself but as a means to the higher value of happiness, that achievement does not bring happiness, and that life on the whole is rather difficult, full of suffering and worry, so that the individual has to struggle to gain any peace of mind. (2) *The individual is alone and cannot count much on the support of others.* Thus he felt he had no strong ties to his family and that even in religion the individual had to work out his own salvation, more or less, without much help from the church or God, etc. (3) *Since the individual is on his own, it is his striving that makes the world go round;* e.g., that provides him with the money he must make, that enables him to find the peace and security that religion will provide; and (4) *that leads to progress and the growth of knowledge,* both of which were ideas which were central in Karl's thinking. (5) Since the world is made up of a number of individuals striving for their own goals, *people will naturally compete with each other* which is wrong but which is nevertheless a fact of life and means that *the individual has got to be suspicious of others, particularly of those in positions of authority*, because they may block the individual's efforts to win a place in the world. Since a number of these ideas appear to be in conflict, Karl had worked out a number of solutions which might serve to make his view of life more consistent. For example, the obvious conflict between his ideas about the desirability of happiness for the individual and his ideas about how individuals must strive and compete with each other might be resolved, he thought, either through service occupations, in which a person would be striving hard for the good of others, or, perhaps, at a more unrealistic level, through a change in society in which the law of love would replace competition. In any case, certainly the conflict of being adequately loved and feeling secure in such a necessarily dangerous and competitive world was central to his whole way of thinking about life.

Even this brief description of his ideology suggests that the method may give results useful in understanding the individual case. It may even suggest categories or leading ideas useful in organizing another individual's thoughts as well; that is, in the present instance it looks as if a number of Karl's ideas might also be found to be of central importance to other members of his generation in his particular culture. He has probably given certain special emphasis to some of these ideas because of his own peculiar experiences and motivational structure, but the general content of the ideas may be quite similar to what could be found in a number of other college males of the same age and generation.

This suggests that a second approach to finding out an individual's main ideas would be to start with the culture rather than a representative sample of an individual's thoughts. Thus it would be rather easy to derive his ideas about the individual's responsibility for his own salvation and happiness in this life from the Protestant ethic as it has been described by Max Weber and others. Similarly, the history of pioneer life in a new country as it is stressed still in our schools and folklore would readily give rise to ideas that the individual is more or less alone and must depend on himself rather than others. Technological change and growth is so obvious to nearly every member of this culture that it would indeed be surprising if one had not found in Karl the idea that progress is not only possible but continuous and perhaps even inevitable. Finally, the fact that most Americans are third-generation, as Dr. Mead has put it, means that many have in their immediate family histories some record of individuals who left the old country because of dissatisfaction with autocratic regimes; and, therefore, it is not too surprising to discover in Karl, whose grandparents had been immigrants, the feeling that authority was dangerous, and to be distrusted. A more usual way of talking about this currently is in terms of freedom, freedom from oppression and tyranny, which is certainly a value or thought pattern of major importance to most Americans at the present time. Thus a cultural anthropologist might argue that, had the culture and its history been examined first, the investigator would have been able to predict what Karl's main ideas would be. At the very least, the cultural analysis would show what to look for in the samples of thoughts obtained from any individual member of the culture. On the whole, this seems to be a very useful suggestion, particularly in the present situation where the methods of studying mental content are relatively undeveloped. Certainly it is often easier to pick out the major themes in a culture by contrasting it to other cultures than it is to find these themes by studying different individuals from the same culture.

In fact, clinical psychology, which specifically adopts the second approach, has managed to overlook to a distressing extent the cultural themes in terms of which individuals think. Instead it tends to treat the individual at times as if there were no social reality from which he picked up his ideas. This may lead to unnecessarily dynamic interpretations of belief systems which have a simple basis in objective social reality. Thus, in Karl's case, it would be a mistake to attribute all of his ideas about authority to certain motives arising perhaps out of early experiences he had with his own father and mother. Certainly much of the substance of his ideas about authority comes from the explicit ideology of American culture which also tends to distrust authority. In defense of the clinician, it might be argued that, since most of his patients have a common cultural background, it is not necessary to worry too much about cultural assumptions since both patient and psychologist will unconsciously make the same ones. Even if one were willing to give up part of his job as a scientist, which is to discover what these assumptions are, he would still be in trouble as far as clinical practice is concerned because it is clearly not true that all individuals, even from such a relatively homogeneous culture as one finds in the United States, make the same value assumptions. As Dr. Mead has pointed out, there are Texas, California, New York, middle-class, white, black, adolescent, etc. versions of American culture, to say nothing of Protestant, Catholic, or Jewish versions, where the often unconscious value assumptions are demonstrably different. The psychologist would, if he were willing to try, find the cultural background of a person a useful short cut to discovering what his basic ideas were apt to be, although, of course, it would be necessary to check in each individual case to see whether they were in fact present as predicted.

A third method of measuring schemas includes all those more formal measurement devices characteristic of traditional psychology. At simple sensory or perceptual levels, one may determine adaptation schemas by recourse to standard psychophysical methods. At the cognitive level, one may construct questionnaires aimed at finding out the subject's views on a particular subject. Such structured methods usually require more knowledge of the schemas being measured than the less structured methods, like content analysis, which can be used to discover what the foci of mental organization are. Nevertheless, there are many occasions when more precise measures are useful and then advantage is taken of all the excellent questionnaire and judgmental techniques available.

It seems appropriate here to consider a study in the achievement area, partly because it is the area in which some of these matters have been worked out in the most detail and partly because it was used as an illustration in the discussion of motivation. Murray [27] has constructed a questionnaire which consists of statements like the following:

I work like a slave at everything I undertake until I am satisfied with the results.

When a man is no longer anxious to do better than well, he is done for.

A person is asked to indicate the extent to which he agrees or disagrees with such statements as these on a scale varying from +3 to −3. His total score will indicate the extent to which he subscribes to sentiments in which striving for achievement is stressed. In one study, DeCharms *et al.* [12] used nine such statements which intercorrelated highly and then checked to see how individuals who pictured themselves as ambitious and as valuing achievement differed from individuals who scored high on the measure of *n* Achievement. Since most of the statements involved the self, it should be noted that this is part of what has been called the self-schema, all schema not necessarily referring to the self.

What DeCharms found was that the two measures of achievement motivation did not correlate at a very high level, indicating that they were measuring two somewhat different things. The questionnaire measure, which can be labeled "*v* Achievement" for short (the *v* standing for valuing achievement as contrasted with needing achievement), does not predict better performance as the *n* Achievement measure does. What it does appear to be related to is the individual's willingness to be influenced by expert authority, as illustrated in a further study in which *v* Achievement correlated significantly with the number of changes in preferences for paintings a student made which were in the same direction as the treatment given the paintings by his art professor. Also high *v* Achievement was associated with a tendency for individuals to be especially impressed by the adjective "unsuccessful" when it was used, along with a number of other characteristics, to describe a person. That is, this adjective, when imbedded in a number of other positive adjectives, tended to shift the judgment of the subjects with high *v* Achievement more in the unfavorable direction than it did subjects with low *v* Achievement. For those who say they value achievement in themselves, the adjective "unsuccessful" is peculiarly salient. In short, the contrasting picture of *v* Achievement and *n* Achievement is not unlike the one that would be expected if the theoretical assumptions stated above are correct; namely, that subjects learn to value things like achievement somewhat later in life, possibly in school or at school age, as a result of pressure from authority figures who stress the importance of being ambitious, striving, etc. In contrast to the subjects who have high achievement *motives*, these people do not seem to be intrinsically interested in doing a good job for its own sake, but instead appear interested in doing well primarily because other people insist on their doing well and because failure to do well would lead to a disgraceful lack of success. In short, to need success and to value it are two quite different things. The first involves a motive, the second a schema. They are measured in different ways, and the evidence suggests that they may have been learned at different age levels under different kinds of influences.

Note that the example chosen here involves a self-schema, the extent to which the person values achievement and ambition for himself. Theoretically, a self-schema must be distinguished from a schema which does not involve the self. In reference to the latter, again from the achievement area, some data collected by Morrison [25] on college women showed that some of them had strong feelings that women should be allowed to pursue careers after marriage, but often these same women did not themselves want, or feel the need for, a career. On these women, there are three separate and essentially uncorrelated measures in the achievement area. The first, derived from content analysis of imaginative stories, yields an n Achievement score (a *motive*) and will predict performance on various tasks. The second, derived from questionnaire data, and also incidentally from achievement imagery produced in response to pictures of career females, gives an index of the extent to which they think careers are suitable for women (a *schema*). A third, also derived from questionnaire measures, indicates the extent to which they personally value achievement for themselves (a *self-schema*). Thus one must distinguish between a schema, the value of career achievement for women in general, and a self-schema, the valuing of a career for one's self. Unfortunately, it is impossible to say very much about self-schemas, but it should be obvious from this analysis that they are by no means simple consequences of underlying personality variables. In fact, there seems every reason to believe that they are very complexly determined by motives, by general schemas, and the like. So those theorists who rely extensively or exclusively on self-descriptive inventories, the answers to which seem to be largely determined by the self-picture, are probably not collecting the kinds of data which can be readily interpreted theoretically in terms of basic personality variables.

The Classification of Schemas

The final question to be considered deals with whether or not there have been found any suitable ways for classifying or discovering the important schemas which serve to organize a man's thoughts. As indicated previously, this is really a difficult and perhaps impossible task. It may be possible to find the important values for a particular culture, but is there any scheme which will apply to all cultures? Possibilities include everything from Mortimer Adler's attempt to reduce all of the world's philosophy to a hundred or so basic ideas to the cultural anthropologist's "Outline of Cultural Materials" which provides a framework at least for collecting data on various topics from different cultures. In psychology, the scheme which is best known is Spranger's as it has been reduced to test form by Allport and Vernon [2]. What Spranger did was to break down the content of culture into six major areas: theoretical (or scientific), economic, aesthetic, social, political, and religious. Everything a man does or thinks can probably, without too much violence, be classified as belonging to one or more of these culture categories. Then he argued that individuals, for one reason or another, come to value most highly the goals pursued in one or more of these areas. Thus, in the theoretical area, the major goal is truth; in the economic area, it is utility; in aesthetics, it is beauty; in social affairs, it is love or affection; in political matters, it is power; and in religious matters, it is the unity of all experience. Allport and Vernon have constructed questions in each of these six areas, the answers to which will provide scores indicating the strength of the subject's interests in each of these six areas and the extent to which he is influenced by the six major values supposedly reflected in preference for activities in these areas. The scheme has a certain appealing simplicity and has many practical advantages. What it lacks is a method of classifying the particular nature of the ideas or values a person has in each of these areas. The score for intensity of interest does not give a sufficient picture of the content of the interest.

Florence Kluckhohn [21] has adopted a somewhat different approach with the same end in view. She asks how a particular culture has answered certain basic philosophical questions, on the assumption that there are only three major ways in which such questions can be answered. For example, what does the culture believe man's relationship to nature is? Man may be viewed as being *over* nature (e.g., as controlling and directing it to his ends), as *in* nature (e.g., as being part of it), or as *under* nature (e.g., as being a pawn more or less pushed about by forces much greater than himself). Other basic questions include: What is man's essential nature? (Evil, good, or neither.) What is the important time dimension? (Past, present, future.) Etc.

There is no doubt but that it is possible to classify cultures and individuals as to the general stand they take on these issues. The question that remains to be settled is whether or not classifying ideology in this way is useful in accounting for the other things that people do. In other words, the problem here is the same as it was with motivation. In order to decide what motives or what schemas are to be worked with, one needs to find those which will account for as much of the variability of human experience and behavior as possible. It may seem to be a long way off; but, nonetheless, it must remain part of one's scientific faith to believe that, ultimately, there will evolve a kind of periodic table of basic elements in terms of which it will be convenient to summarize the variations in human thought patterns. Possibly one of the most promising approaches for determining what the basic elements are is to proceed developmentally, starting with some of the simple sensory and perceptual schemas, or postures, as Dr. Klein has called them, in terms of which early experience is organized and then proceeding to more complex schemas which may, in the final analysis, simply be elaborations of these more basic ones.

TRAITS

The trait variable probably ought to be reserved primarily to describe the consistencies in behavior or the modes of adjustment which the subject habitually adopts to meet recurrent situations. If the motive construct is to account for the *why* of behavior, and the schema construct for the *what*, then the trait construct is to account for the *how* of behavior. In some respects, traits are the most obvious aspects of personality; they are nearest the surface, most easily identified, and most often used to describe another person. Thus it is said that someone is adaptable, quick-witted, energetic, cold, or whatnot. The term *trait* is being used here in a somewhat more limited sense than Dr. Cattell has used it, since it is felt that other constructs are needed to account for personality whereas the trait construct alone, in its most general sense, suffices for him. As used here, the term refers primarily to what Allport [1] has called expressive or adjustive traits, as contrasted to dynamic traits.

Current State of the Field

Where does trait theory stand today? Perhaps because traits are so easily identified, but probably more because of the importance of learning theory in American psychology, trait psychology is the oldest and best developed approach to personality in this country. Four different types of contributions to trait psychology may be distinguished. First, there is Allport's careful and definitive theoretical analysis of traits, in which he deals with such issues as how large or general traits are, how consistent they are, how they should be named, what types of traits need to be distinguished, and the like. He has also provided a good definition of a trait. For him, it is an endopsychic system which serves to render certain situations equivalent and to guide and direct consistent responses. At the concrete level, for example, a person who is hard-working may be thought of as having a trait which will serve to make many situations perceptually alike in that they are perceived as calling for hard work; and as having a trait which will also serve to make the individual work hard in many different ways, in hoeing the garden, driving his car, pursuing his career, and the like.

Dr. Cattell has taken a somewhat different slant on the trait problem. For him a trait is revealed essentially by the covariation of behavior elements, particularly as revealed by factor analysis. For him the correlation coefficient is the weapon of choice and with it he has developed an elaborate and systematic trait psychology. He has searched most vigorously for the basic or primary traits which psychologists, as scientists, need to assume in order to account for the variety of human behavior. He has started with trait descriptions—with the dictionary—and has used ratings on such descriptions to discover by factor analysis the minimum number of basic traits needed to account for the whole universe of such ratings. Then he has proceeded to questionnaire studies and attempted to find the same basic factors again. Finally, he hopes to find the same factors a third time in an analysis of the behavior of individuals in a wide variety of actual experimental situations.

At least in theory, Cattell feels that we have really solid evidence for the existence of a trait only when it appears in a factor analysis involving each of these three different methods of measurement. The major virtue of this procedure appears to be its stress on the necessity of discovering basic traits in terms of which it is possible to describe the variety of human behavior. Its major defect is suggested by the difficulty he has had in matching factors obtained from ratings and questionnaire studies with those obtained from experimental studies. In the first two cases, the measures involve essentially trait perception, either perception by an outside judge or perception by the subject himself of his own behavior. Now it is possible that there is such a thing as the social psychology of trait perception. People may tend to organize their perception of other people's behavior in ways which reflect their culture or their own values and ideology rather than the "True" way in which personality is organized. As Dr. Mead has suggested, why should ratings based on the English dictionary of trait names give the same factors as the Chinese dictionary? And which is to have priority scientifically?

A clear instance of what may be a temporary social movement in trait psychology is the tendency of a large number of psychologists to think nowadays of an individual's behavior as being organized along an autocratic-democratic dimension. It is quite likely that a factor analysis of these psychologists' ratings of themselves or other people would produce a factor corresponding to this dimension because they tend to think in these terms. Yet it does not seem too farfetched to assume that the tendency to perceive behavior in this way is dictated in part at the present time by certain political and social conditions which may change. The best way to avoid this problem seems to be to work with patterns of behavior as directly measured in Cattell's third experimental approach rather than with judgments of patterns of behavior.

Another group of workers has concentrated heavily on the modes of defense that a subject adopts in dealing with various kinds of threats and anxieties. By and large, psychoanalysts and clinical psychologists are found in this group. They are not so much interested, for example, in whether a person is clever or hard-working as in whether he uses repression or denial as consistent modes of dealing with anxiety. Nevertheless, it is necessary to classify these people as contributors to trait psychology since they are primarily concerned with consistent modes of adjustment; and, furthermore, there are now good measuring instruments for many of the defense mechanisms they speak of, such as Blum's Blacky Test and Rosenzweig's P-F Study. The Rorschach is another clinical instrument which can be used for getting at traits; this time in the perceptual sphere, since the method of analyzing responses involves largely a classification of perceptual modes of approach, whether form-dominated, movement-dominated, or whatnot. The authoritarian personality research group, which Dr. Sanford represents, has stressed the importance of rigidity or intolerance of ambiguity as a mode of defense, although other workers have had difficulty in deciding whether rigidity is an identifiable trait unity *[4, 20]*. Certainly it is not if it is used in all the senses in which psychologists have employed the term.

There is a shading-off here into the fourth group of contributions to trait psychology—much too large to describe in detail—which includes loosely all those empirical studies of particular traits from punctuality to rigidity which have not as yet been integrated into an over-all theory. Here, as is the case with the other variables, a great deal of empirical spadework has to be done before any very useful theory of traits can be developed.

How and When Traits Are Formed

But what is there to be said at this stage by way of systematic treatment of the trait concept? To follow a developmental approach, it has been argued that traits are formed possibly somewhat later, or at least more slowly, than motives or schemas. Again, this is an obvious oversimplification. For example, a baby may begin to learn to adopt smiling as a method of meeting social situations as soon as the innate smiling response drops out, say around the sixth month. If one accepts the limited view of a trait which considers it more or less as a habit, he could imagine that in one child smiling might be a response which is strongly rewarded in that it leads adults to feed the baby or play with it, whereas in another baby nonsmiling or taciturnity might be more rewarded possibly because the mother is anxious and feeds the baby if it is not smiling. In the first instance, smiling may in time, if it continues to be rewarded, come to be a consistent mode of adjustment which the child adopts in social situations whereas in the latter smiling may be a good deal less frequent.

Furthermore, the first child may generalize his smiling behavior and become generally emotionally expressive whereas the second child may continue to be relatively inhibited, so that in time one may speak of the trait of "expressive vs. inhibited emotional expression."

From the imaginary example, it is evident that the learning of traits may begin quite early, sometimes even earlier than the learning of motives or schemas; but, on the other hand, traits probably take longer to mature and to become the stable modes of adjustment they are in adulthood: the learning seems to continue over a longer period of time so that the traits become increasingly strong and increasingly broad as the person grows older. Probably the only justification at all for stating that traits are learned later lies in the fact that they may reach their mature or stable form somewhat later than motives or schemas although, of course, some schemas, such as those included in the philosophy of life, may also mature very late. Thus, expressive traits, such as gait and emotional "openness," may be laid down in early childhood whereas others, like neatness, may be acquired at school age, and still others, like participation in community affairs, may not appear until adulthood.

Since traits have been treated here more or less as learned responses, and since responses are usually thought to be learned through the intervention of some motive and reward, one may well ask the question of what the relationship between a motive and a trait is. The question is especially important because the motive problem has been treated in a somewhat unusual way. At the simplest level, one may continue to assume that, in some as yet not clearly understood way, an affective association (which is a rough definition of a motive) does facilitate the formation of specific stimulus-response connections. So far there is nothing new or different about this. However, this conception of what leads to positive and negative affect does help one to understand how some traits may develop their own internal rewards in a way that leads them to continue after extrinsic rewards and punishments have disappeared.

Allport [1], in particular, has argued that some traits seem to persist in the absence of external motivators. This phenomenon may be rather readily understood in terms of the propositions advanced above about the development of expectation levels and the positive and negative affect arising over slight deviations from those expectation levels. To use a homely example, a child may be threatened or cajoled into brushing his teeth. After he has done it often enough, he may build up a fairly firm expectation level about brushing his teeth such that his omitting it constitutes a major break from expectation and yields negative affect by definition. Similarly, minor variations in the way one performs such an act may continue to yield positive affect. Thus, after an expectation level is developed, the basic elements are present for creating positive and negative affect by deviations from it, and one can readily understand how habits formed for other reasons may continue "under their own steam." Perhaps there is something in the parental argument that, if one forms the habit of going to church while young, he may learn to like it!

Our definition of a trait is somewhat different from the ones given by Cattell or Allport. In terms of Allport's trait definition, one would argue that it is the person's schema or schematic system which determines whether situations are reacted to as equivalent, and to some extent it is the person's motives which guide and direct consistent responses. The trait then must be the consistent response system itself which occurs when situations are viewed as similar and when the subject is similarly motivated.

The formal definition of a trait given by the present writer is as follows: "A trait is the learned tendency of an individual to react as he has reacted more or less successfully in the past in similar situations when similarly motivated." *[23, p. 216]* The phrase "as he has reacted" is not very precise, but refers to a range of similar responses—similarity being defined as expressive or "means" similarity rather than "ends" similarity. The remainder of the definition is the "other things equal" aspect of any formal scientific definition; that is, one could not expect a person to show similar trait behavior unless the situation and his motivation were also somewhat similar to what they had been in the past.

If a person is usually polite in social situations, but perceives a psychologist giving him a test, not as a fellow human being but as a person who might uncover disreputable secrets, then it would not be too surprising if he reacted impolitely to the psychologist. In such a case one may conclude that the perceived situation falls outside the normal range of situations in which he expects the trait to occur. If the subject's motivation is different—for example, he happens to dislike intensely this particular psychologist who is testing him—one might expect also some variation in the normal politeness which he displays. The problem in trait psychology, as Allport has pointed out so well, is to find a maximally useful number of similar situations and similar motivations in which a class of similar responses will occur. Obviously some middle ground is necessary. If the range of situations to be included is too large, then the trait becomes inconsistent; and, if it is too small, then the trait may be highly consistent (for example, brushing one's teeth every morning). However, consistency is obtained too often at the price of insufficient generality to be scientifically economical.

Measuring Traits

This brings the discussion to the measurement problem. How does one determine whether a particular person has a given trait? Usually he asks the person a number of questions about his behavior, or he asks someone else to judge whether the person displays that behavior; but, as has been seen above, the drawback of either of these procedures is that it may be contaminated by conscious or unconscious assumptions which the judge makes. Thus the ideal method is simply to observe for the presence of the response system in question under a variety of similar test situations. Few trait studies have employed this method directly or, when they have, they have often not found much evidence for a general trait. Thus, on the negative side, there are studies like Hartshorne and May's on honesty [16], and several recent studies of rigidity [4, 20] where in no case could much evidence for general traits be found. One might object to these studies on the grounds that the "other things equal" part of the trait definition given above was not strictly observed.

Motivation, in particular, may well have varied in the different, supposedly similar testing situations. On the positive side, there are such classical studies as Allport and Vernon's investigation of expressive movements [3], in which, for example, they found pretty good evidence for general trait dimensions of "energetic vs. weak" and "expansive vs. restrained." Again, on theoretical grounds, one might argue the reason that they did find evidence for such general traits is that the situation does remain fairly constant; that is, the situation of moving a physique of given shape and size through space, acting against gravity, etc. Moreover, the motivation remains constant; that is, it is difficult to imagine what motives, other than simply pleasing the experimenter by performing a variety of tasks, could have entered to distort the types of movements made in the test situations used by Allport and Vernon. By way of contrast, consider the variety of possible motives involved in testing for rigidity, when it has been common practice to threaten subjects in various ways in order to see whether or not they become rigid in their responses. It is at least a plausible hypothesis that much of the measurement of traits has been severely handicapped by lack of control of motivational and situational variables. In future research, both should be held constant so far as possible, or at least held within a limited range of variation.

What about factor analysis as a method of measurement, particularly since it has been so ably advocated by Dr. Cattell? The writer feels that factor analysis is a method of measurement which is valuable to the extent that it follows one's theoretical conclusions rather than creates them. For example, in the present instance it is clear that factor analysis will give rather meaningless results provided it does not obey the "other things equal" aspect of the trait definition given above. If the measurements which go into factor analysis are contaminated by testing which is done under a wide variety of motivating conditions, or if the measurements involve judgments of traits either by the subject or by others, then the results are not likely to give pure measures of any particular trait. On the other hand, if measurements are carefully made under controlled conditions, factor analysis should certainly be a superior method of discovering covariation of response elements. From a somewhat more analytic point of view, the current type of factor discovered is a strange conglomeration of motives, schemas, and traits, and as such is not particularly useful in describing personality. But it is readily recognized that, for those who, like Dr. Cattell, do not make the same breakdown into basic personality variables, the method may seem the only way of finding basic unities in terms of which they can describe the variety of human behavior.

The Classification of Traits

Perhaps a good way of comparing the writer's approach with Dr. Cattell's is to present together, as in Table 1, the list of traits obtained by the two methods, recognizing, of course, that in both cases the list is tentative. On the left-hand side are listed the fifteen traits for which it is felt there is pretty good evidence in the literature based on a variety of studies. Nearly every trait has been found several times by independent methods of study *[23, p. 231]*. On the right-hand side are Dr. Cattell's basic factors, which he has found in several different studies involving both ratings and self-descriptive inventories. They have been put opposite traits on the left, wherever possible, to show similarities, but such a procedure is a difficult one to carry out because under consideration here are two different conceptions as to what a trait is. Thus, it can be seen that trait descriptions on the left are restricted to specific response systems in line with the theoretical definition given above, whereas Cattell's factors overlap a variety of response systems. In the former, Trait 2, "expansive vs. restrained" refers to bodily movements whether of arm, leg, trunk, or whatnot. It is possible, but apparently not yet demonstrated, that this movement trait may be similar to Trait 11, "expressive vs. inhibited," as far as emotional life is concerned; that is, most expansive people may also express their emotions freely. However, in the absence of evidence that this is so, it seems preferable to stick more closely to the empirical evidence that there are two separate identifiable traits. And incidentally, the fact that *ratings* of expressiveness and expansiveness might correlate could not be taken as evidence that the traits are similar, since it might only mean that they were *perceived* as related.

On the other hand, Cattell's factor called "cyclothymia vs. schizothymia" cuts across both emotion and movement, and it is difficult to find out from the original measurements whether emotion or movement is actually involved because the measurements involve ratings or self-descriptions in which the two may be lumped together in the judge's mind. From this writer's point of view, Cattell's factors are too complex and not easily identified with particular types of behavior. For instance, they contain a number of subtraits, some of fairly low saturation, which refer to response systems so diverse as to be hard to imagine under a single heading.

Table 1

Basic traits as isolated by McClelland and Cattell

RESPONSE SYSTEM	MC CLELLAND [23, p. 231]	CATTELL
A. Moving	1) Energetic vs. Weak	H. Immunity vs. Reactivity to Threat
	2) Expansive vs. Restrained	I. Mollity vs. Durity
B. Thinking	3) Wholistic vs. Analytic	C. Neurotic General Emotionality vs. Ego Strength
	4) Symbolic Style (visual, verbal, etc.)	A. Cyclothymia vs. Schizothymia
	5) Fluent vs. Inhibited	F. Surgency vs. Desurgency
	6) Inner vs. Outer Orientation	M. Ease vs. Concern
C. Performing	7) Variable vs. Even	E. Dominance-Ascendance vs. Submissiveness
	8) Flexible vs. Rigid	G. Superego Strength vs. Dependent, Noncompulsive Character
	9) Persistent vs. Distractable	B. General Mental Capacity vs. Mental Defect
D. Emoting	10) Labile vs. Even-tempered	K. Socialized, Cultured Mind vs. Boorishness
	11) Expressive vs. Inhibited	L. Trustful Cyclothymia vs. Paranoia
	12) Cheerful vs. Depressed	N. Sophistication vs. Simplicity
E. Interacting	13) Gregarious vs. Autonomous	
	14) Assertive vs. Submissive	
F. Conforming	15) Conscientious vs. Not Conscientious	

But after all, it is a question of utility, and time alone will tell which type of approach psychologists ultimately find more useful in economically describing the variety of consistent behavior which people show. At least it is clear that both approaches have the same end in view: both want to find the basic conceptual units which will economically describe people's behavior. The methods of getting there are, simply, different. One prefers what seems to be a somewhat simpler "trait by trait" discovery whereas the other prefers a more global, direct approach in which somewhat larger and more complex trait units are obtained. It is possible that pursuit of *both* methods energetically may ultimately lead to better insights into the trait problem.

CONCLUSION

In conclusion, it remains only to summarize briefly what has been done. The task of a science of personality, as of any science, is to account for a multitude of particulars with as few general constructs and laws as possible. In personality, this task is more complicated than with other sciences for several reasons. In the first place, there are two types of universes to generalize about: one, the universe of all people's behavior, and the other, the total behavior of each individual in the universe. It does not follow automatically that constructs useful in describing the first universe will apply equally well in describing the behavior of a particular individual. In the second place, it may be, as it is commonly asserted, that human behavior is intrinsically more variable than the response elements of other universes of discourse. It certainly seems to be.

The task being defined, it has been argued that there are three basic, different types of constructs which need to be used to describe our universe. The first of these, *motivation*, is used roughly to describe the *why* of behavior; the second, *schema*, is used to account for the *what*, or content dimension of mind; and the third, *trait*, is used to describe *how* people adapt consistently to similar situations. Within each of these general categories of constructs, one must identify particular motives, particular schemas, and particular traits which are useful in summarizing the behavior of particular individuals and which, at the same time, are not so limited in scope that they will apply only to a few such individuals. Thus, when it has been argued that the achievement motive has been identified as a type of motive which can be used scientifically to describe a variety of behavior in concrete individuals, it has been asserted at the same time that it is a useful construct for describing the behavior of individuals in a variety of, if not all, human cultures. A similar case can be made for such schemas as "perception of cause" or "impulse control," and for such traits as "cheerful vs. depressed" or "expansive vs. restrained." With this definition of the task of personality theorists, there has been an attempt to show how each of the members of this symposium has contributed to the solution of problems which arise in the course of the advance toward what seems an impossibly distant goal at the present time. Thus, the psychoanalysts like Dr. Bellak have contributed largely in the motivational sphere; cultural anthropologists like Dr. Mead, in the sphere of ideas and values; and so on. Each has contributed through vigorous pursuit of some aspect of personality which he considers to be of importance, and it does seem evident that vigorous and honest pursuit of truth by any means contributes toward the reaching of a final goal. It is for this reason that little time has been spent in confronting the various theorists with difficulties of their approaches or with the contradictions implicit in different approaches. Science should not be conceived primarily as an argument between people but as an argument between people and nature. Inconsistencies in what different people are doing are admissible and there is little point in arguing about such inconsistencies so long as each individual is making some contribution to a better or more economical description of the variety which is human personality. Psychology is still a young science, and the psychology of personality even younger. There is a long way to go before the goal outlined above is even roughly approximated; but if the contributions presented herein are taken as a sign, the science is advancing, and, given time and favorable world conditions, psychologists may expect some really solid progress in the next fifty years.

BIBLIOGRAPHY

1. ALLPORT, G. W. *Personality, a Psychological Interpretation.* New York: Holt, 1937.
2. ———, & VERNON, P. E. *A Study of Values.* Boston: Houghton Mifflin, 1931.
3. ———, & VERNON, P. E. *Studies in Expressive Movement.* New York: Macmillan, 1933.
4. APPLEZWEIG, D. G. Some Determinants of Behavioral Rigidity. *J. abnorm. soc. Psychol.,* 1954, 49, 224-28.
5. ATKINSON, J. W. The Achievement Motive and Recall of Interrupted and Completed Tasks. *J. exp. Psychol.,* 1953, 46, 381-90.
6. BARTLETT, F. C. *Remembering: A Study in Experimental and Social Psychology.* Cambridge: Cambridge University Press, 1932.
7. BROWN, J. S. Problems Presented by the Concept of Acquired Drives, in *Current Theory and Research in Motivation.* Lincoln: Nebraska University Press, 1953.
8. BROWN, R. W. A Determinant of the Relationship between Rigidity and Authoritarianism. *J. abnorm. soc. Psychol.,* 1953, 48, 469-76.
9. CHILD, I. L., POTTER, E. H., & LEVINE, E. M. Children's Textbooks and Personality Development: An Exploration in the Social Psychology of Education. *Psychol. Monogr.,* 1946, No. 279.
10. CLARK, R. A. The Projective Measurement of Experimentally Induced Levels of Sexual Motivation. *J. exp. Psychol.,* 1952, 44, 391-99.
11. DeCHARMS, R. Behavioral Differences between Achievement Values and Achievement Motivation. (Master's thesis, Wesleyan University, 1954.)
12. ———, MORRISON, H. W., REITMAN, W., & McCLELLAND, D. C. Behavioral Correlates of Directly and Indirectly Measured Achievement Motivation, in *Contributions to a Psychology of Motivation,* ed. D. C. McClelland. New York: Appleton-Century-Crofts, 1955.
13. DOLLARD, J., & MILLER, N. E. *Personality and Psychotherapy.* New York: McGraw-Hill, 1950.
14. FRENKEL-BRUNSWIK, E. Psychoanalysis and the Unity of Science. *Proc. Amer. Acad. Sci.,* 1954, 80, 271-350.
15. HABER, R. The Sensory Determinants of Affect. (Master's thesis, Wesleyan University, 1954.)
16. HARTSHORNE, H., & MAY, M. A. Studies in Deceit, in *Studies*

in the Nature of Character, 2 vols. New York: Macmillan, 1928.

17. HEBB, D. O.   *The Organization of Behavior*. New York: Wiley, 1949.

18. HOLLINGWORTH, H. L.   The Accuracy of Movement. *Arch. Psychol.*, N. Y., 1909, 2, No. 13.

19. JOST, A.   Die Assoziationsfestigkeit in ihrer Abhängigkeit von der Verteilung der Wiederholungen. *Z. Psychol.*, 1897, 14, 436-72.

20. KLEEMEIER, R. W., & DUDEK, F. J.   A Factorial Investigation of Flexibility. *Educ. psychol. Measmt.*, 1950, 10, 107-18.

21. KLUCKHOHN, F. R.   Dominant and Substitute Profiles of Cultural Orientations: Their Significance for the Analysis of Social Stratification. *Social Forces*, 1950, 28, 376-93.

22. KNAPP, R. H., & GOODRICH, H. B.   *The Origins of American Scientists*. Chicago: University of Chicago Press, 1952.

23. McCLELLAND, D. C.   *Personality*. New York: Dryden, 1951.

24. ——, ATKINSON, J. W., CLARK, R. A., & LOWELL, E. L.   *The Achievement Motive*. New York: Appleton-Century-Crofts, 1953.

25. MORRISON, H. W.   Validity and Behavioral Correlates of Female Need for Achievement. (Master's thesis, Wesleyan University, 1954.)

26. MOWRER, O. H.   *Learning Theory and Personality Dynamics*. New York: Ronald Press, 1950.

27. MURRAY, H. A.   *Explorations in Personality*. New York: Oxford University Press, 1938.

28. SHIPLEY, T. E., JR., & VEROFF, J.   A Projective Measure of Need for Affiliation. *J. exp. Psychol.*, 1952, 43, 349-56.

29. WOLFENSTEIN, M., & LEITES, N.   *Movies: A Psychological Study*. Glencoe, Ill.: Free Press, 1950.

INDEX

A

Abnormal behavior, surface traits recognized, in, 79
Abraham, K., 11, 15
Accuracy, defined, 144
Achievement:
  measurement of, 348-349
  valuing vs. needing, 349-350
Achievement motive, 333-335, 336
Acting out, 4
Activated ideas, 186
Activated intentions, 146
Adaptation level, 338, 343
Adelson, J., 300
Adler, Mortimer, 351
Adolescent-adult genitality, 19-20
  period of, 14
Adorno, T. W., 47, 262, 263, 268, 289
Adult sexual drive, 14
Adventuresomeness, 90
Aesthetic culture area, 351
Affective association, 356

Aggression, 36-40, 325
  and anal ejection, 40
  authoritarian, 271, 275
  conflict, types of, 37
  neutralization of, 38
  processes that modify, 37-38
Aggression motive, 337
Agoraphobia, 25
Alertness, attitude of, 160
Alexander, F., 34
Allport, G. W., 123, 213, 326, 331, 351, 353, 356, 357, 358, 359
Ambivalence, 25
America:
  father in, 233
  fear of external danger, 229
  parent-child interaction in, 231, 232
American, stereotype of, 221
American character, 216-217
American Jewish Committee, Department of Scientific Research, 262-263

Jost, A., 328
Judgment, good, 28-29

K

Kardiner, A., 237
Kates, S., 303
Kaufman, F., 6
Klein, George S., 121, 172, 323, 338, 339
Klein, Melanie, 26
Kluckhorn, Florence, 351
Knapp, R. H., 342
Kohler, Iwo, 132-133
Köhler, W., 176, 177
Kraepelin, E., 80, 84
Krech, D., 139, 172
Kretschmer, E., 84, 85
Kris, E., 31, 56
Kuder Richardson formula, 285

L

Language, 341
  studies of languages, 244
  symbolism of, 81
Lashley, K. S., 14, 27, 34
Latency period, 13, 18-19
Layering effect, 328
L-data, 79
Leadership, 87
  roles, 300-304
Learning:
  early, importance of, 328-329
  methods of, 240
Learning theory, 203, 235-236
  perceptual, 23-24
Leites, Nathan, 229, 340
Lepchas, study of, 237
Lesbians, 16
Levinson, Daniel, 261, 262, 263, 279, 286, 300, 303
Levinson, Maria, 280
Lewin, Bertram, 49
Lewin, Kurt, 20, 43, 146, 147, 157, 301
Lewis, O., 206
Lexicogographic scaling, 105
Liberal, genuine, 290-291
Liberman, A. M., 111

Libido:
  amount of, 20
  defined, 7
  as drive energy, 11
  pre-Freudian meaning, 11
Libido theory, 11-25
  conception of learning implicit in, 23-25
  description of, 11-12
  economic assumptions, 7
  libidinal aims or modes of pleasure finding, 14-20
  libidinal object-choices and cathexis, 20-23
  libidinal zones, 12-14
  research, 54-55
Life record or behavior rating material, 79
Light, B., 109
Linn, L., 27, 29
Linton, R., 237
Literal perception, 135-136, 138
Lobotomies, 29
Loewenthal, Leo, 268
Lorenz, K., 243
Love motive, 337
Lowell, E. L., 333
Luria experiments, 58

M

MacArthur, Gen. Douglas, 297
MacDougall, W., 110
McCandless, B., 296
McCarthyism, 301
McClelland, D. C., 111, 321, 361
McCuloch, W. S., 27
McGee, H., 299
Madariaga, S. de, 205-206
Mahler, M., 20, 22
Malaria, resistance to, 225
Malmo, R. B., 160, 163
Manipulativeness, 293
Manipulative pattern, 289
Mankind, psychic unity of, 224-225
Manners:
  changing standards in, 244-245
  studies of, 244
Manus, 227, 240